JEWISH AND CHRISTIAN TEXTS IN CONTEXTS AND
RELATED STUDIES SERIES

Series Executive Editor
James H. Charlesworth

Editorial Board of Advisors
Motti Aviam, Michael Davis, Casey Elledge, Loren Johns, Amy-Jill Levine,
Lee Mcdonald, Lidia Novakovic, Gerbern Oegema, Henry Rietz, Brent Strawn

Cyprus within the Biblical World

Are Borders Barriers?

Edited by
J. H. Charlesworth and J. G. R. Pruszinski

Sponsored and Funded by the Foundation on Judaism
and Christian Origins

T&T CLARK
Bloomsbury Publishing Plc
50 Bedford Square, London, WC1B 3DP, UK
1385 Broadway, New York, NY 10018, USA
29 Earlsfort Terrace, Dublin 2, Ireland

BLOOMSBURY, T&T CLARK and the T&T Clark logo are trademarks of Bloomsbury Publishing Plc

First published in Great Britain 2021
This paperback edition published 2023

Copyright © J. H. Charlesworth, J. G. R. Pruszinski and contributors, 2021

J. H. Charlesworth and J. G. R. Pruszinski have asserted their right under the Copyright, Designs and Patents Act, 1988, to be identified as editors of this work.

All rights reserved. No part of this publication may be reproduced or transmitted in any form or by any means, electronic or mechanical, including photocopying, recording, or any information storage or retrieval system, without prior permission in writing from the publishers.

Bloomsbury Publishing Plc does not have any control over, or responsibility for, any third-party websites referred to or in this book. All internet addresses given in this book were correct at the time of going to press. The author and publisher regret any inconvenience caused if addresses have changed or sites have ceased to exist, but can accept no responsibility for any such changes.

A catalogue record for this book is available from the British Library.

Library of Congress Cataloging-in-Publication Data
Names: Charlesworth, James H, editor. | Pruszinski, Jolyon G. R., editor.
Title: Cyprus within the Biblical world : are borders barriers? / edited by J. H. Charlesworth and J. G. R. Pruszinski ; sponsored and funded by the Foundation on Judaism and Christian Origins.
Description: New York : T&T Clark, 2021. | Series: Jewish and christian texts; 32 | Includes bibliographical references and index. |
Summary: "This volume moves discussion of ancient Israelite culture beyond concepts of isolation and borders, factoring in already well-known insights from classical studies and ancient history that take greater account of the impressive connections between all the countries bordering the Mediterranean sea"– Provided by publisher.
Identifiers: LCCN 2020048394 (print) | LCCN 2020048395 (ebook) | ISBN 9780567694904 (hardback) | ISBN 9780567694911 (pdf) | ISBN 9780567694935 (epub)
Subjects: LCSH: Bible–History of contemporary events | Bible–Criticism, interpretation, etc. | Jews–History. | Cyprus–History. | Cyprus–Antiquities. | Palestine–History. | Palestine–Antiquities.
Classification: LCC BS635.3 .C97 2021 (print) | LCC BS635.3 (ebook) | DDC 220.95/0093937–dc23
LC record available at https://lccn.loc.gov/2020048394
LC ebook record available at https://lccn.loc.gov/2020048395

ISBN:	HB:	978-0-5676-9490-4
	PB:	978-0-5676-9947-3
	ePDF:	978-0-5676-9491-1
	ePUB:	978-0-5676-9493-5

Typeset by Integra Software Services Pvt Ltd.

To find out more about our authors and books visit www.bloomsbury.com and sign up for our newsletters.

Contents

List of Figures	vi
List of Maps	ix
List of Contributors	x
Preface: Planning the Cyprus Congress	xi
Foreword	xiii
Archaeological Periods of the Levant	xvi
Archaeological Periods of Cyprus	xvi
List of Abbreviations	xx

	Is Cyprus a Neglected Dimension of Biblical Research and Are Borders Barriers? *James H. Charlesworth*	1
1	Cyprus and the Land of Israel: The Mediterranean as a Bridge and the Diverse Consequences of Cultural Contact *Avraham Faust*	25
2	"In Sorrow Thou Shalt Bring Forth Children": Archaeological Perspectives on Delivery Practices in Canaan and Cyprus *Rona Avissar Lewis*	41
3	Cyprus and the Shore of Israel during the Persian Period: According to Metal Finds *Kamil Sari*	55
4	Did Lazarus Flee Jerusalem for Cyprus? *James H. Charlesworth*	65
5	Barnabas: The Levite from Cyprus *Konstantinos Th. Zarras*	83
6	Levites on Cyprus—Not Only in the Jerusalem Temple *James H. Charlesworth*	93
7	Meeting the Romans: The Encounter of Paul and Sergius Paulus according to Acts *Kathy Ehrensperger*	103
8	The Motivations for Paul's Choice of Mission Areas *William S. Campbell*	115
9	Cyprus and Early Christianity: Did Everybody Know Everybody? *Dale C. Allison, Jr.*	127
10	Visions of Cyprus: A Phenomenological Background to Jewish and Christian Scripture *Jolyon G. R. Pruszinski*	147
	Conclusions Regarding Cyprus and the Holy Land in the Biblical Period *James H. Charlesworth and Jolyon G. R. Pruszinski*	171
	Cyprus and the Holy Land in History, Archaeology, and Scripture: A Selected Bibliography *Jolyon G. R. Pruszinski*	173

Ancient Sources Index	196
Modern Authors Index	207
Subject Index	213

Figures

P.1	Professor Charlesworth, President Syllouris, Archbishop Chrysostomous, Asher Ben Artzi, and Lea Berkuz discussing the Congress	xi
P.2	Planning the Cyprus Congress with President of the Parliament of Cyprus. Left to right: Ben Artzi, the Honorable Demetris Syllouris, Charlesworth, and Berkuz	xii
F.1	Sunset during the Cyprus Congress (JHC)	xiii
F.2	The Cyprus Congress, June 2018	xiv
F.3	A Cypriot terracotta juglet, Iron Age II. *c.* eighth century BCE; found in the Holy Land (JHC)	xv
0.1	Bronze Aphrodite, Jerusalem, first century CE (Charlesworth Collection in Princeton, JHC)	2
0.2	*Petra tou Romiou* (JHC)	4
0.3	An inscription found beneath houses and west of the Temple in Jerusalem (JHC)	7
0.4	Jupiter, from the time of Cleopatra and Herod the Great (courtesy of the Hermitage; JHC)	8
0.5	The "traditional" pillar on which Paul was allegedly flogged on Cyprus (JHC)	10
0.6	Aphrodite (courtesy of Hermitage; image by JHC)	11
0.7	Bronze Aphrodite (Roman) (courtesy of the Hermitage; JHC)	17
0.8	The remains of the Roman harbor at Caesarea Maritima, looking westward (JHC)	18
1.1	A map showing the distribution of Late Bronze Age Cypriot imports in the land of Israel (prepared by Haggai Cohen Klonymus on the basis of data collected by Aaron Greener)	26
1.2	Sample of Cypro-Phoenician pottery (BoR) (based on Schreiber [2003] and prepared by Michal Marmelshtein and Sivan Landenberg)	28
1.3	Ashdod Ware plate (prepared by Michal Marmelshtein and Sivan Landenberg)	29
1.4	A composite aerial photograph of Building 101 at Tel ʻEton (photographed by Sky View and Griffin Aerial Imaging, edited by Yair Sapir; courtesy of the Tel ʻEton Archaeological Expedition)	32

1.5	A photograph of Room 101C (Building 101), in which over thirty storage jars were unearthed, apparently used to store liquids (photographed by Avraham Faust; courtesy of the Tel 'Eton Archaeological Expedition)	32
1.6	A plate of typical vessels from Building 101 (drawn by Yulia Rodman; courtesy of the Tel 'Eton Archaeological Expedition). No imported pottery nor decorated vessels were unearthed in this structure	33
1.7	Access analysis of a typical four-room house	36
2.1	Ostracon of delivery. From Deir El-Medina (the New Kingdom)	45
2.2	Iron Age II pillar figurine. From Mount Zion excavations, Jerusalem (courtesy of the Mount Zion excavation, Shimon Gibson)	47
2.3	Iron Age III figurine of a sitting pregnant woman. From Tell es-Safi, Israel. Now at the Istanbul Archaeological Museum (photo: Avissar Lewis)	48
2.4	Early Cypriot or Middle Cypriot period Kourotrophos clay figurine of a woman nurturing a baby, Lapithos tomb 307B	49
2.5	Cypro-Archaic figurines depict delivery, Lapithos, Cyprus	50
2.6	Hellenistic period figurine depicts delivery, temple of Golgoi, Cyprus	50
3.1	Weapons	56
3.2	Parallels from Cyprus	57
3.3	Bowls (Israel)	58
3.4	Bowls (Parallels from Cyprus)	58
3.5	Situla	59
3.6	Ladles	59
3.7	Furniture and its monumental depictions	59
3.8	Jewelry (earrings)	61
3.9	Location of Persian period metal finds, Israeli littoral and interior	63
4.1	"The skull and bones of Lazarus" in Larnaca's Church of Lazarus (JHC)	67
4.2	Agios Lazaros in Larnaca (JHC)	71
4.3	The Tomb of Lazarus in Bethany (with JHC)	72
4.4	Roman Ruins in Salamis (JHC)	74
4.5	The harbor at Caesarea Maritima, looking toward Cyprus (JHC)	77
4.6	The raising of Lazarus, Nativity of Christ Church in Arbanassi, Bulgaria, 1639 (photo: John W. Welch, used with permission)	77
6.1	The Roman gymnasium in Salamis (JHC)	95
6.2	Amulet from Nea Paphos, Cyprus (photo: Marcin Iwan)	98
10.1	Line of sight between Marseille and Canigou	148
10.2	Canigou Effect	148

10.3	Calendrical conditions for sunset alignment between Marseille and Mt. Canigou	149
10.4	Line of sight between Mt. Zaphon and Cypriot Mt. Olympus	150
10.5	Calendrical conditions for sunset alignment between Jebel Aqra and Cypriot Mt. Olympus	151
10.6	Satellite photo of a dust storm. Clouds over Cypriot Mt. Olympus formed by orographic lift	152
10.7	View south to Jebel Aqra/Zaphon/Kasios from the Turkish coast to the north	152

Maps

Map 1 Cyprus					xvii
Map 2 The Eastern Mediterranean		xviii

Contributors

Dale C. Allison, Jr.	Princeton Theological Seminary
Rona Avissar Lewis	Hebrew University
Asher Ben Artzi	INTERPOL Israel, Emeritus
William S. Campbell	University of Wales, Trinity Saint David
James H. Charlesworth	Princeton Theological Seminary
Kathy Ehrensperger	University of Potsdam, Abraham Geiger Kolleg
Avraham Faust	Bar-Ilan University
Jolyon G. R. Pruszinski	Princeton University
Kamil Sari	Israel Antiquities Authority
Konstantinos Th. Zarras	National and Kapodistrian University of Athens

Preface: Planning the Cyprus Congress

When my friend, Professor Charlesworth, began to create our seminar on Cyprus, I wondered: "Why Cyprus?" Was it because from ancient times Cyprus was an important cultural and economic center? Was it because from earliest times every political power that emerged sought to control Cyprus and make it part of its own power base? Was Cyprus' importance for a seminar due to the strategic location of this small island? Charlesworth has been fascinated with the Egyptians, Persians, Greeks, and Romans. Was that fascination driving his agenda?

I knew, moreover, that from the Bronze Age Cyprus (*Alashiya* in its ancient name) was coveted by the *Hittites*, the *People of the Sea*, the *Phoenicians*, and the *Pharaohs*. Cyprus is mentioned in the *Amarna Letters*, in the Bible, and even in Jewish prayers.

Figure P.1 Professor Charlesworth, President Syllouris, Archbishop Chrysostomous, Asher Ben Artzi, and Lea Berkuz discussing the Congress.

Figure P.2 Planning the Cyprus Congress with President of the Parliament of Cyprus. Left to right: Ben Artzi, the Honorable Demetris Syllouris, Charlesworth, and Berkuz.

Do these facts not help explain why there was a need to have a congress focused on Cyprus in antiquity?

Even in the modern era this small island attracts local empires and political powers. Notably, in recent decades all intelligence services consider holding representatives on this island. It is centrally located for nations to the East, West, South, and North. Is that why we are to prepare a seminar on Cyprus?

The "birth pains" of the seminar absorbed three years of planning. During this time we—Lea Berkuz, Professor Charlesworth, and I—met with the Commissioner of the Cyprus Police, the Mayor of Larnaca, the Archbishop of Cyprus, the Director of the Nicosia Museum, and the Director of the Larnaca Museum. Most importantly, we enjoyed a day-long meeting with the President of the Parliament and his staff. All of these preliminary meetings contributed to the success of the seminar.

Now, Charlesworth, Berkuz, and I wish to thank all these distinguished dignitaries for their suggestions, insights, and support. We all would be pleased if this volume would be accepted as our special thanks. We intend to draw attention to a most wonderful and historically important island. Cyprus has played, and continues to play, a unique role in world history. It is time that a congress met on Cyprus so that distinguished experts may discuss its importance in history, in biblical studies, and in the emergence of Christianity. The earliest history of Christianity is found in "the Acts of the Apostles." In Luke's composition, Cyprus plays a role for the spread of both early Judaism and Christianity. We are most pleased to help clarify the importance of Cyprus for major historical developments; admittedly many subjects could not be included in our limited focus, but they were often evident in our discussions in the seminar, during meals, and on the bus from Larnaca to Paphos.

Asher Ben Artzi
Co-convener of the Cyprus Congress
Chief Superintendent, Ret., Israel Police and International Police & Security
Consultant, Managing Director

Foreword

In June 2018, scholars met on Cyprus to discuss the importance of that island for a better comprehension of Jewish and Christian origins. The scholars were from the United States, Great Britain, Cyprus, Israel, Germany, Greece, and Denmark. Ten scholars have polished their presentations for the present publication. Those present concurred that we must more carefully perceive that *borders are not barriers*. Scholars, merchants, and soldiers flowed eastward from Cyprus to Palestine from antiquity to the present. Others crossed the border of the Mediterranean Sea westward from Canaan and the land of Israel. Canaanites, Palestinians, Israelites, and Jews traveled eastward and westward, sometimes to Cyprus.

The island can be exceptionally peaceful and inviting. Often, one imagines Cyprus might resemble Paradise on earth. From the nearby eastern coast of the Holy Land

Figure F.1 Sunset during the Cyprus Congress (JHC).

and Syria, early and modern scholars might have been stimulated by pondering that the island reflects the Island of the Blessed Ones made famous in the first- or second-century composition by that name. Such reflections on the imaginations of early Jews and Christians are provided by Pruszinski.

On behalf of those who attended or spoke at the Cyprus Congress let me share our insights. Numerous times we concurred that Cyprus was more connected than divorced from the Land of the Bible, Canaan, Palestine, and Israel. Those living in "the Promised Land" enjoyed Cypriot wine, now found in archaeological excavations, if only in the residue of marked amphorae. A Dead Sea Scroll most likely refers to a special wine that was made famous by those on Cyprus.[2] Attractive[3] pottery from Cyprus was revered in Palestine, most notably from the Bronze Age through the Roman Period. Cypriot copper-alloyed weapons were used by those who defended the Davidic Monarchy and fought later with the Hasmoneans and Zealots. While Babylon was far to the East, while Rome and Spain were far to the West, Cyprus was nearby. The coast of Palestine and Israel was no obstacle for traveling Cypriots; the Mediterranean coast was not a serious hindrance to Israelites and Jews who needed or wished to visit Cyprus. Rather, the Mediterranean served as a highway for commerce. As A. Faust and K. Sari clarify, the Mediterranean was a bridge that stimulated cultural contact: the border was not a barrier during the Persian Period.

These essays are not focused on Cyprus only but are concerned to emphasize that not all borders are barriers. The following chapters include historical reflections on Canaan, Palestine, ancient Israel, and Cyprus. Sometimes what is beyond a border

Figure F.2 The Cyprus Congress, June 2018.[1]

Figure F.3 A Cypriot terracota juglet, Iron Age II. *c.* eighth century BCE; found in the Holy Land (JHC).

is appreciated inside that border. The edge of the Mediterranean is a border like the wall of a city. It may keep people within and sometimes "undesirables" out, but coasts and walls are liminal spaces that only partially define outside and inside. Avissar Lewis brings into focus the delivery of children in Canaan and Cyprus and how examinations of those locations are mutually illuminating. The historical study of the Levites, Lazarus, Paul, and Barnabas demands inclusion in perspective on Cyprus, as Charlesworth, Zarras, Ehrensperger, Campbell, and Allison demonstrate.

I wish now to acknowledge that the exceptional success of the Cyprus Congress is due to those who prepared polished papers and stimulated insights. Many thanks to Kyra N. Pruszinski for furnishing several of the illustrations for the book. Lea Berkuz, and especially Asher Ben Artzi, helped me choose the best hotel, itinerary, and to include dignitaries within Cyprus. The management of the Palm Beach Hotel provided assistants, pleasing accommodations, and a seminar room. The expenses of the Cyprus Congress were covered by the Foundation on Judaism and Christian Origins; its president, vice president, treasurer, and members of the Board of Trustees were actively involved. They are respectively James Charlesworth, John Hoffmann, Lea Berkuz, Lamar Barden, and Linda Wall.

James H. Charlesworth
Princeton
June 2019

Archaeological Periods of the Levant

Neolithic Period	8500 BCE–4500 BCE
Chalcolithic Period	4500 BCE–3200 BCE
Early Bronze Age I	3200 BCE–3000 BCE
Early Bronze Age II	3000 BCE–2700 BCE
Early Bronze Age III	2700 BCE–2350 BCE
Early Bronze Age IV	2350 BCE–2200 BCE
Middle Bronze Age I	2200 BCE–2000 BCE
Middle Bronze Age IIA	2000 BCE–1800 BCE
Middle Bronze Age IIB-C	1800 BCE–1550 BCE
Late Bronze Age	1550 BCE–1200 BCE
Iron Age I	1200 BCE–1000 BCE
Iron Age II	1000 BCE–700 BCE
Iron Age III	700 BCE–586 BCE
Persian Period	586 BCE–332 BCE
Hellenistic Period	332 BCE–37 BCE
Roman Period I (Herodian)	37 BCE–70 CE
Roman Period II	70 CE–180 CE
Roman Period III	180 CE–324 CE
Byzantine Period I	324 CE–451 CE
Byzantine Period II	451 CE–640 CE
Early Arab Period	640 CE–1099 CE
Crusader Period	1099 CE–1291 CE

Archaeological Periods of Cyprus

Neolithic Period	10th to 5th millennia BCE
Chalcolithic Period	3900 BCE–2500 BCE
Early Bronze Age	2500 BCE–2000 BCE
Middle Bronze Age	2000 BCE–1650 BCE
Late Bronze Age	1650 BCE–1050 BCE
Geometric Period	1050 BCE–750 BCE
Archaic Period	750 BCE–475 BCE
Classical Period	475 BCE–312 BCE
Hellenistic Period	312 BCE–58 BCE
Roman Period	58 BCE–395 CE

(Pilides and Papadimitriou, 2012)

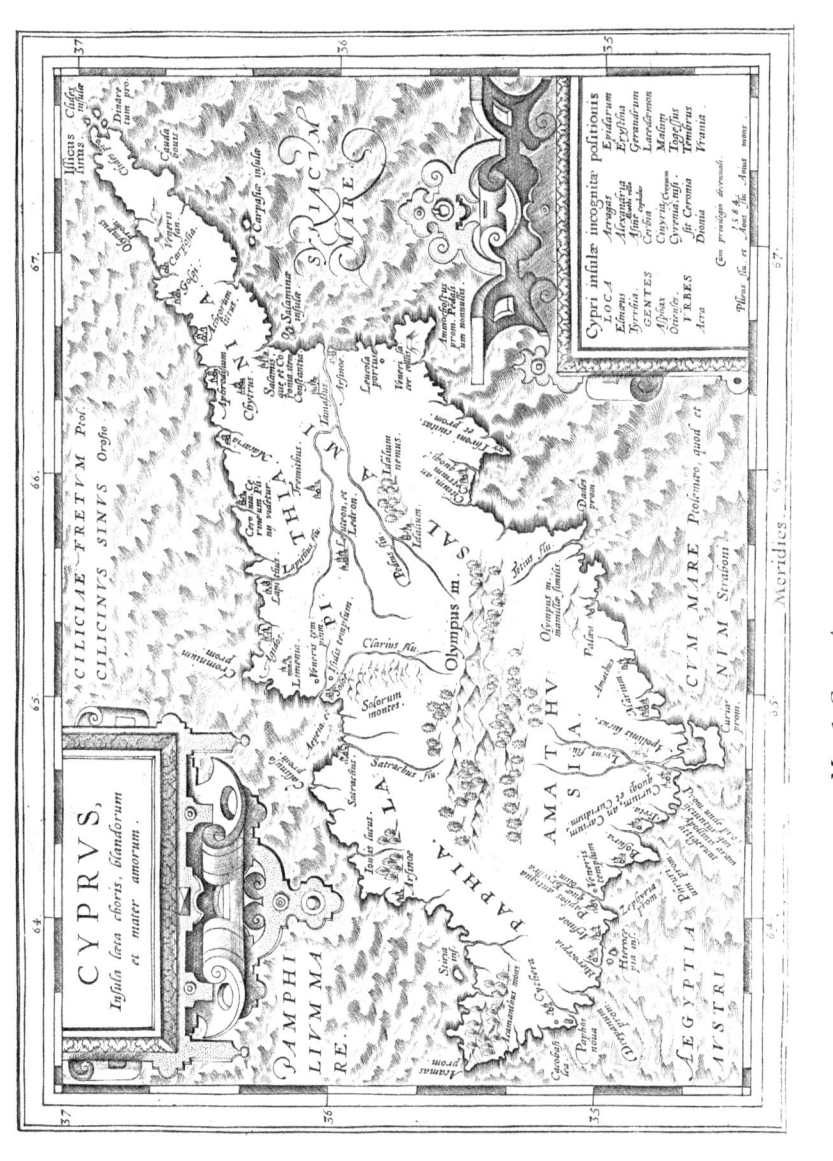

Map 1 Cyprus[4]

Map 2 The Eastern Mediterranean[5]

Notes

1   Photo E. S. Pruszinski. First row, left to right: 1 Superintendent Thomas Hadjikyriacou (Deputy Commander of Larnaca Police), 2 Asher Ben Artzi (Chief Superintendent, Ret., Israel Police and International Police & Security Consultant), 3 James Charlesworth (Princeton, FJCO), 4 HE Demetris Syllouris (President of Cyprus Parliament), 5 HE Archbishop Timotheos (Metropolitan of Vostra), 6 Linda Wall (USA, FJCO). Second row, left to right: 7 Ellen Aagaard Petersen (Denmark), 8 Jolyon Pruszinski (Princeton), 9 Kathy Ehrensperger (Berlin), 10 Bill Campbell (Wales), 11 Peter Ashdjian (Director of Pierides Museum, Larnaca), 12 John Hoffmann (USA, FJCO). Third row, left to right: 13 Lea Berkuz (Israel, FJCO), 14 Kamil Sari (Israel), 15 Jason Iasonides (Vice Mayor of Larnaca), 16 Avraham Faust (Israel), 17 Rona Avissar Lewis (Israel). Fourth row, left to right: 18 Lamar Barden (USA, FJCO), 19 Dale Allison (Princeton), 20 Tassos Panayiotou (Ret. Chief of Cyprus Police), 21 Anders Klostergaard Petersen (Denmark), and 22 Robert Deutsch (Israel). Not pictured: Konstantinos Th. Zarras (Greece); John W. Welch (USA), who provided an appendix to Chapter 4.
2   This reading is found in a forthcoming volume of the PTS DSS Project.
3   Sometimes painted.
4   Detail of "Insular Aliquot Aegaei Maris Antiqua Descrip" by Abraham Ortelius, 1584. Edited for presentation (image by user Balkanique, courtesy of Wikimedia Commons).
5   Detail of "Descriptio peregrinationis d. Pauli apostoli.: exhibens loca fere omnia tam in Novo Testamento quam in Actis Apostolorum memorata" by Abraham Ortelius and Peter van den Keere, 1652. Edited for presentation (image by Special Collections of the University of Amsterdam, courtesy of Wikimedia Commons).

Abbreviations

General

ar	Aramaic
BCE	before the Common Era
BnF	Bibliotèque Nationale de France
BoR	Black on Red (pottery)
c.	circa
cf.	compare
CE	Common Era
CG IA	Cypriot Geometric Period IA
ch(s).	chapter(s)
Cod. Par. Gr.	Codex Parisinus Graece
col.	column
diss.	dissertation
f.	following
ff.	and the following pages or lines
FJCO	Foundation on Judaism and Christian Origins
fn.	footnote
frg(s).	fragment(s)
gk.	Greek
ibid.	ibidem ("in the same source")
id.	idem ("by the same author")
L	Gospel of Luke's special material
LC IIIB	Late Cypriot Bronze Age IIIB
LPDW	Late Philistine Decorated Ware
LXX	Septuagint
M	Gospel of Matthew's special material

MS	manuscript
n(n).	note(s)
NASA	National Aeronautics and Space Administration
p(p).	page(s)
Q	*Quelle* (German for "source")
s.v.	under the word
syr.	Syriac
v(v).	verse(s)

Hebrew Bible/Old Testament

Gen	Genesis
Exod	Exodus
Lev	Leviticus
Num	Numbers
Deut	Deuteronomy
Josh	Joshua
Judg	Judges
Ruth	Ruth
1–2 Sam	1–2 Samuel
1–2 Kgs	1–2 Kings
1–2 Chr	1–2 Chronicles
Ezra	Ezra
Neh	Nehemiah
Esth	Esther
Job	Job
Ps	Psalm
Prov	Proverbs
Eccl	Ecclesiastes
Song	Song of Songs
Isa	Isaiah

Jer	Jeremiah
Lam	Lamentations
Ezek	Ezekiel
Dan	Daniel
Hos	Hosea
Joel	Joel
Amos	Amos
Obad	Obadiah
Jonah	Jonah
Mic	Micah
Nah	Nahum
Hab	Habakkuk
Zeph	Zephaniah
Hag	Haggai
Zech	Zechariah
Mal	Malachi

New Testament

Matt	Matthew
Mark	Mark
Luke	Luke
John	John
Acts	Acts
Rom	Romans
1–2 Cor	1–2 Corinthians
Gal	Galatians
Eph	Ephesians
Phil	Philippians
Col	Colossians

1–2 Thess	1–2 Thessalonians
1–2 Tim	1–2 Timothy
Titus	Titus
Phlm	Philemon
Heb	Hebrews
Jas	James
1–2 Pet	1–2 Peter
1-2-3 John	1-2-3 John
Jude	Jude
Rev	Revelation

Old Testament Apocrypha and Pseudepigrapha

1-2-3 En.	1-2-3 *Enoch*
1-2-3-4 Macc.	1-2-3-4 *Maccabees*
Apoc. Mos.	*Apocalypse of Moses*
HistRech	*History of the Rechabites*
Jub.	*Jubilees*
LAE	*Life of Adam and Eve*
Pr. Jac.	*Prayer of Jacob*
T. Levi	*Testament of Levi*
Sir.	Sirach
Tob.	Tobit

Dead Sea Scrolls

1QS (1Q28)	*Serek Hayaḥad* or *Rule of the Community*
4QpIsaᵃ (1Q161)	*Isaiah Pesher*ᵃ
4QBéat (4Q525)	*Beatitudes*
CD	*Damascus Document*

Rabbinic Texts

ARN A	*The Fathers According to Rabbi Nathan*, Version A
b.	Babylonian Talmud
b.Kerithot	Babylonian Talmud, tractate Kerithot ("extirpation")
b. Ṣot.	Babylonian Talmud, tractate Sotah ("adulteress")
TgPsJonathan	Targum Pseudo-Jonathan

Papyri and Ostraca

pKahun and Gurob	Francis Llewellyn Griffith, *The Petrie Papyri, Hieratic Papyri from Kahun and Gurob*, 2 vols. (London: Bernard Quaritch, 1897–8).
pRam. (Gardiner)	Alan H. Gardiner, *The Ramesseum Papyri* (London: OUP, 1955).

Greek and Latin Works

Aen.	*Aeneid*	Virgil
Aet.	*De Aeternitate Mundi*	Philo
Ann.	*Annales*	Tacitus
Ant.	*Antiquitates Judaicae*	Josephus
De Incarn.	*De incarnatione*	Epiphanius
Deipn.	*Deipnosophistae*	Athenaeus
Dial.	*Dialogus cum Tryphone*	Justin
Ep.	*Epistulae*	Cyprian
Epig.	*Epigrammaton libri*	Martial
Geogr.	*Geographica*	Ptolemy
Geogr.	*Geographica*	Strabo
Gorg.	*Gorgias*	Plato
Haer.	*Adversus haereses*	Irenaeus
Haer.	*Refutatio omnium haeresium*	Hippolytus of Rome

H.E.	*Historia ecclesiastica*	Eusebius
Hel.	*Helena*	Euripedes
Hist.	*Historia*	Dio Chrysostom
Hist.	*Historiae*	Herodotus
Hom.	*Homilia*	Pseudo-Clement
J.W.	*Jewish War*	Josephus
Menex.	*Menexenus*	Plato
Metam.	*Metamorphōseōn synagōge*	Antoninus Liberalis
Ol.	*Olympionikai*	Pindar
Op.	*Opera et dies*	Hesiod
Or.	*Oratio*	Libanius
Quis div.	*Quis dives salvetur*	Clement of Alexandria
Recogn.	*Recognitiones*	Pseudo-Clement
Sert.	*Sertorius*	Plutarch
Spec.	*De Specialibus Legibus*	Philo
Strom.	*Stromateis*	Clement of Alexandria
Symp.	*Symposium*	Plato
Vigil.	*Adversus Vigilantium*	Jerome
Vit. Ant.	*Vita Antonii*	Plutarch
Vita. Apoll.	*Vita Apollonii*	Philostratus

Modern Publications

AASOR	Annual of the American Schools of Oriental Research
AB	Anchor Bible
ABD	*Anchor Bible Dictionary.* Ed. D. N. Freedman. 6 vols. New York: Doubleday, 1992
ABSA	*Annual of the British School at Athens*
ASOR	American Schools of Oriental Research
BA	*Biblical Archaeologist*

BAR	*Biblical Archaeology Review*
BASOR	*Bulletin of the American Schools of Oriental Research*
BBB	Bonner biblische Beiträge
BBET	Beiträge zur biblischen Exegese und Theologie
BBR	*Bulletin for Biblical Research*
BDAG	W. Bauer, F. W. Danker, W. F. Arndt, and F. W. Gingrich, *Greek-English Lexicon of the New Testament and Other Early Christian Literature*. 3rd ed. Chicago: University of Chicago Press, 2000.
BETL	Bibliotheca Ephemeridum Theologicarum Lovaniensium
BGBE	Beiträge zur Geschichte der biblischen Exegese
BNTC	Black's New Testament Commentaries
BTS	*Bible et terre sainte*
BWANT	Beiträge zur Wissenschaft vom Alten und Neuen Testament
BZNW	Beihefte zur Zeitschrift für die neutestamentliche Wissenschaft
CIL	Corpus Inscriptionum Latinarum
ErIsr	*Eretz-Israel*
ETL	Ephemerides Theologicae Lovanienses
ExpTim	*Expository Times*
FRLANT	Forschungen zur Religion und Literatur des Alten und Neuen Testaments
HTKNT	Herders Theologischer Kommentar zum Neuen Testament
HTS	Harvard Theological Studies
ICC	International Critical Commentary
IEJ	*Israel Exploration Journal*
IES	Israel Exploration Society
JBL	*Journal of Biblical Literature*
JETS	*Journal of the Evangelical Theological Society*
JNES	*Journal of Near Eastern Studies*
JSNT	*Journal for the Study of the New Testament*
JSNTSS	Journal for the Study of the New Testament: Supplement Series
JSOT	*Journal for the Study of the Old Testament*

JSOTSup	Journal for the Study of the Old Testament: Supplement Series
KAV	Kommentar zu den Apostolischen Vätern
LA	*Liber Annuus*
LCL	Loeb Classical Library
LNTS	Library of New Testament Studies (formerly JSNTSup)
MTSR	*Method and Theory in the Study of Religion*
NEA	*Near Eastern Archaeology*
NovTSup	Supplements to Novum Testamentum
NRSV	New Revised Standard Version
NTL	New Testament Library
NTOA	Novum Testamentum et Orbis Antiquus
NTS	*New Testament Studies*
OEANE	Oxford Encyclopedia of Archaeology in the Near East. Ed. Eric M. Meyers. 5 vols. New York: Oxford University Press, 1997.
OTP	*The Old Testament Pseudepigrapha*. Edited by James H. Charlesworth. 2 vols. New York: Doubleday, 1983–5.
OUP	Oxford University Press
PEQ	*Palestine Exploration Quarterly*
PG	Patrologia Graeca (e.g., Patrologiae Cursus Completus: Series Graeca). Edited by J.-P. Migne. 166 vols. Paris, 1857–66.
PSBF	Publications of the Studium Biblicum Franciscanum
PTSDSSP	Princeton Theological Seminary Dead Sea Scrolls Project
PUP	Princeton University Press
QD	Quaestiones disputatae
RB	*Revue biblique*
RGG	*Religion in Geschichte und Gegenwart.* 2nd ed. Ed. Hermann Gunkel. 5 vols. Tübingen: Mohr Siebeck, 1927–31. 3rd ed. Ed. Kurt Galling. 7 vols. Tübingen: Mohr Siebeck, 1957–65.
SAC	Studies in Antiquity and Christianity
SBL	Society of Biblical Literature
SCM	SCM Press
SJOT	*Scandinavian Journal of the Old Testament*

SNTW	Studies in the New Testament and Its World
SPCK	SPCK Press
TA	*Tel Aviv*
TD	*Theology Digest*
TDNT	*Theological Dictionary of the New Testament.* Edited by Gerhard Kittel and Gerhard Friedrich. Translated by Geoffrey W. Bromiley. 10 vols. Grand Rapids: Eerdmans, 1964–76.
ThViat	*Theologia Viatorum*
UF	*Ugarit-Forschungen*
WBC	Word Biblical Commentary
WUNT	Wissenschaftliche Untersuchungen zum Neuen Testament
ZAW	*Zeitschrift für die alttestamentliche Wissenschaft*
ZNW	*Zeitschrift für die neutestamentliche Wissenschaft und die Kunde der älteren Kirche*

Is Cyprus a Neglected Dimension of Biblical Research and Are Borders Barriers?

James H. Charlesworth

This chapter evolves in three stages. First, I explore the significance of Cyprus in history. Second, I summarize the influences of Cyprus and Cypriot products for a better understanding of Jewish and Christian texts. Third, I focus on why borders may not be barriers.

What Is the Significance of Cyprus in History?

In such popularly influential reference sites as Wikipedia and Infoplease, Cyprus is discussed without any reference to the Bible and the scientific study of the biblical world. With the possible exception of Lone W. Sørensen, who refers to Palestine as "sites towards the south" of North Syria, no mention is made of Palestine or the land of Israel in *Res Maritimae: Cyprus and the Eastern Mediterranean from Prehistory to Late Antiquity*.[1] The members of the present congress seek to correct this misperception of the significance of Cyprus for biblical research. Readers will observe how important Cyprus was for biblical studies. In contrast to scholars focused on the Bible, the historians, history of religion experts, and those exploring mythology and art highlight Cyprus;[2] one significant reason is the widespread perception in antiquity that the island is the birthplace of Aphrodite.

The island must no longer be ignored in the study of the Bible, early Judaism, and Christian origins.[3] It is the most prominent island in the northeastern Mediterranean, measuring about 150 miles from west to east and 40 miles from south to north. It is only about 60 miles from the coast of Syria.[4] The island is also close to Tyre and Antioch, two major cities in early Judaism and Christian origins. No less than eight millennia of human habitation are evident on Cyprus.[5] Conceivably, we may salute Cyprus as a special place in which West meets East and where Africa and Ethiopia touch Asia and Turkey.[6]

Michal Dayagi-Mendels, Tamar and Teddy Kollek Chief Curator of Archaeology at the Israel Museum (emeritus), succinctly describes the geography of the biblical world that, as we shall see, in our view, includes Cyprus:

Figure 0.1 Bronze Aphrodite, Jerusalem, first century CE (Charlesworth Collection in Princeton, JHC).

The Land of Israel, situated along the Eastern Mediterranean coast between Lebanon and Syria in the north and Egypt in the south, has been home to people of different cultures for more than one and a half million years. In Hebrew, it is often simply referred to as "the Land." Over the course of this period, its boundaries and name have shifted and changed many times. The strategic location of the Land of Israel—at the crossroads of north and south, east and west—has played a major role in shaping its destiny.[7]

Two points in this insightful report need to be emphasized. First, Dayagi-Mendels refers to "people of different cultures." Some of these were from the East or Parthia and Adiabene. A pearl and gold earring with two emeralds, perhaps belonging to Queen Helena of Adiabene, was recovered in Old Jerusalem in the area in which the palace of the kings and queens of Adiabene was located, according to Josephus (*J.W.* 5.253).[8]

Others were from the West, including Cyprus. As will become obvious now and in subsequent chapters, pottery, weapons of copper and bronze, and other *realia* emanating from Cyprus have been found in excavations in Israel.[9] Special wine from Cyprus was coveted by early Jews living in ancient Palestine (see my following discussion of resinated wine).

Second, Dayagi-Mendels mentions that the "boundaries and name" of "the Land" have "shifted and changed many times." All know that the Jordan River on the east of the so-called Holy Land did not provide a boundary for biblical geography; intermittently, from Moses to Herod the Great, the Promised Land included Trans-Jordan. Likewise, the Mediterranean coast was not an impenetrable barrier. Ships arrived upon the coast of the Land for millennia from the North, South, and especially the West. The closest island to Palestine or Israel is Cyprus. Conceivably, Cyprus could be considered an extension of "the Holy Land" as Cypriots and Cypriot ware[10] were involved in the history of the Bible and its people, especially from Abraham to Paul. *Realia* found in excavations in Israel proves the importance of Cypriot products to Israelite and Jewish cultures.

The monumental tower at Jericho antedates 8000 BCE.[11] The same date can be given to the earliest evidence of humans on Cyprus. For example, a statuette dating from about 8200 BCE was found at Khirokitia, Cyprus; it is carved from volcanic rock (andesite).[12] No one should deny it is possible that the influences from Cyprus were occurring in Palestine as early as 11,000 years ago. In assessing what remains from antiquity, it is wise to ponder that a dearth of evidence is not evidence of no contact.

According to Herodotus (7.90), Cyprus was colonized from Greece, Phoenicia, and Ethiopia. Referring to the plundering of the temple of Aphrodite at Ashkelon by the Scythians (1.105), Herodotus states that her temple in Cyprus was an offshoot from that ancient foundation, as reported by the Cyprians themselves. Phoenicians founded it at "Cythera," on arriving from Syria. The dates of the earliest Phoenician settlements on Cyprus are unknown, but the island was a major center of creativity and influence before the time of Moses or circa 1800 BCE.

According to ancient mythology preserved by Hesiod, while the Greeks honored the Dikteon Cave[13] and the Ideon Cave on Crete as the birthplace of Zeus,[14] they celebrated the birth of Aphrodite, the goddess of love and beauty, on Cyprus.[15] Most likely, that is why Aphrodite is also known as "Kypris." According to ancient myths, she appeared out of sea foam on the southern coast of Cyprus. The site is known as *Petra tou Romiou*. From "the Rock of the Romans," she was transferred to dry land in a shell.[16]

Many ancient works of art depict Aphrodite (who is also Venus) emerging in a shell from the sea. This mythic event is highlighted in paintings displayed now in the Louvre in Paris, the State Hermitage Museum in Saint Petersburg, and elsewhere. One example is riveting; it is a fourth-century BCE pottery vessel that depicts Aphrodite inside a shell; it was found in the Phanagoria cemetery in the Taman Peninsula at the north end of the Black Sea. Many art connoisseurs know the marvelous depiction of *The Birth of Venus* by Sandro Botticelli, created between 1484 and 1486 CE. Frequently, a statue of Aphrodite in bronze or clay adorned the desks and homes of the wealthy throughout the Levant, including—as we know from archaeology—in Caesarea Maritima and Jerusalem.[17]

Citium, known otherwise as Kition, was a major city from which the Phoenicians entered the "land of Israel." Archaeologists have discovered that the earliest evidence of life on Citium is an Aegean colony that dates from the Mycenaean Age or from 1400 to

Figure 0.2 *Petra tou Romiou* (JHC).

1100 BCE. The name "Citium" came to be used for the city on the southeastern coast and also for the entire island. Proof that boundaries may not necessarily be barriers is the fact that Citium was part of the Assyrian Empire, under Sargon II. During the Greek revolts of the fifth and fourth centuries BCE, many on Cyprus sided with the Persians. Remaining influential during the following centuries, and a center for Greeks and Romans, Citium was abandoned for Larnaca due to silting and earthquakes.[18]

Why is a congress devoted to Cyprus and the Bible significantly fundamental and for whom? First, while congresses devoted to Egypt, Iran, Turkey, Greece, Italy, Israel, and other ancient civilizations have been popular and well known, no international congress has been devoted to Cyprus and its specific importance for biblical studies. That is a major desideratum especially when Cyprus has been influential on human history for millennia, providing archaeological evidence of human achievements on Cyprus for every period from the tenth century BCE through 395 BCE.[19] This final year is when Theodosius I died, having made Christianity the official religion of the Roman Empire. In February 313 CE, Romans officially tolerated religions such as Christianity with the Edict of Milan. The earliest extant mention of Christianity on Cyprus is a mosaic inscription in the Building of Eustolios, Kourion, of the fifth century CE. It announces the edifice is protected by the venerated symbols of the Christ.[20]

Second, a congress focused on Cyprus in antiquity is important to historians and biblical scholars because the island was the gateway to the East for Libya, Italy, and Greece. Cyprus was also the gateway to the West for those in the East. Culture and commodities moved from the East, including the northeast, to the West. In antiquity, Cyprus was ruled by Egyptians, Assyrians, Phoenicians, Hittites, Greeks, and Romans. The eastern transportation of wine, cedar, glass, defining literature (especially from Greece and Rome), and other commodities was often via Cyprus. The western flow of silk, spices, rubies, defining literature, and other commodities from Iran, Persia,[21] China, and India passed frequently through Cyprus to the West, finally to Spain and later Britain. More attention should be focused on perceiving Cyprus as a major hub of world commerce from the Bronze Age[22] to the Roman period (and subsequently until the invention of the airplane). Much later, the Nestorians helped shape world culture from Famagusta, Cyprus, to Beijing, China.

Third, the flow of internationally important commodities by boat placed Cyprus at the hub of ancient shipbuilding. Many ships were designed and manufactured on Cyprus and served commercial and military purposes. The forests on Cyprus provided timber for shipbuilding. The attractive harbors on Cyprus were strategically placed above Egypt, below Asia Minor, and west of Syria and Palestine. Few countries were so important in antiquity for maritime commerce as Cyprus. Cypriots were heralded as sailors and shipbuilders by Herodotus, Strabo, and Pliny the Elder. In the fourth century CE, Ammianus Marcellinus saluted Cyprus as "far removed from the main land" and blessed with harbors. The Cyprians built "cargo ships from the very keel to the topmast sails" (*Res Gestae* 14 8.14).[23]

Fourth, the cultures of ancient Palestine and Israel were impacted by commodities from Cyprus. John Strange argued persuasively that "Caphtor," found in Amos 9:7, means "Cyprus" and dates the immigration of Cypriots or Philistines to Canaan about 1300 or 1200 BCE. This date is not distant from the immigration of Joshua and the Hebrews from the east or Jordan Valley.[24]

By the third millennium BCE, the discovery of copper on Cyprus brought about a major cultural change on Cyprus and subsequently on civilizations to the East and West.[25] Cyprus was named in Greek *kupros*, or "copper," and copper and bronze (a mixture of copper and tin) weapons and utensils were often made on Cyprus or crafted elsewhere from metal mined on Cyprus. Thanks to archaeological research on Cyprus, we know that copper was dominant until about 2000 BCE; then, the much more durable bronze defined the production of weapons and other objects. Since no tin was available on Cyprus, it was imported from the East or Asia Minor. The Early Bronze Age on Cyprus can be dated from perhaps 2500 to 1900 BCE.[26]

Subsequently, Cyprus helped define the production of copper and bronze in the Mediterranean world. The Mycenaeans, who came to Cyprus peacefully about 1100 BCE, perhaps as refugees from Crete, colonized Cyprus and their Greek culture replaced the earlier culture and languages. The influx of the skilled Mycenaeans enhanced mining and the economy on Cyprus. They helped to define the culture of Enkomi, the first major "city" on Cyprus.[27] It appeared most likely in the seventeenth century BCE and was abandoned by about the eleventh century BCE; the inhabitants moved to the coast and to Salamis. Examples of the wealth of Enkomi are three pieces of gold jewelry from the thirteenth century BCE: a gold necklace, a gold-plated bronze ring, and gold earrings.[28] Gold jewelry from Idalion proves the wealth of Cyprus before and during the twelfth century BCE and is displayed in Berlin.[29]

A unique Cypriot culture followed the Mycenaean incursion. It antedated the Syro-Palestinian influences from Tyre, Sidon, Byblos, and even Israel and its monarchy. The Cypriot vessels and ceramic creations and art influenced Canaanite culture and were followed by local copies in Palestine. The peaceful relations between Cyprus and Phoenicia increased the links between Cyprus and ancient Israel. The Phoenicians settled in Kition,[30] Cyprus, about 850 BCE. Like some cities on the coast of Palestine, Kition essentially became a Phoenician colony. The later Assyrian destruction of ancient Israel in the eighth and seventh centuries BCE was also felt on Cyprus. An inscription of Sargon II mentions cutting down "all my foes from Yatnana," which is Cyprus. A stele found in Kition, now in Berlin, mentions the subjugation of Cyprus by the Assyrians.[31]

After a period of relative peace, Cyprus was conquered again. In 586 BCE, Pharaoh Amasis took control of the island. His success was heralded by Herodotus who claimed that Amasis "was the first conqueror of Cyprus" (*Hist.* 2.182). According to Diodorus of Sicily, Pharaoh Amasis was beneficial to those on Cyprus, "adorning many temples with noteworthy votive offerings" (*Bibliotheca Historica* 1.68, 6).[32] Egyptian influences on Cyprus are evident today in the museums on Cyprus.[33]

Subsequently, the Persians conquered Palestine and Cyprus. The Persian Empire, due to relatively peaceful activities, united those in Palestine and Cyprus. According to Xenophon, the Cypriots enthusiastically supported the Persians (*Cyropaedia* 7 4.1-2).[34] However, many of the Cypriots, probably influenced by the Greeks, revolted against the Persians from 499 to 497 BCE, according to Herodotus (*Hist.* 5.104). About 470 BCE, Kition and most of Cyprus was ruled by Persians who sought to eradicate the influence of Greek culture.

Greek culture, nevertheless, would remain fundamental on Cyprus. Even though the Greek language appeared on Cyprus before 1200 BCE and became dominant about 1000, King Evagoras (*c.* 410–374 BCE) officially shifted the language of Cyprus from the Cypriot Syllabic Script to Greek and invited Greek philosophers to Cyprus from Athens.[35] At Kition, the most famous philosophers included Zeno of Kition (*c.* 336–265)[36] and Eudemus (who probably died in 353 or 370 BCE and is known as "Eudemus of Rhodes"),[37] who was a student and friend of Aristotle. During the Hellenistic and Roman periods, Greek drama shaped life on Cyprus, as is evident from terracotta masks for actors,[38] but most of the Cypriot poems and dramatic works are now lost.

In 333 BCE, Alexander the Great defeated Darius III. He took Tyre with the help of kings from Cyprus.[39] The Ptolemies ruled Cyprus from the end of the fourth century until the Romans annexed it.

With the end of the Punic Wars and the defeat of Carthage in 148 BCE, Rome moved eastward and began to control Cyprus. Eventually Cyprus became a Roman province in 58 BCE. The most famous of the Roman governors was Cicero (51–50 BCE). Julius Caesar gave Cyprus back to the Ptolemies about 48 or 47 BCE. Roman domination in Cyprus and Jerusalem is well documented and obvious to all who read this volume.

The inscription (FRET[ENSIS]) refers to the Tenth Legion (Legio X Fretensis) that was created by Gaius Octavius in about 41 BCE; it provides sufficient evidence of Rome's domination of the Middle East. After the burning of Jerusalem in 70 CE, the Tenth Legion controlled the area. In 79 CE, Vesuvius obliterated Pompeii (Venus' city),

Figure 0.3 An inscription found beneath houses and west of the Temple in Jerusalem (JHC).

Herculaneum (Hercules' glory), and other cities nearby present-day Naples. We have only apocalyptists (esp. the authors of *4 Ezra* and *2 Baruch*) to lament the burning of Jerusalem, but Martial in 88 CE composed a four-couplet poem about the devastation of southwestern Italy in 79 CE:

> This is Vesuvius, which only yesterday was green with umbrageous vines;
> Here, squeezed in the press the noble grape filled the vats.
> These are the heights which Bacchus loved more than the hills of Nysa;
> On this mountain the satyrs still danced yesterday.
> Here was the city of Venus, which she preferred to Sparta;
> Here was the city whose name resounded the glory of Hercules.
> And now lies buried in flames and dull ashes.
> Even the gods would have wished not to have had the power to cause such a
>   catastrophe.[40]

The Latin *hoc nuper Satyri monte dedere choros* is a lament Jeremiah and the authors of *4 Ezra* and *2 Baruch* would appreciate.

Enamored by Cleopatra's beauty and intelligence (she knew over ten languages, including Hebrew), Julius Caesar virtually made her queen of Cyprus. Antony concurred.[41] This impression is evident on coins on which Cleopatra, as Aphrodite, holds Caesarion, Julius Caesar's son. Following Cleopatra and Mark Antony's apparent suicide in 30 BCE, Cyprus again became a Roman province.

Returning to the importance of copper for Cyprus, it is important to note that at least four million tons of slag have been found at the foot of the Troodos range. What is its significance? Probably, K. Hadjidemetriou is correct to conclude that "at least two hundred thousand tons of copper ore were produced in ancient Cyprus. This huge production undoubtedly renders Cyprus the biggest centre of copper ore production in antiquity."[43]

While some of the weapons used by those who led military campaigns in ancient Palestine from Joshua to David may have been made from Cypriote bronze or copper, it would be misleading to assume that the weapons used by Solomon must have been made on Cyprus. The copper mines at Timna, in southern Palestine, are datable to Solomon's period and he might have found them more suitable than the mines on Cyprus. Thus, perhaps these Timna mines would be the major source of copper and bronze for the monarchy of Solomon and those who followed him, even though they most likely belonged to the Egyptians.[44]

Our sessions indicated the need to focus on many questions. For example, scholars should discuss if Cyprus gave its name to copper or if "copper" derives from the Sumerians who had previously crafted the name "copper," *kubar*. Was this Sumerian name simply transferred to Cyprus? If so, it would again define the island as the source

Figure 0.4 Jupiter, from the time of Cleopatra and Herod the Great (courtesy of the Hermitage; JHC).[42]

of copper. Any answers should be informed by Pliny the Elder; he referred to "Cyprian copper" as *aes cyprium*.

Many examples of glass and pottery made in Cyprus have been found in ancient Palestine from the Late Bronze Age to the early Byzantine period.[45] The Bilbel jar was shaped by Cypriots and helped define jars in ancient Palestine especially in the Bronze Age and the Iron Age. Cypriot glass was cherished in Palestine and Canaanites and Israelites created a type of Cypriote ware known as faux Cypriot glass. Many examples of glass made on Cyprus or influenced by Cypriot models have been found in Palestine from the late Persian period through the Roman period.[46]

Fifth, Cyprus was a major hub for travel to the West. The spread of Christianity highlights the importance of Cyprus. Paul visited Cyprus on his first missionary journey (Acts 13):

> Therefore, being sent out by the Holy Spirit, they [Saul (Paul) and Barnabas] went down to Seleucia; and from there they sailed to Cyprus (ἐκεῖθέν τε ἀπέπλευσαν εἰς Κύπρον). And having arrived in Salamis, they proclaimed the word of God in the synagogues of the Jews.
>
> (Acts 13:4-5)

According to the author of Acts, Paul and Barnabas trekked through Cyprus from Salamis (the traditional site of Barnabas' birth and martyrdom)[47] on the east coast to Paphos on the west coast (Acts 13:6). They probably took the southern route that extended for about 115 miles. In Paphos, Sergius Paulus, the proconsul on Cyprus, is reported to have rejected the advice of the magician named Bar-Jesus (Elymas) and heard Paul and Barnabas. Astonished by the teaching about the Lord (ἐπὶ τῇ διδαχῇ τοῦ κυρίου), he is reported to have "believed" (ἐπίστευσεν) in Acts 13:12.[48]

Where was Paul scourged thirty-nine times (according to 2 Cor 11:24)? We are told he was whipped five times but we do not know where. By supplying a site for one of the floggings, local legends developed that Paul was whipped in Paphos. The report or tradition is evident neither in the New Testament (noticeably absent in Acts and Paul's letters) nor in the New Testament Apocrypha (not even in the *Acts of Paul*). A pillar commemorating this apocryphal story is located outside the church known as *Agia Kiraki*; the church dates from about 1500 CE but is built on the ruins of the fourth-century *Panagia Chrysopolitissa Basilica*.

What happened to Barnabas? A legend circulated that Bar-Jesus incited some Jews to kill Barnabas.[49] Legends often color or define history on Cyprus; scholars do not have data that allows them to answer this question and related questions. We scholars are "slaves" to what has survived from antiquity.

The author of Acts highlighted Cyprus as "Christianity" moved westward from Palestine. Barnabas and Mark preached on Cyprus after their break with Paul (Acts 15:37-41). Hadrian, during his reign from 117 to 138 CE, banished both Jews and Christians from Cyprus, though the ban was short-lived.

Commodities, notably wine, elegant pottery, copper, and bronze helped define the culture within ancient Palestine. These essential *realia* were highlighted when Strabo celebrated the importance of Cyprus:

Figure 0.5 The "traditional" pillar on which Paul was allegedly flogged on Cyprus (JHC).

> Cyprus's fertility exceeds that of any other island. It is rich in wine and oil and produces sufficient grain. There are also rich copper mines near Tamassos, … Eratosthenes says that in the old days the woods were so vast that one could not cultivate fields, for there were too many trees. [50]
>
> (*Geogr.* 14 6.5)

Cyprus' importance is placarded by the specialists whose participation and research define the following chapters. These scholars clarify why a congress on Cyprus and the Bible is now fundamentally important.

Figure 0.6 Aphrodite (courtesy of Hermitage; image by JHC).

Is Cyprus a Neglected Dimension of Research into Jewish and Christian Texts?

Too many scholars incorrectly report or assume that the island called "Cyprus" is not mentioned in the Hebrew Bible (the Old Testament). The island in antiquity was known by numerous names; among them, the most prominent are "Kittim" and "Elishah."

The author of Numbers describes ships from Cyprus or "from Kittim" (כתים; Num 24:24). In a tirade against Israel, God, according to Jeremiah, is understandably more favorable to "the coasts of Cyprus" or better "the islands of the Kittim" (איי כתיים; Jer 2:10) than to the chosen people. The island is mentioned twice by Ezekiel:

> From oak trees of Bashan
> they made your oars;
> they made your oars (or deck) of pines

from the coasts of Cyprus (or isles of Kittim; מאיי כתים)
inlaid with ivory,
they made your decks. (Ezek 27:6)

The noun for "Cyprus" is "Kittim" (כתים). The Greek translation (LXX) is "from the islands of Kittim" (ἀπὸ νήσων τῶν Χετείμ). The other name for Cyprus appears in Ezek 7:7; it is "Elishah" (Hebrew) or "Elisai" in Greek.

In a lamentation over Tyre, composed in poetic Hebrew *qinah* rhythm, Ezekiel chose to highlight Cyprus as he delineated the origin of woods chosen to build a ship that is a metaphor for Tyre. Cyprus was thus heralded by Ezekiel as a land that produced wood or "pine," and such was often inlaid with ivory.

The composer of 1 Chronicles discusses the descendants of Javan. He names "Elishah, Tarshish, Kittim, and Rodanim" (1 Chr 1:7). Searching for "Cyprus" in the Hebrew Bible requires focusing on all its various names in the Hebrew Bible and Septuagint.

According to the author of Dan 11:30, "ships of Kittim shall come against" the *bête noire* Antiochus IV (175–164 BCE). The noun "Kittim" denotes powerful armies from the West; perhaps readers assumed the Romans were intended but Cyprus may be involved as an intermediate stage. According to the author of 1 Macc 1:1, the "land of the Kittim" seems to refer to the Greeks who are led by Alexander the Great. Greeks also seem to be identified as "Kittim" in 1 Macc 8:5. The fourth-century BCE ostraca from Idumaea mention the date according to the year of "Alexander the King" (אלכסנדר מלכא).[51] While "Kittim" are mentioned in the Qumran Scrolls, usually the term refers to Romans, though one passage in the *Pesharim* may refer to Cyprus as the land of the Kittim. This meaning seems apparent in *Isaiah Pesher 4*:

> [… "and the th]ickets of [the forest will be hacked down] with an axe, and Lebanon together with a mighty one [will fall." They are the] Kittim, wh[o] will fa[ll] by the hand of Israel. And the Poor Ones of […] all the nations, and the mighty ones will be filled with terror, and [their] cour[age] will dissolve [… "And those who are lofty] in stature will be cut down." They are the mighty ones of the Kitt[im …]d "and the thickets of [the] forest will be hacked down with an axe." Th[ey are]⁰m for the battle of the Kittim. [VACAT] "And Lebanon (together) with a mi[ghty one will fall." They are the] Kittim, who will be giv[en] into the hand of his great ones […]
>
> 4QpIsaᵃ frgs. 8-10, col. 3, lines 6-12.[52]

Some at Qumran may have imagined the texts to refer to those on Kitium, Cyprus. The reference to "thickets" and "the forest" might reflect the wide reputation of abundant forests on Cyprus. Under the Hasmoneans, "Israel" could easily have been imagined to have defeated the Kittim. The references to "Lebanon" bring into focus Cyprus, not Rome. Of course, some at Qumran would imagine that someday Israel will be able to defeat the seemingly invincible might of Rome.

"Cyprus," specifically, is mentioned in the New Testament but only eight times in Acts (Acts 4:36; 11:19, 20; 13:4; 15:39; 21:3, 16; and 27:4). From these passages, we obtain many insights. Joses, surnamed Barnabas by the apostles, was a Levite from Cyprus.[53] All of us would like to know more about Levites on Cyprus.[54] Was Barnabas born a Levite on Cyprus,[55] as Paul was apparently born a Pharisee in Tarsus?[56] Almost always, we rightly assume a Levite is one officiating in the Temple and living in Jerusalem or nearby.[57] Aaron and his sons, according to the P Source, and the sons of Zadok, according to Ezekiel, were the descendants of Levi who were to protect the holiness of the priests and of the Temple. The Levites and their vestments helped to define the Temple.[58]

Is Ludger Schenke correct to conclude that Barnabas was gifted in Hebrew and Aramaic, had mastered Jewish traditions, and had served in the Temple?[59] Or is Kollmann on target, in rejecting Schenke's interpretation, concluding that all we know is that Barnabas took pride in being a descendant of Levi?[60] Who offers the most insightful explanation? We are offered, again, the maximalist and minimalist recreations of the past. Do we have additional reliable historical information regarding Barnabas?

Nothing more about Barnabas' Levite connection is obtained from studying references to him by the early scholars of the church; for example, Pseudo-Clement adds only that Barnabas was a "Hebrew" (*Hom.* 1 9.1; *Recogn.* 1. 7.7).[61] If the author of John is accurate in reporting Jesus spent months in Jerusalem,[62] especially before his crucifixion, then Epiphanius, Clement of Alexandria, Eusebius, and *Pseudo-Clement* may preserve reliable historical traditions that Barnabas knew the historical Jesus.[63] Barnabas may have met Jesus in Jerusalem and in the Temple but that does not prove he had followed Jesus in the late twenties.

After Jesus' crucifixion, many followers would probably flee Jerusalem (Acts 11:19), including perhaps Lazarus.[64] After the persecutions that followed the martyrdom of Stephen, disciples of Jesus fled to many places, most notably Galilee, Antioch, Rome, and Cyprus, preaching the word of God.

In summary, the men of Cyprus preached concerning Jesus in Antioch (Acts 11:19-20). Saul (Paul) and Barnabas sailed to Cyprus (Acts 13:4). Barnabas left Paul, took Mark, and sailed to Cyprus (Acts 15:39). Paul and a companion sailed east of Cyprus to Tyre (Acts 21:3). Paul meets Mnason of Cyprus, "an old disciple," on the way to Jerusalem (Acts 21:15-16). Paul sails for Italy by Cyprus (Acts 27:4).[65] That island was in focus for the spreading of the Good News about Jesus from the earliest decades of what would be recognized as "Christianity."

Two Speculations

I conclude this chapter with two speculations. First, are the Kittim in the Dead Sea Scrolls a name derived from Kitium in Cyprus? To begin exploring answers to such a question, we should begin with the occurrences of "Kittim" in the Hebrew scriptures. First, we ask what area or place is suggested by "Kittim"?

The broad meaning of "Kittim" is found in Genesis 10:
ובני יון אלישה ותרשיש כתים ודדנים

And the sons of Javan: Elishah and Tarshish, the Kit[t]im and the Dodanim
(Gen 10:4)

In this verse the noun "Kittim" refers to the descendants of Javan; thus, the noun is a generic reference to the Greeks and Romans. Perhaps, Kittim once denoted the geographical area defined by the Mediterranean coasts. It thus includes the islands, all of them, including Cyprus. The inclusive meaning appears again in 1 Chr 1:7. In this passage, the noun includes Spain, Sicily, southern Italy, and the Greek islands. As the noun Kittim evolved over time it obtained a more focused meaning. That is, eventually Kittim denoted specifically the island of Cyprus. The author of Isa 23:1 and 12 mentions "Cyprus." Ezekiel, in 27:6 and 7, knows the noun "Cyprus" and some readers may grasp that he indicates it is situated between Bashan and the isles of Elisha. Ezekiel highlights the importance of the forests of Cyprus: "they made your deck of pines from the coasts of Cyprus" (Ezek 27:6 [NRSV]). In his sixteenth-century map, *Sacrae Geographiae*, Benedictus Arias Montanus shows "Kithim" as an island off the southern coast of Asia Minor and provides the name of the island in Latin and Hebrew. He uses the term כתים.[66]

Some references in the Hebrew scriptures specify the ships made on Kittim, Cyprus. The author of Num 24:24 mentions that ships will come from the coast of Kittim and they will afflict Asshur and Eber. The author of Dan 11:30 mentions the ships coming from Kittim, and that term seems to denote the general Mediterranean coast. Josephus, our most important historian of the first century CE, reported that "Cyprus" (Κύπρος) provides the name "Chethim" (Χεθίμ) which the "Hebrews" give "to all islands and to most maritime countries" (*Ant.* 1, 128).

A Proposed Restoration in Fragment 24: Resinated [wine] and all those drin[king ...]

Second, does "resinated wine" appear in the Qumran Scroll 4Q525? My restoration of this fragment highlights the resinated wine associated with Cyprus. Among the fragments of 4Q525, fragment 24 challenges Qumran experts. What is the most appealing scientific restoration of the end of line seven so that line eight begins with שרף? These consonants are usually taken to denote a verb: "it burned." With this rendering, we lose a flow of thought. The consonants are followed by "and all those drin[king ...]." In the next fragment we find in line four: "[... do not be a glutton and drun]kard" (Frag. 25.4). We all know that "drunkard" specifies a person who habitually overeats and over drinks, resulting in the loss of wisdom. The translation "it burned" is widely accepted. We should explore whether there is another meaning and if so does it restore some meaning in the context?

It is best to recognize another meaning of שרף (meaning "resin" or "resinated"). The meaning is extant in early Jewish Aramaic and can be found in Jastro and TgPsJonathan of Gen 37:25 and 43:11. Resinated wine is pungent and is known for "burning" the tongue; that insight helps explain the Hebrew etymology of "resinated."

יַיִן שָׂרָף or "resinated wine" was not always made from grapes; it was often made from beets, grains, and potatoes. It was a potent alcoholic drink, causing drunkenness as with hard liquor today.

How, then, should one make sense of Fragment 24.7-8? Should the end of line seven be restored to obtain: שרף [יין]?[67] For יַיִן שָׂרָף, see Even-Shoshan's lexicon (vol. 3, p. 969): "resinated wine." The restoration would thus indicate "[resinated] wine." This term designates a popular wine for many in Greece and Cyprus especially in the famous brand today called "Retsina Malamatina." This wine obtains a flavor from the "resin" from a tree (often pine). Resinated wine is usually at least 12 percent alcohol and may have been higher in antiquity. It was potent and caused drunkenness; most likely the burning sensation gave rise to join יין with שרף (in modern Hebrew, יי"ש is the abbreviation for "resinated wine").

The proposed restoration brings cogency to the next words: "and all those drin[king ....]" The reconstruction harmonizes with the next fragment: "[... do not be a glutton and drun]kard." Thus, the author of this Wisdom text seems to warn his readers to avoid the drunkenness caused by "resinated wine." The author knows Proverbs 23:

> Hear, my child, and be wise,
> and direct your mind in the way.
> Do not be among winebibbers [אַל־תְּהִי בְסֹבְאֵי־יָיִן],
> or among gluttonous eaters of meat;
> for the drunkard and the glutton will come to poverty,
> and drowsiness will clothe them with rags.
> (Prov 23:19-21 [NRSV]; cf. Sir 31:29; Tob 4:15])

Perhaps skeptics might retort to this obvious and attractive restoration that "resinated wine" denotes a modern drink. They would need to be informed that the earliest evidence of a virtually identical potent fermentation seems to be 9000 years ago in northern China; the drink was not wine but an alcoholic drink made from rice, honey, and wild fruit. Wine may have been discovered, perhaps accidentally, about 8000 years ago by a Neolithic culture, the Shulaveri-Shomu, in what is now Georgia,[68] according to excavations and biochemical research.[69] The earliest evidence of resinated wine seems to be 7000 years ago. Wine was found in a Neolithic jar dating from about 5400 to 5000 BCE. It was found in Iran's northern Zagros Mountains at Hajji Firuz Tepe. The jar contained the remnants of "resin" (the yellowish oleoresin of the *pistacia atlantica*) and tartaric acid (the remains of wine).

How did the resin get into the wine? It is surmised that the "resin" was used to inhibit bacteria from growing and mask an offensive odor.[70] Resinated wine dating from 3150 BCE has been found in Egypt. Patrick E. McGovern, a specialist in biomolecular research,[71] agrees with the archaeologists who excavated a tomb in Egypt. They were astounded to find resinated wine in 700 jars left in the burial of King Scorpion I, one of the first kings of Egypt. Most likely resinated wine was produced in northern Greece by at least the third millennium BCE.[72] It is relatively certain that resin was used to preserve the wine. Critics hard to convince might claim now that resinated wine was known in earliest antiquity and modernity but not during the time of early Judaism.

Resinated wine was indeed known in the first century CE. In *De Re Rustica* 12.20.3 and 12.22.2, Lucius Columella (4–70 CE), probably the most popular writer on agriculture in the Roman period, mentioned it. In *Naturalis Historia* 14.124 and 16.60, Pliny the Elder (23–79 CE) also referred to this potent drink. Apparently unaware of the earliest use of resin to preserve wine from spoiling, Greek and Roman scholars claim that the resin inadvertently transferred to the wine from the pine resin that was used to seal amphorae. Both explanations may be correct for the respective times; that debate is not important. What is important is the fact that we have abundant evidence, archaeologically and textually, that resinated wine was desirable and praised from 5000 BCE to at least the end of the first century (and, of course, until today for those who have a special taste for it).

In summary, the scientific evidence is abundant for the antiquity and ubiquity of resinated wine. It was known in the Mediterranean world and the Middle East thousands of years before and about a century after a Jew inscribed 4Q525, "Beatitudes." This special wine was known throughout the Middle East and the author of 4Q525 may well have been familiar with it since he lived somewhere in Palestine and not in the reclusive Qumran community. The restoration, שרף [יין], is justifiable historically, archaeologically, philologically, and contextually. Most early Jews would know that "resinated wine" was a product from Cyprus.

The main objection to the restoration may be the paucity of יין שרף in Hebrew or Aramaic before 70 CE. The force of such an objection must be judged in light of three facts. First, many restorations of Qumran texts have no precedent. Second, we may have only 10 percent of the words known to Isaiah, Jeremiah, and Nehemiah since, when writing, an author selects only a few words known in his society. Third, we have less than 8 percent of the inscribed leather or papyrus that was in the eleven caves in 68 CE and one cannot claim that the expression cannot be partly preserved in the hundreds of tiny Qumran fragments with few consonants or indecipherable portions of scrolls.

These comments do not mean the restoration is certain; all restorations are hypothetical. The advantage of the restoration is obvious: for the first time the text not only makes sense but is also harmonious with the *Tendenzen* of biblically inspired Wisdom documents.

Coming to my conclusion, as I have prepared this chapter, I felt like I was wandering in *terra incognita*. Cyprus is an island that deserves more scholarly studies. It is now virtually impossible to comprehend all that should be known archaeologically, textually, and historically about Cyprus.

Our first question prompted us to ponder if Cyprus is a neglected dimension of biblical research. We may conclude that while Babylonia, Persia, Syria, Egypt, Asia Minor, Greece, Ethiopia, and Italy have often been in central focus of biblical research, Cyprus has been relatively out of sight. One purpose of the present symposium is to bring Cyprus into focus for biblical research.

Figure 0.7 Bronze Aphrodite (Roman) (courtesy of the Hermitage; JHC).[73]

Are Borders Barriers?

Finally, we may focus on the main issue before the congress: Are borders barriers? Frequently, biblical savants mention "borders" within the land of Israel.[74] For us, the focus is on the assumption that the Mediterranean Sea on the West and (less so) the Jordan River on the East were not only borders but barriers. Let us concentrate on the second of these first: Did the biblical authors imagine the Jordan River and Valley to be a barrier?

The Jordan River and Valley is often perceived to be only a border, not a barrier.[75] During the late Bronze Age, Joshua crossed the border of the Jordan River; it was never described as a dangerous border as was the Negev far to the south. During the Iron Age, Israelites often moved across the Jordan and sometimes settled there. The kingdoms of David and Solomon included the area from Dor on the western coast to Damascus to the east—obviously far beyond the Jordan. During the times of Jeroboam I and Rehoboam, "Judah" included the land from Lachish on the border of Philistia to cities north of Moab and east of the Jordan. During the period of the Hasmoneans, Kinnereth, Jordan, and the Salt Sea were not barriers. For example,

Figure 0.8 The remains of the Roman harbor at Caesarea Maritima, looking westward (JHC).

recently anchors, remains of boats, a lighthouse, and docks have been found on the western shores of the Dead Sea, proving that Jews crossed the Dead Sea; it was no barrier. Thus, throughout biblical history, the River Jordan may have been a minor border but it was no barrier.

The Mediterranean, in contrast, was often considered a border *and* a barrier by scholars, but a focus on Cyprus in biblical history helps all perceive that the western border of Palestine was not a barrier. Ancient accounts and excavations at Dor, Ashkelon, Ashdod, and Gaza, as well as Roman remains at Caesarea Maritima, prove that the border was porous. In antiquity, invasions from the West continued from the time of the Philistines to that of the Romans. The incursions from the West were earlier with the Egyptians; and Egyptian military outposts are known at Beth Shean.[76] Caesarea Maritima, beginning with Herod the Great, witnesses to vast amounts of influence from many areas to the West; it defined a border but not a barrier.[77]

It has become obvious that to speak about the land of the Bible is to include the people who came to the land of the Bible. They came from the East, beginning with Abraham, and continued from the West with the Egyptians, Phoenicians, Greeks, and Romans. These western people were influential and they include Barnabas of Cyprus.

Borders that are barriers can cease being obstacles for travelers. For example, after the Second World War, the borders between countries in Europe were barriers.

Travelers had to go through checkpoints that were often excruciatingly demanding. Now, one moves from England to Poland crossing borders that no longer have barriers.

Crossing the border between west and east Berlin was a painful and sometimes terrifying experience, as one walked through "Check Point Charlie" and looked up at machine guns aimed down upon you. Once the border was a barrier, but it is now gone and has disappeared into the bustling modern city.

Copper or copper alloys were used widely in the Levant to make vessels (Exod 27:3), tools, jewelry, musical instruments (1 Chr 15:19), and military equipment. From the discovery of Iron Age weapons in and near Jerusalem, we can surmise that some of David's fighters used weapons made of bronze that emanated from Cyprus. In early Judaism, most of the coins made by the Palestinian Jews were made of copper or bronze. The famous widow's mite was a Jewish prutah which contained copper (Matt 10:9; Mark 12:42; Luke 21:2). Copper often denotes or implies Cyprus.

The land of ancient Palestine had few copper resources. As already mentioned, a copper mine has been located at *Timna*. The mine is along Wadi Arabah in southern Palestine, but it was operated by Egyptians and not King Solomon. Furthermore, furnaces for smelting copper have been found in such places as Beth-Shemesh, Tell Qasile, and Ai (1 Kgs 7:14, 45-46). It is probable that in antiquity the most abundant source for copper was Cyprus.[78] By at least the fourth century BCE, copper smelting can be discerned at Idylion on Cyprus.[79] Thus, when we hold a bronze weapon or prutah found in ancient Palestine we may be touching a product from Cyprus. Perhaps such an experience helps us realize that the western Mediterranean edge of Palestine was a border but not a barrier.

We may now answer our second question. Sometimes borders are barriers. At other times, borders are not barriers. The Mediterranean must not be portrayed, or perceived, as a barrier to the West for Palestinians or to the East for those in Greece and Italy; the "Great Sea" provided a highway or gateway between two different cultures: the West and the East.

Some major questions have been brought into focus and answered. Now I shall conclude with questions raised about Cyprus and biblical history:

- Is the brilliant creativity seen in early Cypriote art due to wealth from copper?
- Did copper get its name from Cyprus?
- Did Saul, David, and Solomon use weapons made on Cyprus or from Cypriot material?
- How and in what ways is Cyprus important for biblical history?
- Did Cypriots fashion new boats and help the Persians, then the Greeks, and later Herod?
- Who used the word "Kittim" and what did it signify, by whom and when?
- Was Barnabas a Levite from Cyprus as the author of Acts claims?
- Why would "Levites" be on Cyprus?
- What can we know historically about Lazarus going to Cyprus?
- Did Paul convert Sergius Paulus?
- Did Jews stone Barnabas?
- Was Paul the first to bring "Christianity" to Cyprus?

Suffice it now to conclude this beginning with questions that remain challenging and stimulating. How many more perspectives and questions will be raised by the following exploratory chapters?

Notes

1. Stuart Swiny et al., eds., *Res Maritimae: Cyprus and the Eastern Mediterranean from Prehistory to Late Antiquity* (ASOR Archaeological Reports 04; Atlanta: Scholars Press, 1997).
2. One excellent recently published example is Laura Nasrallah, Charalambos Bakirtzis, and AnneMarie Luijendijk, eds., *From Roman to Early Christian Cyprus*, WUNT 437 (Tübingen: Mohr Siebeck, 2020). The focus of that volume is largely the period of Late Antiquity and is less specifically oriented toward the biblical period and biblical studies.
3. In this volume, see D. C. Allison, "Cyprus and Early Christianity: Did Everybody Know Everybody?"
4. See the challenging and insightful chapter in this collection by Jolyon Glenn Rivoir Pruszinski. With the requisite atmospheric conditions, a person in Syria might see the high mountain on Cyprus.
5. See the concise and authoritative introduction and color images in Vassos Karageorghis, *Cyprus Museum and Archaeological Sites on Cyprus* (Athens: Ekdotike Athenon S.A., 1985).
6. I am indebted to the entries on "Cyprus" in *Easton's Bible Dictionary*, in *Fausset's Bible Dictionary*, in *Nave's Topical Bible*, in *Smith's Bible Dictionary*, and entries in other authoritative dictionaries focused on biblical studies.
7. M. Dayagi-Mendels, "Introduction," in *Chronicles of the Land: Archaeology in the Israel Museum Jerusalem*, edited by Dayagi-Mendels and Silvia Rozenberg (Jerusalem: The Israel Museum, 2010), p. 7.
8. R. Steven Notley and Jeffrey P. Garcia, "Queen Helena's Jerusalem Palace—In a Parking Lot?" *BAR* 40 (May/June 2014): 28–39, 62–5; the image of the pearl and gold earring with two emeralds is on p. 39.
9. In the present volume, see A. Faust, "Cyprus and the Land of Israel: The Mediterranean as a Bridge and the Diverse Consequences of Cultural Contact."
10. See the core-formed bottle and juglets that were made in Egypt or Cyprus (more likely). For color images, see *Chronicles of the Land*, pp. 300–1.
11. See the image in J. H. Charlesworth and Michael Medina, *Walking through the Land of the Bible: Historical 3D Adventure* (Jerusalem: The Hebrew University Magnes Press, 2014), p. 115.
12. See the image on p. 13 and the discussion on pp. 12–19 in K. Hadjidemetriou, *A History of Cyprus*, 2nd ed. (Nicosia: I. G. Kassoulides & Sons, Ltd., 2007).
13. Archaeological evidence suggests that human presence in the Dikteon Cave began in the Neolithic period and continued for the past 6000 years. It also was apparently a center for the worship of Zeus from the early Minoan period or from 2000 to 700 BCE.
14. H. Whipps claims that archaeological evidence indicates some Greeks believed Zeus was worshipped and believed to have been born on Mount Lykaion in Arcadia since the supreme god was celebrated there before 3000 BCE. Whipps, "Mythic Birthplace of Zeus Said Found," *LiveScience* (February 9, 2000).

15 Stephanie L. Budin rightly argues against a fertility-only interpretation of Aphrodite. She was a powerful and erotic symbol of sexual pleasure. See her "Creating a Goddess of Sex," in *Engendering Aphrodite: Women and Society in Ancient Cyprus*, edited by D. Bolger and N. Serwint, ASOR Archaeological Reports 07 (Boston: ASOR, 2002), pp. 315–24.
16 According to Hesiod, *Theogony*, 195, Aphrodite was born in the sea off of Cythera, Cyprus, from the foam (in Greek, *aphros*). The foam was created from the genitals of Uranus. Also, see Homer 5 and Plato, *Symposium* 180e. Aphrodite was sexually active. According to the *Odyssey*, she commits adultery with Ares, and according to the *First Homeric Hymn to Aphrodite*, she enjoys sex with the shepherd named Anchises.
17 In the Charlesworth collection are bronze and clay statues of Aphrodite dating from the Persian, Greek, and Roman periods.
18 "Citium," in *Encyclopedia Britannica*; the contribution was by "the editors."
19 For a table of archaeological ages, see "Archaeological Periods of Cyprus" earlier in this volume.
20 See the color image in Despina Pilides and Nikolas Papadimitriou, eds., *Ancient Cyprus: Cultures in Dialogue* (Nicosia: Department of Antiquities, Cyprus, 2012), p. 72.
21 In the volume just cited. See also K. Sari, "Cyprus and the Shore of Israel during the Persian Period."
22 Athienou began no earlier than the sixteenth century BCE. See Trude Dothan and Amnon Ben-Tor, *Excavations at Athienou, Cyprus 1971–1972*, Qedem 16 (Jerusalem: Institute of Archaeology, Hebrew University of Jerusalem 1983).
23 (Rolfe, LCL 300). I am indebted to Hadjidemetriou, "Navigation, Religion and Letters in Historical Times," *A History of Cyprus*, pp. 111–12.
24 John Strange, *Caphtor/Keftiu: A New Investigation*, Acta Theologica Danica 14 (Leiden: Brill, 1980).
25 Karageorghis, *Cyprus Museum and Archaeological Sites on Cyprus*, p. 6.
26 See Hadjidemetriou, *A History of Cyprus*, p. 25.
27 For images of Enkomi, see Karageorghis, *Cyprus Museum and Archaeological Sites on Cyprus*, p. 20.
28 See Karageorghis, *Cyprus Museum and Archaeological Sites on Cyprus*, images on pp. 40 and 41. Also, see the eleventh-century royal gold scepter from Kourion on p. 43 and the eleventh-century gold diadem from Enkomi on the same page.
29 See the color images and helpful discussions in Sylvia Brehme et al., *Ancient Cypriote Art in Berlin* (Nicosia: A. G. Leventis Foundation and the Staatliche Museen zu Berlin, 2001). Note esp. Gertrud Platz-Horster, "Jewellery" on pp. 67–9. Note the spelling of "Jewellery"; it is on the page and the table of contents.
30 See the publications in V. Karageorghis and M. Demas, *Excavations at Kition V* (Nicosia: Department of Antiquities Cyprus, 1985).
31 (Oldfather, LCL 279). For the text, see Hadjidemetriou, *A History of Cyprus*, p. 52.
32 I am indebted to the research published by Hadjidemetriou, *A History of Cyprus*, pp. 48 to 57.
33 See especially the following: Vassos Karageorghis, *The Cyprus: Ancient Monuments* (Nicosia: C. Epiphaniou Publications, Ltd., 1989); Karageorghis, *The Cyprus Museum* (Nicosia: C. Epiphaniou Publications Ltd., 1989); Pilides and Papadimitriou, *Ancient Cyprus: Cultures in Dialogue*. The first two publications are designed for a popular audience.

34   I am indebted to Hadjidemetriou for much of this summary.
35   See C. P. Georgiades, *History of Cyprus* (Nicosia: Demetrakis Christophorou, 1993), pp. 75–6.
36   See Jos J. Mark, "Zeno of Citium," *Ancient History Encyclopedia* (February 15, 2011).
37   Little is known about Eudemus' life and writings. His lone remaining writing is a fragment of a letter to Theophrastus, who defeated Eudemus by becoming Aristotle's successor as head of the *Lyceum*; it discusses an interpretation of Aristotle's *Physics*; see Simplicius, *Phys*. 923.
38   For images of the theaters of Soloi, Salamis, and Kourion, see Karageorghis, *Cyprus Museum and Archaeological Sites on Cyprus*, pp. 24, 27, 31.
39   I am indebted to the information on Cyprus found in the *Encyclopædia Britanica*.
40   Martial *Epig* 4.441; for the Latin text and English translation, see Grete Stefani, ed., *Man and the Environment in the Territory of Vesuvius: The Antiquarium of Boscoreale*, Archeologia Vesuviana (Pompeii: Flavius Edizioni Pompeii, 2010), p. 120. Also see M. Gigante, *Il fungo sul Vesuvio secondo Plinio il Giovane* (Rome, 1989).
41   See Plutarch *Vit. Ant.* 36.3; Dio Chrysostom, *Hist.* 49 32.5; a reliable discussion is found in Bernd Kollmann, *Joseph Barnabas: His Life and Legacy*, translated by M. Henry (Collegeville, MN: Liturgical Press, 2004), pp. 4–5.
42   See images of the "Jupiter Hall," in *The Hermitage*, edited by Maria Lyzhenkova and Valery Fateyev (St. Petersburg: P-s Art Publishers, 2008), pp. 134–5.
43   Hadjidemetriou, *A History of Cyprus*, p. 23.
44   A. Kalman, "Timna Copper Mines Dated to King Solomon Era," *The Times of Israel* (September 8, 2013). J. Bonazzo, "Scientists Just Discovered a Major Part of King Solomon's 3,000-Year-Old Mines," *Observer* (January 27, 2017). The Timna Valley is about 15 miles north of Eilat. The site is not mentioned in the Bible. The "Timna" mentioned in Judges 14 is further north of Solomon's mines.
45   Notably, see the MetPublication: *The Cesnola Collection of Cypriot Art*, https://www.metmuseum.org/art/metpublications/The_Cesnola_Collection_of_Cypriot_Stone_Sculpture.
46   Sometimes it is difficult to decide if a glass object was made in Egypt for "Egyptians' Cypriote clientele" or was produced in "a local Cypriote glass industry." See esp. Dan Barag in Yael Israeli, *Ancient Glass in the Israel Museum: The Eliahu Dobkin Collection and Other Gifts* (Jerusalem: The Israel Museum, 2003), p. 36; also see p. 39: no evidence that glass was produced "in Cyprus or Canaan during the Late Bronze Age." Also see Maud Spaer, *Ancient Glass in the Israel Museum* (Jerusalem: The Israel Museum, 2001), p. 234. Spaer discusses glass that was manufactured on Cyprus (p. 25). For decades, archaeologists have discussed with me glass found in controlled excavations in Israel and that the pieces were from Cyprus. Valuable information is presented in D. B. Harden, *Catalogue of Greek and Roman Glass in the British Museum* 1 (London, 1981), pp. 31–7. I am indebted to Spaer for this bibliographical information.
47   In this volume, see K. Zarras, "Barnabas: The Levite from Cyprus."
48   In the following pages, see K. Ehrensperger, "Meeting the Romans: The Encounter of Paul and Sergius Paulus on Cyprus according to Acts."
49   See *Patrologia Series Graeca* 86, 189.
50   I am grateful to Kollmann, *Joseph Barnabas*, for this information; see p. 5.
51   Israel Eph'al and Joseph Naveh, *Aramaic Ostraca of the Fourth Century BC from Idumaea* (Jerusalem: The Magnes Press, the Hebrew University, and the Israel Exploration Society, 1996); see ostraca 111 and 112 on p. 58 (transcription) and p. 59 (images).

52 Maurya P. Horgan in PTSDSSP, vol. 6B, pp. 92–5. Quotations are from Isaiah 10.
53 Misleading is the use of the term "the Levitical Diaspora." The term created by Martin North, and used by Lawrence Stager and Jeremy M. Hutton, refers to the Levitical cities in the land of Israel. See Hutton's chapter in *Levites and Priests in Biblical History and Tradition*, edited by M. Leuchter and J. M. Hutton, SBL Ancient Israel and Its Literature 9 (Atlanta: SBL, 2011).
54 The issue does not concern most of those who have published on the Levites, including A. H. J. Gunneweg, *Leviten und Priester*, FRLANT 89 (Göttingen: Vandenhoeck & Ruprecht, 1965); R. Nurmela, *The Levites*, South Florida Studies in the History of Judaism 193 (Atlanta: Scholars Press, 1998); Leuchter and Hutton, eds., *Levites and Priests in Biblical History and Tradition*.
55 On Barnabas, see E. Haenchen, "Barnabas," *RGG* 1 (1957): 879; M. Hengel and A. M. Schemer, *Paul between Damascus and Antioch* (London: SCM, 1997), pp. 205–24; Ch. Markschies, "Barnabas," *Der Neue Paul: Enzyklopädie der Antike* 2 (1997): 452; J. B. Daniels, "Barnabas," *ABD* 1 (1992): 610–11. A solid short study is by Kollmann, *Joseph Barnabas*.
56 Since Alexander of Cyprus' *Laudatio Barnabae apostoli* is late (sixth century CE), we may not assume the report is historical and without embellishment. See P. Van Deun, ed., *Sancti Barnabae Apostoli Laudatio*, Corpus Christianorum Series Graeca 26 (Leuven: University Press, 1993).
57 Generally, see J. H. Charlesworth, "Introduction: Devotion to and Worship in Jerusalem's Temple," in *Jesus and Temple: Textual and Archaeological Explorations*, edited by J. H. Charlesworth (Minneapolis: Fortress Press, 2014), pp. 1–17.
58 A solid discussion is provided by Menahem Haran in *Temples and Temple Service in Ancient Israel* (Winona Lake, IN: Eisenbrauns, 1985).
59 L. Schenke, *Die Urgemeinde: Geschichtliche und theologische Entwicklung* (Stuttgart: Kohlhammer, 1990).
60 Kollmann, *Joseph Barnabas*, p. 7.
61 For a discussion of legends about Barnabas, see O. Braunsberger, *Der Apostel Barnabas: Sein Leben und der ihm beigelegte-Brief* (Mainz: Florian Kupferberg, 1876), pp. 20–3.
62 See Charlesworth, *Jesus as Mirrored in John: The Genius in the New Testament* (London: T&T Clark, 2019).
63 Clement of Alexandria, *Stromateis* 2 116.3; Eusebius, *H.E.* 1 12.1; 2 1.4; Epiphanius, *De Incarn.* 4.4; *Panarion* 20. Kollmann concludes that Jesus was in Jerusalem only once and probably never met Barnabas. Kollmann, *Joseph Barnabas*, p. 9. I am impressed by the evidence in John that Jesus spent many months in Jerusalem. If so, one cannot insist that Jesus and Barnabas never met.
64 See my chapter on this possibility in this book.
65 See W. S. Campbell, "Sailing Past Cyprus: The Motivation for Paul's Choice of Mission Areas." Chapter 8, this volume.
66 Nahman Ran, ed., נתיבים לארץ ישראל (Tel Aviv: אמנות ארץ ישראל, 1987), pp. 76–7.
67 For a morphology similar to ין שרף, see חמר ין, "fermenting wine," as in Ps 75:9.
68 Shulaveri is northeast of Lake Van and south of Tbilisi. The place is located 41° 21' 48" North and 44° 49' and 46" East.
69 See Paul Salopek, "Ghost of the Vine: In Georgia, Science Probes the Roots of Winemaking," *National Geographic* (April 14, 2015), https://www.nationalgeographic.org/projects/out-of-eden-walk/articles/2015-04-ghost-of-the-vine/.
70 See Patrick E. McGovern, Donald L. Glusker, Lawrence J. Exner, and Mary M. Voigt, "Neolithic Resinated Wine," *Nature* 381.6582 (June 6, 1996): 480–1. Also see,

P. E. McGovern, S. J. Fleming, and S. H. Katz, eds., *The Origins and Ancient History of Wine* (Luxembourg, 1995).

71 Patrick E. McGovern is Scientific Director of the Biomolecular Archaeology Project for Cuisine, Fermented Beverages, and Health at the University of Pennsylvania Museum in Philadelphia.

72 See Patrick E. McGovern, *Ancient Wine: The Search for the Origins of Viniculture* (Princeton: Princeton University Press, 2003), pp. 296–7.

73 Photographed and published with gratitude, thanks to Mikhail Piotrovsky, Director of the Hermitage Museum.

74 The tendency is understandable when experts focus on the evolution of biblical traditions. An example would be Nadav Na'aman, *Borders and Districts in Biblical Historiography*, Jerusalem Biblical Studies (Jerusalem: Simor, 1986).

75 See esp. Moshe Weinfeld, "The Extent of the Promised Land: The Status of Transjordan," in *Das Land Israel in biblischer Zeit*, edited by G. Strecker (Göttingen: Vandenhoeck & Ruprecht, 1983), pp. 59–75; David Jobling, "'The Jordan a Boundary': Transjordan in Israel's Ideological Geography," in *The Sense of Biblical Narrative*, JSOTSup 39 (Sheffield: JSOT Press, 1986), vol. 2, pp. 88–133, 142–7; Hutton, "Southern, Northern, and Transjordanian Perspectives," in *Religious Diversity in Ancient Israel and Judah*, edited by F. Stavrakopoulou and J. Barton (London/New York: T&T Clark, 2010), pp. 160–1.

76 For images and discussions of Caesarea Maritima, Beth Shean, and other sites, see Charlesworth and Medina, *Walking through the Land of the Bible: Historical 3D Adventure*.

77 Most publications about these facts are well known; one that needs highlighting is the Hendler Collection. All of the objects collected together were discovered in the Caesarea dunes by Yochanan Hendler and his sons. See Shua Amorai-Stark and Malka Hershkovitz, *Ancient Gems, Finger Rings and Seal Boxes from Caesarea Maritima: The Hendler Collection* (Tel Aviv, 2015, published privately in a handsome book).

78 I am indebted to B. S. Hummel, "Copper," in *Eerdmans Dictionary of the Bible*, edited by D. N. Freedman, A. C. Myers, and A. B. Beck (Grand Rapids, MI: Eerdmans, 2000), vol. 1, p. 278.

79 See L. E. Stager, *American Expedition to Idalion, Cyprus*, edited by L. E. Stager, A. Walker, and G. E. Wright, Supplement to the Bulletin of the American Schools of Oriental Research 18 (Cambridge, MA: ASOR, 1974), p. 82.

1

Cyprus and the Land of Israel

The Mediterranean as a Bridge and the Diverse Consequences of Cultural Contact

Avraham Faust

From at least the early second millennium BCE, the eastern Mediterranean served more as a bridge than a barrier, and it appears as if the land of Israel and Cyprus maintained continuous maritime connections ever since. This relationship is best exemplified in pottery, and from the Middle Bronze Age[1] onwards, ceramic objects manufactured on Cyprus were almost always present in the Southern Levant, often in large quantities. Cypriote influence can further be seen in local imitations that were quite popular in various periods.

Contacts, however, can produce a variety of outcomes, and in addition to the importation of actual artifacts, and evidence of their emulation by indigenous potters, some local groups reacted in other ways and even rejected the foreign imports. In this chapter, I briefly present the overall pattern of continued contacts between Cyprus and Canaan during the second and first millennia BCE and will then focus on two specific and distinct Iron Age phenomena—the Ashdod Ware of the southern coastal plain and the Israelite avoidance of imported pottery—each reflecting a different outcome of cultural interaction.

Cypriot Pottery in the Land of Israel during the Second and the Beginning of the First Millennium BCE: Setting the Scene

It is not my aim in this chapter to summarize the history of Cypriot importations to the land of Israel, and the brief summary below is meant to serve as a background for the more detailed discussion of the Iron Age reactions to intercultural trade.

Significant contacts, and a growing number of Cypriot imports, are clearly evident in the Middle Bronze Age, with the number of imports peaking toward the end of this period.[2] Importation continued in the Late Bronze Age (Figure 1.1), increasing with time until reaching a peak in the thirteenth century BCE,[3] when the entire eastern

Mediterranean became significantly integrated into a complex web of political and economic relations.[4]

It is commonly agreed that international trade ceased during the late thirteenth century,[5] but recent evidence suggests that as far as Cyprus' relations with the Southern Levant are concerned there was only a decline, and trade contacts continued throughout the era. This decline is clearly manifested in northern ports like Tyre and Dor, where connections were intense,[6] but also in other regions, like Philistia, where influences are clear, reflecting continued contacts between the new settlers in Israel's southern coastal plain and their contemporaries in Cyprus.[7]

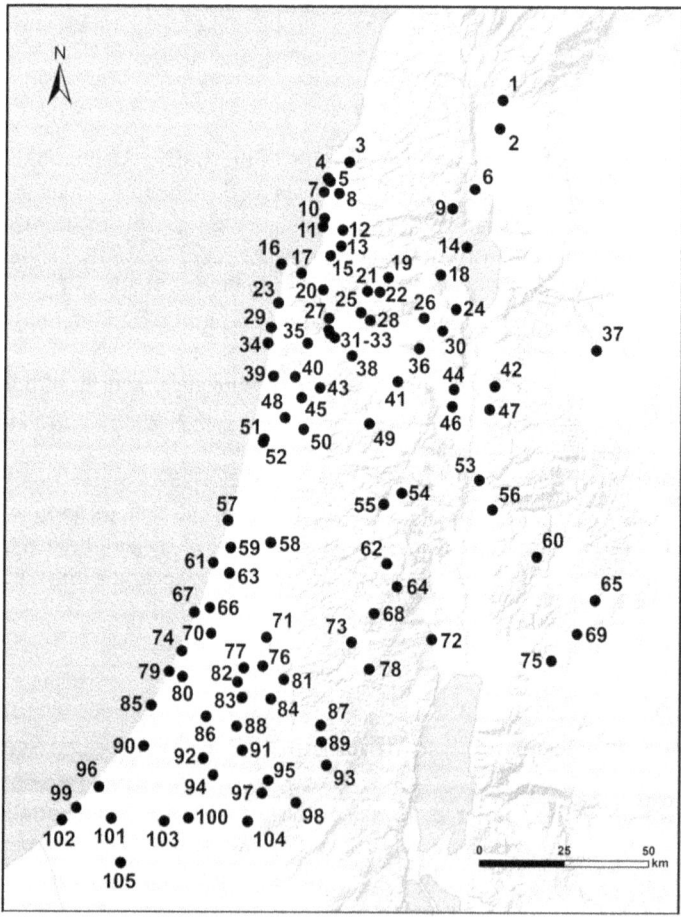

Figure 1.1 A map showing the distribution of Late Bronze Age Cypriot imports in the land of Israel (prepared by Haggai Cohen Klonymus on the basis of data collected by Aaron Greener).

Key

1 Dan	36 Afula	71 Gezer
2 Anafa	37 Fukhar	72 Jericho
3 Hanita	38 Megiddo	73 Gibeon
4 Akhziv	39 Mevorakh	74 Mor
5 Gesher HaZiv	40 Sit Leila	75 Heshban
6 Hazor	41 Ta'anach	76 Batash
7 Nahariyah	42 Abu Kharaz	77 Miqne
8 Kabri	43 Ara	78 Jerusalem
9 Safed	44 Beth Shean	79 Ashdod (southern beach)
10 Acco (Persian gardens)	45 Esur	80 Ashdod
11 Acco	46 Rehov	81 Beth Shemesh
12 Uza	47 Pella	82 Harasim
13 Kison	48 Zeror	83 Zafit
14 Chinnereth	49 Dothan	84 Azekah
15 Aphek (N)	50 Jatt	85 Ashkelon
16 Shiqmona	51 Hefer	86 Zippor
17 Abu Hawam	52 Ma'abarot	87 Gedor
18 Qarney Hittin	53 Sa'idiyeh	88 Zayit
19 Wawiyat	54 Far'ah (N)	89 Beth Zur
20 Regev	55 Shechem	90 Netiv Ha'asara
21 Yiftah'el	56 Deir 'Alla	91 Lachish
22 En Zippori	57 Michal	92 Hesi
23 Megadim	58 Aphek (S)	93 Hebron
24 Yin'am	59 Gerisa	94 Nagila
25 Nazareth	60 Umm ad Dananir	95 Eton
26 Zelef	61 Jaffa	96 Ajjul
27 Qashish	62 Shilo	97 Beit Mirsim
28 Ein el-Hilu	63 Azor	98 Rabud
29 Nami	64 Ein Samiyeh	99 Deir el-Balah
30 Rekhesh	65 Amman	100 Sera'
31 Yoqne'am	66 Humra	101 Jemmeh
32 Qiri	67 Palmachim/Yavneh Yam	102 Ridan
33 Abu Zureik	68 Bethel	103 Haror
34 Dor	69 Umeiri	104 Halif
35 En Haggit	70 Yavneh	105 Far'ah (S)

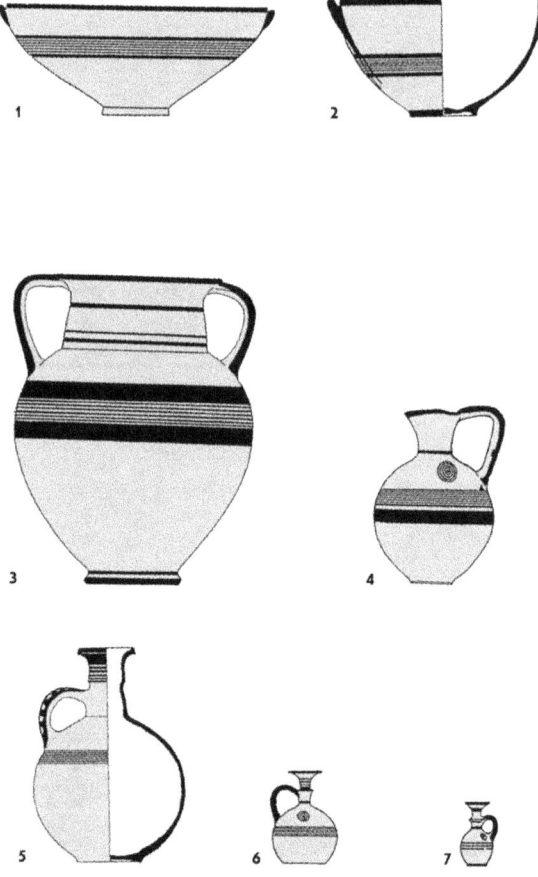

Figure 1.2 Sample of Cypro-Phoenician pottery (BoR) (based on Schreiber [2003] and prepared by Michal Marmelshtein and Sivan Landenberg).

Key

#	Type	Redrawn after:
1	BoR I	Schreiber 2003: Fig. 3:2
2	BoR II	Schreiber 2003: Fig. 4:13
3	BoR I	Schreiber 2003: Fig. 3:17
4	BoR I	Schreiber 2003: Fig. 3:11
5	BoR I	Schreiber 2003: Fig. 3:18
6	BoR II	Schreiber 2003: Fig. 4:21
7	BoR I	Schreiber 2003: Fig. 3:9

International trade resumed on a larger scale during the Iron II, and Cypriot pottery is again found in an increasing number of sites throughout the region.[8] Iron II imports include various families (e.g., bichrome) but most common is the Black on Red (BoR) pottery, also known as Cypro-Phoenician pottery (Figure 1.2).[9] BoR pottery is found throughout the region, and it appears that Ashdod Ware (Figure 1.3, and see below), common in the south, is a local imitation of this form.[10]

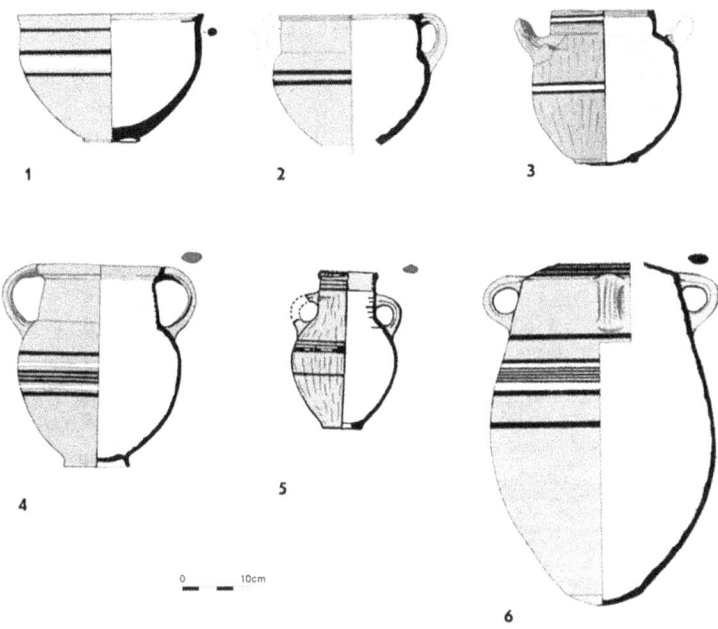

Figure 1.3 Ashdod Ware plate (prepared by Michal Marmelshtein and Sivan Landenberg).

Key

#	Type	Site	Stratum	Redrawn after:
1	Krater	Gezer	3	Dever 1986: Fig. 47:3
2	Krater	Ashdod	XA	Ben-Shlomo 2006: Fig. 1.26:12
3	Krater	Ashdod	7b	Dothan and Porath 1982: Fig. 20:2
4	Krater	Ashdod	8	Dothan and Porath 1982: Fig. 14:14
5	Amphora	Tel 'Amal	IV	Levy and Edelstein 1972: Fig. 11:6
6	Storage jar	Ashdod	3b	Dothan 1971: Fig. 43:5

Cypriot Imports during the Iron II and the Local Reactions to International Trade

Iron Age II in the Southern Levant is one of the best archaeologically known periods in history. Not only is the region the most studied in the world,[11] but Iron II is extremely well represented even in the Southern Levant. This period was marked by a demographic peak[12] and usually constitutes the uppermost layer of significant occupation on most mounds. Hence, strata from this era are found in most sites and are often widely exposed. In addition, this is a "historical" period, and we also have (relative to previous eras) a wealth of textual information, both biblical and extra-biblical. All these factors have made the period both interesting to scholars and well suited to detailed social studies.[13]

In the following pages I would like to focus on two phenomena that are of interest in the context of studying the relations between Cyprus and the Southern Levant: (1) the Ashdod Ware of the southern coastal plain and (2) the Israelite ceramic assemblage.

Ashdod Ware and Cyprus

In the Iron IIA a new type of pottery appears mainly in the southern coastal plain—Ashdod Ware (Figure 1.3, sometimes also known as Late Philistine Decorated Ware [LPDW]).[14] Dothan and Freedman (1967, 130–2), who first identified this group, noted the similarity between Ashdod and Cypro-Phoenician pottery but added that "there are differences significant enough to warrant giving the category a special name 'Ashdod ware.'" Ben-Shlomo (2005, 185) defined this class of pottery in the following words: "Ashdod Ware pottery is characterized by red slip, horizontal wheel or vertical hand burnish and black and white decoration. The forms are chiefly large kraters or closed vessels."[15]

As far as the decoration is concerned, Ashdod Ware presents a complete break from the Aegean-inspired tradition which originated in the Mycenaean IIIC. As Ben-Shlomo (2010, 174) wrote, the decoration is "lacking any Aegean-Style motifs."[16] Not only is the inspiration of the new decoration not to be found in the traditional Philistine style, but as observed already when this pottery was first identified as a new type of ware, the decorative tradition from which the Ashdod pottery is derived is related to the Phoenician and Cypriot style of decoration (Figure 1.2). Thus, according to Dothan and Freedman (1967, 130),[17] "the style, the decoration, and the finish of these vessels … bear a resemblance to Cypro-Phoenician ware," adding that (132) "Among the decorated pottery found, most vessels seem akin to Cypro-Phoenician and black-on-red ware, but all appear to have been made locally." Kempinski (1983, 77) simply wrote that the Ashdod Ware is "a local variant of the 'Black on Red' ware." And Kang and Garfinkel (2009, 156) suggested that this was a reaction to development in the Phoenician world, adding (156): "Ashdod Ware decoration is probably a localized reaction of Philistine culture to much wider developments in pottery style toward the end of the Iron I." This new Iron II decoration is divorced from the Iron I Philistine, Aegean-inspired decoration and belongs to the Phoenician sphere.

This is not the place to discuss the changes in Philistia at any length,[18] but it is quite clear that the local population imitated the Cypriot pottery as part of a much broader change in which the Philistine economy was incorporated within the growing Phoenician economy of the Iron Age[19] and was influenced by it. While in Iron I the Philistines maintained high boundaries with their neighbors, these were drastically reduced in Iron II.[20] The Iron II Philistine material culture indicates integration rather than separation, and the Philistines' strategy of boundary maintenance was transformed from fighting for hegemony and acting as the "neighborhood bully" into peaceful integration and being one of the neighbors.[21]

The Cypriot impact, as part of the larger economic changes brought about by the Phoenician economic success, can therefore be seen in the larger political and socioeconomic shifts in Philistia, as well as, symbolically, in the new pottery form adopted there.

This is one possible reaction to contacts and trade—influence, emulation, and integration.

Israelite Pottery and International Trade

A completely different type of reaction to the international trade can be seen in Israelite society.

A well-known trait of the Israelite ceramic assemblage is the lack (or extreme rarity) of imported pottery.[22] Obviously, this trait is much more significant in Iron II, following the resumption of trade in the eastern Mediterranean, but is manifested in the Iron Age I by the almost total absence of Philistine pottery in the highlands. In Iron II, this is reflected in the rarity in imports in most sites and their absence altogether in other sites. The extreme rarity of imported pottery was not a result of lack of trade, because sites—and often even buildings—in which no imported pottery was found provide various evidence for large-scale trade, including Mediterranean and even Nile fish, imported wood (e.g., cedar), and more.[23] Notably, it cannot be suggested that this was a result of poverty, not only because pottery is not a good indicator of wealth[24] but also because imported pottery is absent from rich households, where other evidence for trade is present. Building 101 at Tel 'Eton exemplifies the phenomenon.

Building 101 is an elite dwelling (Figure 1.4). It is 225 square meters in size on the ground floor only, and it had (at least) one more story over parts of it. It was built on the highest part of the mound using high-quality materials, including ashlar stones and cedars, and boasted many surpluses (Figure 1.5). The wealth of the inhabitants was also expressed in the faunal remains, which included a large percentage of wild animals and fish.[25] Still although almost 200 complete vessels were unearthed there, not a single imported vessel was found (Figure 1.6).

So why don't we have imported ceramics? In order to understand this absence we must broaden our discussion and look for additional patterns.

Interestingly, the absence, or rarity, of imported pottery was accompanied by a similar trait—the absence (or extreme rarity, to be more precise) of decoration on the pottery manufactured in ancient Israel. This phenomenon is also well known to modern scholarship. The lack of painted decoration on Iron I highland pottery has been noticed by practically all scholars dealing with the Settlement phenomenon[26] and was usually explained by the low standards of living and the hardship of life in the small highland

Figure 1.4 A composite aerial photograph of Building 101 at Tel 'Eton (photographed by Sky View and Griffin Aerial Imaging, edited by Yair Sapir; courtesy of the Tel 'Eton Archaeological Expedition).

Figure 1.5 A photograph of Room 101C (Building 101), in which over thirty storage jars were unearthed, apparently used to store liquids (photographed by Avraham Faust; courtesy of the Tel 'Eton Archaeological Expedition).

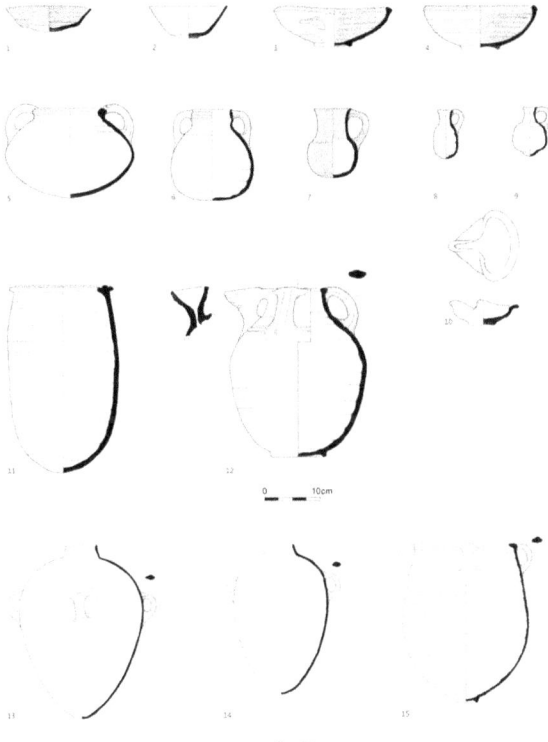

Figure 1.6 A plate of typical vessels from Building 101 (drawn by Yulia Rodman; courtesy of the Tel 'Eton Archaeological Expedition). No imported pottery nor decorated vessels were unearthed in this structure.

Key

No.	Vessel	Reg. No.	Locus	Description
1	Bowl	10195	1052	Red slip inside and outside, wheel burnish inside
2	Bowl	10247-8	1042	
3	Bowl	10469-1	1115	Red slip inside and on the upper part outside, horizontal hand burnish inside
4	Bowl	10150-13	1042	Red slip inside and on rim, horizontal hand burnish inside
5	Cooking-pot	10126-1	1036	
6	Cooking-pot	10179	1042	

7	Jug	10135-3	1036	Red slip outside and on the upper half inside
8	Juglet	10233.01	1063	
9	Juglet	10287.01	1042	Black-gray clay
10	Lamp	10239.04	1036	
11	Hole-mouth	10147-5	1042	
12	Spouted jar	10912-9	1247	
13	Storage jar	10264.01	1056	
14	Storage jar	10147-4	1042	
15	Hole-mouth storage jar	10930-6	1247	

villages of this era.[27] The tradition of not decorating pottery persisted, however, and the conspicuous absence of decoration on the pottery manufactured in the kingdoms of Israel and Judah during Iron Age II is also well known to scholars.[28] Indeed, the finds in the aforementioned Building 101 did not include a single decorated vessel. The reasons behind this remarkable pattern were not often systematically addressed. Notably, unlike the situation in Iron Age I, it cannot be claimed that a low standard of living is responsible for the lack of decoration in Iron Age II, as the standard of living was, at least in some cases (including in Building 101), extremely high.[29]

Notably, the lack of decoration on ceramics in ancient Israel is unique and stands in sharp contrast to both the contemporary pottery of the nearby regions of Cyprus, Phoenicia, Philistia, Midian, Moab, and Edom[30] and the second millennium BCE Canaanite tradition.[31] This absence must be meaningful, therefore, and one has to search for its explanation along social and cultural lines.

It is quite clear that the rarity of imports and the rarity of decoration are related. Why did the Israelites avoid both? Pottery, like all other artifacts, is used to convey messages, and while the issue cannot be discussed here at any length,[32] it appears that the pottery used in Israelite settlement played part of the group's boundary maintenance and ethnic negotiations.[33] What, however, was the message transmitted by the use of simple, undecorated pottery and by the avoidance of imported pottery?

It seems to me that the message was one of simplicity and perhaps also part of a broader message of egalitarianism (see below). A similar phenomenon of lack of decoration, though in a completely different time and place, was observed by Ivor Noël Hume (1974, 108), who noticed that the earliest English delftware (in London) was usually elaborately decorated. After the civil war, however, potters began to produce undecorated plain vessels. Only after the restoration in 1660 did decorated pottery become popular again. Deetz (1996, 81) summarized this trend: "Puritans' attitudes toward decoration of everyday objects might have had an effect on the delftware industry in the London area in the form of reduction of the amount of decorated pottery before the restoration." He, furthermore, attributes the lack of decoration on various artifacts in Anglo-America to Puritan attitudes (Deetz, 81–2). It seems to me that the situation here was somewhat similar.

Interestingly, various scholars, on the basis of biblical texts, claimed that Israelite society had such an ideology.[34] While the texts are problematic sources, and each interpretation is met with counterinterpretations, the ancient Israelites' material culture seems more straightforward. An ethos of simplicity and egalitarianism is indeed expressed in many additional material traits,[35] and in the following I would like to discuss a few of these.

Pottery Repertoire: Much had been written about the continuity of pottery forms from the Late Bronze Age to the Iron Age.[36] It is clear, however, that the ceramic repertoire in the Israelite settlements in the highlands is extremely limited when compared to both Iron Age I lowlands and the Late Bronze Age throughout the region.[37] It is interesting to quote Bunimovitz and Yasur Landau (1996, 96), who also observed the "*poorness and isolation reflected in the Israelite assemblage.*" They raised the possibility that this is a "*hint at ideological behavior*" (emphasis in original). While the issue was not elaborated, it is clear that in contrast to the use of an elaborated assemblage, a limited repertoire can be easily used to convey similar messages of simplicity and egalitarianism.[38]

Rarity of Temples: The absence of temples in the Iron Age I highland villages is also very noticeable. While temples are abundant during the Late Bronze Age,[39] they disappear from the archaeological record of the Iron Age highlands.[40] It should be stressed that this cannot be attributed to the rural nature of the highland sites, as temples in villages existed in many periods, both before and after Iron Age I,[41] and, furthermore, temples are also absent from most cities in Iron II Israel and Judah.[42] The lack of real temples and, accordingly, temple personnel (it is likely that there were local priests, etc.) might also be a result of an egalitarian ideology that rejected overt signs of hierarchy.[43]

Four-Room House: As claimed elsewhere,[44] an egalitarian ideology is reflected in the plan of the four-room house. This can be seen most clearly in an analysis of movement within this house. The four-room plan enables easy access to every room and is lacking any hierarchy in the structuring of the rooms; unlike other dwellings there are hardly any movement restrictions, and once in the central room, one can go directly to the desired space (Figure 1.7). Again, this seems to reflect an ideology of egalitarianism.

Lack of Royal Inscriptions: A phenomenon that was little discussed in the past is the lack of royal inscriptions in the kingdoms of Israel and Judah (unlike previous traits this one is relevant only for Iron Age II). The territories of the kingdoms of Israel and Judah were excavated to a much larger extent than any other polity in the region and have indeed yielded much larger quantities of finds of various sorts. For example, Israel and Judah produced more ostraca than any other state in the region.[45] When one examines the quantity of royal inscriptions, however, the situation changes dramatically. Although not abundant in any polity, all the states in the region yielded such inscriptions,[46] with the exception of Israel and Judah (e.g., Na'aman 2002, 94; Hallo 2003, xxiii–xxvi; Rendsburg 2007).[47] We are witnessing a strange pattern, in

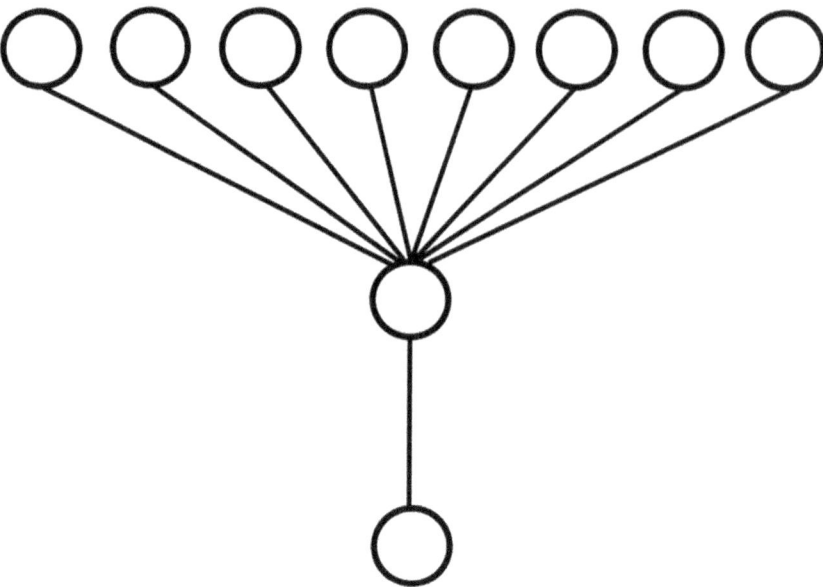

Figure 1.7 Access analysis of a typical four-room house.

which the polities that were excavated much more intensively than all the others, and whose finds are much more numerous, are (as yet) lacking royal inscriptions.[48]

This pattern cannot be an accident, as the large number of excavations indicates. I believe that in accordance with the aforementioned traits, the society under discussion did not generally approve of this genre.[49]

The Lack of Burials: Hardly any Iron Age burials are known in the highlands prior to the eighth century BCE, an issue discussed at length by Kletter (2002) and myself.[50] This stands in sharp contrast to the Late Bronze Age in all parts of the country[51] and to the Iron Age I–IIA in the lowlands.[52] Tombs and burials are an important channel for the transmission of messages of social difference and status, and they certainly served this purpose in the Late Bronze Age.[53] While there was a variety of burial types in Late Bronze Age Canaan, which could have resulted from any of several reasons (of which social hierarchy is but one), even the "multiple cave burials" that characterized the highlands throughout most of the second millennium BCE were extremely rare during Iron I,[54] therefore breaking the continuity that prevailed through wide segments of Canaanite society for almost 800 years.[55] Even if a few Iron I burials are identified in the highlands,[56] the general pattern is striking: during the Late Bronze Age the highlands were only sparsely settled but many tombs are known,[57] while during the Iron Age I–IIA the area was filled with settlements, but such burials are practically absent.[58]

It is likely that almost all individuals during this period (and area) were buried in simple inhumations;[59] the lack of any observable burials is a clear reflection of an egalitarian ideology and exhibits a sharp contrast to Late Bronze Age Canaanite traditions. As burials have an important social role, they are a chief vehicle through which such an ideology can be expressed and channeled.[60]

This is not the place to discuss any of these traits in detail, as each of them deserves an article of its own,[61] but the important thing is that they all attest to the same phenomenon. The highland population of Iron Age I had an ideology of egalitarianism and simplicity, and this ethos continued well into Iron Age II.[62] While not a direct reaction to interaction with Cypriot pottery, the aversion for imports is a related phenomenon.

The Rarity of Imports in Context: The aversion to imported pottery was part of a larger system of worldviews that can be exemplified in other phenomena as well, including settlement patterns. Thus, although the Sharon was the only part of the coastal plain controlled by the Israelites, and one could expect heavy investment there due to the great importance of maritime trade at the time, settlement in the region was at a nadir during the eighth century BCE, probably for cultural reasons.[63] This attitude can be seen not only in the reduction of the number of sites and their sizes but also in the surprising finds at Dor, the main port on the central coastal plain, where Gilboa, Sharon, and Bloch-Smith (2015, 71) noted that "in the mid-to-late-9th-century BC, most probably under the Omrides, the town of Dor underwent a thorough programme of urban renovation … The new centre was heavily fortified … A series of public structures stood on the south, and extensive open spaces replaced previous domestic quarters," adding that "an economic revolution accompanied this urban one—namely the disruption of nearly all of Dor's traditional inter-regional interaction spheres, especially maritime ones with Cyprus and Egypt. Dor's new administrative centre looked mainly inland, rather than to the sea."

The same attitude is expressed in other realms, including language. Thus, the Israelites had a negative view of the sea (the channel for maritime trade), and the word "sea" (*yam*) itself had a very negative meaning.[64] The Israelite also preferred to avoid the west, associated with the sea (the west was also called *yam*), and oriented their houses to other directions and mainly the east.[65]

Moreover, it appears as if, at times at least, the Israelites also had a negative attitude toward trade and many of its products. The most common term in biblical Hebrew for one who engages in trade is "a Canaanite." Canaanites were obviously not viewed positively in the Iron Age society which produced much of the Bible. Whether most traders were Canaanites or not, the term indicates that the trading profession was viewed negatively. In King and Stager's (2001, 190) words: "At least in their propaganda the Israelites were condescending toward traders and commerce." This negative attitude is also reflected in the extreme rarity of imported pottery in most Israelite sites, discussed above.

Thus, Israelite reaction to trade is just another type of reaction to contact, that is, rejection and avoidance.

The Mediterranean as a Bridge and the Diverse Consequences of Contact

Despite ups and downs, contacts between Cyprus and the Southern Levant during the second and first millennium BCE never really ceased, exhibiting the mediating nature of the Mediterranean, bridging between the two regions and enabling cultural contact.

Cypriot pottery was imported to the land of Israel continuously during the second millennium BCE, although some decline is evident toward the end of the millennium (during the southern Levantine Iron I or the LC IIIB-CG IA[66] in Cyprus). In the early Iron II, international trade resumed on a larger scale, and this is exemplified by various imports, for example, the BoR pottery.

It is in this period, when our data is far more detailed, that we can see a number of interesting processes, showing that contact does not necessarily result in similarity (Eriksen 2013, 23). In some regions (Philistia) the impact of contact was so great that we witness not only importation of actual vessels but the emergence of a new pottery family, emulating it. This is of course a direct result of the contacts across the Mediterranean.

In some other regions, namely in Israelite sites, this pottery—like other types of imported ware—was practically avoided. This avoidance was not a direct reaction to Cypriot influence but rather part of the broader Israelite experience with contact with other groups. Still, even if it was a result of contact with other "foreign" groups (i.e., non-Cypriot), this experience was extended to Israelites' reaction to Cypriot imports.

Thus, in Iron II we can see two opposite reactions to international contact and trade: adoption and avoidance. One way or the other, it is important to stress that avoidance can only exist when there is contact between groups, and even the Israelite aversion to the use of imports, while clearly part of a much wider "mind-set," should be attributed to contact with other cultures.

Notes

1   For a table of archaeological periods, see "Archaeological Periods of the Levant" earlier in this volume.
2   Frankel (2014, 491); see also Greener (2015, 41). For full bibliographic notes, see the concluding bibliography in this volume.
3   Gonen (1992b, 236–9); Killebrew (2005); Greener (2015).
4   Gonen (1992b, 247); Killebrew (2005); Bunimovitz (in press).
5   E.g., Ward and Joukowsky (1992); see also Cline (2014).
6   E.g., Aubet (2014, 713); Steel (2014, 587); Gilboa (2014); (2015); Gilboa, Waiman-Barak, and Sharon (2015).
7   E.g., Bunimovitz (1998); Killebrew (2005); see also Master, Mountjoy, and Mommsen (2015); Sherratt (2003).
8   E.g., Gilboa (2015); Iacovou (2014).
9   E.g., Schreiber (2003); Gilboa (2015); Iacovou (2014).
10 E.g., Dothan and Freedman (1967, 130); Schreiber (2003, 13); Kempinski (1983, 77); Faust (2015).
11 For some numbers, see Faust and Safrai (2005); (2015).
12 Broshi and Finkelstein (1992).
13 E.g., Reviv (1993); Faust (2012).
14 Ben-Shlomo et al. (2004), and see below.
15 Elsewhere, Ben-Shlomo et al. (2004, 2–3) used what appears to be a more encompassing definition, including "(1) Iron Age IIA coastal forms; (2) thick, dark red slip; (3) meticulous vertical hand burnish; and (4) painted black and/or white decoration (usually bands)," adding that "although not all of these features must

appear together, at least two should" (see also Shai and Maeir 2012, 348). It seems to me, however, that the most important characteristic of the Ashdod Ware is the decoration (#4 above)—in the absence of the painted black and/or white decoration I do not think we could consider the vessels as part of this family. Additionally, while the phenomenon clearly centers on Philistia, it is not limited to this area and hence the term "Philistine" (as in LPDW) is somewhat problematic, as it denotes ethnic association and also suggests continuity with the Iron I Aegean-inspired pottery of Philistia, which as we shall presently see does not exist.

16 Cf., Dothan (1982, 218); Uziel (2007, 169).
17 Also Ben-Shlomo (2006, 23, 69); Schreiber (2003, 13).
18 See Faust (2015); Faust and Lev-Tov (2011; 2014); and additional literature.
19 For the Phoenicians, see, e.g., Aubet (2001; 2014); Elayi (2013).
20 E.g., Faust (2013b; 2015) and many references.
21 Faust (2013b; 2015) for discussion and references.
22 E.g., Dever (1995, 204); Bloch-Smith and Alpert Nakhai (1999, 76).
23 See Faust (2006a; 2006b) and many references.
24 E.g., Vickers and Gill (1994).
25 E.g., Faust et al. (2017); Faust and Katz (2017); Sapir, Avraham, and Faust (2018).
26 E.g., Dever (1995, 205); Mazar (1985a, 69); (1992b, 290); Bloch-Smith and Alpert Nakhai (1999, 76); King and Stager (2001, 139).
27 This argument is very problematic, as many "simple" societies (including those much simpler than the Israelite society of the Iron I) decorate their pottery. Furthermore, a functional explanation does not negate a social or cognitive one, and the dichotomy is artificial (see Hodder and Hutson 2003, 71; Jones 1997, 110–27). While not mutually exclusive, the presence of a functional explanation for past behavior makes it very difficult for scholars to ascribe it to any other kind of explanation. The absence of a functional explanation, however, makes the need for another form of explanation more apparent.
28 Barkay (1992, 354); Aharoni (1982, 177); Franken and Steiner (1990, 91); Dever (1997, 465); Lapp (1992, 442).
29 E.g., Campbell (1994); Faust (1999; 2012); Faust et al. (2017).
30 E.g., Barkay (1992, 325, 326, 336–8, 354, 358); E. Mazar (1985); Ben-Shlomo, Shai, and Maeir (2004).
31 E.g., Franken and London (1995).
32 E.g., David et al. (1988); Braun (1991); Faust (2006b).
33 E.g., Faust (2006a; 2006b).
34 E.g., Lods (1932); Wolf (1947); Albright (1961, 119); Mendenhall (1962); Kelso (1968, 48); Speiser (1971); Gordis (1971, 45–60); Humphrey (1978); Gottwald (1979); Lenski (1980); Cross (1988); Dever (1992); Berman (2008); Shapira (2009).
35 Such accordance between various facets of culture is expected; see Deetz (1996); David et al. (1988, 378); Hodder and Hutson (2003).
36 Most notably by Dever, e.g. (1993; 1995); see also Kletter (2002, 33), and additional references.
37 E.g., Albright (1961, 119); Esse (1991, 109; 1992, 94–5); Dever (1995, 204–5); Mazar (1992b, 290–2); King and Stager (2001, 139).
38 Note that the limited repertoire phenomenon is relevant only for Iron I, and this specific trait disappears in the transition to Iron II, when Israelite society became more stratified.
39 E.g., Gonen (1992b, 222–32); Mazar (1992a).

40 E.g., Bloch-Smith and Alpert Nakhai (1999, 76); Mazar (1992b, 298).
41 E.g., Faust (2000, 6, 14; 2005, 112, 116, 119, and additional references).
42 Faust (2010); see also Alpert Nakhai (2015, 90–3, 95); Dever (2017, 497, 503); Meyers (2017, 11); Farber (2018, 441).
43 See also Dever (1995, 205).
44 Bunimovitz and Faust (2002; 2003); Faust and Bunimovitz (2003); (2014).
45 E.g., Ahituv (1992).
46 E.g., Gitin, Dothan, and Naveh (1997); Biran and Naveh (1993); (1995); McCarter (1996, 84–96) and many others.
47 The Siloam Inscription, despite the nice script, does not even mention the king and cannot be regarded as royal in this sense.
48 Such inscriptions were clearly present in some special circumstances, for example, in non-Israelite regions of the kingdom of Israel (note that Na'aman 2002, 94, expects such inscriptions to be found in the future). The general pattern, however, is clear, and it is not likely to be affected by future discoveries (and I assume some inscriptions will eventually be found).
49 See also Stein (1994); Blanton (1998, 162) for a similar interpretation in a different context.
50 Faust (2004; 2011); see also Tappy (1995, 65–6); Ilan (1997a, 385; 1997b, 220); Barkay (1994, 160, note 211); Dever (2003).
51 Highlands and lowlands; e.g., Gonen (1992a); Gonen (1992b, 240–5).
52 Bloch-Smith (1992); Kletter (2002).
53 E.g., Bunimovitz (1995, 326).
54 Gonen (1992b, 245).
55 Bunimovitz (1995, 331).
56 Bloch-Smith (2004); see also Livingstone (2002).
57 Gonen (1992a); Gonen (1992b, 240–5); see also Eisenstadt, Arabas, and Ablas (2004); Peleg and Eisenstadt (2004); Peleg (2004).
58 For reasons for the emergence of the Judahite tomb in the eighth century BCE, see Faust and Bunimovitz 2008. We must note that in the kingdom of Israel the tradition of burying only in simple inhumations prevailed until its destruction in the eighth century BCE.
59 Faust (2004; 2011).
60 For examples where burials reflect an egalitarian ethos, although the society is highly stratified, see Metcalf and Huntington (1991, 134) for Saudi Arabia and Parker Pearson (1982) for England. For a detailed discussion, see Faust 2004; 2011 and additional references.
61 See also Faust (2002; 2006; 2010; 2011).
62 It must be stressed that having a certain ideology does not necessarily mean that reality followed. No society is truly egalitarian, and the Israelite society was clearly not, especially during the Iron Age II (the period of the Monarchy). The ideology influenced many traits, as we have seen here, but reality was different.
63 Faust (2011; 2018, and many references).
64 Lewis (1993, 335); see also Stoltz (1995, 1397–8); Keel (1978, 23, 35, 49, 50, 55, 73–5); Faust (2011; 2018, for discussion and references).
65 E.g., Faust (2001).
66 LC IIIB-CG IA refers to the Late Cypriot Bronze Age IIIB through the Cypriot Geometric Period IA.

2

"In Sorrow Thou Shalt Bring Forth Children": Archaeological Perspectives on Delivery Practices in Canaan and Cyprus

Rona Avissar Lewis

Introduction (Research Framework)

Children have always been a major component of every society; no culture can perpetuate itself without children. Taking this into consideration, one may be surprised by the fact that very little has been written on children in connection with ancient societies. This has begun to change over the past few decades[1] but, there is much more about this issue to be explored.

This chapter deals with the subject of childbirth and delivery in Canaan and Cyprus from the Middle Bronze Age to the Iron Age (the second millennium to the sixth century BCE). This is a relatively long time in human history when examining culture and could potentially raise skepticism since archaeologists usually deal with shorter periods within specific geographical regions. However, due to the fact that we know little about this issue, I think that surveying the practice of delivery over a long period of time, and in two different geographical regions, will enable us to identify differences, even though it is likely that people in both Canaan and Cyprus shared the same basic physical and emotional needs.[2] Unfortunately, the main difficulty in studying these geographic areas during these periods is that we do not have many written sources dealing directly with this subject. Archaeology provides us with important information, but it must be used wisely and one must always keep in mind that it cannot furnish a complete picture. Therefore, only a multidisciplinary approach and a wide perspective on the subject can give us new insights and ideas on the issue.

The research framework involved in such a study includes gathering information from diverse disciplines, including sociology, education, child rearing, psychology, anthropology, and ethnography. Examination must be made of historical texts from the different periods and cultures, household archaeology, and artistic representations from different periods and geographical areas in light of information from archaeology and its subdisciplines. From these sources, broad commonalities are being identified and fuller understanding can be gained. This requires working through various research disciplines and making deductions and interpretations from source material.[3]

Fertility

In the Bible the very first blessing, and a very substantial one, is to have children. This is seen in Gen 1:27-28: "Male and female created He them. And God blessed them, and God said unto them, 'Be fruitful, and multiply, and replenish the earth, and subdue it.'" In Gen 9:1, 7: "And God blessed Noah and his sons, and said unto them, 'Be fruitful, and multiply, and replenish the earth … And you, be ye fruitful, and multiply; bring forth abundantly in the earth, and multiply therein.'" In Gen 22:17: "In blessing I will bless thee, and in multiplying I will multiply thy seed as the stars of the heaven, and as the sand which is upon the sea shore." Having children is described as a blessing to the people and to every couple, highlighting the importance of children both to every family and to the population in general.

It is clear from poems, magical spells, letters, and medical documents from the ancient Near East that societies such as the Egyptians, Babylonians, Acadians, Sumerians, Hittites, Ugarits, and the Israelites knew not only how to conceive, of course, but also about the connection between the lack of a menstrual cycle and conception.[4] In Egyptian mythology, Osiris took his sister Isis and "placed her on [his] phallus," and she became pregnant.[5] Moreover, in addition to the physical aspect, there were many rituals relating to pregnancy including better days for childbirth. For instance, on the twenty-fifth of the month, the festival day of Ishtar, it was believed the deity would take care of the child and its wealth. There are also medical papyri[6] which describe details and signs that someone is pregnant, such as the color of the skin or the condition of the breasts; the rate of the heartbeat and the effect of a pregnant woman's urine on weeds and seeds.[7]

Fertility was a major issue in ancient times (and to this day of course), and there are many biblical stories about infertile women. In many of these stories, the couple prays to God and the woman later bears a child. These include stories of the forefathers, such as Sarah and Abraham (Genesis 17); God intercedes and she gave birth to Isaac. Rebekah and Isaac also pray (Genesis 24, 26, 27) and then Rebekah gives birth to Esau and Jacob. It is written that a woman who bears children is deemed fortunate and happy (Gen 29:32-34, 30:20). In the ancient Near East, an infertile woman was considered unfortunate and downcast and as such had a lower status, as fertility was part not only of her self-esteem but of her worth to the community (even if the problem was with the man) and infertility was a reason for which a husband could divorce a woman or take another wife.[8] It is very reasonable that a family, particularly the woman, would do everything they could in order to have a child, including prayers and cultic practices, so it is not surprising to find many female figurines connected to fertility.

The fear of infertility, miscarriages, stillbirths, and the death of a baby or mother during childbirth has been part of the human experience throughout history. The woman, and indeed the whole family, was helpless in these situations and believed that gods, goddesses, deities, and demons were in charge of the entire process—from conception and pregnancy all the way through to childbirth—and could help them through these challenges. It was believed that these gods, goddess deities, and demons were the ones who protected (or harmed) both the woman and the baby. In order to intervene, people prayed, offered sacrifices, drank potions, wore amulets, made and worshipped figurines, and practiced ritual ceremonies throughout the pregnancy.[9]

How Many Children?

Today, scholars learn about infant mortality and the causes of death from modern statistical rates, but it is hard to know much about the death rate and the causes of infant deaths in the ancient world. This may only be done through models, estimations, anthropological studies, and archaeological excavations of children's graves (although it is rare to find buried children's bones because they are much more fragile than those of grown-ups). It is estimated that only around 15 percent of all children's graves have been found.

According to various studies, from the Epipaleolithic until the nineteenth century, the mortality rate of children under a year old was between 30 percent and 40 percent, and the mortality rate of children under 10 years old was as high as 30 percent.[10]

In Europe in the Middle Ages (in different areas there were different rates) only one out of four to five babies survived until the age of one; until the age of two, mortality rates were between 16 percent and 49 percent;[11] in Russia at the beginning of the nineteenth century, the mortality rate of children under the age of five was 50 percent; in Japan at the beginning of the twentieth century, it was a bit less than 50 percent; and in Athens, Greece, during the same period, it was between 25 percent and 30 percent. Although the mortality rate of babies and children was very high, they were still the majority in every population.[12]

So how many did survive? Between 1960 and 2000, children (0–14 years) were 30 percent to 40 percent of the world population. In 2016, children were 25.4 percent of the world population and 41 percent of the population in Africa. In Israel, they were only 27.5 percent of the population; in Cyprus, just 15.6 percent of the population.[13] It has often been assumed that there were crowds and crowds of little children in antiquity, but was this really the situation? In a study of 177 documents[14] from the Neo-Assyrian period (800–600 BCE), it was found that 447 families are mentioned; in 327 of these families (73 percent of all the families) there are details about the number of children. On average, there were 3.71 people per family, two families had fourteen to fifteen persons, eleven families had eight people, thirty-four families had six to seven people, ninety-five families had four to five people, and 185 families (57 percent of the families) had two to three people per family.[15] Very similar rates are seen in an annuity list of workers in Babylonia from the Post-Chaldean period (1158–722 BCE). In this case, there are details about the families of the workers, brothers, and children under the worker's authority. Children under the age of 15–16 were part of the family and lived with it; half of the families had only one child, and one-third of the families had two children.[16] According to ethnographic studies of agricultural societies, households contained between three and seven people, with an average of five people per family.[17] Therefore, we can estimate that the average family had three children.

The Delivery

The delivery was very important and could be dangerous to both the mother and the baby. Genesis 3:16 explains the pang of childbirth as due to the fact that Eve gave Adam to eat from the fruit of the forbidden tree of knowledge: "Unto the woman he said, I will greatly multiply thy sorrow and thy conception; in sorrow thou shalt bring forth children." There are also stories in the Bible in which the woman died during the delivery, such as Rachel while delivering Benjamin (Gen 35:16-20).

How did the woman give birth? One of the very interesting descriptions of a woman giving birth can be seen in Exod 1:16: "And he said, 'When ye do the office of a midwife to the Hebrew women, and see them upon the stools; if it be a son, then ye shall kill him: but if it be a daughter, then she shall live.'" But the phrase "upon the stool" is originally in Hebrew עַל-הָאָבְנָיִם and its translation to English should be "on the potter's wheel." Rashi explains this phrase as "the women's stool."[18] Metzudat Zion (the David Aletschueler commentary on the Bible) explains: the potter has the wheel to make the ceramic, and there is a wheel especially for the women.[19] This means either a stool or a few stones arranged like a stool. However, it is more appropriate to look at this phrase according to Egyptian mythology about the god Khnum, who formed the bodies of new children on his potter's wheel.[20] In 1 Samuel it is written that delivery took place in a "bowed" position: "And his daughter-in-law, Phinehas' wife, was with child, near to be delivered; and when she heard the tidings that the ark of God was taken, and that her father-in-law and her husband were dead, she bowed herself and brought forth; for her pains came suddenly upon her" (1 Sam 4:19).

In Mesopotamian[21] traditions there are a few goddesses (such as Gee-Sin) that help at the time of the delivery, while there are some demons (such as Pazuzu and Lamashtu) that cause trouble during the delivery. Therefore, one needs to pray and give offerings so they will not hurt the mother and the newborn.[22] In written sources from Mesopotamia it is very common to describe deliveries as being done on stone installations so the birthing women can either sit or lean on them at the time of the delivery.[23] In the Atra-hasis (1:281-295) it is written that in the house of the pregnant women, the midwife makes a round symbol with flour and arranges a few stones for the birth to take place upon it. After the delivery, the stone installation stays in its position for another nine days for the Nintu Mami (a goddess who is in charge of the delivery).

Among ancient Egyptian traditions, there are a few goddesses and gods in charge of the delivery and baby (e.g., Hathor, Bes, Tawrat, and Isis) to which the woman should pray and make offerings for a successful process. According to written sources, and mainly depictions, from Egypt there were two main ways to deliver: on a stool or on a stone installation. The upper class would use a special room for delivery; it was called a *Mammisi* (in Coptic, the "place of the delivery"), which was built near the palace or the temple (from the eighth century BCE to the fourth century CE). This was the site

Archaeological Perspectives on Delivery Practices 45

of weddings and the delivery of kings and was also believed to be a place where gods and goddesses were born and married.

An installation built from bricks was found at the Abydos mayoral residence, with depictions of a mother and newborn.[25] A few ostraca with descriptions of delivery on a stool were found at Deir El-Medina (from the New Kingdom). On one ostracon, there is a depiction of a naked woman breastfeeding a newborn. The woman is sitting on a stool, her hair is tied, the image seemingly depicting a ceremony or cultic practice performed immediately after delivery (Figure 2.1). On another ostracon, a naked woman is sitting on a stool or bed, breastfeeding the newborn. Her hair is tied and a young naked woman is holding a mirror for the mother.[26] Backhouse argues that the existence of three very similar ostraca gives, and perhaps suggests a continuity of, meaning. They cannot be meaningless, nor could they be drafts for wall paintings, because they are full of detail and colored. Therefore, she claims that these are a sort of stelae, standing objects with meaning, possibly amulets for blessings and the support of the goddess for the delivery and the baby.[27]

Figure 2.1 Ostracon of delivery. From Deir El-Medina (the New Kingdom).[24]

In Canaan, there are no depictions of delivery, but according to the Bible and other written sources from the region, as well as traditions from Egypt and Mesopotamia, it is very likely that the delivery occurred on a stool, on a stone installation, or while bowed (either with or without a midwife's help). Although there are no descriptions of the delivery, there are many types of female figurines, which are understood as related to fertility due to the emphasis on organs relating to fertility. In most of these figurines, it is impossible to determine at which stage of the birth process these figurines were associated. Clay figurines depicting women in Canaan in different periods were found mainly in households, but also in cultic places. Each period has a distinct type of fertility figurine. Frontal nudity is a main characteristic of these figurines, which may be erotic or may be a symbol of fertility.

In the Middle Bronze Age II,[28] fertility figurines are almost absent from the material culture. However, one figurine made of gold leaf has been found. It depicts a pregnant woman or goddess with one hand on her belly, the other hand resting along the side of her body (such as from Gezer). Other figurines (such as from Tel el-Agul) depict a female figure with both hands under her breasts.[29]

In the Late Bronze Age, the image of a naked goddess is relatively common on figurines. There are some pendants with similar depictions of a naked goddess made of bronze leaf, with punctured holes indicating female genitalia, such as from Tel el-Agul.[30] Some of these naked goddess figurines are shown while holding their breasts with the hands (at Lachish, for example).[31] On the other hand, it is very rare to find figurines of a woman breastfeeding. Until now, only three such figurines (all made from the same mold) have been found—an almost complete one at Revadim and broken ones at Tel Harasim and Aphek. These figurines depict two babies on the woman's belly, but it is not clear if this is to show two born babies being breastfed or two unborn fetuses in the womb.[32] At Beth Shean, Deir el-Balah, and Tell Tenim from the Late Bronze Age, figurines of a naked woman holding babies have been found. However, these were found in sites that were under substantial Egyptian influence and in some cases were even Egyptian strongholds. Therefore, it is very likely that these figurines depict the well-known image of Isis and Horus by means of the local Canaanite naked goddesses.[33]

At a few sites in Canaan dating to Iron Age I, a small number of female figurines have been found, but the Philistines are known to have produced many seated woman figurines (Ashdoda type); two exceptional ones, of a suckling bond, were found in Iron Age I Ashkelon and are connected to the influence of Mycenaean tradition.[34]

Very common among the figurines from Iron Age II are pillar figurines (Figure 2.2) that portray a naked woman with emphasized (hand-supported) breasts.[35] There are a few Iron Age figurines showing a woman and baby, but these are very rare. One pillar figurine, from Tell Beit Mirsim, depicts a woman carrying a baby on her back; two figurines from Lachish and Samaria depict a sitting goddess with a child on her lap.[36] The figurine from Tel Beit Mirsim is unique while the other two are very likely related to Egyptian influence.

In Iron Age III, figurines (Figure 2.3) of a sitting pregnant woman have been found in many sites.[37] In all these figurines, the female sex organs and genitalia are dominant or emphasized; this emphasis can be explained as a characteristic depiction of a

Archaeological Perspectives on Delivery Practices 47

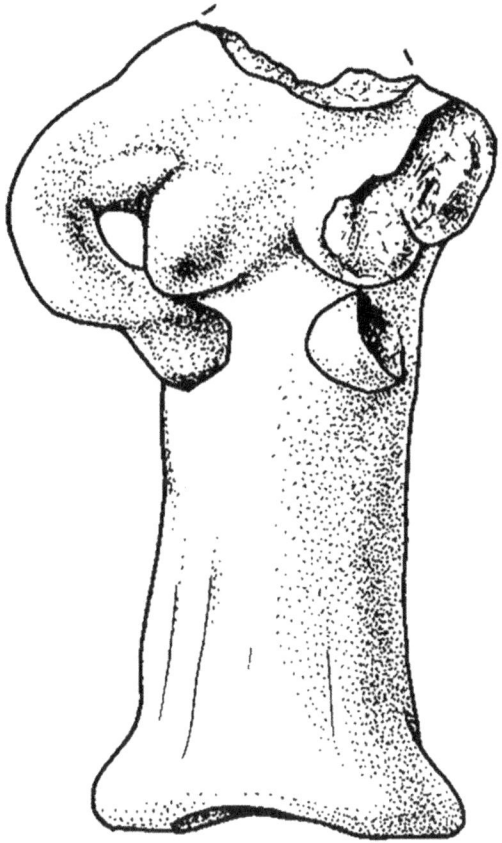

Figure 2.2 Iron Age II pillar figurine. From Mount Zion excavations, Jerusalem (courtesy of the Mount Zion excavation, Shimon Gibson).

goddess, as this is a long-standing representational tradition of naked women. In my opinion, however, these should be explained as part of household cultic activity which contains aspects of daily life, with fertility as a major component. In any case, these figurines show household cultic activity as likely oriented toward fertility as a whole and toward female fertility in particular, suggesting an interest in helping women conceive or succeed in delivery.[38]

In Cyprus, while no written sources about this subject have been found, a substantial amount of Kourotrophoi, clay figurines of a woman nurturing a baby (Figure 2.4), have been found. These female figurines have been found in adult graves, child graves, and domestic contexts. In the Early Cypriot Bronze period to the Middle Cypriot Bronze period,[40] the figurine often has a rectangular body shape and the head has shaped eyes and a nose but no mouth; the infant is usually held in the right hand; sometimes the figurines have defined breasts; gender is not always depicted in the figurines, but it is common that they depict women.[41] Many archaeologists prior to Budin have suggested

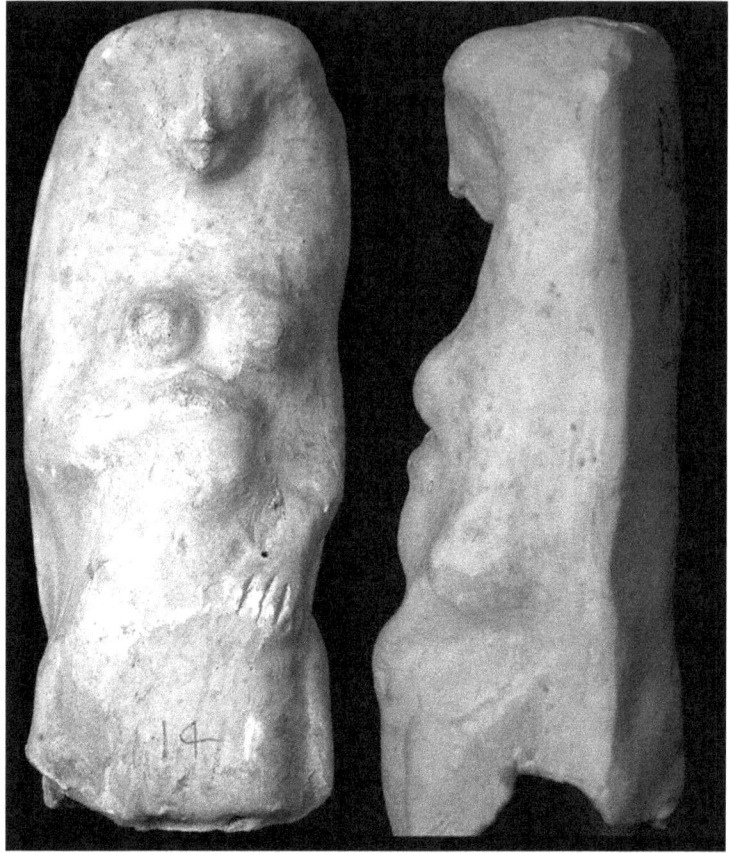

Figure 2.3 Iron Age III figurine of a sitting pregnant woman. From Tell es-Safi, Israel. Now at the Istanbul Archaeological Museum (photo: Avissar Lewis).

that these figurines depict the Mother Goddess, which started as an indigenous cult in Cyprus and was later influenced by different cultures and called Kypris/Aphrodite as the goddess in charge of the security of the afterlife (mainly of children), of women's fertility,[42] and of the fertility of nature.[43]

In the Early Cypriot Bronze period until the Late Cypriot Bronze period, most of the intact figurines which are not from archaeological excavations have some similarities of style to those found in excavations; most of them are standing but holding the baby in their left arm;[44] some are breastfeeding the baby. These are understood to symbolize a connection with eternity.[45]

Another common Cypriot group of figurines depicts the delivery itself. These are mainly from the Cypro-Archaic Period through the Hellenistic and Cypro-Classical periods. In figurines from the earlier periods, the pregnant women depicted are bowing on the floor and being helped by two other women (Figure 2.5): One is sitting behind the mother holding her hands on her waist and the other woman, the midwife,

Figure 2.4 Early Cypriot or Middle Cypriot period Kourotrophos clay figurine of a woman nurturing a baby, Lapithos tomb 307B.[39]

is helping the mother from the front, holding the newborn.[48] In later periods, some of the figurines are actually cut into limestone. Typically, the mother is sitting or lying on a couch or bed (Figure 2.6); the woman behind her is putting her arms on the mother's shoulders and the other woman, the midwife again, is in front of her holding the baby.[49] The referenced figurine and a few other limestone-carved figurines with childbirth scenes were found in the temple of Golgoi and can therefore be attributed to the old Cypriot mother goddess who was worshipped as a protector of childbirth and Kourotrophos.[50] Were the other ceramic figurines, and the earlier ones, part of the cult of Cypriot Aphrodite, the mother goddess, or examples of household cultic fertility figurines?

50   *Cyprus within the Biblical World*

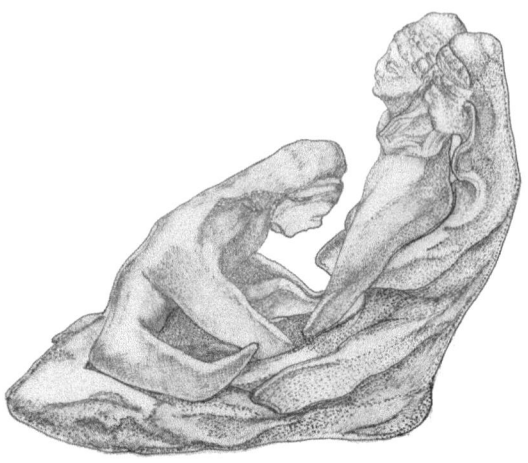

Figure 2.5 Cypro-Archaic figurines depict delivery, Lapithos, Cyprus.[46]

Figure 2.6 Hellenistic period figurine depicts delivery, temple of Golgoi, Cyprus.[47]

Discussion

There are several ways to explain the frequent appearance of these female figurines in ancient societies: they may be symbols of a specific god, or goddess; they may have served as a form of cultic prayer in clay; they may symbolize wishes and thoughts; they may be connected with magic rituals. The fact that the majority of the clay figurines were found in houses and graves suggests that they are connected to the household and to issues connected to individuals' wishes or problems.

As previously noted, delivery was a very important aspect in women's lives; in Cyprus and Canaan, we find that delivery occurred while bowing or on a stool with or without a midwife. This is also known from different traditional societies in the area and anthropological studies from different parts of the world.[51]

The different material culture of Cyprus and Canaan regarding this issue is intriguing. During those periods in Canaan, there are many examples of figurines of naked women, pregnant women, and fertile women with their fertility organs emphasized. There are a few figurines with suckling babies or with a child sitting on a woman's lap, but they are likely associated with a different cultural influence and not a local tradition. However, unlike in other places, none of the figurines depict the time of the delivery itself.[52] Though the delivery itself is not shown, it is very likely that these figurines are related to fertility and to the processes leading to delivery. On the contrary, in Cyprus, though there is no written evidence, the material culture clearly shows the importance of delivery and the processes surrounding it. There are many figurines that show delivery and many others which connect to conceiving, pregnancy, and breastfeeding. It is very likely that these were produced because there are specific goddesses connected to these child-bearing stages and that it was believed that the figurines would help the mother at the time of the delivery.

This difference cannot be explained by a lack of fear of problems at the time of the delivery in Canaan; as shown earlier, in the Bible there are stories of women who died at the time of the delivery, and there is an emphasis on the importance of fertility and the child, just as in every other place in the world. There are several possible explanations for the absence of delivery figurines in Canaan: (a) different ways of thinking, including the idea that female figurines symbolize the different stages of a woman's needs and as such also delivery; (b) different gender that made the figurine: if men made the figurines rather than women, they would not have known how to depict delivery, since they were absent when it occurred.[53] If this is true, it suggests that in Cyprus, women made their own figurines;[54] (c) a taboo in Canaan on delivery, and as such there were no depictions of the process; (d) different beliefs, such as no interference of the goddesses with delivery because it is very delicate; (e) the women of Canaan delivered with midwives, and the midwife would bring the figurine deities for the process.[55]

Notes

1. The advances are mainly due to the feminist movement, female researchers, gender studies, research on child development, the psychology of children, ethnographic studies, sociological research, and archaeological subdisciplines such as Household Archaeology and the Archaeology of Children and Childhood.
2. Needs such as approaches to deal with fears, dilemmas, family subsistence, and overcoming challenges related to delivery; needs which still exist today despite progress in medical science.
3. Avissar Lewis (2010: 3–33, 2016, 2018: 242–5, 2019: 17–20).
4. Janssen and Janssen (1990: 1); Stol (2000: 1–5, 17–26); Livingstone (2007: 17).
5. Sarcophagus Text, Utterance 366 § 632; R. O. Faulkner, trans., *The Ancient Egyptian Pyramid Texts* (London: Oxford University Press, 1969).
6. See, e.g., pKahun and Gurob (prescriptions 21–23) and pRam. IV (Gardiner, C 2-3).
7. Robins (1993: 77–9); Janssen and Janssen (1990: 1–2); Reiner (1982: 124–38).
8. Cameron and Kuhrt (1993); Harris (2000: 7); Seibert (1974: 16); Marsman (2003: 192–9); Depla (1994: 48–9).
9. Marsman (2003: 199); Lichty (1971: 23); Beckman (1982: texts 5, 7); Stol (2000: 49–59); Janssen and Janssen (1990: 1); Robins (1993: 75–83); Burrows (1941: 218–21); Willett (2009: 93–4).
10. Harrington (2007: 60); Chamberlain (2006: 81–4); Stone (1977: 63–4); Hassan (1975: 42); Lillehammer (1989: 100–2); Goodman and Armelagos (1990: 226–7); Belfer-Cohen, Schepartz, and Arensberg (1991: 412); Kimbel, Lavi, Rak, and Hovers (1995: 50–3); Garroway (2014: 219–22); Bikai and Perry (2001: 62–4, figure 2.3); Smith, Bornemann, and Zias (1981: 110, 118). For more information on children's graves in Israel, see Garroway (2014: 219–22); for more information on children's graves in Cyprus, see Lorentz (2002: 208).
11. Stone (1977: 66–70).
12. Kelly (1995: 207–8); Cunningham (1995: 90–7); Stone (1977: 63–4); Kamen (1984: 26); Lancy (2008: 53–5).
13. Statistical data gleaned from cbs.gov.il; data.worldbank.org; esa.un.org/Graphs/DemographicProfiles; statista.com/world-population-by-age-and-region; indexmundi.com/world/age.
14. The documents dealt with four main subjects: legal issues, administrative documents, legal documents, and letters.
15. Galil (2007: 104, 259, 287).
16. Gehlken (2005: 104).
17. Chamberlain (2006: 50–2); Stager and King (2001: 43).
18. Rashi on Exodus 1:16.
19. יש אֲבָנִים שמיוחדים ליוצר חרס ויש שהוא המיוחד אל היולד
20. Wilkinson (2003: 229).
21. The phrase "Mesopotamian tradition" is a general description because we are dealing with a wide range of time periods.
22. Marsman (2003: 199–201); Lichty (1971: 23–4); Stol (2000: 59–74); Harris (2000: 8); Seibert (1974: 28); Willett (2009: 82–4).
23. Stol (2000: 118–22); Beckman (1982: texts 1, 2, 5, 6 7); Beckman (1983: 250); Marsman (2003: 231); Livingstone (2007: 17).
24. Based with changes on Backhouse, J., Figure 2.2 from "Figures Ostraca from Deir El-Medina," in *Current Research in Egyptology 2011 Proceedings of the Twelfth Annual*

Symposium Which Took Place at Durham University, United Kingdom, March 2011. Edited by H. Abd El Gawad, N. Andrews, M. Correas-Amador, V. Tamorri, and J. Taylor (Oxford & Oakville: Oxbow Books, 2015).

25 Janssen and Janssen (1990: 3–7); Shaw and Nicholson (2002: 169); Robins (1993: 83).
26 Robins (1993: 83); Janssen and Janssen (1990: 8–9).
27 Backhouse (2015: 32–6).
28 For date ranges on archaeological periods, see "Archaeological Periods of the Levant" in this volume.
29 Keel and Uehlinger (1998: 34–6, fig. 25a, 25b).
30 Keel and Uehlinger (1998: 54–6, fig. 49).
31 Keel and Uehlinger (1998: 66–7, fig. 69).
32 Keel and Uehlinger (1998: 72–5, fig. 82); Budin (2011: 165–70).
33 Keel and Uehlinger (1998: 84–5, fig. 103); Budin (2011: 161–5).
34 Press (2012: 71, 74. No. 59, 66).
35 Kletter (1996); Zevit (2001: 273–4); Keel and Uehlinger (1998: 330–5).
36 Keel and Uehlinger (1998: 333, fig. 326, 327, 328).
37 Keel and Uehlinger (1998: 377–9, fig. 365).
38 Burrows (1941: 218–21); Willett (2009: 93–4); Kletter (1996: 73); Fowler (1985: 333–43).
39 After: Karageorghis, V. (2006). *Aspects of Everyday Life in Ancient Cyprus, Iconographic Representations*, p. 47, fig. 37. Nicosia: A. G. Leventis Foundation.
40 For date ranges on archaeological periods, see "Archaeological Periods of Cyprus" in this volume.
41 Budin (2011: 229–36).
42 Some of the Kourotrophoi were part of clay vessels.
43 Though Budin herself disputes the value of this identification (Budin, 2011: 242–3).
44 As opposed to the right arm, which is typical of those found in excavations.
45 Budin (2011: 31–3, 243–5); Price (1978: 90–9); Ulbrich (2015: 201–7); Olsen (1998: 384); Merrillees (1988: 55); Karageorghis (2006: fig. 35–38, fig. 66–67).
46 Based with changes on Karageorghis, V. (2006). *Aspects of Everyday Life in Ancient Cyprus, Iconographic Representations*, p. 204, fig. 217. Nicosia: A. G. Leventis Foundation.
47 After: Karageorghis, V. (2006). *Aspects of Everyday Life in Ancient Cyprus, Iconographic Representations*, p. 220, fig. 235. Nicosia: A. G. Leventis Foundation.
48 Karageorghis (2006: 204–6, fig. 217–20).
49 Karageorghis (2006: 218–20, fig. 233–235); Lorentz (2002: 206).
50 Vandervondelen (2002: 151–3).
51 Granqvist (1947: 59–61, 72); Erikson (1950: 98–101); Van Gennep (1972: 41–9).
52 Which is very interesting. While there are many Cypriot and Egyptian influences in Canaan known through commodities, vessels, and iconography, there do not appear to be any examples of influence in this vein.
53 Viezel (2018).
54 Or men were present.
55 Even as they were not preserved in the archaeological record.

3

Cyprus and the Shore of Israel during the Persian Period: According to Metal Finds

Kamil Sari

Introduction

This chapter describes the relation between Cyprus and the shore of Israel during the Persian period, as expressed in metal finds. The analysis is based on field research conducted in 2011.[1] The research examined metal objects found during archaeological excavations in Israel compared with parallel finds from Cyprus. Based on these data this chapter will describe the Israeli finds and their parallels from Cyprus, and then discuss implications and conclusions.

Historical Background

The evidence of material culture unearthed in archaeological excavations suggests a division of the country (of Israeli land) into two regions: the mountain area of Judea and Transjordan, which were influenced by the Assyrians, Babylonians, and Egyptians on the one hand, and the Galilee and the coastal plain which were subjected to Phoenician influence on the other. This evidence correlates well with historical information from the literary record stating that during the Persian period the Phoenician cities of Tyre and Sidon, which ruled the Levantine coast, had a significant cultural influence on it. The Israeli shore and Cyprus were included in the fifth satrapy as described by Herodotus: "The fifth province was … all Phoenice, and the part of Syria called Palestine, and Cyprus" (*Historiae* 3.91).[2]

This simultaneous influence over both Palestine and Cyprus is most evident in some pottery types and Phoenician metal jewelry. The Phoenicians were known as excellent metal craftsmen and they imported copper for their metal production, especially for metal bowls, from Cyprus (Harden, 1963).

The Finds

The metal objects tested in this research included 952 objects, which were divided into groups according to function: weapons, tools, objects of daily use, and jewelry. The objects were arranged in a catalog according to physical details: length, width, weight, and chemical analysis results. In each group additional subjects were addressed, such as typology and comparison with other Persian period metal finds from Mediterranean cities. In this treatment, the focus will be on comparison with finds from Cyprus.

Weapon Finds

The weapons tested in this research (see Figure 3.1) included mainly arrowheads, armor scales, and one helmet found in the sea near Haifa. Another helmet found near Ashkelon and two swords found at Ashdod and Shiqmona (along the Israeli shore) have been published elsewhere and are not included in this study. The majority of discovered weapons are arrowheads, with only a few swords.

The arrowheads include three types. The first type includes the flat, leaf-shaped arrowheads of the Iron Age, usually made of iron (see Figure 3.1(a–b)). These were replaced by the second type during the Persian period (sixth century BCE) in the lands of modern-day Israel: bronze Irano-Scythian arrowheads (see Figure 3.1(c–d)). These also appear in places such as Iran, Tarsus, Turkey, and elsewhere during the Iron Age. Similar objects (see Figure 3.2) were found in archaeological excavations in Cyprus and present a good parallel for dating. A new type of arrowhead, the third type, appears in the Hellenistic period and has marked wing tips and a midrib.

The helmet found in Haifa (see Figure 3.1(e)) during the marine work has no archaeological context but was dated according to similar helmets such as the one found during archaeological excavation in Kouklia (see Figure 3.2(d)). It can therefore be dated to the fifth century BCE.

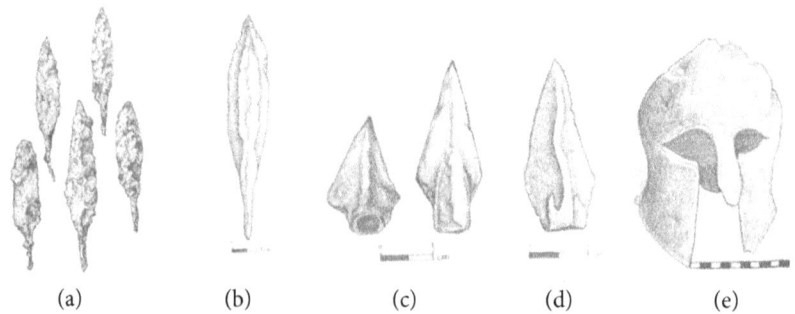

(a) (b) (c) (d) (e)

Figure 3.1 Weapons.[3]

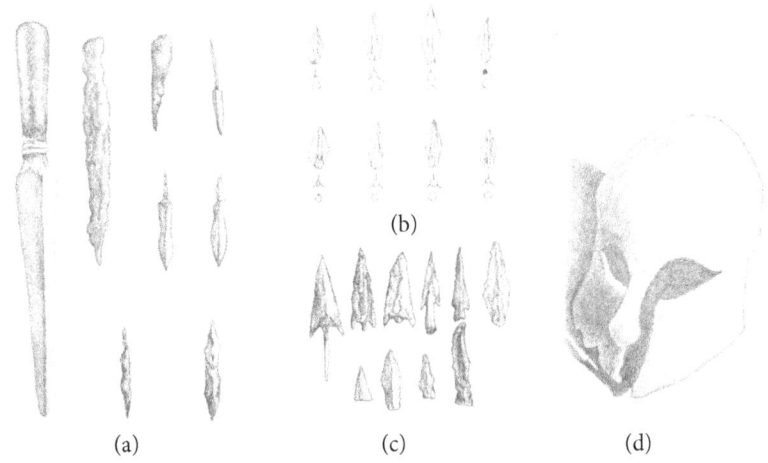

Figure 3.2 Parallels from Cyprus.⁴

Daily Use Object Finds

The biggest group among the finds consists of "daily use" objects including such things as bowls, vessels, furniture, nails, needles, sickles, and fish hooks. For this chapter, I have given only an example of a portion of the assemblage, choosing to highlight bowls, similar vessels, and furniture.

A variety of bowls have been found and can be divided generally into two groups: decorated and nondecorated ones. The nondecorated bowls seem to be the earliest ones from Assyrian origin. Generally, they are slight, shallow, and most of them have an omphalos in the base (see Figure 3.3(a–c)). They likely date to the ninth century BCE of the Persian period, during which time this type of bowl became deeper with an angle in the mid part of the body (Figure 3.3(d)). Decorated bowls appear during the Persian period. These are typically very similar in shape to the earlier, slighter ones but include decoration of plant leaves, generally the lotus plant (see Figure 3.4).

Parallel finds from Cyprus date to the seventh to fourth century BCE. These are similar in shape and decoration to the objects from the Israeli shore. The origin of these bowls is unknown, but we can assume that they were produced in the East and from there spread toward the West (including Cyprus).

Another group of daily use objects includes the "situla"—a small jug used for medicine, perfume, or Kohal (an ancient eye cosmetic). Some of them are made of bronze (like the ones from Metspe Yamim, see Figure 3.5(b)), others of silver (Figure 3.5(a), jug from Tel Gezer).

Parallels and similarity in objects by typology and decoration can also be found among the ladles group (Figure 3.6(a–g): ladles from Israel and Figure 3.6(h): parallel

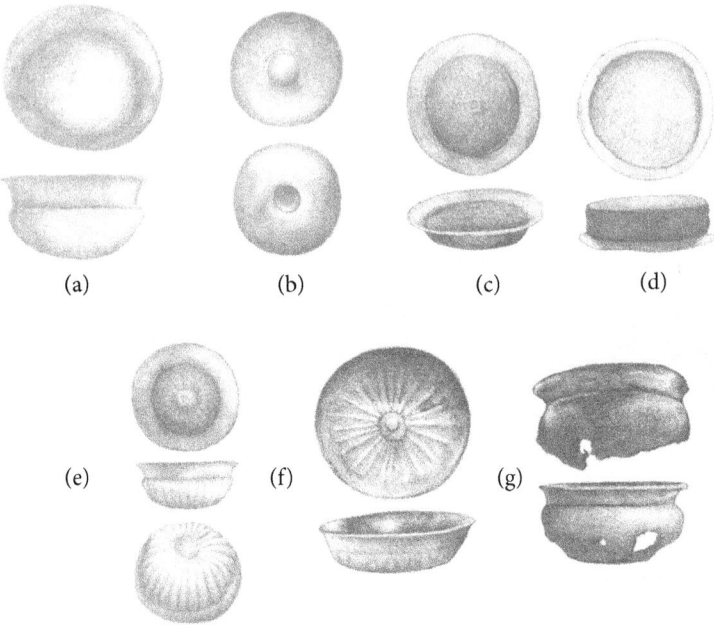

Figure 3.3 Bowls (Israel).[5]

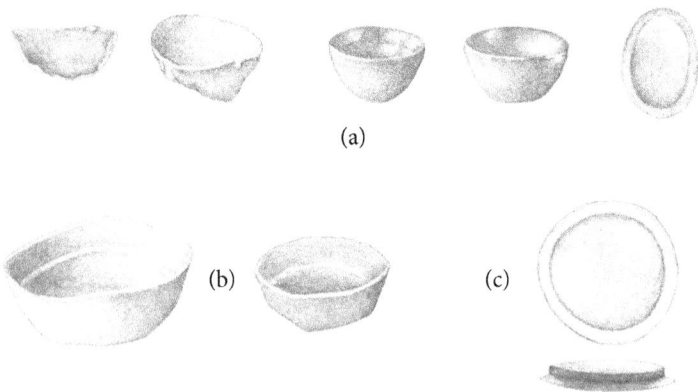

Figure 3.4 Bowls (Parallels from Cyprus).[6]

from Cyprus). In this case, the finds from both Israel and Cyprus-based excavations are dated to the same period. Interestingly, furniture finds from the Israel littoral have no parallels found in metal objects on Cyprus, and the only parallels come from inscriptions such as are present in the decoration of the city walls in Persepolis (see Figure 3.7).

Cyprus and Israel during the Persian Period   59

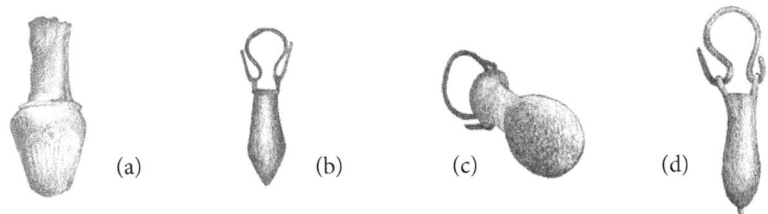

Figure 3.5 Situla.[7]

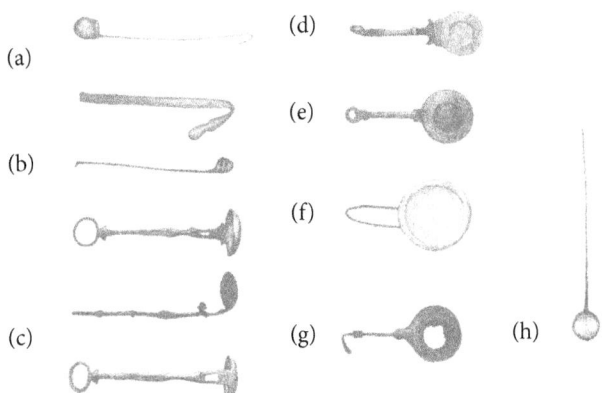

Figure 3.6 Ladles.[8]

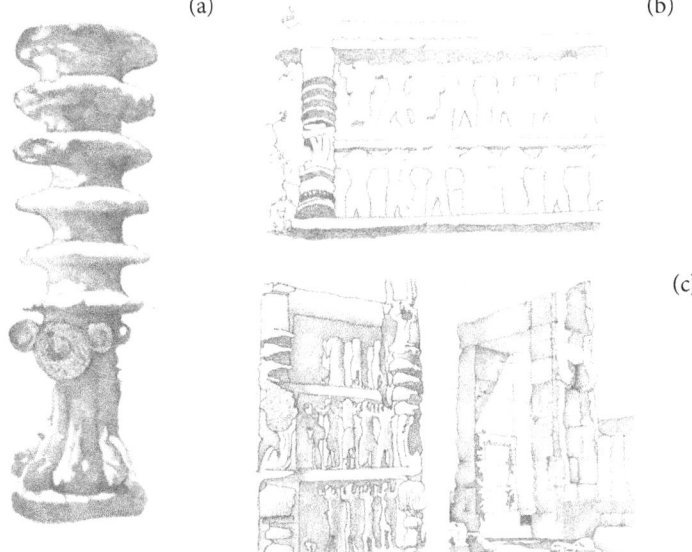

Figure 3.7 Furniture and its monumental depictions.[9]

Discussion and Conclusion

According to the data presented on metal object finds, a few facts can be observed in considering the relations between Cyprus and the Israel littoral during the Persian period. Similarities and differences can be identified on several levels.

New Weapons

According to typology, these metal finds support the historical information about the importance of the coast during the Persian period. During this period the bronze Irano-Scythian arrowhead (Figure 3.1(c–d)) replaced the flat, leaf-shaped arrowheads of the Iron Age (Figure 3.1(a–b)), usually made of iron. This arrowhead tip is known outside of Israel earlier. The Indo-Scythian arrowhead had appeared already during the Iron Age: examples are known from Iran, Tarsus, Turkey, and elsewhere but not in Israel. A new type of arrowhead appears in the Hellenistic period that has wing tips and a midrib. The appearance of this arrowhead at Paphos, Cyprus (during the Persian siege), and in Israel emphasizes that these weapons are a likely indicator of new people in the area. All discovered daily use objects (jewelry, pottery, and glass) were likely imported through trade. Only weapons, which were the soldier's private possession, are a sign of new occupation. According to this theory, it is not surprising to find most of the weapons on the coast, as it was the thoroughfare used most by the Persians on their way to their wars with Greece and Egypt.

Dating

As pertaining to dating, the presence of similar objects in different locations enables study of the history and development of those objects. The parallels from Cyprus come from a good dated complex. For example, while the arrowheads found in Israel dated generally to the fifth century BCE according to the loci in which they were found, the same type of arrowheads were found during the excavations in Paphos (Figure 3.2(b)) and can be dated to the years 498/497 BCE, that is, during the Persian siege.

In addition, we should emphasize that in Cyprus the iron, flat-leaf arrowhead (such as those found in Kakopetria and dated to the fifth century BCE [Figure 3.2(a)]) also existed prior to the Irano-Scythian arrowheads. This is a commonality with the development of arrowheads along the Israeli coast at the same period.

Concerning the daily use objects: while in Israel several different types of bowls seem to date from the Persian period (Figure 3.3), the same objects appear earlier in Cyprus (Figure 3.4). This correlation can help us in dating the daily use objects. Further, it seems that some of these objects were in use for long periods of time in essentially the same shape. This fact makes it very difficult for the archaeologist to base dates on metal objects only, and good dating must be based on several types of finds.

Production

A typological and material examination of the metal objects (especially the daily use objects) demonstrates that cultural influence and functionality of the objects were the main considerations in the manufacturing processes. Objects that were clearly used for work, such as sickles, hammers, and hoes, had similar shapes throughout antiquity. Sickles, a semicircle tool sharpened on one side, for example, all had the same shape during the Iron Age, the Persian period, and the Hellenistic era. Sickles found in the lands of modern-day Israel are similar to objects found outside Israel.

In examining bowl production, it can be noted that the decorated ones (such as in Figure 3.3(c–g)) display attributes from different cultures, which may indicate that these bowls were made by the Phoenicians.

Further supporting evidence for the contention that most of the metal objects were produced by the Phoenicians can be found with the jewelry (Figure 3.8); furthermore, objects found in Israeli lands and Cyprus are all similar to jewelry found in Phoenician tombs dating to the sixth and fifth centuries BCE.

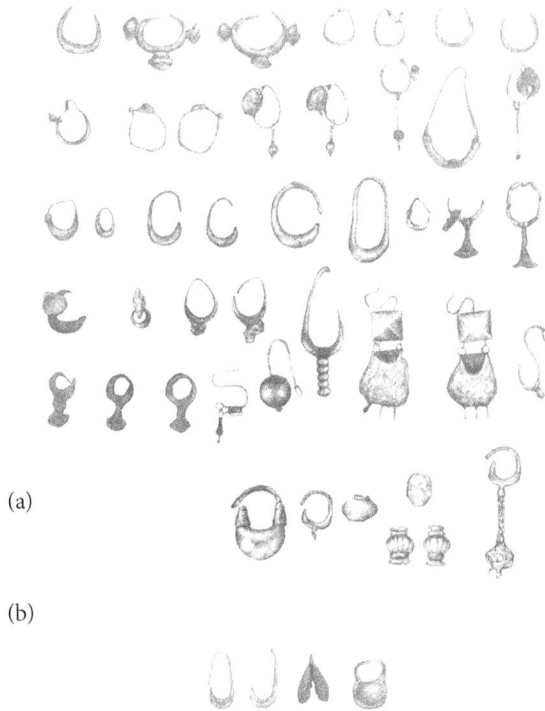

(a)

(b)

Figure 3.8 Jewelry (earrings).[10]

The importance of shape and final decoration can especially be noticed in vessels (Figure 3.5) and furniture. Since these objects were visible in daily life, they afforded the opportunity to convey many kinds of messages and emphases: markers of beauty, power and ruling (the lion motif), and wealth (objects made from gold or silver) are prominent.

The cultural influence of the civilization that ruled the area is apparent in the final shape and decorations of found objects. Finds from important cities, such as Samaria, were decorated with Persian motifs in the Persian cultural tradition. However, along the coast Phoenician influence can be noted on similar objects.

The function of objects was the main consideration in determining the materials they were made from: iron was suitable for objects like knives, sickles, and ploughs because of its resistance to wear. In fact, after the discovery of iron in the Iron Age, this has been the material of choice for these types of objects to this day.

Geographic environment was considered as well during the manufacturing process: nails and needles at coastal sites were produced from pure copper, because it has a better resistance to corrosion. These objects underwent mechanical treatment after casting. This included beating with a hammer and annealing for obtaining the desired degree of hardness.

Jewelry included earrings, bracelets, rings, fibulae, hair rings, and beads. Two major types can be discerned: decorated and undecorated objects. Decorative motifs include animals and geometric shapes. Chronologically, these objects are dated to the Persian period and are similar to objects from other sites in the Mediterranean. Phoenician objects are similar to those discovered at Israeli coastal sites. This could indicate that Phoenicians produced these metal objects. However, Persian cultural influences can also be noticed in jewelry and in Phoenician production.

Technologically, the difference between small and large objects can be noticed in the production method: while small objects such as beads and rings are only cast, large objects such as fibulae were treated mechanically by hammering and annealing after the casting procedure to obtain the final shape.

Most of the metal objects found during excavations in Israel (around 70 percent) come from coastal sites. About 600 objects come from the two coastal sites of "Atlit and Tel Michal" and only a few objects are from inland and mountain sites such as the major cities of Nablus and Samaria. It is important to stress that Persian period sites have been excavated all over Israel and not only on the coast.

I believe that this geographic distribution of metal finds is directly related to the importance of the coastline for the Persian Empire during their military expeditions against Egypt and the naval warfare against Greece. This, in fact, gave great importance to the coastal strip and likely resulted in an increase in settlement density and a proportional settlement decrease in the mountains and inland.

The historical sources for this period (mainly Herodotus) support this claim. In this context we can see the connection to Cyprus during the Persian period since, according to Herodotus, both regions were included in the fifth satrapy (Herodotus 3.89).

There are obvious similarities in shape between the found metal objects in these respective locations which indicate Phoenician influence in both places. On the one hand, the finds from Cyprus provide a good general dating parallel for the objects from Israeli littoral, while on the other hand, finds such as the arrowheads from Paphos (dated to 498/497 BCE) can provide very specific dating support to finds from Israel.

The similarity of finds in Cyprus and at the Israeli littoral lead to the conclusion that Cyprus exerted a significant influence on the material culture of the Israeli littoral during the Persian period; in short, the metal finds examined in this study support the historical sources that describe the "Phoenician" impact on the coastal strip.

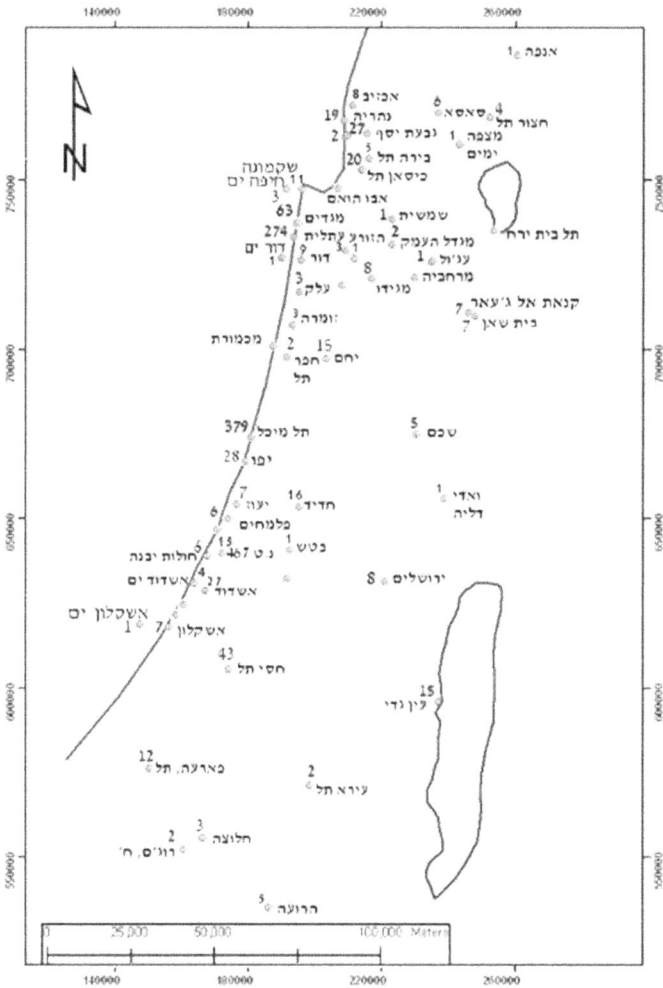

Figure 3.9 Location of Persian period metal finds, Israeli littoral and interior.[11]

Notes

1. See Figure 3.9 for the geographic location of Israeli littoral sites.
2. Henderson, LCL.
3. 3.1(a): Group of arrowheads; 3.1(b): Object no. 90–481, Site: Tel Michal; 3.1(c): Object no. 601204, Site: Tel Michal; 3.1(d): Object no. 32–383, Site: Atlit; 3.1(e): Helmet from Haifa. Courtesy: Israeli Antiquities Authority. Artist's renderings K. N. Pruszinski.
4. 3.2(a): Kakopetria, fifth century BCE (adapted from V. Karageorghis, 1977, Plate LXXII); 3.2(b): Paphos, 498/497 BCE; 3.2(c): Ancient Corinth, fourth century BCE; 3.2(d): Kouklia, fifth century BCE. Artist's renderings K.N. Pruszinski.
5. 3.3(a): Naplos; 3.3(b): Achziv; 3.3(c): Tel Michal; 3.3(d): Jaffa; 3.3(e): Zieta; 3.3(f): Tell el-Farah; 3.3(g): Gezer. Courtesy: Israel Antiquities Authority. Artist's renderings K. N. Pruszinski.
6. 3.4(a): Amathus, Cyprus, 600–325 BCE; 3.4(b): Kornos, Cyprus, 510–450 BCE (adapted from M. Loulloupis, 1967, Plate XXVII); 3.4(c): Kakopetria, Cyprus, fifth century BCE. Artist's renderings K. N. Pruszinski.
7. 3.5(a): Tel Gezer; 3.5(b): Metspe Yamim; 3.5(c): Jordan; 3.5(d): Amathus, Cyprus. Artist's renderings K. N. Pruszinski
8. 3.6(a): Haifa, underwater (two views of one ladle: full ladle [top] and handle); 3.6(b): Tel Michal; 3.6(c): Tell el-Farah (three views of one ladle); 3.6(d): Ibdan -Nablus; 3.6(e): Dor; 3.6(f): Nablus; 3.6(g): Nablus; 3.6(h): Amathus, Cyprus. Courtesy: Israel Antiquities Authority. Artist's renderings K. N. Pruszinski
9. 3.7(a): Object no. 70–92–619, Samaria, Persian period, lion's foot decoration, courtesy: Israel Antiquities Authority; 3.7(b): Darius' Tomb, Naqsh-e Rostam, lion's foot decoration; 3.7(c) Persepolis, city gate, lion's foot decoration. Artist's renderings K. N. Pruszinski.
10. 3.8(a): Kouklia, Cyprus (adapted from S. Hadjisavvas, 2001, p. 94); 3.8(b): Israeli shore finds, courtesy: Israel Antiquities Authority. Artist's renderings K. N. Pruszinski.
11. Courtesy: Israel Antiquities Authority.

4

Did Lazarus Flee Jerusalem for Cyprus?

James H. Charlesworth

During the early centuries of the Common Era, Christians built in Larnaca, Cyprus, a church dedicated to Lazarus, whom the early followers of Jesus believed had been raised from the dead by Jesus. The name is an abbreviation of the Hebrew "El-azar" which means "God helped."

The name "Lazarus" signifies two people in the New Testament. One is a beggar who is featured in a parable preserved by Luke (16:19-31). "Lazarus" is the only proper name to appear in Jesus' parables.[1] Most importantly for us now, according to the Gospel of John, Lazarus is the man whom Jesus revived from the dead in Bethany, a small village to the east of Jerusalem just over the Mount of Olives. As we know from the *Temple Scroll* and Jerome, Lazarus' home was situated where sick people were located. Does that inform our speculations regarding Lazarus' sickness?[2]

At the outset, we should ponder if the Lazarus story in John is redactional and thus not historical or if it may, behind the theological editing, preserve an event that happened before 30 CE. Scholars are divided on the historicity of the story about Lazarus found in chapter eleven of the Gospel of John. Many concur that it was created by the Fourth Evangelist (whoever he may be) and built from earlier traditions in the Gospels, notably Jesus' resuscitations of those who had apparently died.[3] It clearly is placed near the conclusion of John's Gospel, especially in an early edition without the addition of chapters 15–17 and 21. And the Evangelist contrasts Lazarus' resuscitation from the dead—he is bound in cloths and walks out of a closed tomb after four days—with Jesus' resurrection—his clothes remain neatly folded in the empty tomb and Jesus' exit is neither described nor imagined but it is after three days. The Evangelist most likely strives to illustrate Jesus' claim, only in John, that he is the resurrection and the life (John 11:25).

Some scholars perceive a historical kernel in the Johannine account in chapter eleven. Johannine redaction, with theological and Christological embellishments, is obvious in each pericope of John and some of them ultimately derive from a historical event. According to a growing number of Johannine experts, John is no longer relegated as the latest Gospel. It is most likely a multilayered Gospel that preserves a version that could be remnants of the earliest Gospel.[4] The Lazarus account belongs to the *Signs Source* that considerably antedates the Gospel of John and took shape in Palestine perhaps in the forties. Lazarus may have enjoyed a special relation with Jesus and that led the author to state that he is one "loved" by Jesus (John 11:3, 5, 36) and is Jesus' friend (John 11:11). If this aspect of the story is trustworthy, then the account probably has a historical kernel. The account does not mention "Pharisees" and highlights Jesus' opposition as "the high priest." These terms antedate 70 CE, after which the Pharisees alone succeed as Jewish leaders in Jerusalem and nearby. The "Pharisees" are mentioned later in John 11:57 but that looks like a much later, post-70 CE, addition to John. Lazarus may seem at first glance to be in central focus but he does nothing, receives no dialogue, and never confesses belief in Jesus. As Raymond E. Collins observes: "This Lazarus ... is one of the principal named disciples in the Fourth Gospel, even though his role is admittedly a passive one. He never makes an explicit profession of faith in Jesus, nor does he even speak. The gospel shows no particular interest in his person or his personal history."[5] Perhaps I may be among the minority of scholars who perceive a historical person called "Lazarus" behind the Gospel of John, but the Johannine editing and theological developments probably mask a real episode. Why would a scholar conclude the full account is fabricated when Lazarus is marginalized and is astoundingly passive? The account comes from the *Signs Source* and that is our earliest source for Jesus' miracles. The sociological and archaeological description fits only pre-70 CE Judea and Jerusalem. Jesus was thought to have raised people from the dead according to the other Gospels, notably Jairus' daughter (Mark 5:21-43; Matt 9:18-25; Luke 8:40-56) and the resuscitation of the widow's son in Nain (Luke 7:11-17). Resuscitation is plausible since we have proof that in antiquity sometimes a person was thought to be dead but was alive in an anatomical coma without discernible heartbeat. Jesus clearly resisted the supreme authority and claims of the high priests, a fact which is assumed by and colors the Lazarus story. If Jesus raised one from the dead, many Jews would believe he was from God and most likely the Messiah. Political and priestly authorities could not allow such threats to their power to continue. Historical verisimilitude and the pre-50 CE date of the *Signs Source* override the unsophisticated claim that if only one Evangelist records an event it is probably an evangelical creation. I shall assume that it is possible that behind the Lazarus story in the Gospel of John is a historical person named Lazarus who was resuscitated by Jesus. Lazarus' connection with Mary and Martha, who are not doubted to be historical women, and the fact that Lazarus is not one of the Twelve impress me as aspects of John 11 that are not part of the tradition created for the kerygma. I shall proceed with the recognition that the story is a Johannine masterpiece but preserves reflections on a historical event.

On Cyprus, relics purported to be Lazarus' skull and bones are shown to pilgrims, parishioners, and tourists. Did Lazarus flee Judea and die on Cyprus? Is this simply an early medieval legend as in the *Golden Legend* that dates from the thirteenth century and confuses Mary, Lazarus' sister, with Mary Magdalene? The tradition in the Gospel of John seems clear but why would a church in honor of Lazarus be built on Cyprus? Is there some historical truth to the claim that Lazarus went from Bethany to Cyprus and died there? Is the belief that Lazarus died on Cyprus merely legendary or is there residual history in it?[6] And how would we know that? Such an account is found neither in the New Testament nor in any of the documents assigned to the New Testament Apocrypha.

Figure 4.1 "The skull and bones of Lazarus" in Larnaca's Church of Lazarus (JHC).

When Luke introduces Jesus' visit to the home of Mary and Martha, he significantly edits his traditions. Luke merely mentions "a village" near Jerusalem in which Mary and Martha lived. According to Luke, Martha complains that Mary is not helping to serve the guests but only attends to her master. Jesus replied: "Mary has chosen the good portion" (Luke 10:38-42; verse 42 quoted). Luke does not supply the name of the village. He also does not suggest that the sisters have a brother, namely Lazarus; and no scribe added these specifications as variants to the established text.

The author and editors of John preserve appreciably more details about Jesus in Judea. In John 11:1-44, readers are informed of the sickness and eventual death of Lazarus. And the author adds that Jesus loved Lazarus. Jesus plans to travel to Bethany, where Mary, Martha, and Lazarus live, despite his disciples warning that Judean Jews are seeking to stone him (11:8). Thomas, a spokesman for the Twelve, suggests that all proceed into the danger zone and die with Jesus (11:16). The disciples contemplate that Lazarus is not dead but sleeping; Jesus states: "Lazarus is dead" (11:14). The narrator adds that Lazarus had been in the tomb "four days" (11:17) and allows Jesus to announce that he is "the resurrection and the life."

In John 11:38-44, the narrator insists that Lazarus is resuscitated by Jesus. He repeats that Lazarus has been in the tomb four days and will now stink. The exceptional details are either from an eyewitness or a gifted narrator. The story emphasizes that God's glory was revealed and that God, the Father, hears Jesus and has "sent" him. Jesus shouts, and although bound by hands and feet, Lazarus walks out of the tomb to Jesus. As Raymond E. Brown and Craig S. Keener observe, Lazarus' ability to walk when bound is due to the supernatural nature of the miracle.[7]

According to John 11:45-57, many Judean Jews now believe in Jesus because they witnessed Jesus' actions and unparalleled power. Other Jews go to the Pharisees and chief priests; they convene the Sanhedrin (11:47). All agree that Jesus performed "many signs" (11:47) and must be stopped or everyone will believe in him. That belief will force the Romans to destroy "our holy place and our nation" (11:48). Astoundingly, Caiaphas is given the gift of prophecy and claims that Jesus is to "die for the people," the Jews. Jesus flees Judea and settles in Ephraim. Passover is near, many pilgrims flood into Jerusalem, and the chief priests and Pharisees seek information how to arrest Jesus (11:57).

According to John 12:1-8, Jesus returns to Bethany. Lazarus enjoys supper with Jesus. It is six days before Passover. Martha serves but Mary anoints Jesus' feet with a "costly ointment." Judas, who is reported to be the one who is not only the group's treasurer but a thief, claims that the expensive nard should have been sold and the money distributed to the poor.

According to John 12:9-11, the narrator explains the plot to kill Lazarus. The chief priests seek to kill Lazarus because too many Jews were leaving them and believing in Jesus.

The account preserves amazing details from pre-70 CE Judaism. The author and editors leave no doubt that Jesus raised Lazarus from the dead, that many Judean Jews leave the Temple authorities and believe Jesus, and that the Temple authorities are committed to finding Lazarus in order to kill him. If the account appeared only after 70 CE, a critic would have expected Pharisees, the only group of Jews that survive 70 CE, to be at least mentioned.

Lazarus remains poorly defined. He is a figure who is devoid of a clear personality or any action. The account is not embellished; there is no reason to dismiss the account as a post-70 CE creation or an allegory.[8] If before 70 CE in Palestine, Stephen and James were martyred and Paul has to flee for his life from Jerusalem and the leading Jewish authorities, then a historian can comprehend why Lazarus also would have faced a polemical environment. No one should doubt that the "resurrection" of Lazarus would cause a major rift between the priests and Jesus' group. The narrator also leaves no doubt that if Jesus raised Lazarus from the dead then he had the power to raise others who had died. That would be a powerful message in Jerusalem at Passover. The average Jew would become excited by such claims or experiences.

No author or editor focuses a spotlight on Lazarus. He remains unrecognizable. He says nothing. While Mary and Martha appear as distinct personalities, Lazarus has no distinguishing features. He is only the recipient of Jesus' miraculous action. Despite the attention given to Lazarus narratively, the focus is on Jesus, not Lazarus. Jesus is the One who is declared to be "the resurrection and the life." Lazarus is important primarily because of what Jesus has done to him and the powers revealed in the "sign" (John 12:18). The chief priests and Pharisees are portrayed as evil men who seek to kill not only Jesus but also Lazarus (12:10).

The story about Lazarus in John is the longest miracle recorded in the New Testament. It is also from the *Signs Source*. Perhaps, the "sign" (τὸ σημεῖον) concluded that pre-Johannine source that takes us back into the period before 50 CE. Recall John 12:

> The reason why the crowd went to meet him (Jesus) was that they heard this: He had performed the sign (ὅτι ἤκουσαν τοῦτο αὐτὸν πεποιηκέναι τὸ σημεῖον). (John 12:18)

Do we not have a historical claim that antedates each of the Gospels? The passage is not only from one witness; it is a narrative that displays an author and at least an editor. Johannine specialists concur that the author of the *Signs Source* is not the author of the Gospel of John.

The separate Lucan and Johannine stories of a man named "Lazarus" were conflated in medieval iconography. That identity also occurs in the minds of some biblical readers; they imagine that Luke and John preserve versions of the same "Lazarus." The misleading identity is highlighted, for example, in scenes found in many churches, specifically in the portal of St. Trophîme at Arles, the church at Avallon, in the portal at Vézelay, and portals of Autun Cathedral.[9] Thus, such conflation shaped the imagination of medieval Christians in Burgundy and Provence.

As John Meier demonstrated in *A Marginal Jew*, the Lazarus story has a long history and begins early; it has historical dimensions and may well go back to a pre-Easter miracle "in the life of the historical Jesus."[10] To recapitulate, Jesus revives Lazarus and many Judean Jews begin to believe in Jesus. The Judean leaders, especially the chief priests, concur that they must kill Jesus and Lazarus.

Lazarus must flee Judea or be killed. He would not flee East as the road to Jericho was taxing and too precipitous for a man who had been in a burial cave for four days. That road eastward would be filled not only with Roman soldiers but also with those who planned to kill Lazarus. He would not flee South as Judean Jews filled the hills and valleys and the roads were treacherous. He could flee North but he would face Samaritans and they sometimes kill Judean Jews, especially those who worshipped on Zion and not Gerizim. The road northward is also hazardous and fluctuates between demandingly steep inclines and descents.

Lazarus probably fled westward, descended to the Sharon and northward on paved roads to Caesarea Maritima where there was safety amid a cosmopolitan world. The Romans and Roman soldiers in this port city did not, at that time, face the crises from crowds that dominated Jerusalem. From the coast Lazarus would probably not sail to Alexandria, because of the problems among the Jews there (as we know from Philo); he most likely took a ship to the closest island: Cyprus. That area was not then defined by riots or wars as in the past. The Greeks and then the Romans had brought peace and prosperity to a very wealthy island defined by abundant forests and copper. These reflections provide similitude to the Lazarus' story. Yet, a historian must ponder if our speculative reconstruction of Lazarus' life is grounded in history and reliable traditions.

Our imagination[11] is supported by early Christian sources. According to these sources, Lazarus fled to Cyprus (and not to other places). In the words of Metropolitan Chrysostomos of Kition, Lazarus was "the first bishop of ancient Kition and patron Saint of Larnaca."[12] Stavros S. Fotiou discusses the many sermons and exegetical comments about Lazarus' "resurrection" by Jesus, especially those delivered by the following famous men:[13]

Hippolytus of Rome,
John Chrysostom,
Cyril of Alexandria,
Amphilochius of Iconium,

Proclus of Constantinople,
Basil of Seleucia,
Romanos the Melodist,
Andrew of Crete,
John of Euboea,
Theodore of Studios,
Euthymius Zigabenus,
Theophylact of Bulgaria,
Theophanes Kerameus, and
Damascenus of Studios.

Some of the accounts are not far from Lazarus' own time. Hippolytus of Rome lived from about 170 to 235/6 CE, and he was famous for his extensive knowledge. In *Against Noetus* 18, Hippolytus, who was deeply influenced by the Gospel of John, stressed belief in One God but two persons. He affirmed that Jesus raised Lazarus from the dead after he had been in the tomb for four days. Hippolytus supplies no independent tradition and is interpreting John. Does Hippolytus have corroborating evidence or is he merely preaching from John?

Most of these comments are included with liturgical celebrations, and we all know that liturgy is not the best source of history. Do any of these authors know historical information that would increase the plausibility that Lazarus fled Judea for Cyprus?

The early Christian traditions are summarized in *St. Lazarus and His Church in Larnaca* by Stavros S. Fotiou. According to him, shortly after Pentecost, Lazarus fled to Cyprus from the environs of Jerusalem because powerful Judean Jews sought to kill him. Why? It is because many Jews believed Lazarus' "resurrection" proved Jesus was the Christ and divine. Fotiou continues:

> In order to escape his persecution, Lazarus found refuge in Cyprus and dwelled in Kition, an ancient city with an important history. Apostles Barnabas and Paul met Lazarus in Kition, during their first Apostolic Mission in Cyprus (around 46 A.D.), and ordained him as the first bishop of Kition.[14]

Perhaps there is some reliable history in this account;[15] Kition, as mentioned already, is an ancient city with an impressive history.[16] Some scholars may agree with this judgment by Fotiou. But the same scholars will probably reject the historicity of the legend that Lazarus eventually met Mary, the mother of Jesus, on Cyprus.[17] Historians, however, must admit that we have no early information of what happened to Mary, Jesus' mother, and Mary Magdalene, after the asides in the early chapters of Acts.

As previously mentioned and illustrated, on Cyprus a skull and alleged bones of Lazarus are displayed in the church of Agios Lazaros. Some may assume these bones prove that Lazarus fled to Cyprus since in 890 "his tomb" was discovered and in 1972 human remains were found under the altar of this church.[18]

What other sources for evaluating Lazarus' escape from Judea and death exist? The legend that Lazarus fled to Provence, France, and died there after becoming bishop of Marseilles derives from late and unreliable historical sources, as in the *Golden Legend*.

Figure 4.2 Agios Lazaros in Larnaca (JHC).

It appears first in the *Otia imperialia* of 1212[19] and later is reported by a French traveler, Seigneur de Villamount, about 1589.[20] That tradition also claims Lazarus was beheaded and so died a martyr's death, and further, that his bones were eventually taken to the church of Saint Lazarus in Avallon.[21]

What about the claims related to Lazarus' tomb in Bethany, modern el-'Azariyeh (which in Arabic preserves the Greek *Lazarion*), on the eastern side of the Mount of Olives and less than two miles from Jerusalem? The location is defined by tombs dating from about the sixth century BCE to the fourteenth century CE. Archaeological remains of pottery, houses, wine-presses, cisterns, and silos date from the Persian, Hellenistic, Roman, and Byzantine periods.

The site is now revered by Christians and Muslims. Tombs from the first century CE have been located near the cave in which pilgrims are shown the tomb of Lazarus. Did Lazarus die in Palestine? Was he buried finally near where he was earlier buried and resuscitated by Jesus? The claims that Lazarus was finally buried in Bethany date from the fourth century CE and that is after the Council of Nicea in 325. Eusebius of Caesarea, shortly after 325,[22] and the Bordeaux pilgrim, in about 333, mention a tomb of Lazarus,[23] but it may be the one in which he was buried for four days. If no evidence exists before this date then we must contemplate the creation of holy sites by pilgrims, representing the triumphant church. Proclamations by ecclesiastical authorities who do not understand archaeology or early church history should fall on deaf ears. No archaeological evidence enhances the Bethany claim and in 390 Jerome is the first one

Figure 4.3 The Tomb of Lazarus in Bethany (with JHC).

to mention a church of Lazarus, the *Lazarium*, in Bethany.[24] No church seems to have existed to honor Lazarus before the end of the fourth century.

All who visit Lazarus' Church in Larnaca are shown some of the alleged bones of Lazarus, as mentioned already. According to medieval traditions, other bones of Lazarus were transferred from Cyprus to Constantinople in the ninth and tenth centuries by Emperor Leo VI. They eventually were placed in the famous Hagia Sophia, according to some traditions, or in a monastery named after Lazarus in Constantinople, according to others.[25]

Is it possible that Lazarus fled the death threats of Judean Jewish leaders and arrived in Cyprus? If so, the time would antedate Paul's mission to Cyprus. Lazarus' arrival could be datable as early as 30 CE, the time of Jesus' crucifixion, or slightly later. After the claims that Jesus had been raised by God, Lazarus, if still near Jerusalem, would probably have had to flee for his own safety. Shortly after the crucifixion of Jesus, Stephen will be stoned. That occurred in the early or mid-thirties. The social setting was dangerous for Jesus' followers. If Lazarus were still in Judea, he would be forced to flee Judea. He would have had only two options: remain and be stoned or flee to a safe location.

The political climate in and near Jerusalem was electric. Authorities feared the supernatural power of Jesus. As the gifted lawyer John W. Welch, a specialist on ancient Jewish law, demonstrated, the claims that Jesus raised Lazarus from the dead demonstrated awesome numinous power to many Jews and opened Jesus up to the Roman and Jewish charges of *maleficium* and *maiestas*: that is, these political leaders could charge Jesus with sorcery, magic, and occult practices.[26]

There does seem to be some reliable historical verisimilitude in the Lazarus traditions preserved on Cyprus, but that is not tantamount to historical proof. In estimating the historical veracity in the Lazarus traditions, thinkers should read, or reread, Walter Bauer's insight that early Christians sought to claim their village, town, or city was founded by an apostle or benefited from the presence of a Saint.[27] All a historian can claim is that Cyprus seems to have the best and earliest claims for Lazarus' final years. What additional valuable information is preserved by the earliest scholars of the church?

If resurrection is the return to life of someone who died and will never die again, then Jesus did not resurrect Lazarus from the dead. If Jesus did not "raise" Lazarus but revived (or resuscitated) him because he was not completely dead, then he would eventually die again. According to all traditions, biblical and patristic, Lazarus revived at Jesus' call and then died sometime later. In *On the Four-day [Dead] Lazarus* (PG 132, 513B), John Chrysostom argues that Jesus delayed his trip to Bethany until Lazarus had been dead four days:

> But now, on purpose, he [Jesus] is waiting for Lazarus' death, he voluntarily delays his presence there, so as to reveal his victory over death before his own struggle with death. Therefore, he delays for three days, so that on the one hand the death of Lazarus will not be disputed and on the other hand the Jews will be present when the tomb is opened, in order to convert those who persecute him into preachers of the miracle.[28]

As I mentioned in my introductory chapter, Salamis was a major and wealthy city in northeast Cyprus.[29] In 480 BCE, a Greek fleet of ships defeated the mighty Persians in the straits of Salamis. After the death of Alexander the Great in 323 BCE, the city became part of the Ptolemaic Empire that was centered in Egypt.

On the "first" missionary journey of Paul, he and Barnabas sailed from Antioch to Salamis. According to the traditions in Acts, there were both a Jewish community and synagogues in this city:

> They [Barnabas and Paul] went down [from Antioch] to Seleucia; and from there they sailed to Cyprus. And when arriving in Salamis, they proclaimed the word of God in the synagogues of the Jews. And they also had John to assist (them). When they had gone through the whole island until Paphos, they met a certain magician, a Jewish false prophet, named Bar-Jesus. He was with the proconsul, Sergius Paulus, an intelligent man, who summoned Barnabas and Saul and sought to hear the word of God. (Acts 13:4-7)

Figure 4.4 Roman Ruins in Salamis (JHC).

Salamis was renamed "Constantia" by Emperor Constantine II (337–361 CE). A famous Christian scholar, Epiphanius, became Bishop of Constantia. He was born in Palestine, near Eleutheropolis,[30] a major city in Judea that means "free city." Epiphanius had been trained in Egypt.

According to his *Panarion* 37.6, Epiphanius (367–403 CE) reported that Lazarus lived for thirty years in Judea and thirty years in Kitium, the home of the earlier Greek philosopher named Zeno.[31] Epiphanius may have written more about Lazarus, but many of his writings are lost. Almost identical traditions about Lazarus are found in later Greek authorities, including Saint John of Euroia, the Patriarchate of Antioch (*c.* 744 CE), and Saint Theodoros of Stoudites (759–826 CE). As previously intimated, the tradition that Lazarus was a "martyr" is late and dubious.

Summary. Many who are convinced of history in the Lazarus pericope will be impressed by the insights of the brilliant scholar B. F. Westcott. Here is what he reported from his exploration of the Gospel of John:

> 3. Numerous minute touches mark the fullness of personal knowledge, or the impression of an eye-witness: for example, the relation of the family to Jesus (*v.* 5); the delay of two days (6); the exact position of Bethany (18); the presence of Jews (19); the secret message (28); the title "the Master" (*id.*); the pause of Jesus (30); the following of the Jews (31), and their weeping (33); the prostration of Mary (32); the successive phases of the Lord's emotion (33, 35, 38); the appearance of Lazarus (44).

4. Not less remarkable than this definiteness of detail are the silences, the omissions, in the narrative; for example, as to the return of the messenger (v. 4); the message to Mary (27 f.); the welcome of the restored brother (44). Under this head too may be classed the unexpected turns of expression: for example, "unto Judæa" (v. 7), vv. 11 f., v. 37.

5. That however which is most impressive in the narrative, as a history, is its dramatic vividness; and this in different respects. There is a clear individuality in the persons. Thomas stands out characteristically from the apostles. Martha and Mary, alike in their convictions, are distinguished in the manner of shewing them. Then again there is a living revelation of character in the course of the narrative; Martha reflects the influence of the Lord's words. The Jews are tried and separated. And above all the Lord is seen throughout, absolutely one in His supreme freedom, perfectly human and perfectly divine, so that it is felt that there is no want of harmony between His tears and His life-giving command.[32]

What seems to be the wisest explanation of the Lazarus episode? First, some experts might argue that since the "resurrection" of Lazarus appears only in John, it probably did not happen. There is no "multiple attestation;" and that method helps protect against assuming as historical an event that is not corroborated by other authors. These critics would continue to suggest, most likely, that the Lazarus story was created in the latter half of the first century CE to prove that Jesus represents "the resurrection and the life" (John 11:24). These critics would conclude that the author is motivated by theology, not history.

Second, other New Testament scholars might claim that the raising of Lazarus was so well known that only John needed to report it. Scholars know that authors who seek to be historians tend to describe what is not widely known or not comprehended. It was too obvious to report that Jesus raised Lazarus since all believers and nonbelievers knew that Jesus caused dissensions within Palestinian Judaism and that Jesus' followers were persecuted. Moreover, only John tends to report miracles in and near Jerusalem. No credible historian doubts the crucifixion of Jesus and the stoning of Stephen. To report the Lazarus episode would draw attention to the problems Jesus caused within Judaism; and the Evangelists and Paul wanted to portray Jesus as a loving Messiah. Perhaps, the polemical tsunamis caused by the event and its retelling could have been avoided so the proclamations about Jesus might be heard and contemplated.

Third, no one in Judea and Galilee may have known what happened to Lazarus. He was weak. He was facing martyrdom. He may have fled under the radar of the leading authorities within the Temple. With Mary and Martha, he could escape, perhaps during the night, from Jerusalem. And that metropolitan city at Passover was filling with tens of thousands of pilgrims from all directions; they poured into Jerusalem and its environs to celebrate the greatest feast in the Holy City as Torah demanded (John 11:55). If Lazarus felt the dangers at that time, he would have immediately fled from Jerusalem. The precise moments were optimal; it would be virtually impossible to find Lazarus as he fled westward and down to the coast. The road was packed with pilgrims pouring into the Holy City.

Fourth, the author of Acts did not report the Lazarus episode; he also did not describe what happened to most of Jesus' disciples and followers. He was focused, almost blindly, on the missionary journeys of Peter and Paul.

These reflections are presented in what I deem an ascending order of historical probability. John makes it clear that many Jews were believing in Jesus because of Lazarus. If Jesus did "raise" Lazarus, then it is probable that many of those in Judea would believe that Jesus was far more powerful than the high priests—that is, those who, according to John, sought to kill Lazarus (John 11:45-48; 12:9).

No early evidence of Lazarus seems to remain from the first century, according to academicians. Earthquakes, fires, the Persian invasion of 614 CE, and the later Muslim invasions destroyed churches and their texts and icons in and near Jerusalem.[33]

Research in Cyprus reminds us all that to find a symbol of a cross from antiquity may be no evidence of Christianity. For example, "cross-like images" centuries before Christianity have been found on Cyprus.[34] They date from the Chalcolithic period or about from 3900 to 2500 BCE.

Conclusion

The Lazarus that Jesus resuscitated is mentioned only in the Gospel of John. Why is he not mentioned in Acts? Is it because the book is about the life of Peter and then Paul and because Lazarus had already fled to Cyprus? Why is Lazarus not mentioned by Mark in the Gospel assigned to him? Is it because this Gospel was dependent on what Mark remembered Peter had told him in Rome and Peter was not one who preached in Cyprus?

Can we trust the historical accuracy of John? In the past, many experts concluded that it is the latest Gospel and shaped primarily by theological concerns. Recent scholarship and archaeological discoveries,[35] however, have proved that John preserves a vast number of independent traditions and they have as much a right to being historically reliable as any passage in Mark. There is a new perspective about John presented by New Testament experts in the Society of Biblical Literature and the Studiorum Novi Testamenti Societas. As I have tried to demonstrate in *Jesus as Mirrored in John*, the Fourth Gospel preserves a vast number of independent traditions that are historically reliable. For example, the pools of Bethzatha and Siloam are pre-70 CE and are situated precisely where only John situates them, north and south of the Temple Mount. Portions of John are so topographically and architecturally accurate that sections of it must antedate the destruction of Jerusalem in 70 CE. The *realia* described in John have been hidden from view until modern excavations. Experts agree that John reflects more than one edition; perhaps the first edition of John was composed in Jerusalem before 70 CE. If so, the accuracy of traditions about Lazarus would have been known to the author of John.

Did Lazarus flee Jerusalem for Cyprus? Scholars seldom discuss certainty. It is conceivable that Lazarus fled Jerusalem in the thirties of the first century CE. He was in danger. Jesus had been crucified. Jesus' disciples, no longer the Twelve, hid from

Did Lazarus Flee Jerusalem for Cyprus? 77

Figure 4.5 The harbor at Caesarea Maritima, looking toward Cyprus (JHC).

Figure 4.6 The raising of Lazarus, Nativity of Christ Church in Arbanassi, Bulgaria, 1639 (photo: John W. Welch, used with permission).[38]

persecutors (John 20) and Stephen was stoned. When Paul believed that Jesus was the Christ, he had to flee Jerusalem for his life. Lazarus should be no exception. Cyprus would be a good choice for him. It was not far from Caesarea Maritima, where he could find protection.[36] And it was a home of various types of Jews and Gentiles who enjoyed tolerance and significant wealth.[37] Sadducees who denied any possibility of resurrection and wanted to protect the sanctity of the Temple would care less about someone who fled to Cyprus and Kition (now Larnaca) and would have no impetus to pursue Lazarus.

Notes

1. Raymond F. Collins, "Lazarus," *ABD* 4.265.
2. See the discussion and bibliographical notes in James H. Charlesworth, *Jesus as Mirrored in John* (London, New York: T&T Clark, 2019), p. 38, note 58.
3. See, e.g., K. Pearce, "The Lucan Origins of the Raising of Lazarus," *ExpTim* 96 (1985): 359–61. J. Kremer, "The Awakening of Lazarus," *TD* 33 (1986): 135–8. Joseph Wagner, *Auferstehung und Leben: Joh 11, 1-12, 19 als Spiegel johannischer Redaktions-und Theologiegeschichte* (Regensburg: F. Pustet, 1988).
4. See the various treatments of this issue in James H. Charlesworth and Jolyon G. R. Pruszinski, eds., *Jesus Research: The Gospel of John in Historical Inquiry*, Jewish and Christian Texts 26 (London: T&T Clark, 2019), and Charlesworth, *Jesus as Mirrored in John: The Genius in the New Testament*.
5. Collins, "Lazarus," *ABD* 4.265.
6. For further reflections, see Philip F. Esler, *Lazarus* (Philadelphia: Fortress, 2006).
7. Raymond E. Brown, *The Gospel according to John*, AB 29A (Garden City: Doubleday, 1970), vol. 1, p. 427, and Craig S. Keener, *The Gospel of John* (Peabody, MA: Hendrickson, 2003), vol. 2, p. 850.
8. William Barclay concluded that the Lazarus pericope is an allegory. See Barclay, *And He Had Compassion on Them* (1955), pp. 211–29.
9. See Richard Hamann, "Lazarus in Heaven," *The Burlington Magazine for Connoisseurs* 63.364 (July 1933): 3–5, 8–11. See the summary in "Lazarus," newworldencyclopedia.org.
10. John P. Meier, *A Marginal Jew: Rethinking the Historical Jesus* (New York, London: Doubleday, 1994), vol. 2, p. 831.
11. Paintings and icons highlight Jesus' miraculous raising of Lazarus. For example, an early seventeenth-century scene in the left margin of the icon called "Virgin of Vladimir with Festivals" illustrates many elements depicted or imagined from pondering Jesus' raising of Lazarus according to John 11. In the icon, now in the Tretyakov Gallery in Moscow, one sees the following: (1) on the left: An artist depicts Jesus with his right hand raised. Behind him are a large number of his apostles (it is impossible to count the hidden heads). A book appears to be in Jesus' left hand. (2) Before Jesus, Mary and Martha bow to the ground; the one in white holds Lazarus' face cloth. (3) Behind the two women is a man holding the door to the tomb or the lid of the sarcophagus. (4) Above this man and parallel to Jesus is Lazarus who is standing before the opened door of the tomb; he is wrapped in white

linen and bound by red cords. A Jew is depicted unwrapping Lazarus. (5) Mary, Martha, Lazarus, and one apostle stare at Jesus. (6) Four men with turbans watch the scene from above (perhaps from heaven. They may be Moses, Elijah, Enoch, and Abraham). (7) Jesus and Lazarus are the main characters and only they have halos. Lazarus appears strong and upright and in blazing white; his adoration is directed to his Lord. The icon was crafted in the workshop of the Stroganov family in Solvychegodsk. A color image is found on p. 123 in A. Kostsova, *The Subjects of Early Russian Icons* (Saint Petersburg: Iskusstvo Publishers, 1994).

12   Metropolitan of Kition, "Foreword," in Stavros S. Fotiou, *St. Lazarus and His Church in Larnaca*, translated by Andreas P. Vittis (Larnaca, 2016 [no publisher cited]). See the bibliography on pp. 83–9; no recent critical study is listed for Lazarus.
13   Fotiou, *St. Lazarus*, pp. 20–1.
14   Ibid., p. 23.
15   Legends are often not separated from history, even if it is elusive, by many authors. Katia Hadjidemetriour, in *A History of Cyprus* (p. 108): "The Cypriot Jews, who reacted against Barnabas' work, arrested him and stoned him to death in Salamis (A.D. 57). John buried his dead body near Salamis and placed Matthew's gospel on his chest." Most experts do not date Matthew so early.
16   See Marguerite Yon et al., "Kition in the Tenth to Fourth Centuries B.C.," *Bulletin of the American Schools of Oriental Research* (November 1997). Kition and Enkomi share the same history. See the attractive summary of Kition by Vassos Karageorghis, *The Cyprus Ancient Monuments* (Nicosia: C. Epiphaniou Publications, 1989), pp. 52–5.
17   See the numerous sources for this legend discussed by Fotiou, *St. Lazarus*, pp. 75–6.
18   See newworldencyclopedia.org.
19   See Charalampos G. Chotzakoglou, *Church of Saint Lazarus in Larnaka* (Lefkosia: Thekona Printing Works, LTD, 2004), pp. 18–23. See the picture of the putative prison of Lazarus in Marseilles on p. 21.
20   See Seigneur de Villamont's claim in Fotiou, *St. Lazarus*, p. 29.
21   See Chotzakoglou, *Church of Saint Lazarus in Larnaka*, p. 19. The author rightly judges this late tradition to be unhistorical.
22   Eusebius, *Onomastikon* 58, lines 15–17. For the report of excavations in Bethany, see S. J. Saller, *Excavations at Bethany (1949–53)*, PSBF 12 (Jerusalem: Franciscan, 1957), S. Loffreda, "Due tombe a Betania presso le Suore della Nigrizia," *LA* 19 (1969): 349–66, and Loffreda, "La tomba n. 3 presso le Suore della Nigrizia a Betania," *LA* 24 (1974): 142–69.
23   See Jerome Murphy-O'Connor, "Bethany," in *The Holy Land: An Oxford Archaeological Guide from Earliest Times to 1700*, 4th ed. (Oxford: Oxford University Press, 1998), pp. 133–5.
24   The claims were rejected long ago. For example, see "Bethany," in *The Catholic Encyclopedia*, edited by Charles Herbermann (New York: Robert Appleton Co., 1913).
25   See the clear discussion in Chotzakoglou, *Church of Saint Lazarus in Larnaka*, p. 15.
26   John J. Welch, "Miracles, *Maleficium*, and *Maiestas* in the Trial of Jesus," in *Jesus and Archaeology*, edited by J. H. Charlesworth (Grand Rapids: Eerdmans, 2006), pp. 349–83.

27 Walter Bauer, *Orthodoxy and Heresy in Earliest Christianity*, edited by R. Kraft and G. Krodel (Philadelphia: Fortress, 1971). Bauer's work is foundational but he does not discuss Cyprus, Sergius Paulus, Elymas, or Lazarus.
28 Stavros S. Fotiou, *St. Lazarus and His Church in Larnaca*, translated by A. P. Vittis (Larnaca: The Ecclesiastical Committee of the Holy Church of St Lazarus, 2016), p. 21.
29 Vassos Karageorghis, *Salamis in Cyprus, Homeric, Hellenistic and Roman* (New York: Thames and Hudson, 1969). Also see his lengthy bibliography in D. Pilides and N. Papadimitriou, eds., *Ancient Cyprus: Cultures in Dialogue* (Nicosia: Department of Antiquities, Cyprus, 2012), p. 277.
30 It received that name from Septimus Severus in 200 CE; its former name was Beth Gabra. It was prominent in the First Jewish War; see Josephus, *J.W.* 4.8.1.
31 A historian has no means to access such numbers. It appears, however, to represent numerology (the creation of meaning by numbers) and not historical calculation or knowledge. Was it thought that Jesus was crucified in 30 CE and Lazarus would have to flee Palestine in 30?
32 Brooke F. Westcott, *The Gospel according to St. John*, edited by Arthur Westcott (London: J. Murray, 1908), p. 163.
33 For a discussion of the few images that remain, see Athanasios Papageorgiou and Ioannis A. Eliades, *Guide to the Byzantine Museum and Art Gallery of the Archbishop Makarios III Foundation* (Nicosia: Byzantine Museum of the Archbishop Makarios III Foundation, 2008), pp. 26–33. As far as I know, no image of Lazarus exists from the early centuries of Christianity in Cyprus.
34 Crosses that antedate the Israelite Monarchy in the tenth century BCE are part of the collection at the Pierides Museum in Larnaca, Cyprus.
35 See Charlesworth, *Jesus as Mirrored in John: The Genius in the New Testament*; see chapter six: "Archaeological Discoveries Supporting the Historicity of John's Traditions."
36 See Charlesworth, "Cesarea Maritima," in *The Millennium Guide for Pilgrims to the Holy Land* (North Richland Hills, Texas: BIBAL Press, 2000), pp. 62–5.
37 Between the well-known sculptors, Phidias and Praxiteles, is an anonymous master who left us an image of Aphrodite. It was found in the Roman Gymnasium at Salamis. For a colored image, see Vassos Karageorghis, *The Cyprus Museum* (Nicosia: Epiphaniou Publications, 1989), p. 106.
38 John W. Welch: "Viewers will notice Jesus in the center, with his right hand blessing Lazarus who is awakened, who comes forth from the stone-tomb, with his burial shroud beginning to unwind. Lazarus has a gold halo, indicating his holy discipleship, soon to become St. Lazarus. Jesus's left hand appears to be receiving the message that Lazarus had died. The women in red and black are apparently Mary and Martha. Behind Jesus are eleven disciples, Judas not to be shown. In the lower right, a servant is moving away the stone that had covered the entrance to the tomb. In the top-center are depicted the walls around Jerusalem and the inner Temple enclosed with the flaming altar of sacrifice on the left, Caiaphas with three other chief priests or Pharisees, and two structures, perhaps the Holy Place and the Holy of Holies, to the right. They have been told by eyewitnesses about Jesus's raising of Lazarus in Bethany, just on the other side of the Mount of Olives, not far from Jerusalem. Caiaphas will soon convene the Sanhedrin. They will debate what to do next in the face of this most impressive sign and miracle that threatens to lead everyone in Jerusalem to follow Jesus. Even miracle workers can be convicted of leading people

into apostasy under Deuteronomy 13. And so, Caiaphas ruled that it was better for Jesus to be executed than for a riot to break out and for the holy city and Temple to be taken away by the Romans. A warrant for his capture was sent out, and Lazarus also was found worthy of death, apparently convicted of complicity with Jesus in working some kind of ploy to deceive the people."

5

Barnabas: The Levite from Cyprus

Konstantinos Th. Zarras

It is the deeds of great and well-known men that turn the wheels of history. Celebrated, they set an example and they are admired by all. Like beacons, they shed light on the paths of ordinary people and their lives echo in the ages. Yet, in their long wanderings deep into the mists of half-told tales and murmurs between the lines of eroded texts, oftentimes historians find traces of other men destined to dwell in the shadow of their more famed protagonists. The Apostle Paul is considered by some as the true founder of Christianity and thousands of studies have been written on his person and on his mission. No doubt, he helped spread the word to the Gentile world more than anyone else and he is credited accordingly. And as is the case in many similar instances, the phenomenon called Paul was formed and forged by the greater and lesser losses and sacrifices of many other brothers and sisters—brothers largely unknown or barely studied. Barnabas, the Levite from Cyprus, the first to feature and to further the Apostle Paul, is such a case.

Though Jewish communities were found in many areas around the Mediterranean, in many of their societies, a full picture or account of their lives, trades, and doings is very far from complete. The communities that present enough witnesses in order to draw a sketch are those of Rome, Syria, Cyrenaica, and Asia Minor,[1] but not of Cyprus. The island of Aphrodite, Cyprus,[2] "the third largest island in the Mediterranean,"[3] lies in the eastern Mediterranean like a giant ship or like a human hand pointing to the northern part of Levant. Perhaps not without meaning, one may also imagine that by its northeastern peninsula Cyprus seems to point toward the direction of Antioch and Tarsus—places of great importance when considered in light of the events that followed at that time. Its distance is only a few hundred miles from the land of Israel and only 60 miles away from the Syrian coast. Thence, it is easy to travel to and fro. Inscriptions unearthed in Kition (today's Larnaca) and dated in the fourth century BCE witness the presence of Jews in Cyprus at least from the Persian period.[4] Later on, since Cyprus belonged to the Ptolemaic rule, it is highly probable that when Ptolemaeus I Lagos in 301 BCE, after his campaign to Palestine, ordered the transportation of thousands of Jews, due to the island's proximity, many should have moved there, too.[5] During the times of Cleopatra and her son Ptolemy Lathyrus, Josephus (*Ant.* 13.10.4) passes down that the Jews in Cyprus were in prosperity. After all, the Ptolemies called for slaves and soldiers from all of their lands, including Asia Minor, Crete, and Cyprus;[6] and the Jewish communities also responded.

Rich in copper, as Josephus has it (*Ant.* 16.4.5), in addition to her strategic place in eastern Mediterranean, Cyprus presented one further strong element of interest to the Romans. After his being victorious over Anthony and Cleopatra, Octavian placed Cyprus "under his direct control in 30 BC" and the island was made "a senatorial province governed by a proconsul who was chosen annually" "in 22 BC."[7] Both Ptolemies and Romans offered a significant level of autonomy to the Jewish communities in the Diaspora and raised no objection to their following of their religious duties. As in other areas of Jewish Diaspora in the eastern Mediterranean, their Cypriot communities were "fully Hellenized," yet in close contact with Jerusalem.[8]

Needless to say, the more recent the sources, the more information available. Therefore, there are various other sources that mention the presence of Jews in Cyprus.[9] In Acts 13:5 there is a reference in the plural (ἐν ταῖς συναγωγαῖς τῶν Ἰουδαίων) to synagogues in Salamis, one of the largest cities in Cyprus. Salamis was a rich and busy port, actually the main port, exporting copper, timber, and corn.[10] According to Acts 11:19, after the killing of Stephanus, the earliest Judeo-Christian communities were formed in Phoenicia, Cyprus, and Antioch, spreading the word only to Jews.[11] These were of the Nazarene sect (τῶν Ναζωραίων αἱρέσεως, Acts 24:5).[12] The εἰ μὴ μόνον Ἰουδαίοις in Acts 11:19, together with the early decision to preach in Cyprus, is a strong indication that there were many Jewish communities and synagogues there. Philo[13] asserts that not only the mainland in Greece was strong in the colonies of Jews but the islands of Euboea, Cyprus, and Crete, as well (καὶ οὐ μόνον αἱ ἤπειροι μεσταὶ τῶν Ἰουδαϊκῶν ἀποικιῶν εἰσιν, ἀλλὰ καὶ νήσων αἱ δοκιμώταται, Εὔβοια, Κύπρος, Κρήτη). The fact that Paul and Barnabas are mentioned in Acts 13:6 as having gone through the island preaching until they had reached Paphos (διελθόντες δὲ ὅλην τὴν νῆσον ἄχρι Πάφου), the then capital on the other side of the island,[14] together with the element that they would preach only to the Jews (Acts 11:19), proves that there were many Jewish communities to visit.

Unfortunately, the uprisings of 115–117 CE brought deep changes in the Jewish Diaspora, changes that mattered a lot and lasted, sometimes plunging Jewry in the pains of challenges to survival.[15] Salamis must have been destroyed completely during the uprising.[16] After the turmoil, the Roman emperor Trajan banned Jews forever from Cyprus.[17] Dio Cassius is the only historian who provides commentary on that disastrous event:

ἔν τε Αἰγύπτῳ πολλὰ ἔδρασαν ὅμοια καὶ ἐν τῇ Κύπρῳ, ἡγουμένου τινός σφισιν Ἀρτεμίωνος· καὶ ἀπώλοντο καὶ ἐκεῖ μυριάδες τέσσαρες καὶ εἴκοσι. καὶ διὰ τοῦτ' οὐδενὶ Ἰουδαίῳ ἐπιβῆναι αὐτῆς ἔξεστιν, ἀλλὰ κἂν ἀνέμῳ τις βιασθεὶς ἐς τὴν νῆσον ἐκπέσῃ θανατοῦται. ἀλλ' Ἰουδαίους μὲν ἄλλοι τε καὶ Λούσιος ὑπὸ Τραϊανοῦ πεμφθεὶς κατεστρέψατο.[18]

Yet, this edict must have been annulled during the reign of Antoninus Pius (138–161 CE).

As it has been written, "The Levites remain somewhat of a mystery."[19] Though they were distanced from their more glorious past and from the sacrificial ritual per se, during the Second Temple their status was still high.[20] It is characteristic that they are totally absent from later books, like Ben Sira and I Maccabees. In the services they acted as helpers to the priests. Though initially they were very close to them, now they acted as gatekeepers[21] and choir members, while they took care of other things, like keeping the ritually unclean and the aliens away from the holy ground.[22] It is very interesting that in the *Mishnah* (Middoth 2:5-6) the Levites are mentioned as acting only as singers, as music players, and during the rituals they acted from a special elevated platform (the *dukhan*). They are also mentioned as stationed in another level altogether (at "chambers beneath the Court of the Israelites"). According to Josephus (*Ant.* 20.216), following a rule from the Sanhedrin, the Levites were finally permitted to wear the white priestly linen attire, but that came to pass only for a brief period of time, since the Temple was destroyed soon after by the Romans. After the destruction of the Temple in 70 CE they were demoted to a lesser role. Even so, their glory never faded totally. Thus, in Clement's letter to the Corinthians (40.5) appears the phrase λαϊκὸς ἄνθρωπος, indicating the difference between the priests and Levites. In the same letter to the Corinthians, Clement likens the Levitical hierarchy (chs. 40–41) to the church and the "body of Christ." He also likens it to the order of the universe and the human body (chs. 37–38). Let us also remember that Jerome *(Epistulae* 52.5) likened the Levites to the clergy of the Christians.[23]

Given that Diaspora Jewry and especially priests and Levites remained closely tied to the Temple in Jerusalem, one may surmise that they could travel there to attend to their service. In the Yerushalmi (Yoma 4:5) it is mentioned that "Cyprus wine, three seahs and three qabs"[24] should be sent from the island to the Temple at Jerusalem. And possibly, this wine traveled together with such people of the Levitical temple personnel.

Christian beginnings in Cyprus are connected to the flight of some of Jesus' followers there, after the stoning of Stephanus (*c.* 37 CE), and are considered as synonymous to the work of Barnabas, Saul/Paul, and Mark (or, Ἰωάννην, Barnabas' cousin)[25] there around 45 CE.[26] The joining with Mark took place while in Jerusalem (Acts 12:25–13:3), where Mark's mother, Mary, held church meetings in her house (Acts 12:12).[27] Perhaps because of his relations to the priestly caste or maybe for his ministry in the Temple, Barnabas the Levite seemed to travel a lot to Jerusalem. Most probably not from Aaronic or Zaddokite descent, he might have offered his service in the Temple as a guardian, a singer, or helping in the animal slaughtering.[28]

According to Acts 4:36, Barnabas[29] came from Cyprus (Salamis); therefore, he was a Jew of the Diaspora. His name was Joseph (Ἰωσὴφ), a Levite, whom the apostles called Barnabas (υἱὸς παρακλήσεως,[30] which means "son of encouragement" or "son of consolation" or even "son of prophecy"). He was not one of the twelve initial disciples and apostles, but surely he was one of the earliest to come into faith to Jesus Christ.[31] In Acts (4:36-37) he is said to have sold some of his property he owned in Jerusalem and donated the sum of the money to the apostles in Jerusalem.[32] Acts 11:24 presents Barnabas as a good man, strong in faith and full of the Holy Spirit (ἀνὴρ ἀγαθὸς καὶ πλήρης πνεύματος ἁγίου καὶ πίστεως). The fact that he was a man of high financial status, yet he chose to work, as Paul did (Acts 4:36; 23:16), proves that he was a man of integrity that cared to offer an example to his brothers without laying the burden of his sustenance on their shoulders. Thus, he seems to be a real model of the true and faithful, a man for whom his name met his mission in life. Perhaps that is why Barnabas is mentioned twenty-four times in Acts and five times in the epistles of Paul.[33] In Acts 14:14 he is called an "apostle" together with Paul. The fact that in Acts (11:27-30; 12:25) he is the one (with Saul) who brings the famine offerings from Antioch[34] to Jerusalem proves the importance of his position there. What's more, since Barnabas is sent from Jerusalem to Antioch (Acts 11:22-23), it is obvious that he was thought to be a person suitable to speak to people from another cultural environment. His Cypriot home must have contributed to his cosmopolitanism; therefore, it seems perfectly natural that he would be the one to send to the converts from the Hellenized Jews and Greeks at Antioch.

The truth is we do not have information about the latter part of Barnabas' life and work. What we do have is bits of material from the sphere of legend. Thus, it is highly debatable by scholars that he was chosen to be one of the seventy direct disciples of Jesus in Luke 10:1.[35] His supposed authorship of the Epistle to the Hebrews (by Tertullian, in his *De Pudicitia* 20), attributed to Paul himself by some, is also dubious, as is the support for Clement of Alexandria's claim for his authorship of the so-called *Epistle of Barnabas* (actually, a second-century work).[36] Still, it is only in a late document, the *Acts of Barnabas* (fifth to sixth century), that we find a story about his final efforts to spread the word in Cyprus and about his martyrdom. According to *Acts of Barnabas* (23), he was killed in Salamis in 55[37] or in Syria in 61 CE by hostile Jews.[38] Although highly debated, tradition has it that the first bishop in Cyprus, Heraclides, after Barnabas, was supposedly ordained by him and Paul.

Though possible, Barnabas studying together with a younger Saul under Gamaliel[39] is unfounded and in all probability belongs in the sphere of folklore. Even so, albeit Gal 1:13-17, in all probability, Barnabas must have played a significant role in mentoring Saul theologically. There is no doubt that Saul learned a lot watching the older Barnabas.[40]

Therefore, not surprisingly, Barnabas came to be one of the earliest apostles, one of the pillars of the church in Antioch, and a companion to Saul/Paul[41] during the initial phase of his mission to the Gentile world.[42] Like their older Jewish officials, they seem to have formed a kind of a זוג,[43] a pair in cooperation and service. After all, both of them shared a love for their people and their religion, where they excelled, Barnabas a Levite, Saul a Pharisee. Even more, it seems that during the first missionary journey of Paul, Barnabas might have been the "initial leader."[44] The fact that in Acts his name is mentioned before Saul's[45] proves his seniority to the "apostle of the nations." It has also been maintained that Luke fashioned Paul's mission after that of Barnabas.[46]

Barnabas' importance is clearly proven in Acts 9:27-28, when he brings with him and introduces Saul/Paul[47] to the other disciples. Actually, due to his earlier hostility for the church (Acts 7:58; 8:1-3), the disciples were very hesitant in accepting Saul as a μαθητής (Acts 9:26). Then, Paul is accepted in the inner circle of the Jerusalem brothers mostly thanks to Barnabas' trust in him. Still, in Acts 11:25-26 it is Barnabas (the one who sought, found, and brought Saul to Antioch and into the newly found church there) and Saul together who instructed the neophytes for one year. And it was Barnabas who went to the Jerusalem council of apostles and elders with Paul, when the issue on Law and circumcision arose (Acts 15:1-35). Here the text of Acts 15:12 leaves us with the impression that Barnabas spoke first or that his merit was higher than Paul's. In any case, at least initially, Barnabas' name is mentioned first.[48]

Barnabas' high position in the church of Jerusalem may also be detected in Acts 11:19-26, where he is chosen as their representative to those in Antioch-on-the-Orontes.[49] Even more importantly, Barnabas and Paul are singled out for proclaiming the good news by the Holy Spirit (Acts 13:2). They sailed from Seleucia to Cyprus[50] and afterwards they traveled to many Jewish communities in central Asia Minor. Together they managed to convert the proconsul Lucius Sergius Paulus and to stun Elymas, a Jewish sorcerer and false prophet, who seemed to be a regular in his court (see Acts 13:6-11). A similar miracle was conducted by Paul in Lystra, where Paul through the Holy Spirit healed a crippled man. There the crowd compared them to gods, calling Barnabas Zeus and Paul Hermes (Acts 14:8-18).[51] They even wanted to offer sacrifices to them.[52] The attribution of these specific names should carry some meaning here, betraying some crucial elements concerning the appearance and/or the conduct of the two. Hermes was a god of eloquence,[53] speed, literacy, a pedagogue, and a psychopompus (a soul guide for the deceased). Zeus, on the other hand, the king of the Olympian gods, though many a time meek and slow in anger, was a more commanding and powerful icon. Of course, Hermes answers to Zeus and not vice versa.[54] Then, calling Barnabas after Zeus might mean that his attitude and posture was even more imposing than Paul's,[55] an indication that he was taken to be the leader of the two.

By and large it remains a mystery why bringing Mark with them in their subsequent travels brought a serious discord (a παροξυσμός) with Paul (Acts 15:37-39)[56] and—after fifteen years of working together—a finale and a parting of the ways to their concerted effort and mission[57] (although in good spirit, as is shown in 1 Cor 9:6). From then on Paul travels with Silas, while Barnabas with Mark (Acts 15:36-40). Here Barnabas seems ready to offer Mark a second chance,[58] but Paul resists strongly. Surely, real causes run deeper and had to do with more serious issues than those indicated by the text of Acts. Another disagreement between the two was concerning the rules of table-fellowship concerning the converts from the Gentiles. In Antioch, when Peter decided against it, Barnabas the Levite sided with him and on this matter turned against his companion.[59] Since it is not mentioned that Paul persuaded them on his view like he did earlier in Jerusalem, one may suppose that in this battle he failed. Therefore, the grounds for their parting would likely have been theological, and more specifically, related to the validity of Jewish laws concerning contact with the nations. And when Paul left Antioch, he followed his way. Perhaps Paul was afraid that Mark would be like-minded to Barnabas (since a relative) and thus present obstacles to his mission as Paul perceived it to be unfolding.

All things considered, Barnabas' role as a companion to Paul should not be underestimated. Though not favored by modern scholarship, at least not as much as Paul and Peter, Barnabas was a true soft force during his life and mission. It is quite probable that his teaching and his character exerted a deep influence on the first churches, both in Antioch and in Jerusalem. According to Acts (13:43, 48; 14:1; 15:2) Barnabas' and Paul's mission was successful, since many took heed and became believers in the teachings of Jesus of Nazareth. He was there when Paul needed him the most: when he had to confront the apostles and gain confidence during his initial travels preaching the good news. It cannot be doubted that Barnabas helped greatly in Paul's maturing in the faith. Perhaps Paul's success in persuading the apostles and the elders in Jerusalem against the prerequisite of the circumcision for the converts from the Gentiles owed something to the meek appearance of Barnabas when they traveled and presented their case together in front of them.[60] Then, undoubtedly, Barnabas presented characteristics of a true leader that seeks not to bring glory to himself but only to serve others and spread the word.[61] He was a true cosmopolitan, feeling comfortable both in Jerusalem and at Antioch or Salamis. From this point of view, he might have exerted significant influence on the younger Saul, the "apostle to the nations." In persuading the disciples to accept Saul/Paul, Barnabas played a pivotal role. Taking into consideration the enormous impact of Paul's mission for the expansion of the Christian faith, it should be noted that on *that* day Barnabas was the true protagonist and the one who helped usher in a new era for the world.

In one of his comments on Acts 11:25-30, Gregory of Nazianzus maintained that Barnabas should be "indebted" to Paul, since he was chosen to be his companion. Yet, Branch is quite right when he turns the argument around, concluding that according to the biblical account it was "*Barnabas* [the one who] chose Saul/Paul and championed him."[62] That is why it has been written that "it was Barnabas who made him [Paul] a leading member of the church at Antioch and shared with him his task of teaching (Acts 11:25-6; 13:1)."[63] Thus, in the person of Barnabas many traits converge to form a truly composite yet harmonious personality. A Hebrew, a Levite, a man of the world, a "people's person," a traveler, and a cosmopolitan, he acted in a most efficient way as a mediator between people, places, and eras.

Notes

1   J. M. G. Barclay, *Jews in the Mediterranean Diaspora: From Alexander to Trajan (323 BCE-117 CE)* (Edinburgh: T&T Clark, 1996), p. 231. Also, Er. S. Gruen, *Diaspora: Jews amidst Greeks and Romans* (Cambridge, MA: Harvard University Press, 2004), p. 2. Here I need to extend my heartiest thanks to my friend and colleague Haralampos Atmatzides for reading the manuscript and sharing some really interesting thoughts.
2   The Greek name "Cyprus" brought forth the term for copper, a mineral the island was famed and rich for. Elsewhere, Cyprus is called Kittim (Jer 1:10), too.
3   R. G. Branch, "Barnabas: Early Church Leader and Model of Encouragement," *In die Skriflig* 41.2 (2007): 299.
4   See 1 Macc 15:23; 2 Macc 12:2. Also, Ευανθία Πολύβιου, *Οι Ιουδαίοι στην Αρχαία Κύπρο: Απόστολοι, ραββίνοι, μάγοι, επαναστάτες*. Χρονικό Δ/6, 7/4/2018 (Ev. Polyviou, *Jews in Ancient Cyprus: Apostles, Rabbis, Magicians, Rebels*, in Greek), p. 4.
5   *Epistle of Aristeas* 12–14. Josephus, *Ant*. 12.3-7. Also in Polyviou, *Jews in Ancient Cyprus: Apostles, Rabbis, Magicians, Rebels*, in Greek, p. 5. Also, for a brief discussion, see the information in G. Vermes, F. Millar, and M. Goodman, *The History of the Jewish People in the Age of Jesus Christ (175 B.C.-AD 135)*, vol. II, part 1 (Edinburgh: T&T Clark, 1986), pp. 68–9.
6   Barclay, *Jews in the Mediterranean Diaspora*, p. 22.
7   Branch, "Barnabas: Early Church Leader and Model of Encouragement," p. 299.
8   Polyviou, *Jews in Ancient Cyprus: Apostles, Rabbis, Magicians, Rebels*, in Greek, p. 15.

9   See 1 Macc 15:23. Philo, *Legatio ad Gaiam* 282. Acts 4:36, 11:20. Josephus, *Ant.* 13.284–287. Also, Gruen, *Diaspora: Jews amidst Greeks and Romans*, p. 108.
10 Ev. Polyviou, "The Jewish Diaspora in Cyprus in Roman Times: The Limitations of Evidence," *Κυπριακαί Σπουδαί (Cypriot Studies)* 75 (2011): 69–84, here 72 (in English). Greek mythology has it that Salamis was founded soon after the Trojan War by the son of Telamon, Teucer, and named after the island of Salamis that is close to Athens.
11 Acts 11:19, Οἱ μὲν οὖν διασπαρέντες ἀπὸ τῆς θλίψεως τῆς γενομένης ἐπὶ Στεφάνῳ διῆλθον ἕως Φοινίκης καὶ Κύπρου καὶ Ἀντιοχείας μηδενὶ λαλοῦντες τὸν λόγον εἰ μὴ μόνον Ἰουδαίοις.
12 Of course, the term αἱρέσεως has nothing to do with the meaning attached to it after the Christian Synods in the fourth and fifth centuries CE—that is, of heresy.
13 Philo, *Legatio ad Gaium* 282.3.
14 Romans chose Paphos instead of Salamis.
15 Barclay, *Jews in the Mediterranean Diaspora*, p. 78; in the places of uprising, Jews seemed to act in concert or as for a common cause (see p. 424). Barclay calls the heat of those uprisings a "mad fury" (see p. 258).
16 Polyviou, "The Jewish Diaspora in Cyprus in Roman Times: The Limitations of Evidence," p. 72.
17 J. Efron, S. Weitzman, and M. Lehmann, *The Jews: A History* (London/New York: Routledge, 2016), p. 97. The witness of the Roman historian Dio Cassius (*Historiae Romanae* 68.32) reveals a Jewish community in Cyprus with a lot of population, able to destroy the city of Salamis and its Greco-Roman population (also, in Polyviou, *Jews in Ancient Cyprus: Apostles, Rabbis, Magicians, Rebels*, in Greek, pp. 4 and 20).
18 Dio Cassius, *Historiae Romanae* 68.32.3. "In Egypt, too, they perpetrated many similar outrages, and in Cyprus, under the leadership of a certain Artemion. There, also, two hundred and forty thousand perished, and for this reason no Jew may set foot on that island, but even if one of them is driven upon its shores by a storm he is put to death. Among others who subdued the Jews was Lusius, who was sent by Trajan" (Henderson, LCL). Of course, the 240,000 dead he mentions as victims of the wrath of the Jews must be an outright exaggeration.
19 M. Leuchter, "From Levite to Maskil in the Persian and Hellenistic Eras," in *Levites and Priests in Biblical History and Tradition*, edited by M. Leuchter and J. M. Hutton (Atlanta: Society of Biblical Literature, 2011), p. 215.
20 For the role and history of the Levites, see the collective volume by M. Leuchter and J. M. Hutton, eds., *Levites and Priests in Biblical History and Tradition* (Atlanta: Society of Biblical Literature, 2011), and especially the last contribution therein, M. Leuchter, "From Levite to Maskil in the Persian and Hellenistic Eras," pp. 215–32.
21 See also Josephus, *Ant.* 20.218.
22 Mentioned also by Philo, *Spec.* 156.
23 Still, when Cyprian (*Ep.* 1.1) needed to support the view that clergy should not have to work, he referred to the Levites and their living from the tithes. What's more, one may find parallels between the *Apostolic Church Order* (15–29) and some of the Qumranite texts—namely, CD 13:2-11, 1QS 6:8-11, and 1QS 8:1-3.
24 Jacob Neusner's translation. See also b.Kerithot 6a.
25 See Col 4:10, where he is called Μᾶρκος ὁ ἀνεψιὸς Βαρναβᾶ.
26 See Polyviou, "The Jewish Diaspora in Cyprus in Roman Times: The Limitations of Evidence," p. 70.
27 This is the house Peter used as a refuge after his escape from prison.

28 Branch, "Barnabas: Early Church Leader and Model of Encouragement," p. 298.
29 There are "29 New Testament entries about Barnabas"; see Branch, "Barnabas: Early Church Leader and Model of Encouragement," p. 318.
30 The term παρακλήσεως is akin to παράκλητος, thus betraying a link to the work or the influence of the Holy Spirit. See also Branch, "Barnabas: Early Church Leader and Model of Encouragement," p. 300, n. 7.
31 J. D. G. Dunn, *Beginning from Jerusalem: Christianity in the Making*, vol. 2 (Grand Rapids, MI: Eerdmans, 2009), p. 183.
32 See Dunn, *Beginning from Jerusalem: Christianity in the Making*, 2.169, 211–12.
33 Also in Branch, "Barnabas: Early Church Leader and Model of Encouragement," p. 297.
34 At that time, Syrian Antioch was the third city in population and wealth in the Roman Empire, with Rome and Alexandria in the first and second place respectively. On the issue of the famine, see Dunn, *Beginning from Jerusalem: Christianity in the Making*, 2.375–77.
35 See Clement of Alexandria, *Strom.* 2:20.116.3.5: τὸν ἀποστολικὸν Βαρνάβαν (ὃ δὲ τῶν ἑβδομήκοντα ἦν καὶ συνεργὸς τοῦ Παύλου).
36 See Clement of Alexandria, *Strom.* 2.6, 7. The most probable dating is either during 96–98 CE or 132–135 CE. On extra-canonical traditions on Barnabas, see also Branch, "Barnabas: Early Church Leader and Model of Encouragement," pp. 301–3.
37 Branch, "Barnabas: Early Church Leader and Model of Encouragement," p. 301.
38 Polyviou, "The Jewish Diaspora in Cyprus in Roman Times: The Limitations of Evidence," p. 71.
39 Branch, "Barnabas: Early Church Leader and Model of Encouragement," p. 301.
40 It is believed that at least initially it was Barnabas who planned their journeys; see M. J. Borg and J. D. Crossan, *The First Paul: Reclaiming the Radical Visionary behind the Church's Conservative Icon* (San Francisco: HarperOne, 2010), p. 78.
41 The fact that both Barnabas and Saul carry a contribution to the brothers in Jerusalem during the famine (Acts 11:27-30) proves that they were the "pillars" of the Antiochene church. See also Gal 2:9-10.
42 But, concerning Paul's second mission to Galatia and Cyprus, see Borg and Crossan, *The First Paul: Reclaiming the Radical Visionary behind the Church's Conservative Icon*, p. 77, too.
43 The Hebrew term זוג comes from the Greek ζεύγος, that is, the "pair."
44 Branch, "Barnabas: Early Church Leader and Model of Encouragement," p. 299. Also, Dunn, *Beginning from Jerusalem: Christianity in the Making*, 2.419.
45 Even in Gal 2:9 Barnabas' name comes first.
46 Borg and Crossan, *The First Paul: Reclaiming the Radical Visionary behind the Church's Conservative Icon*, p. 79; later Paul changed his strategy completely (p. 85).
47 Saul's name changes to Paul after a miraculous event, when in Paphos he blinds sorcerer Elymas and causes the conversion of the proconsul Sergius Paulus (Acts 13:8-12). The event presents all the elements of a rite of passage, especially the new name given to him (Acts 13:9 and 13) and the here-to-fore recognition of his new status. That is why from now on Paul is mentioned before Barnabas (see Acts 13:43, 46, 50). On the name change, see also Dunn, *Beginning from Jerusalem: Christianity in the Making*, 2.423-24.
48 See Acts 11:19-26; 12:25–13:3; 13:4-12.
49 Perhaps Barnabas owned some property in Antioch, too; see Dunn, *Beginning from Jerusalem: Christianity in the Making*, 2.302.

50. On their mission in Cyprus, see Dunn, *Beginning from Jerusalem: Christianity in the Making*, 2.419-24.
51. Inscriptions unearthed at Sedasa, a place close to Lystra, and dated to the mid-third century CE prove that Zeus and Hermes, the spokesman of the gods, were worshipped in the Lycaonian Galatia. Gods visiting humans is very old; see Homer, *Odyssey* 17.485–87.
52. According to a legend written down by Ovid (*Metamorphoses* 8.618-724), long ago Zeus and Hermes came down to earth, in Phrygia, dressed like men and seeking for a place to sleep. Most of the people denied their hospitality to the god of hospitality and only a couple of poor people accepted them in their hut. Perhaps, the people at Lystra interpreted the presence of the two along the lines of the legend.
53. To Iamblichus (*On the Mysteries* 1.1), Hermes was Θεὸς ὁ τῶν λόγων ἡγεμών, Ἑρμῆς ("god, the ruler of speech, Hermes").
54. See Borg and Crossan, *The First Paul: Reclaiming the Radical Visionary behind the Church's Conservative Icon*, pp. 77–8.
55. See also Branch, "Barnabas: Early Church Leader and Model of Encouragement," p. 298.
56. Mark had deserted both of them during their mission in Pamphylia and returned to Jerusalem (Acts 13:13). Later Paul and Mark reconciled with each other and co-operated (2 Tim 4:11).
57. This is the so-called "Antioch incident" (see Gal 2:11-13).
58. Due to his constant trust to their true potential, Barnabas is called a "people person;" see Branch, "Barnabas: Early Church Leader and Model of Encouragement," p. 306.
59. See Gal 2:11-13. Though initially Cephas was eating together with the Gentiles, when men from James arrived, he withdrew and practiced differently. Galatians 2:13 calls this behavior "hypocrisy" (Βαρναβᾶς συναπήχθη αὐτῶν τῇ ὑποκρίσει). Here Paul seems to be in shock, since he writes "even Barnabas" (ὥστε καὶ Βαρναβᾶς). See Borg and Crossan, *The First Paul: Reclaiming the Radical Visionary behind the Church's Conservative Icon*, p. 80. On the issue, see Dunn, *Beginning from Jerusalem: Christianity in the Making*, 2.318-19.
60. See Acts 15:1-3, 22-32.
61. He is called "a key leader" in Branch, "Barnabas: Early Church Leader and Model of Encouragement," p. 319.
62. Branch, "Barnabas: Early Church Leader and Model of Encouragement," p. 318 (author's italics).
63. Kl. Haacker, "Paul's Life," in *The Cambridge Companion to St Paul*, edited by J. D. G. Dunn (Cambridge: Cambridge University Press, 2004), p. 26.

6

Levites on Cyprus—Not Only in the Jerusalem Temple

James H. Charlesworth

In the previous chapter of this volume, Professor Konstantinos Th. Zarras discusses the Levite from Cyprus named Barnabas. The purpose of this chapter is to explore—as briefly as possible—what can be known about Levites on Cyprus. Is it historically accurate to imagine Levites on Cyprus? What can be known about Levites outside the land of Israel? Scholars have not adequately explored this area of research, although they know the report in Acts that Barnabas is a nickname for Joseph who was a Levite from Cyprus. Note Acts 4:

> **36** Ἰωσὴφ δὲ ὁ ἐπικληθεὶς Βαρναβᾶς ἀπὸ τῶν ἀποστόλων, ὅ ἐστιν μεθερμηνευόμενον υἱὸς παρακλήσεως, Λευίτης, Κύπριος τῷ γένει, **37** ὑπάρχοντος αὐτῷ ἀγροῦ πωλήσας ἤνεγκεν τὸ χρῆμα καὶ ἔθηκεν πρὸς τοὺς πόδας τῶν ἀποστόλων.
>
> **36** There was a Levite, a native of Cyprus, Joseph, to whom the apostles gave the name Barnabas (which means "son of encouragement"). **37** He sold a field that belonged to him, then brought the money, and laid it at the apostles' feet.
>
> (NRSV)

Pondering that Barnabas was a Levite from Cyprus, should we not contemplate the geographical distribution of the Levites? Have too many assumed Levites were those who served in the Jerusalem Temple? It will become obvious that Levites did not live only in Jerusalem.

Some Levites lived within the Essene Community at Qumran in Judea. It is widely assumed that all Levites resided in the land of Israel and probably near the Temple in Jerusalem. Yet, Acts indicates that some Levites lived on Cyprus. Is that even conceivable?

The Levites were assistants to the Aaronite priests in the Temple and subservient to them. The Priestly Code (viz., Genesis 17; Exod 12:1-20, 43-49; 28; 29:1-37; Leviticus 1–16) and Ezekiel report that the priesthood is bifurcated into two ranks. The sons of Aaron were the superior group (Exodus 28–29). The Levites were a lower class of priests (Num 3:2-13; 8:14-19). Ezekiel adds that the Levites are second-class priests due to apostasy (44:10-14) and they are not allowed to perform the duties of the priests in the Temple (44:13). Yet, these reports cannot be harmonized with other passages.

In the TANAKH (or Old Testament), the Levites are related traditionally to the Aaronites, since Aaron is a descendent of Levi (Exod 6:16-20) and thus all Aaronite priests are within the tribe of Levi (Num 18:2; 26:58-59). The authors of the Priestly Code do not call Levites priests. Thus, three sources in the Torah, the Priestly Code, the Deuteronomist, and Ezekiel 40-48, often concur but more often present contrasting views of the Levites and Aaronites. For example, Deuteronomy does not indicate any rank within the priesthood; that portrayal contrasts markedly with the Priestly Code and Ezekiel.[1]

David's High Priest Zadok was an Aaronite and a Levite; that is, Zadok was a descendant of Aaron and head of the Levites (1 Chr 27:17).[2] One tends, then, to assume that the Levites lived only in ancient Palestine notably in "Levitical cities" or, according to the well-known phrase, "Levitical Diaspora." This phrase was made famous by Martin North, Lawrence Stager, and particularly Jeremy M. Hutton who, in featuring the phrase, denoted "Levitical cities" within Palestine.[3]

Usually, "Diaspora" in the study of early Judaism and Christian origins denotes Jews living outside Palestine in the East and in the West. It is obvious that the study of Levites became myopic, focusing only on the so-called Promised Land, Israel.[4]

The authors and editors of the Pentateuch seem to indicate that all Cohens and Levites are from the Tribe of Levi. With attractive perception, Menahem Haran clarifies that "all the Pentateuchal sources agree as to the principle that the priesthood is confined to the tribe of Levi." Haran continues by exploring "what part of the tribe of Levi actually held priestly office" and could Levites outside "the priestly group" ascend to the functions reserved for priests.[5] Thus, not all descendants of Levi were priests and these blurred distinctions cause confusion in comprehending such passages as Exod 6:25, Lev 25:32, Num 35:2, and Josh 21:3-7. Perhaps one may contemplate that all priests were Levites but not all Levites were priests;[6] and that distinction is clear in Jesus' Parable of the Good Samaritan in which "a priest" and then "a Levite" passed by opposite the wounded man (Luke 10:25-37).

The explanations of Levites according to Numbers 3 to 4 confuse distinctions between the Tabernacle of Moses and the Temple of Solomon. I would agree that Levites assisted priests (Num 1:50; 3:6, 8; 16:9; 1 Chr 9:22, 26-27; 23:2-4, 28; Ezra 3:8-9) and cared for the courts (as the LXX reports about David's sons). The Levites also assisted in interpreting Torah (Neh 8:7; 9:2; 2 Chr 17:7-9; 35:3).

The Levites went through some form of training that prepared them for special services in the Temple. According to early traditions, they shaved the whole body, received the laying on of hands, were presented to God, and later offered sacrifices (Num 8:5-13). The selected and consecrated Levites, who were at least thirty years old (Num 4:1-3), were in charge of liturgy, chanting, and music in the Temple. Most Levites—especially in the renovated Herodian Temple—apparently lived in the Temple chambers and many were musicians (1 Chr 9:33). The Levites were also civil servants who controlled records and Temple gates and entrances.

According to the later Priestly documents in the Pentateuch, David divided the sons of Levi into three groups. The Gershonites had been in charge of the skins covering the Tabernacle. The Qohathites administered all things related to the furniture in the Temple, especially the ark and the table of showbread. The Merarites were custodians of the Temple pillars and other structures. It is unknown how their duties in the Tabernacle evolved from the time of Aaron to the celebrations in the Solomonic Temple and then in the Herodian Temple. On the one hand, no one, to our knowledge, wrote down the evolution of Levite duties; on the other hand, the author of Numbers 3 and 4 of course had no knowledge of phenomena that postdated him.

Prior to the Babylonian Exile in the sixth century BCE, the priests, descendants of Levi, were those who controlled all sacrifices (Leviticus 1), blessed the people (Deut 10:8; 21:5), and carried the ark (Deut 10:8; 31:9, 25). Within Second Temple Judaism, the priests were the aristocrats and powerful ruling class; they were represented by Annas who served officially as "High Priest" from about 6 to 15 CE but remained a powerful "High Priest" emeritus until his death sometime about 40 CE.

These reflections prove why most scholars assume the Levites were limited to and defined by the Temple. They had, however, a more complex history. Fortunately, my present task is more focused and limited. I am interested in Levites on Cyprus. Unless they resided in Cyprus and traveled to the Jerusalem Temple during a seasonal arrangement, Cyprian "Levites" cannot have been those special ministers in the Temple as implied in Num 8:16-18. Perhaps they had left Jerusalem and performed religious services in the synagogues in Salamis. We do not know how many synagogues existed

Figure 6.1 The Roman gymnasium in Salamis (JHC).

in Salamis or on Cyprus, but the plural noun "the synagogues of the Jews" (focusing on Salamis) is clear in Acts 13:5. Unfortunately, the Jewish riots of 115–117, as K. Zarras notes in his chapter, brought an end to these synagogues on Cyprus, but most likely Antoninus Pius (138–161) annulled Trajan's ban of Jews from Cyprus. We should imagine many Jewish communities on Cyprus, proving again that the border of ancient Palestine was no closed barrier.

What would Levites be doing on Cyprus? What was their purpose on that large island? How long had they been on Cyprus before the time of Barnabas? How often did Cypriot Levites make a pilgrimage to the Temple? In the Jerusalem cult, did any Levite from Cyprus have as much prestige as those living in Jerusalem? These and other questions arise with the present study.

Levites Today Outside Israel

Today, there are about 240,000 "Levites" living in Israel and 200,000 in the United States, so we would be wrong to imagine a Levite must be expected to live in Israel either today or in antiquity. In antiquity, many in Samaria claimed to be Levites and Cohens; and today the Samaritans proudly claim their High Priest descends from Aaron.

Levi was the third son of Jacob and Leah (Gen 29:34); the Tribe of Levi is the traditional source of the sons of Aaron, the Levites. Here is the traditional genealogy according to the Pentateuch and the *Testaments of the Twelve Patriarchs*: Levi's sons were Gershon, Kohath, and Merari. Kohath's sons were Amram, Izhr, Hebron, and Uzziel. Amram's children were Aaron, Moses, and Miriam.

During the sojourn in Egypt, Levites were with Aaron. During the time of early Judaism (or circa 300 BCE to 70 CE), Levites were not only in the Temple. The Qumran scrolls prove the presence of Levites within the Qumran community and most likely in other Essene communities throughout the land of Israel. Within the Qumran Scrolls we frequently read about "the Sons of Aaron," "the Sons of Zadok," and "the Sons of Levi." Recall the unique honor offered the Levites by those who revered them in CD MS A 4.2-4:

> "The priests" are the penitents of Israel who depart(ed) from the land of Judah, ("the Levites" are those) who accompany them, and "the Sons of Zadok" are the chosen ones of Israel, those called by name, who stand in the end of days.
> (Baumgarten and Schwartz in PTSDSSP 2, p. 19)

Among the Qumran Scrolls are versions of the following: *Visions of Amram*[a-g] (4Q543-49), *Pseudepigraphon of Benjamin ar* (4Q538), *Vision and Testament of Jacob ar* (4Q537), *Testament of Joseph ar* (4Q539), *Testament of Judah* (3Q7, 4Q484), *Testament of Levi* (1Q21, 4Q213, 4Q213[a-b], 4Q214, 4Q214[a-b]), *Apocryphon of Levi* (4Q541), *Pseudepigraphon of Levi* (4Q540), *Testament of Naphtali* (4Q215), *Testament of Qahat ar* (4Q542).[7] No specialist should assume these early Jewish documents were all composed at Qumran, though many were edited finally in the Qumran Scriptorium.

These compositions prove the importance of the sons of Jacob and especially the Levites in pre-70 CE Palestinian Judaism. The *Testament of Levi* is preserved in more than one recension and other "quasi-testaments" are attributed to Levi. Thus, we should not place a barrier on the influence and existence of the Levites. I have every reason to conclude they were living on Cyprus and in Egypt; as is so clear, the Jewish sects were not exclusively localized in ancient Palestine.

Suffice it now to perceive that the brief words introducing Barnabas prove that Levites could be found on Cyprus. That helps us grasp, as I have stated in many publications, that the Jewish sects were not confined to Palestine, the land east of the Mediterranean. Many Jewish groups are known outside Palestine. Paul was born a "Pharisee" in Tarsus so this dominant sociological group was not limited by Palestine's coastline. Samaritans are now known to have lived on Delos. Philo's reference to the "Therapeutae" suggests to many experts that types of Essenes were present in Egypt. Perhaps most of all, the Jewish group that proves that borders are not barriers is the Palestinian Jewish Movement. It began in Galilee but spread throughout the known world, including Parthia, India, Ethiopia, Egypt, Libya, Turkey, Greece, Italy, and elsewhere. The Mediterranean Sea was clearly a border, but it was no barrier.

From Cyprus: Ancient Greek Palindrome

This brief summary of Levites and other Jews on Cyprus benefits from a discovery in 2011 in Nea Paphos, Cyprus, by archaeologists from the Institute of Archaeology at Jagiellonian University in Krakow, Poland.[8] A 1500-year-old dark gray siltstone amulet, a palindrome, has been unearthed in the agora. A palindrome amulet reads the same backwards as forwards—as in MOM or James Joyce's masterful onomatopoeic palindrome in *Ulysses*: "tattarrattat." The inscription is in Greek and contains fifty-nine letters.[9] Here is the transcription of the Greek palindrome:[10]

IAEW
BAΦPENEM
OYNOΘIΛAPI
KNIΦIAEYE
AIΦINKIPAΛ
IΘONYOME
NEPΦABW
EAI

The script of the final line is not clear due to the reduced margins. Notice how the letters at the top mirror (reverse) those beginning at the bottom.

The amulet may be translated as follows: "Iahweh is the bearer of the secret name, the lion of Re secure in his shrine."[11] The palindrome most likely belonged to Jews, since "Iahweh" (IAEW) is the well-known Tetragrammaton, YHWH. As Joachim Śliwa observed: "The first four letters pose no difficulty in interpretation as they form the Iaeo/Iahweh word, a more precise rendition of the Hebrew *tetragrammaton* than the more frequent Iao (Ganschinietz 1914: 700–1; Brashear 1995: 3587)."[12] This ineffable name YHWH is indeed for Jews "the secret name." In the Qumran Scrolls, YHWH sometimes appears in an ancient script (*palaeo hebrew*) and four dots (....) to warn readers not to pronounce the Creator's sacred name.

The Cypriot Jews who revered the amulet were syncretistic believers in YHWH. They were probably not monotheists but henotheists, believing in the existence of other gods, such as "the lion of Re secure in his shrine," who may be imagined to be YHWH or another god.

On the opposite side of the amulet are symbolic representations of Osiris, the well-known Egyptian god of reincarnation and the afterlife, and Harpocrates, the Greek god of silence. In addition, a serpent is depicted facing Harpocrates. Someone also depicted a cynocephalus, a mythical creature with a dog's head. It is holding a paw to the lips, perhaps mimicking the god of silence.[13] As Joachim Śliwa stated: "We can find no justification for the cynocephalus's gesture of raising its right paw to its lips in a manner similar to Harpocrates." No one doubts that this amulet represents the beliefs of the common person in antiquity. The author is not gifted and seems to misunderstand mythology. In terms of ancient symbolism, the cynocephalus should raise its paws in adoration of Harpocrates and the latter god is typically shown sitting on a lotus flower, not a stool.

Figure 6.2 Amulet from Nea Paphos, Cyprus (photo: Marcin Iwan).

Joachim Śliwa discerns, rightly, Egyptian influence: "It must be stated that the depiction is fairly unskilled and schematic. It is iconographically based on Egyptian sources, but these sources were not fully understood by the creator of the amulet" (p. 295). What I find missing in all studies of the amulet is its Jewish character. IAEW is the way Greek-speaking Jews transcribed the Hebrew noun YHWH; they also may have mistakenly pronounced the ineffable Tetragrammaton. The amulet is similar to the *Prayer of Jacob*:

> You who sit [upon] the s[er]pen[t] gods,
> the [God who s]i[t]s [upon the s]un, *Iaō*.
> (Pr. Jac. 10-11; JHC in *OTP* 2.721)

As in the Cyprus Amulet, a serpent is aligned with God's name.

The Jewish origin and pre-Mishnaic character of the *Prayer of Jacob* is obvious; note other lines of the prayer: "Father of (the) Patria[rch]s ... He who showed favor to [Abr]aham by [giving the] kingd[om to him]." All doubts should be removed that IAEW or *Iaō* is a Jewish-Greek way of writing the Tetragrammaton, YHWH. The equation was clarified by Pauly-Wissowa and Urbach.[14] In *Psalm* VIII, Jerome explains that "*Iaō*" can be pronounced "Yaho." The equation is widely accepted; for example, in *Verus Israel* (p. 400) Simon suggested that *Iaō* equals YHWH. Thus, I would disagree with Joachim Śliwa in ascertaining that the Paphos Amulet reflects "Hellenistic magic" and consider a Jewish context, though no doubt many Jews on Cyprus were influenced by magic and magicians like Elymas of Paphos (Acts 13:8). Śliwa also may be leaning toward such an interpretation when he judged, wisely, that "the amulet found at Paphos seems to belong to a group of gems coming from a Syrian-Palestine worship of the late 5th century AD (Spier 2007: 109–14)."[15]

Many early Jews and Christians continued to place their faith in ancient gods and superstitions in a bid to protect themselves from misfortunes and demons. As the director of the excavations at Paphos, Ewdoksia Papuci-Wladyka, perceived, the amulet proves again that Christians lived among devotees of older religions (but I would not call them pagans).[16] I would add that the owner was a "Jewish-Christian" or a Jew. To assume these beliefs were heretical would be anachronistic for some nonbiblical and non-Rabbinic Jews and some Christians before Nicea in 325 CE. As Walter Bauer stressed, heresy often prevailed before and alongside what would later be judged "orthodox."[17]

Conclusion

By pondering the existence of Levites on Cyprus we begin to explore the borders of "the Holy Land" called ancient Palestine and learn that Jewish groups and sects defined more than Palestinian Judaism. Hellenistic Judaism, as I have tried to show for decades, is not a geographical term; it is a chronological concept. The term refers to the types of Judaism that can be observed in the Hellenistic period. We may now more accurately perceive that while the Temple almost always defined borders and barriers (even inside the consecutive borders within), and most Levites were circumscribed by the Temple, other Levites were present in locales far distant from the Temple, though still powerfully defined by its theologically magnetic cult. Barnabas, a Levite from Cyprus, traveled across the borders of ancient Palestine and ascended up to the Jerusalem Temple to participate with his fellow Jews in the only sanctioned place for worship.

Notes

1   See the discussion in Risto Nurmela, *The Levites: Their Emergence as a Second-Class Priesthood*, South Florida Studies in the History of Judaism 193 (Atlanta: Scholars Press, 1998).
2   Frank M. Cross perceived a distinction between "Mushite Levites" and "Aaronid Priests." See his *Canaanite Myth and Hebrew Epic* (Cambridge, MA: Harvard University Press, 1973), pp. 195–215. In contrast, Baruch Halpern observes impressive variates among the "Levites." See his "Levitic Participation in the Reform Cult of Jeroboam I," *JBL* 95 (1976): 31–42.
3   J. M. Hutton, "The Levitical Diaspora (II): Modern Perspectives on the Levitical Cities Lists (A Review of Opinions)," in *Levites and Priests in Biblical History and Tradition*, edited by M. Leuchter and J. M. Hutton, SBL Ancient Israel and Its Literature 9 (Atlanta: SBL, 2011), pp. 45–81.
4   I note three major exceptions: Moshe Weinfeld, "The Extent of the Promised Land: The Status of Transjordan," in *Das Land Israel in biblischer Zeit*, edited by G. Strecker (Göttingen: Vandenhoeck & Ruprecht, 1983), pp. 59–75; David Jobling, "'The Jordan a Boundary': Transjordan in Israel's Ideological Geography," in *The Sense of Biblical Narrative*, JSOTSup 39 (Sheffield: JSOT Press, 1986), vol. 2, pp. 88–133, 142–7; Hutton, "Southern, Northern, and Transjordanian Perspectives," in *Religious Diversity in Ancient Israel and Judah*, edited by F. Stavrakopoulou and J. Barton (London/New York: T&T Clark, 2010), pp. 160–1.
5   M. Haran, *Temples and Temple Service in Ancient Israel* (Winona Lake: Eisenbrauns, 1985), p. 84.
6   According to 2 Sam 8:18, David's sons were "priests" (כהנים). Conceivably, the priesthood may not have been limited to Levites during David's reign and power. The Septuagint has a different version: καὶ οἱ υἱοὶ Δαυιδ αὐλάρχαι ἦσαν, "and the sons of David were court princes."
7   The introductions, texts, and translations of each of these titles (and the reason for more representative titles) will appear in a forthcoming volume in the Princeton Dead Sea Scrolls Project.
8   Sarah Griffiths, "Mysterious 1,500-year-old Charm Unearthed: Palindrome Amulet that Reads the Same Backwards AND Forwards Sheds Light on Ancient Religious Beliefs," *Mailonline* (January 5, 2015). David Freeman, "Strange 'Magical' Amulet Has Scientists Buzzing," *Huffington Post* (January 7, 2015), contains images of the front and back of the amulet). The publications on the Cyprus Amulet I could find were preliminary announcements often by journalists. The most reliable publication is as follows: Joachim Śliwa, "Magical Amulet from Paphos with the ιαεω- Palindrome," *Studies in Ancient Art and Civilization* 17 (2013): 293–301. He reports that the amulet was discovered on July 23, 2011, in Trench II, Area 2 (Room 5), in the upper, late Roman layer. He dates the amulet to the "5th–6th century AD."

9   The amulet is 1.4 inches by 1.6 inches or 34.9 millimeters by 41.2 millimeters. See Owen Jarus, "Ancient Amulet Discovered with Curious Palindrome Inscription," *Live Science* (January 1, 2015), https://www.livescience.com/49239-ancient-amulet-palindrome-inscription.html. Also see April Holloway (a pen name for Joanna Gillan), "Ancient Greek Amulet with Strange Palindrome Inscription Discovered in Cyprus," *Ancient Origins* (January 2, 2015).
10 I am indebted to Joachim Śliwa who accurately transcribed the script; see his article in *Studies in Ancient Art and Civilization* 17 (2013): 297.
11 Professor Joachim Śliwa noted that the inscriber twice inscribed "p" instead of "v." The alleged mistake may also be due to different pronunciations of these consonants. I often discovered philology affects spelling, especially in the Upper Nile manuscripts.
12 Joachim Śliwa in *Studies in Ancient Art and Civilization* 17 (2013): 298.
13 For an image of the etchings, see Owen Jarus in *Live Science* (January 1, 2015).
14 See my notes in *OTP* 2.721, note l.
15 Joachim Śliwa in *Studies in Ancient Art and Civilization* 17 (2013): 298.
16 Professor Papuci-Wladyka may be reached at Paphos Agora Project Instytut Archeologii UJ ul. Gołębia 11 31-007 Kraków. On the web, see Paphos Agora Project.
17 Walter Bauer, *Orthodoxy and Heresy in Earliest Christianity*, edited by R. A. Kraft and G. Krodel (Philadelphia: Fortress, 1971).

7

Meeting the Romans: The Encounter of Paul and Sergius Paulus according to Acts

Kathy Ehrensperger

According to the narrative of Acts, Saul is being introduced to the world of Rome in Cyprus by meeting the proconsul Sergius Paulus in Paphos. It is also here that for the first time his other name, Παῦλος (Paul), is mentioned and that the focus on his role in the Christ-movement for those from the nations moves to center stage. The Roman aspect of Saul/ Paul's activities is developed from here on by the author of Acts, with numerous further encounters with Roman officials (e.g., Acts 21:37-39; 24:10-27; 25:6-12), to eventually culminate in Saul/Paul's arrival and proclamation of the gospel with courage unhindered in Rome itself (Acts 28:31). I will argue in this chapter that in the narrative strategy of Acts, the events in Cyprus are presented as a crucial stepping stone on Paul's way into the world of Rome and the spreading of the gospel to the center of political power.

Acts 13 has been noted as a key chapter in the narrative structure of the book of Acts in that the focus shifts from Peter and Jerusalem as the center of activities in chapters 1–12 to Paul and the nations from then on.[1] However, the small narrative of 13:4-12 has been underestimated in my view,[2] in that it actually encompasses (in narrative form) the program of the Pauline mission according to Acts with the key characters exemplifying some key aspects of that mission. And although perceived from a different perspective and at a later period, analogies to the image that Paul himself presents in his undisputed letters can be found.

A Narratological Reading

The focus of my contribution will be on the key characters of this short narrative, the so-called "Jew" Bar Jesus, the Roman Sergius Paulus, and Saul/Paul, and on the interaction between these three. My approach is thus informed by narratology rather than the quest for "historical proof" in this narrative, although I assume that historical aspects are to some extent relevant to understand the narrative plot of that scene.

I take Acts as a secondary source when compared with Paul's undisputed letters, a theological narrative of the second generation, which integrates some historical memories but is mainly concerned with the theological dimension that is conveyed in narrative form.

It is interesting that the first named non-Jew Saul/Paul meets according to the narrative of Acts is a Roman official of elite status, most likely of senatorial rank. This actually presents an analogy to the narrative of Peter and Cornelius (Acts 10–11), which presents the first non-Jewish Christ-follower as a member of the Roman elite as well, although Paul's Roman is of significantly higher status than Peter's. The author of Acts most likely intended to create an analogy between Peter and Paul here.[3]

After this meeting Paul's Roman name is used without exception in the narrative, and not only that, with the use of this Roman name also his role changes. From now on he is the one almost exclusively named first in the subsequent chapters when he and Barnabas travel together (which they always do until the end of chapter 15, where they part company).[4] So it is likely that something significant is indicated in this encounter between these three characters in Paphos which deserves closer attention. That the encounter happens in Paphos makes good sense as Paphos was the capital of the Roman province of Cyprus in the first century CE. It was of strategic importance with its harbor to the west, open to the sea routes to Rome and Alexandria. It is thought that Paphos represented the more western-oriented part of the island, with a high percentage of imports from Italy and Rome itself, while the eastern part of the island with Salamis as its center was eastern-oriented. Ceramic and numismatic remains provide indications to such an orientation.[5] Thus a series of coins minted under Augustus had two different reverse images: the temple of Aphrodite at Palaipaphos and the temple of Zeus at Salamis. Hence, in historical perspective, Paphos is the obvious place of an encounter with the highest Roman magistrate.

The fact that Paul's first specific encounter with a representative of the non-Jewish nations is with a Roman official in this narrative is interesting for a number of reasons:

First, there can be no doubt when we consider Paul's undisputed letters that the Roman context was significant for him. The letters he writes are addressed to Christ-followers from the nations who live in Roman colonies (like Corinth and Philippi), are closely linked with Roman domination (like Galatia and Thessalonica), or are in Rome itself. That the Roman context also eventually plays a prominent role in the depiction of Paul's activities in the narrative of Acts should thus not come as a surprise. Through his letters we learn that Paul travels in the Roman world and sets up Christ-following groups in Roman-dominated places. The narrative of Acts depicts an image of him[6] precisely in this sociocultural and political context. This Roman context has often been underestimated compared with all the literature that compares his writing to Greek traditions. Note that I avoid using the compound Greco-Roman. There existed no blended Greco-Roman culture or identity[7] or sense of "Greekness and Romanness as a seamless pair"[8] in antiquity. Greeks and Romans were very much aware of the difference in their traditions and played off these differences in sometimes polemical exchanges, as, for instance, in the *Tusculan Disputations* in which Cicero maintains:

> I have thought it an employment worthy of me to illustrate them in the Latin tongue: not because philosophy could not be understood in the Greek language, or by the teaching of Greek masters; but it has always been my opinion, that our countrymen have, in some instances, made wiser discoveries than the Greeks, with

reference to those subjects which they have considered worthy of devoting their attention to, and in others have improved upon their discoveries, so that in one way or other we surpass them on every point: for, with regard to the manners and habits of private life, and family and domestic affairs, we certainly manage them with more elegance, and better than they did; and as to our republic, that our ancestors have, beyond all dispute, formed on better customs and laws. What shall I say of our military affairs; in which our ancestors have been most eminent in valour, and still more so in discipline? As to those things which are attained not by study, but nature, neither Greece, nor any nation, is comparable to us: for what people has displayed such gravity, such steadiness, such greatness of soul, probity, faith—such distinguished virtue of every kind, as to be equal to our ancestors.

(1.1.2)[9]

Hence the narrative strategy of Acts coheres in that sense with the prevalence of the Roman context in which Paul operates according to his own writings.[10]

The second interesting point in the narrative is the fact that this Roman magistrate shows an interest in Jewish tradition. This coheres with some of our historical knowledge of specific interest in Jewish tradition by so-called Godfearers and Sympathizers,[11] and the long-standing, if ambiguous, relationships between Rome and Judea certainly since the time of the Maccabees.[12]

The third interesting point in this encounter is the fact that there is a debate among Jews (i.e., Paul, Barnabas, and Bar Jesus/Elymas) about what to tell this pagan sympathizer about Jewish tradition.

The Triangular Encounter

After Barnabas and Saul have been commissioned by the community in Antioch for the work to which they had been called by God (Acts 13:1-3, 47), they set out on their task and perform some work in the east of the island of Cyprus (13:5). But then they travel west to Paphos, and the first specifically named person they meet is a Jewish *magos*, Bar Jesus/Elymas (13:6). The second named person is the proconsul Sergius Paulus, in whose company the Jewish *magos* is found (13:7). The latter is with the proconsul because the Roman has an interest in, or because the *magos* had attracted the Roman's interest in, Jewish tradition. There is no description of the venue or setting in which these protagonists meet. Maybe it was that of a banquet which included some philosophical discussion. This "intelligent" Roman magistrate had an interest in other traditions, as seems apparent from his characterization. Whatever the precise setting, though, it is evident that the encounter is envisaged to occur in the proconsul's palace, that is, on pagan ground or in a pagan house.

Bar Jesus is referred to with two labels: the label μάγος is not in itself negative[13] but rather indicates some kind of specialty in relation to transcendent powers generally. The other label ψευδοπροφήτης presents the perspective of the Christ-followers— and since Bar Jesus apparently is not one of them, whatever he says about God and Jewish tradition cannot be right in their eyes. He might well have been a prophet of

Jewish tradition, but in the perspective of Paul and Barnabas, or the Christ-following audience of this narrative, this is categorized as a false claim. Obviously, this man had transmitted Jewish tradition to the Roman magistrate—and Sergius Paulus wished to learn more about it. So, he seems to have taken the chance upon the arrival of other Jews to learn from them about their tradition as well. The μάγος was not pleased with these newcomer compatriots—and tried to turn the attention of the Roman away from the way in which Barnabas and Saul talked about loyalty (πίστις) to the one God.[14] And the debate between the Jews involved here, between Bar Jesus and Paul in particular, is about a deeply intra-Jewish issue concerning an outsider.

Could it be that it concerned the implications of loyalty to the one God as far as non-Jews/Roman officials were concerned since this is the context in which the disagreement emerges? It could be seen as an intra-Jewish competition on how to talk about Jewish tradition to an interested Roman magistrate. It could even be imagined that from the perspective of a Jewish person who was not convinced that Jesus was the Messiah, and hence was not convinced that the time had come when non-Jews would also exclusively worship the one God of Israel, that to convey such a message to a Roman magistrate would be dangerous and even insane. To claim over against a Roman magistrate that someone who had been executed as a rebel against Rome had been raised from the dead and was the Messiah would have sounded like insurrection and could thus have easily been understood to be a risky affair. In Roman perspective, messianic claims were classified as claims to rulership not sanctioned or instigated by Rome and thus considered inherently rebellious as it undermined the claims to hegemonic domination of imperial Rome.[15] As Loveday Alexander notes, "To acknowledge Christ as 'Lord of all' (Acts 10:36) is to enter an alternative sphere of authority that radically deconstructs the emperor's claim to absolute allegiance."[16] Hence the attempt of the *magos* Bar Jesus/Elymas to prevent the dissemination of this gospel could be due to plausible and legitimate rather than distorted motives.

However, even if the *magos*' motives may have been reasonable, this now provides the narrator with the opportunity to present Paul in his new role, named with his Latin name, taking on the lead role in the interaction with the *magos*. Whereas before this scene, Barnabas is consistently named before Saul, from now on Paul is consistently named first, indicating that the hierarchy between the two had changed from this event onwards. There are further relevant aspects to the usage of his Latin name shown when Paul both acts in this leading role and interacts with the world "out there" in the Roman-dominated diaspora, particularly when he interacts with non-Jews.[17] The change is not depicted as a name change in Acts, hence there is no replacement of Paul's Jewish name indicated here but merely that from this moment on, when he directly encounters and interacts with the Roman world, he is referred to with a Roman name.[18] Since Paul is the only key figure in the movement at the time known (also) under a Latin name this can hardly be just a random aspect. I consider this as indicative of the key context within which Paul operated and to which he most likely specifically related, as noted above. Although I am highly skeptical about the assumption of Acts that Paul held Roman citizenship, he, and with him the message he was called to proclaim (Gal 1:15-17; Acts 13:47), is certainly depicted as relevant in relation to the Roman world and the claims of the imperial power.

A Verbal and Nonverbal Intra-Jewish Debate

From here on in the narrative of Acts, Paul is depicted as in charge of the activities concerning the spreading of the message. This is paradigmatically exemplified by his firm look at the *magos*—providing a powerful image of the power of the eyes! The body language is not an addendum to the narrative but key in depicting Paul as in charge now, especially when we remember that in the narrative of the Damascus road experience he loses the power of his eyes, so that he cannot see anything anymore (Acts 9:8-9)! Now, in 13:9, he is in full control of his eyes and sees clearly how the message needs to be conveyed.[19] According to convictions in many cultures around the Mediterranean in antiquity, the steady gaze expresses a firm decision, reflecting a mind which is clear in how things are perceived, and no alternatives are considered anymore: thus, for example, the firm gaze of Aeneas expresses his resistance to Dido's pleas to stay in Carthage (Virg. *Aen*. 4.331-332).[20]

The language in which Paul then addresses his compatriot seems very denigrating—if read according to traditional translations. But in a way it is not all that much different from language used by Paul in Galatians (cf. Gal 1:7; 3:1). He calls Bar Jesus/Elymas someone who deceives and is a fraud (13:10),[21] meaning someone who pretends to be something or who gives someone something which is not authentic. He addresses him as υἱὲ διαβόλου, a potentially highly problematic term when translated as "son of the devil." A translation as "son of a disturber" or "twister" would be perfectly legitimate and indicate a different dimension from what is associated with the term "devil" in Christian tradition. Even so, the question needs to be asked—in whose perspective? Did this *magos* consciously deceive the Roman magistrate, twisting and distorting Jewish tradition or could he actually have been convinced of what he had told him? As mentioned before, it might well be that the denigrating qualification serves the narrative purpose of Acts, which is of course the conviction that the messianic time had begun to dawn with the coming of Christ and hence the relation to people from the nations who embraced this conviction was changing. Bar Jesus then could be seen as representing those Jews who saw things differently. Hence Paul qualifies him as someone who tries to twist or divert "the ways of the Lord" by his non-messianic understanding of Jewish tradition. That he thereby is an ἐχθρὸς δικαιοσύνης may resonate with Rom 11:28 where Paul states that "they are enemies for your sake," meaning that for the time being the fact that not all Jews see things the way Paul and his colleagues saw them has (in mysterious ways) something to do with God's plan. But clearly, they are enemies in a specific way, certainly not enemies of God as the NRSV inserts falsely into its translation of the passage! And as far as election is concerned "they are beloved for the sake of the fathers, for the gifts and the calling of God are irrevocable" (Rom 11:28b-29). For a limited time, as Paul argues here, they are prevented from seeing that the path to righteousness (to the right relation with the one God) has now, in Christ, opened for non-Jews as non-Jews. But this is only so if one is convinced that, now that the age to come was beginning to dawn, non-Jews could be loyal to the one God without becoming Jews. This perception of events and the time in messianic perspective presents a troublesome understanding of Jewish tradition rather than the traditional non-messianic understanding. It certainly led to diverse responses on the part of Jews as well as non-Jews in the first century CE.

Paul's sharp words in Acts 13:10 are supported by action achieved through his words, indicating that his words in this inner-Jewish debate are more powerful than those of the *magos*. Through Paul's words Bar Jesus/Elymas is rendered temporarily blind, that is, he is prevented from seeing what Paul and other Christ-followers can see. The significance of the message is hidden to him. Not being able to see is a familiar *topos* in the Lucan narratives (cf. Luke 10:23; 24:31).[22] Bar Jesus/Elymas is told that he will not be able to see the sun for a while—he will not be illuminated for a while (13:11). It seems that the story is telling the audience that Bar Jesus/Elymas cannot understand the meaning of the Christ event in relation to non-Jews. There is a haze of mist and darkness surrounding him. This "not-seeing," however, is clearly marked as temporally limited. The "not-seeing," that is, "not understanding," will not last forever; it is caused by the hand of the Lord for a specific time. So there is no condemnation or judgment of Bar Jesus/Elymas except that he cannot see for some time. In this respect there is even a similarity to the Paul of Acts, who could not see for a certain, limited time (Acts 9:8-9) and had then needed guidance to come to an understanding of what had happened (9:17-19). Elymas too needs a hand to guide him when he cannot see things clearly anymore, when he cannot see things as he had seen them before. His gait has become unsafe (13:11b). He does not know anymore where his steps carry him. This state of affairs, in terms of the body language already mentioned, indicates some instability of the mind. That is, he is shaken in his convictions and is seeking guidance now that his perception, his way of seeing things, has been challenged fundamentally. The narrative, rather than being judgmental at this point, depicts Elymas as someone who has to reorient himself, not sure where the next steps will take him. But in seeking a guiding hand, some openness to new paths might be indicated. There is certainly some openness for Elymas indicated in the flow of the narrative.

The debate between the Jews in this passage is indicative of the author's perception of the impact of the Christ message. Its proclamation produces a split within Judaism— some are being convinced, while others are not. It is a *topos* which can be found at the beginning of the Gospel of Luke[23] when Simeon tells Mary "This child is destined for the falling and the rising of many in Israel, and to be a sign that will be opposed" (Luke 2:34; cf. also 13:43-45; 17:4) and it is carried through up to the open ending of Acts (καὶ οἱ μὲν ἐπείθοντο τοῖς λεγομένοις, οἱ δὲ ἠπίστουν [28:24]). In Acts 13:1-12 this *topos* is presented for the first time in relation to the activities of Paul. From now on in the narrative, Paul's activities will cause a split in reaction among Jews alongside the winning of some from the nations/ἔθνη. Hence the debate between Paul and Barnabas and the Jewish *magos* Bar Jesus/Elymas is not a random event but a core moment in the narrative of the spreading of the message of the gospel, located on the island of Cyprus.

A Roman Magistrate—Convinced

Moreover, I think it is also no mere coincidence that the debate is presented as happening in front of a Roman magistrate.

The magistrate's reaction to both the words and what happens after Paul had spoken indicates the impact of Paul's interaction with Bar Jesus/Elymas. The question is what precisely caused the Roman, who is characterized as intelligent at the beginning, to actually trust in Paul's and Barnabas's way of transmitting more about Jewish tradition (or as it was formulated at the beginning of the narrative, 'ἐπεζήτησεν ἀκοῦσαι τὸν λόγον τοῦ θεοῦ [13:7]). What was it that convinced him of the version he had heard from Paul? In terms of the words said, there is actually nothing spelled out here about the message or concerning the teaching about which Sergius Paulus was astonished. The words said in the narrative are challenges or rebukes of what Bar Jesus/Elymas said or did, and this is not expressed in explicit words. Of course, it is appropriate to assume that the debate was about the question of time: that is, is it already messianic time, at least a shimmer of a beginning of it, or not?

But the reader needs to assume this from the wider flow of the narrative. The commissioning of Barnabas and Saul precedes this passage—and in more specific words, the reader then only learns in 13:47 what the actual divine commissioning was: οὕτως γὰρ ἐντέταλται ἡμῖν ὁ κύριος· τέθεικά σε εἰς φῶς ἐθνῶν τοῦ εἶναί σε εἰς σωτηρίαν ἕως ἐσχάτου τῆς γῆς ("For so the Lord has commanded us, saying, 'I have set you to be a light for the gentiles, so that you may bring salvation to the ends of the earth'" [NRSV]). Following the events in Paphos, Paul, now in Perge in Pamphylia for the first time in the narrative of Acts, addresses people in a speech (before that the main speaker was Peter—or earlier Stephen). One might infer from this that this is the teaching to which Sergius Paulus reacted, since the narrative explicitly states that Sergius Paulus was "astonished" about the διδαχή, although trust (πίστις) emerged through him "seeing what had happened" (ἰδὼν ὁ ἀνθύπατος τὸ γεγονὸς). Thus, it is not the mere fact that Bar Jesus/Elymas could not see anymore but the entire event (τὸ γεγονὸς) and decisively the διδαχή which is presented as having the transformative impact. Thus, the narrative is twofold: it encompasses the dispute among Jews concerning the right way to talk to non-Jews about the λόγος τοῦ θεοῦ, and there is the location of the scene—"in front of" or possibly "at the palace of" a Roman magistrate.

That it is not just any non-Jew who is convinced here coheres in the narrative flow with Peter also addressing a Roman non-Jew, in his case a soldier, who then gets convinced by the message and accepts it with his entire household. As with the narrative of Cornelius, also here, Sergius Paulus already knows something about Jewish tradition and the λόγος τοῦ θεοῦ when he wishes to learn more about this tradition. Hence the message of the messiah and its implications are heard by a knowledgeable non-Jew, one who has some understanding of Jewish tradition, and therefore can relate to what Barnabas and Paul teach. Knowledge, specifically pre-knowledge, is necessary for a non-Jew to be able to make sense of this messianic message. It does not convince the magistrate out of the blue. The διδαχή is convincing within the context of knowledge about Jewish tradition he already had before.

The magistrate, as a member of the elite, is depicted as recognizing the value of the teaching as something worthy of his level of education. As noted, it is the teaching (διδαχή) that astonishes him, not the sign that Paul's words trigger as such. Otherwise one would assume that it would be mentioned that he was astonished at the power of Paul to render Bar Jesus/Elymas blind or something to that effect. It is the teaching that makes the most significant impression on this intelligent Roman magistrate and, together with the "seeing," causes him to place his trust in *this* Jewish tradition about the arrival of a savior (σωτήρ) named Jesus for the well-being of Israel, a descendant of the royal line of David (implying a royal claim as understood explicitly in Acts 17:7). Unlike other magistrates, who are troubled by this message (Acts 17:8), Sergius Paulus trusts this teaching and declares his loyalty to the one God of Israel. It is unclear whether he fully joins the movement and gets baptized. If there is some realism in this narrative, this is consciously left open. As the proconsul of the province, Sergius Paulus would have had priestly duties. It is difficult to imagine that during his period in office (one year) he would have been able to forsake immediately this important task. Thus, the fact that no baptism is reported here demonstrates the knowledge and understanding of the author of Roman practice.

Accommodation to Imperial Rule?

It has been argued that with scenes like these, the author of Acts tried to demonstrate that the message of the Christ-event was compatible with, and in no ways threatening to, Roman rule and ideology, and further, that it was an attempt at demonstrating that this was a harmless movement which accommodated to, and was compatible with, Roman rule. I consider this a rather unlikely notion given that the message clearly indicated that it related to one crucified, sentenced to death by a Roman magistrate. Admittedly, to leaders in Jerusalem and residents of the city is attributed participation in what led to this crucifixion (13:27), but there is nowhere in Luke-Acts a generalizing accusation of the involvement of Jews in the events that lead to the death of Jesus. Historically, it would have been difficult for leaders in Jerusalem, who were leaders only due to Roman approval and hence were entirely dependent on Roman goodwill to exercise their leadership role, not to intervene when messianic claims were made by, or about, someone by a group of fellow Jews. This would be especially true in Jerusalem, and more especially at the time of Pesach, the city being filled with pilgrims. In Roman perspective, any messianic claim would have been considered as explicitly rebellious. In that sense, the crucifixion was not a misunderstanding on the part of the imperial power, but the logical action that would be taken by it when such a claim was raised. The challenge to the hegemonic imperial claims of Rome was part of the message of Christ, and with the cross being an inherent part of this message, including the vindication of this one crucified by God in the resurrection, the notion of trying to accommodate this message to imperial claims seems inconceivable. However, it is evident from Paul's letters that he operated in the context of Roman colonies and regions with a high Roman presence, thus he must have been familiar with and related to the Roman sociocultural and political world on an everyday basis.

The book of Acts presents Paul as familiar with the Roman world to the extent that encounters with Roman officials seem a thing Paul is comfortable with. He is depicted as being able to have educated conversations with these elite men to the point that he even convinces some of them, as in the scene here with the magistrate Sergius Paulus in Paphos. From a Jewish perspective, there is nothing in this teaching which would deserve death or imprisonment as is stated by Agrippa after the long speeches of Paul before Agrippa and Festus in Acts 25 and 26. It might trigger disputes, but from a Jewish perspective this is an issue of potential disagreement about interpretation and concerned the question of whether one lived already in a time when the messianic age was beginning to dawn or not. The issue is different in Roman perspective as noted. To be a follower of someone who was executed as a rebel against Rome was problematic to say the least and potentially a deadly risk. Thus, I cannot see in what way the author of Acts tried to accommodate the message of the gospel to Roman perceptions with his narrative.

That right at the beginning of Paul's leadership role in the movement, when it comes to teaching the nations, a Roman magistrate is getting convinced of the power of this teaching is remarkable. But rather than being an indication of the message being accommodated to Rome by trying to demonstrate that it was harmless, I think the narrative tries to tell the story the other way round. That Sergius Paulus is astonished by the teaching and trusts in it expresses that the teaching is more powerful than the ideology of imperial Rome. This narrative of a savior king who is fundamentally different from the one proclaimed imperator through the senate by the *populus Romanus*, and who thereby is declared the son of a god, is presented here as capable of convincing a representative of precisely this imperator, someone who had up to this point embodied imperial rule and its ideological claims. The Caesars were attributed titles like "savior," "peacemaker," "lord," and "son of god." The proconsul's transformation into a Christ-follower demonstrates the power of the gospel over such imperial claims of Rome. It is in that sense a counternarrative to the imperial narrative. It is not accommodating to Roman rule but undermining it. If a Roman magistrate converts, and subsequently the narrative claims that other Roman magistrates are not sure what to do with Paul or are told that there is nothing in this message that deserves death or imprisonment, this is either mocking or subverting the Roman perception of the Christ-event. With the proclamation of the Christ as savior king, son of God, resurrected, strong allusions to the claims of the emperors were created. By applying these to this Jewish man, who had been executed on a Roman cross, the Christ-followers implicitly challenged the claim to hegemonic power by the Roman Empire and to their self-perception as having been granted such rulership of the world by the gods. Thus, the embracing of this counter-teaching by the magistrate Sergius Paulus in my view marks the key focus of the author's intention in the depiction of Paul's interaction with the Roman elite: the message of the gospel, this teaching which convinced Sergius Paulus, is more powerful than the ideology of Rome. The ultimate power lies not with Rome and its Imperator (or his representatives) but with the God of Israel, now revealed also to the nations through Christ. This message is proclaimed throughout the empire, beginning from Jerusalem throughout the οἴκουμένη. Cyprus marks a decisive stepping stone in the narrative of Acts about the spreading journey of this message until it arrives in Rome and is freely proclaimed at the heart of the Roman world at the end of narrative: "And he proclaimed the kingdom of God and taught about the Lord Jesus Christ entirely free to speak without hindrance"[24] (Acts 28:31).

Notes

1. Cf. the discussion of the structure of Acts in Richard I. Pervo, *Acts: A Commentary*, Hermeneia (Minneapolis: Fortress, 2009), pp. 20–1.
2. Pervo notes that "these verses present an odd narrative." *Acts*, p. 323.
3. Cf. Pervo, *Acts*, 324.
4. This is so except when they are in Jerusalem (Acts 15:12) and in the letter sent from Jerusalem to Antioch (Acts 15:25) possibly indicating that Barnabas is still presented as the senior colleague as far as Jerusalem is concerned.
5. John Lund, "On the Circulation of Goods in Hellenistic and Early Roman Cyprus: The Ceramic Evidence," in *Panayia Ematousa II: Political, Cultural, Ethnic and Social Relations in Cyprus: Approaches to Regional Studies*, edited by L. Wreidt Sørensen and K. Winther Jacobson (Athens: Danish Institute of Athens, 2006), pp. 31–49.
6. Note the conscious avoidance of the title "apostle" for Paul in Acts, as the author attributes this title only to the Twelve.
7. Cf. the detailed arguments I presented in my *Paul at the Crossroads of Cultures: Theologizing in the Space Between* (London/New York: Bloomsbury T&T Clark 2013), pp. 17–38, 76–83. Similarly, Annette Yoshiko Reed and Nathalie B. Dohrmann, "Rethinking Romanness, Provincializing Christendom," in *Jews, Christians and the Roman Empire in Late Antiquity*, edited by Annette Yoshiko Reed and Nathalie B. Dohrmann (Philadelphia: University of Pennsylvania Press, 2013), pp. 1–21, esp. 4–9.
8. Reed and Dohrmann, "Rethinking Romanness," p. 5.
9. Cf. also my discussion in *Paul at the Crossroads of Cultures: Theologizing in the Space Between*, pp. 76–83. Text of Cicero from *Cicero's Tusculan Disputations*, translated by C. D. Yonge (New York: Harper & Brothers Publishers, 1877).
10. Cf. also J. Brian Tucker, *You Belong to Christ: Paul and the Formation of Social Identity in 1 Corinthians 1-4* (Eugene, OR: Pickwick, 2010), pp. 89–128.
11. Paula Fredriksen, "If It Looks Like a Duck, and It Quacks Like a Duck … On Not Giving Up the Godfearers," in *A Most Reliable Witness: Essays in Honor of Ross Shepard Kraemer*, edited by Susan Ashbrock Harvey et al. (Providence, RI: Brown Judaic Studies, 2015), pp. 25–34.
12. Werner Eck, *Rom und Judaea. Fünf Vorträge zur römischen Herrschaft in Palaestina* (Tübingen: Mohr, 2007); Ernst Baltrusch, *Die Juden und das Römische Reich: Geschichte einer konfliktreichen Beziehung* (Darmstadt: Wissenschaftliche Buchhandlung, 2002).
13. In Matt 2:1 it is translated as "astrologers" or "wise men"!
14. This is how I think πίστις should be translated. Cf. my *Paul at the Crossroads of Cultures*, pp. 160–74.
15. Neil Elliott, *The Arrogance of Nations: Reading Romans in the Shadow of Empire* (Minneapolis: Fortress, 2008); Warren Carter, *The Roman Empire and the New Testament* (Nashville, TN: Abingdon 2005). Cf. also Josephus' account of the turmoil after Herod's death *Ant.* 17.285-95.
16. Loveday Alexander, "Luke's Political Vision," *Interpretation* (July 2012): 283–4, 290.

17 David H. Wenkel, "From Saul to Paul: The Apostle's Name Change and Narrative Identity in Acts 13.9," *Asbury Journal* 66 (2011): 67–76; Stephen B. Chapman, "Saul/Paul: Onomastic Typology and Christian Scripture," in *The Word Leaps the Gap: Essays on Scripture and Theology in Honor of Richard B. Hays*, edited by J. R. Wagner, C. K. Rowe, and Katherine Grieb (Grand Rapids, MI: Eerdmans, 2009), pp. 214–43; Sean McDonough, "Small Change: Saul to Paul, Again," *JBL* 125 (2006): 390.
18 The later onomastic evidence from the Jewish catacombs in Rome suggests that devout Jews were quite content to use, and commemorate one another by, non-Hebrew names. See L.V. Rutgers, "The Jews of Italy, c. 235–638," in *The Cambridge History of Judaism. Vol. IV. The Late Roman-Rabbinic Period*, edited by S. T. Katz (Cambridge: Cambridge University Press, 2006), pp. 492–508, esp. 497.
19 On body language generally, see Anthony Corbell, *Nature Embodied: Gesture in Ancient Rome* (Princeton: Princeton University Press, 2004), and here specifically on the face and the eyes, pp. 144–67. On body language and facial expression in Jewish tradition, see now Catherine Heszer, *Rabbinic Body Language: Non-verbal Communication in Palestinian Rabbinic Literature of Late Antiquity* (Leiden: Brill, 2017), p. 203 ff.
20 Cf. Corbell, *Nature Embodied*, p. 147.
21 πλήρης παντὸς δόλου καὶ πάσης ῥᾳδιουργίας.
22 Cf. Brittany Wilson, "Hearing the Word and Seeing the Light: Voice and Vision in Acts," *JSNT* (2016): 456–81.
23 I see many trajectories which indicate if not the same author then a continuity of tradition between the Gospel of Luke and the book of Acts.
24 My translation—note that παρρησία normally translated as "bold" or similar actually is the technical term for freedom of speech, the right of a free citizen to express his views and, if considered necessary, to speak against unjust authority.

8

The Motivations for Paul's Choice of Mission Areas

William S. Campbell

According to Luke's narrative in Acts 15:36-41, Barnabas and Saul (Paul) emerged as leaders in the Christ-movement to the non-Jews. They remained in Antioch until Paul proposed a return visit to see how the new Christ-followers were progressing in all the cities in which he and Barnabas had previously proclaimed the gospel. Earlier in Acts, it is Barnabas who is mentioned first in the chapter in which they are initially set apart for mission (Acts 13:1-3), followed by "Saul," thereafter "Paul," according to Acts 13:9. Together they went to Seleucia and then to Paphos in Cyprus. But now the order has changed and from henceforth, except at 15:12 and 15:25, it is Paul followed by Barnabas (13:46).

But Paul's travel proposal (which included possible implications for his understanding of mission strategy) was not followed because of disagreement concerning John Mark. The reason given is that Paul did not want to take Mark with them "because he had withdrawn from them in Pamphilia, and had not gone with them to the work" (15:38). As a result, Barnabas took Mark with him and sailed away to Cyprus whereas Paul chose Silas and traveled through Syria and Silicia, strengthening the ἐκκλησίαι (15:39-41).

Is this fuzzy picture deliberately drawn, possibly because Luke does not really have any further information? Or does it give what Luke thought were sufficient clues for his purposes? Is it a debate over how mission should proceed: returning to areas where they had already preached to build up existing congregations or going instead to new areas (and possibly revisiting some congregations en route to these new areas)? Alternatively, was the issue at stake in Mark's earlier withdrawal related to patterns of evangelism, where Mark was closer to Barnabas than to Paul, since Barnabas was happy for Mark to accompany him? What had the previous work together in Antioch revealed to Paul and Barnabas about their differing convictions about patterns of behavior? It seems that Paul is presented as becoming the leader over Barnabas who earlier was regarded as his senior. Is Paul now the leader because he represents what, for the author of Acts, is the way forward but possibly not for Barnabas?

Part I: Toward a Theology of Calling

In Romans 15 Paul gives some clues as to his mission strategy, especially 15:18-21.[1] Paul possibly regarded Jerusalem as both the point of origin of his mission[2] and the earliest center of authority for the Christ-movement, including its later expansion among non-Jews. Thus, Paul may have envisaged himself as working in a circle (κύκλος) from Jerusalem to Illyricum, indicating the scope of his mission. W. Paul Bowers has shown that Paul's global strategy seemed to be based on Roman provinces.[3] Paul appears to be moving westwards in his evangelizing of Roman provinces, in a wide semicircle from Jerusalem round to Spain, to the distant coastlands at the end of the earth in the far West. According to Rodney Stark, Paul probably had a preference for working in large Hellenized urban centers, particularly those with access to the sea and with a large concentration of Jews among the population.[4]

Paul as Pioneer Missionary

The main policy he follows is that he does not build on another apostle's foundation (Rom 15:20). If the ἐκκλησία at Rome had a Jewish foundation (from Jerusalem), might it not have been perceived as within the missionary sphere of Peter rather than that of Paul?[5] It seems that Paul's policy involved the setting up, or establishment, of congregations in the main provincial centers, then moving on after a short period of time (but sometimes staying longer), ultimately leaving them to evangelize their own region.[6] Mission for Paul meant not just proclamation of the gospel but a multidimensional engagement: an integrated reciprocal participation in the lives of his converts, with the goal of getting these to turn to the life of faith and a commitment to the lifestyle associated with this.[7] Thus he states in Rom 15:23 that he has no more room for evangelizing in the East and therefore is heading for the furthest borders of the West via Rome. His eventual targeted audience is not those in Rome, but rather the peoples of Spain, and he seeks the support of those in Rome in this work (προπεμφθῆναι, 15:24).[8]

What is apparent from Paul's travels is that he is very flexible and adaptable in seeking what to do or where to go next, but his goal is global rather than local.[9] Thus he does not seek to undo the work of his predecessors by starting another mission where they have already worked. Like the Qumran community, he relates scripture and current events and thus seeks guidance where issues are unclear or guidance is needed.[10] The first-century exegete searched the scriptures in light of the signs of the times. From scripture one learned the nature of God's purpose and from current events one could learn the signs of its fulfilment. But Paul seems to have a definite plan not to become a leader in a specific location but to press on to new areas with a continuing sense of urgency, to bring in "the fullness of the gentiles" (Rom 11:25).[11] Hence his goal is Spain, not Rome (cf. διαπορευόμενος, 15:24).

A number of scholars have shown that this goal is derived from scriptural prophecies that were obviously well known to Paul in which non-Jews (those from the nations) will, in Paul's interpretation, be brought by him to Jerusalem as an offering. It seems that Paul considers that only when the fullness of the Gentiles happens, that is, when the offering of the Gentiles has been completed once he has reached as far as Tarshish in Spain (mentioned in Isa 66:19), will his own mission be fulfilled.[12] Thus, Paul's mission travels and goals are eschatologically determined by his reading of the scriptures in the current context of events, in accordance with the contemporary Jewish geography/cosmology in relation to the Table of Nations in Genesis;[13] Israel as a light to the nations in Isaiah 66 and other texts whose meanings were actively debated at this time certainly influenced him, even as he developed his own specific reading of some of these.

Theology, Ethnicity, and Mission

Paul's converts are not a haphazard collection of individuals but a specific entity: they function together as representatives of the non-Jewish nations traditionally called "the Gentiles." Although I prefer to use "nations," this does not include the modern concept of nation but could possibly be better designated as distinct "peoples." Paul's pattern seems to have been to plant ἐκκλησίαι in areas hitherto unevangelized and to maintain some minimal pastoral oversight through visits by him and his coworkers as opportunity permitted.[14] But Paul does not appear to intend to become domiciled to a particular city or to pastor only to a particular group of Christ-followers. According to Acts, the men of Cyprus and Cyrene who had heard the gospel came to Antioch and large numbers believed, so Barnabas was sent down from Jerusalem and then went to Tarsus to find Saul to help in the work. Thus, although Barnabas had strong links with Jerusalem, he is introduced in Acts 4:26 as a Levite from Cyprus; and although Saul is from Tarsus, the two worked together for a whole year in Antioch according to Acts 11:19-26. We are not told what Paul was doing prior to being sent for by Barnabas. Was he conducting mission work in Tarsus or elsewhere? The reference to Arabia has been understood by some as a reference to Nabateans. The Nabateans were considered Ishmael's descendants and were thus related Semites. The same was true of the Idumeans, as can be seen in the prophetic promises to the "neighbors" in Jer 12:14-16. Luke, writing a different kind of narrative at a much later period, gives no hint on this topic. But it should be noted that a clear boundary marker in Paul's later, *fully developed mission work* is the abiding covenantal difference between Jew and non-Jew which is not removed by following Christ. This is to say that differing lifestyles are typically followed according to the origin as Jewish or non-Jewish of the groups concerned.

This is one of Paul's fixed points which he says he teaches everywhere in all the ἐκκλησίαι (1 Cor 7:17). The rule is that "everyone should remain in the state in which he was called." If one was called as a Jew he must not attempt to hide the marks of circumcision; if one was called as a non-Jew he must not accept circumcision. The only variation is that if one was called as a slave, they should take their freedom if the opportunity becomes available.

The conclusion of this particular section on calling is 1 Cor 7:24: "So brethren, in whatever calling one was called, there let him remain with God." Weymouth's translation is equally clear: "Where each one stood when called, there, brethren, let him still stand."[15] The calling here does not refer to a profession as a tentmaker or such but only to the call to follow Christ: where one was placed as a Jew or non-Jew there they should remain. As the circumcision of Timothy demonstrates in Acts 16:3, Paul does not oppose circumcision for Jews as such. He opposes the circumcision of non-Jewish Christ-followers, not only because they have in Christ all they require but also because, according to the covenant, of which circumcision is the sign, only Jews, but not Gentiles, need to be circumcised. Circumcision for non-Jews is wrong not because circumcision is nothing[16] but merely because these are not Jews. Since his thought is covenantal throughout, Paul ought not to be portrayed as anti-ethnic,[17] but ethnicity, as with all aspects of life, must be subject to the lordship of Christ.

Paul does say "circumcision is nothing," but since he also says uncircumcision is nothing, 1 Cor 7:19 has to be understood as the rhetorical statement that it is, that is, an exaggerated statement *addressed to non-Jews* to stress that Christ is the ultimate value and all else is as of no value when compared with him. Significantly, circumcision can be used neutrally by Paul simply to refer noncritically to the Jewish people: "Christ became a servant to the circumcised to show God's truthfulness and to confirm the promises given to the patriarchs" (Rom 15:8).

Paul's stance or value system is that whatever one is or has, has second place to loyalty to Christ, even one's wife: "Let those who have wives be as though they had none" (1 Cor 7:29-31). This is living according to the famous ὡς μή, which Bultmann emphasized,[18] which is to say "having," yet living "as if not having." This indicates the entire reevaluation of all things that the call to follow Christ entails for Paul. Those who buy must live as though they had no goods, an ethic which promotes equality among those of differing social levels: the amount of goods they have is of no account since all continue to live, "as having nothing." Thus, Paul is not concerned about some things but indifferent to others. Rather he lives "as if not having all things" and therefore distances himself effectively from all competing objects or value systems, so that Christ should be all and in all. But this criterion of ultimate value in Christ cannot mean simply the giving up of some things and their replacement by others, since the call of God cannot in itself be inconsistent.[19] Thus within the Christ-movement generally, there is greater continuity in value systems and life-patterns among Jewish, as distinct from non-Jewish, Christ-followers, with subsequently differing outcomes within differing groups. It must be clearly recognized that Paul's call for the entire reevaluation of all things has as its primary target the non-Jewish groups who were Paul's addressees, some of whom probably lived in "pagan" households.

As God to Each Has Assigned

It is noteworthy that in 1 Cor 7:17 Paul views the place or point of call as an assignment from God (ὡς ἐμέρισεν ὁ κύριος). This therefore cannot be easily given up or changed. It seems to be part of the "given" over which the individual has no control, and yet it is theologically very important. Thus, if one is not to seek to remove the signs of circumcision but to regard it as an ongoing state in which to live, it may even be regarded by Paul as "keeping the commandments of God" for those of Jewish origin. This is just as it appears in 1 Cor 7:19 where Paul repeats the same formulaic assertion as in Gal 6:15 that "circumcision is nothing." But this time he employs in his response not new creation terminology but rather reference to the commandments of God, which for Paul remain a given. Paul does not advocate indifference to anything,[20] but instead the most serious evaluation of everything, since for him "the time is short," and therefore both circumcision and uncircumcision (i.e., the whole of life) must be reevaluated, as in Phil 3:7-8 where Paul says he counts "everything (πάντα) as loss."

If we compare the Acts narrative with similar statements in Paul's letters[21] concerning Paul's motivation in determining where he should next travel, we find again some factors which seem to be regarded by Paul and his coworkers as a given which can only be accepted. We note three passages in Paul's letters that are connected by the recurrence of the term ἐμέρισεν. In all three there is a given element that is to be regarded as determined by God. In the first of these, 1 Cor 7:17-24, the point of call, we have noted, is assigned by God. The second example is from Rom 12:3 where what God has assigned is described as the "measuring rod of faith." According to Robert Jewett, the primary meaning of μέτρον is "that by which anything is measured" and thus indicates "the norm that each person is provided in the appropriation of the grace God apportions."[22] To each is apportioned charismata that are to act as a measuring rod within the life of the individual and the community.

The third example we note is 2 Cor 10:13 where the emphasis is on the geographical limits that God measured out for different apostles/evangelists. Paul claims, "but we will not boast beyond limit, in other men's labours: but our hope is that as your faith increases, our field among you may be greatly enlarged so that we may preach the gospel in lands beyond you, without boasting in work done in another man's field" (κατὰ τὸ μέτρον τοῦ κανόνος). The implication of this passage in 2 Corinthians 10 is that God is regarded as apportioning spheres of work, to the limits of which Paul seeks to adhere in his mission. He and his associates can only boast over the success in those areas assigned to them, unlike others who boast in themselves rather than in what comes from God (v. 12).

From our brief overview of these passages, we have found that the use of μέτρον here denotes given aspects of Christ-followers' life. In the first instance the given element appears to have more to do with social status—where one is assigned whether as Jew, non-Jew, or slave. In the second it concerns spiritual gifts including leadership qualities and in the third a designated sphere of work. What we will maintain is that despite the freedom and newness of life in Christ in the Pauline mission, *Paul's theology includes a given element*. Christ's followers are not free men (free to do anything they choose), but rather freedmen who know the cost of freedom: they were bought with a price and regard every aspect of their life as emanating from the call of Christ. And Christ is the Messiah of Israel, so the narrative of Israel is one of the most significant of the given factors that continues to influence the pattern of the mission to the nations. The Christ-followers were called to do the will of God, to accommodate to the purpose of God in Christ rather than just to freedom in Christ. They were called, or freed, and equipped so that they could be free to do the work assigned for them. "For he who was called in the Lord as a slave is a freedman of the Lord. Likewise, he who was called as a free man is a slave of Christ" (1 Cor 7:22). Contrary to what is sometimes declared, in the Pauline mission all of life is not open to Christ-followers, but rather only those areas in which they can be free to serve Christ as God has assigned them. As in the case of former slaves, they are not without obligations once they have been freed.[23] Paul and Barnabas are freedmen of Christ who have been called to a task God has assigned them, and they must serve that purpose rather than their own choices or preferences. But how much do the differing backgrounds of Paul and Barnabas affect or influence the pattern of their mission work? If, as we have argued above, Christ-followers differ in life-patterns depending on their origin as Jews or non-Jews, and they are obligated to remain in that status or calling, then how accommodation to difference was negotiated was a crucial issue and thus was also a central point of negotiation in mission strategy and policy. In the second part of this chapter, I want to try to work out what such a theology of calling might imply about Paul's not returning with Barnabas to Cyprus.

Part II: Why Might Paul Not Have Returned?

What I wish to stress is that the New Testament documents do not suggest that it was purely human factors or preferences that determined whether Paul and Barnabas, etc., went or did not go to Cyprus or elsewhere. Luke gives examples of this in Acts and there are similar instances in Paul's letters. In Acts 16:7 it is reported that Paul and Silas "attempted to go into Bithynia, but the Spirit of Jesus did not allow them." A vision of a man from Macedonia is the reason given for going there (16:10). In Acts 21:4 Paul is told through the Spirit not to go on to Jerusalem.

One notable example is in Paul's relations with the Corinthians, who criticized Paul for being unreliable, promising to come while not coming, that is, saying "yes" and "no" at the same time (2 Cor 1:15-2:4). Paul's plans had to change as changed circumstances in differing areas required, but the Corinthians could only see that Paul did not keep to his plans, and Paul has to explain himself. He had wanted to come to see them on his way to Macedonia, and to return via them on his return journey, but did not actually do so. One argument is that he did not come because he wanted to spare them the reprimands he would have had to deliver; that is to say, he changed plans out of kindness to them, to spare them from what happened on a previous painful visit (2 Cor 2:1). Similar issues appear in 2 Cor 8:16-24, where Paul seems to have had to change his plans about who should accompany the collection and his trustworthiness is again called into question.

Paul asserts that he did not make his plans like a worldly man, ready to say "yes" and "no" at the same time. His thesis is that it is not normal human preferences that determine his decisions to come or go, but the needs of the ἐκκλησίαι and what Paul believes God requires him to do in the face of all the circumstances. Thus, he says in 1 Cor 4:19, "But I will come to you soon, if the Lord will."[24] Similarly, Paul says he will return to the Jews of the synagogue at Ephesus, "if the Lord wills" (Acts 18:21).

Whatever devices Luke uses to develop the narrative of Acts, and whatever we think of these, it is clear that he intends to demonstrate that Paul and his coworkers were consciously seeking to do what they thought God wanted them to do, and that the circumstances in which they were operating were of themselves not the only guide to what was best for them to do or the only guide of where to go next. Paul, in his letters, offers a variety of reasons, such as his call as apostle with a particular sphere of service (i.e., among the nations), and he characterizes his changes of plans not merely as expedient but as his willing response to what he thought God was calling him to do.

Paul and Barnabas Agree to Separate

Thus, Paul's separation from Barnabas may have several reasons. It probably resulted from a divergence in mission strategy emerging out of their circumstances and experiences at Antioch. Both Barnabas and he were seeking to plant ἐκκλησίαι among the nations, and connections with Cyprus were early and strong. That Paul went with Silas on a separate mission may indicate that Paul wanted there to be no debate about the freedom of non-Jews, a stance he thought was warranted by the Jerusalem summit meeting (Acts 15). Barnabas was well connected to those in Jerusalem and he may have interpreted the mission strategy differently from Paul, who was emerging as the more powerful leader even though originally Barnabas was recognized as senior to him. Perhaps this separation represents nothing more than a division of labor, but I suspect it indicates that there was more diversity than is obvious from the narratives. Paul reports that when Peter came to Antioch, he opposed Peter "to his face" because of a change of policy, and that even Barnabas was won over by Peter's stance. This I think lies behind the separation of Barnabas and Paul, even though I do not believe that Paul actually broke off relations with Jerusalem because of this incident.[25] Too much is read into a serious disagreement between two apostles and the extant evidence for their advocated patterns of behavior for non-Jews in Christ in their association with Christ-following Jews. The posited role of Paul, attributed to him in the "Antioch Incident," depicting him as the great innovator and sectarian who set up his own independent mission, in my view, serves the theological purposes of a later era. It does not appear to reflect the varied and ongoing divergences of a mixed ethnic movement in the first century in which the attachment to Jewish norms and patterns of behavior were still being negotiated for Gentiles.

To me it seems there were issues of how diverse lifestyles could be accommodated, and Paul, and Peter with Barnabas, took different sides so that it was easier to avoid conflict by working separately. The interesting question is what differing practices and patterns were henceforth promoted or maintained in the two separate mission teams. Thus, we are to assume that John Mark's withdrawal indicates a policy disagreement which meant he would not work with Paul but would work with Barnabas. This may imply that there was some difference in policy also between Paul and Barnabas. This should not be viewed as merely personal preference but an issue strong enough to require a change of mission partner. In other words, it must be a significant issue.

If, as I think likely, one of the points at issue was eating in connection with idolatry, Paul reveals a stance typical of those living in the Diaspora: be as accommodating as you can be about issues in dispute (cf. 1 Corinthians 8 and Romans 14), whereas those with closer links to Jerusalem may have been stricter in their strategies to avoid things sacrificed to idols. This could have been a point of divergence between Barnabas and Paul. It makes more intelligible the issue between Peter and Paul at Antioch. It was not so much the gospel message as such (both apostles were agreed on this) as the appropriate behavior of non-Jewish Christ-followers in relation to idolatry. This reading need not result in the claim that Paul broke off relations with those who differed from him and started his own independent mission as Dunn seeks to argue.[26] This, in my view, depicts Paul as the archetypal sectarian and a bad example for the members of his ἐκκλησίαι.

Diversity Is Original: Differing Convictions Are Acknowledged

It reveals, rather, that even among the early apostles, despite being in agreement about the gospel message itself, there were strong convictions that from the beginning demonstrated the great diversity in patterns of behavior and practice within the Christ-movement as it moved out into the Roman world. It was a new movement and brought great changes with it, but in some aspects of its outreach, despite claims to the contrary, ethnic, geographical, and other issues all still played a part. Thus, it was a movement that, even in Paul's mission to the nations, sought to continue a heritage in which Israel's vocation to become a light to the nations would be fulfilled.[27] In this Paul and Barnabas were deeply involved bringing with them their cultural heritages in a common commitment to Christ for the outreach of the gospel. It may be that their differing affiliations in Jerusalem, Antioch, and the Diaspora also affected the differing patterns of halakhic arrangements they recommended for non-Jews joining the movement. One possible point of divergence is whether the eating together of Jewish and non-Jewish Christ-followers took place in a household where everyone was a Christ-follower, as distinct from a house where only one member had turned to the Lord. The story of Peter in Acts 10 seems to suggest that it was only when the whole household had turned to the Lord and been baptized that it was possible to eat there. That is to say, it is not just who you eat with but where you eat that is the issue.

I summarize here one of the most recent statements on the Antioch incident: that of Paula Fredriksen in her book, *Paul, the Pagans' Apostle*.[28] Before certain men came from James, Peter had originally followed a Diaspora Jewish convention of eating and drinking in a private (though Gentile) domestic setting as long as it did not scandalize another member of the community who was present. But James' men when they came *were* scandalized. They declined to participate at such meals, and Peter withdrew. Peter had been prepared to eat within a pagan household that itself would hold images of gods. Peter, as leader of the mission to the circumcised, was persuaded by James' men to drop this practice.[29]

This summary of the evidence demonstrates that the issue was not with whom one ate but where. As Fredriksen concludes:

> At issue was not the social company—Christ-following gentiles could eat with Christ-following Jews—but the *location of these meals*, and, by extension, the status of what was consumed. Worse, from Paul's point of view, the combined authority of the visitors from Jerusalem and of Peter himself undermined Paul's own authority with the other, local Jewish members of Antioch's ἐκκλησία, even Barnabas (2:13): from now on, members of this mixed community, when eating together, would meet only within Jewish households.[30]

Conclusion

For Peter's mission to the circumcision, eating in non-Jewish households would be exceptional, but for Paul in the Diaspora not to eat in pagan households would render life difficult, and so he gave his consent to the practice. It seems that this is the issue over which John Mark had earlier disagreed with Paul and because of which he had decided to go with Barnabas instead. It is probable that some such issues help explain the points at issue between the "weak" and the "strong" in Romans 14–15.[31] It may not be the food or drink that separates so much as its perceived links with idolatry, whether in its place of origin or consumption. We note that despite clear divisions among the non-Jewish Christ-following groups in Rome, Paul calls for the full acceptance of each by the other, and he makes no suggestion of separation.[32] But in the founding of new ἐκκλησίαι, abiding patterns had to be and were established. Despite what is not explicitly stated about disagreements whether by Luke or in Paul's letters, it seems that Barnabas and Paul with their coworkers sought to maintain a recognition of each other's work, though going their separate ways. This implies an acknowledgment of diversity within mission practice and subsequent life-patterns within the ἐκκλησίαι they founded. It likewise includes a recognition that one should not build on the foundation of another to replace or reform that foundation. Behind this must lie a consciousness of the work of the Spirit working in diverse ways through differing apostles and their coworkers in differing contexts. These would ultimately result in ἐκκλησίαι that diverged in various directions as a result of the demands and challenges the different groups encountered. These challenges contributed to the particular characteristics of local communities of Christ-followers and resulted in a particular form of identity in keeping with the origin, geography, culture, and subsequent history of these groups.[33] Cyprus was close enough to Jerusalem to be part of the initial mission work of Paul and his coworkers and thus to be influenced by their activities.

The narrative of Paul revisiting Cyprus without John Mark may indicate that the pattern of his understanding of proper approaches to diversity within the Christ-following groups would gain a foothold on the island and thereby contribute in significant ways to the shaping of the particular form of Christianity that developed in the eastern part of the empire.

Notes

1. This was first stressed by John Knox (though influenced to some extent by Johannes Munck's *Paul and the Salvation of Mankind*), in his "Romans 15:14-33 and Paul's Conception of His Mission," *JBL* 83 (1964): 1–11.
2. Paul possibly envisaged his travels as constituting a circle with Jerusalem as the starting point and conclusion of his travels, cf. κύκλω in Rom 15:19. Cf. Roger D. Aus, "Paul's Travel Plans for Spain and the 'Full Number of the Gentiles' of Romans 11.25," *Novum Testamentum* 21 (1979): 232–62. E. P. Sanders suggests "arc" rather than "circle" for Paul's missionary vision, *Paul, the Law, and the Jewish People* (Philadelphia: Fortress, 1983), p. 189.
3. Cf. Ksewnija Magda, *Paul's Territoriality and Mission Strategy* (Tübingen: Mohr Siebeck, 2009), pp. 6–7.
4. Cf. Rodney Stark, *Cities of God: The Real Story of How Christianity Became an Urban Movement and Conquered Rome* (New York: HarperOne, 2007), p. 132.
5. Should the ἵνα μὴ ἐπ' ἀλλότριον θεμέλιον οἰκοδομῶ be interpreted as a mere avoidance of overlapping mission areas among apostles generally, or does it possibly refer to the division of labor agreed for the missions of Peter and Paul respectively? It would seem to me strange if there were no agreement about work among Jews in the Diaspora, especially since theological and ethnic implications are involved in the division of labor (contra Sanders, *Paul, the Law and the Jewish People*, pp. 188–90). A parallel issue is whether within Paul's Gentile mission, agreements were agreed about respective spheres of operation, cf. "Universality and Particularity in Paul's Understanding and Strategy of Mission," in my *Unity and Diversity in Christ: Interpreting Paul in Context* (Eugene, OR: Cascade Books, 2013), pp. 187–202.
6. Cf. Robert Jewett, *Romans*, Hermeneia (Minneapolis: Fortress Press, 2007), pp. 914–15.
7. Paul should not be conceived as someone who did not put down roots or make close friendships in the cities he visited; the intensity of Paul's relationships is clearly not entirely determined by the length of his stay, cf. Volker Rabens' stress upon Paul's intense involvement in the forming of Christ in his converts, "Von Jerusalem aus und rings umher … (Röm.15,19). Die paulinische Missionstrategie im Dickicht der Städte," in *Das frühe Christentum und die Stadt*, edited by Reinhard von Bendemann und Markus Tiwald, Hg., BWANT 198 (Stuttgart: Kohlhammer, 2012), pp. 219–37.
8. This is problematic if Peter has not already been in Rome prior to Paul's writing his letter, but it could also mean that the Christ-following groups in Rome had no particular founder that the group just grew from those who had become Christ-followers elsewhere and then moved to live in Rome. In that case Paul is going to Rome to give the non-Jewish Christ-followers a proper foundation, under his leadership as apostle to the nations.
9. Paul's longer-term vision is Spain, but he has to be flexible in his interim plans as these must alter in relation to conditions in the local context in which he was working.
10. Cf. Earle Ellis, "the first century exegete had a two-fold task, to 'search the scriptures' and to discern 'the signs of the times;' from scripture he learned the nature of God's purpose, and from current events he sought indication of their fulfilment," *Paul's Use of the Old Testament* (Grand Rapids, MI: Eerdmans, 1957), p. 135.
11. Paul's use of the Table of Nations in Genesis 10 as well as in Isa 66:18-19 possibly lies behind the travel route that Paul notionally followed in his mission, but there is less agreement on whether Paul had an early mission among the Arabs and in Nabatea all

the way to Petra and Hegra, cf. Magda, *Paul's Territoriality*, pp. 12–15. For a detailed discussion of the Table of Nations, see James Scott, *Paul and the Nations* (Tübingen: Mohr Siebeck, 1995).

12   Cf. Aus, "Paul's Travel-Plans for Spain," pp. 242–50.
13   James S. Scott in his *Paul and the Nations* built on Philip S. Alexander's drawings of a map in the book of Jubilees 8–9 to argue that geography offers solutions concerning Paul's mission strategy; understanding Paul's territoriality is the basis for understanding his strategy. Cf. P. S. Alexander, *Toponymy of the Targumim with Special Reference to the Table of Nations and the Boundaries of the Land of Israel* (Oxford: University of Oxford, 1974). Further, see Magda, *Paul's Territoriality*, pp. 4–7.
14   Cf. Kathy Ehrensperger, *Paul and the Dynamics of Power: Communication and Interaction in the Early Christ-Movement* (London: T&T Clark, 2007), pp. 134–54.
15   R. F. Weymouth, *The New Testament in Modern Speech* (London: James Clarke & Co., 1903).
16   As, e.g., David Horrell, "No Longer Jew or Greek: Paul's Corporate Christology and the Construction of Christianity," in *Christology, Controversy and Community: New Testament Essays in Honour of David R. Catchpole*, edited by David G. Horrell and Christopher M. Tuckett (Leiden: Brill, 2000), pp. 320–44 (here 338).
17   Cf. my *The Nations in the Divine Economy: Paul's Covenantal Hermeneutics and Participation in Christ* (Lanham, MD: Lexington/Fortress Academic, 2018), pp. 129–52.
18   *Theology of the New Testament* (London: SCM, 1955), 1.240.
19   On a biblical concept of continuity, see Frank C. Rüsemann, *Das Alte Testament als Wahrheitsraum des Neuen: Die neue Sicht der christlichen Bibel* (Gütersloh: Gütersloher Verlaghaus, 2011), esp. pp. 255–7.
20   Cf. my essay, "'As Having and as Not Having': Paul, Circumcision and Indifferent Things in 1 Corinthians 7:17–32a," in *Unity and Diversity in Christ*, pp. 106–26.
21   We take into account here the difference between the letters as written by Paul himself and the later accounts in Acts based on reports of the apostle rather than written by Paul.
22   *Romans*, 742.
23   Cf. Paul B. Duff, *Jesus Followers in the Roman Empire* (Grand Rapids, MI: Eerdmans, 2017), pp. 189–92.
24   James MacKnight, *A New Literal Translation from the Original Greek of All the Apostolical Epistles*, 4th ed. (London: Longman & Company, 1809).
25   See my *Paul and the Creation of Christian Identity* (London: T&T Clark, 2008), pp. 38–53.
26   "The New Perspective on Paul," in *Jesus, Paul and the Law: Studies in Mark and Galatians* (London: SPCK, 1990), pp. 183–206 (here 196).
27   This is a dominant theme in my *The Nations in the Divine Economy* (n. 17 above); see esp. Chapter 6, "The Hermeneutics of Commonality and Comparison in 2 Corinthians 3," esp. pp. 160–2.
28   Paula Fredriksen, *Paul, the Pagans' Apostle* (New Haven: Yale University Press, 2017), pp. 96–9.
29   Ibid., p. 99.
30   Ibid.
31   The occurrence of the term οἰκέτης in Rom 14:4 may indicate the fact that some Christ-followers live as house servants in a (pagan) household. Cf. my

"The Addressees of Paul's Letter to the Romans: Assemblies of God in House Churches and Synagogues?" in *Between Gospel and Election: Explorations in the Interpretation of Romans 9-11*, edited by Florian Wilk and J. Ross Wagner, WUNT 257 (Tübingen: Mohr Siebeck, 2010), pp. 146-68 (now also published in *Unity and Diversity in Christ*).

32 The concept of forming one united church in Rome sounds laudable, but Paul's concern is for the well-being of all the Christ-followers, especially "the weak" and so he counsels the strong to care for them rather than dominate or force them to do what they believe is sin for them (Rom 14:19–15:3)

33 Cf. Kathy Ehrensperger, *Paul at the Crossroads of Cultures: Theologizing in the Space-Between* (London, New York: Bloomsbury/T&T Clark, 2015), pp. 105-39.

Cyprus and Early Christianity: Did Everybody Know Everybody?

Dale C. Allison, Jr.

Introduction

The New Testament refers to Cyprus only in Acts and only on a handful of occasions:

Acts 4:36-37: (36) Joseph, who was surnamed by the apostles Barnabas (which means, Son of encouragement) and a Levite and a native of Cyprus, (37) sold a field which belonged to him, and he brought the money and laid it at the apostles' feet.

Acts 11:19-20: (19) Now those who were scattered because of the persecution that arose over Stephen traveled as far as Phoenicia, Cyprus, and Antioch, speaking the word to none except Jews. (20) But some of them, men of Cyprus and Cyrene, when they came to Antioch spoke to the Greeks also, preaching the Lord Jesus.

Acts 13:4-12: (4) Being sent out by the Holy Spirit, they [Barnabas and Paul] went down to Seleucia; and from there they sailed to Cyprus. (5) When they arrived at Salamis, they proclaimed the word of God in the synagogues of the Jews. And they had John to assist them. (6) When they had gone through the whole island as far as Paphos, they came upon a certain magician, a Jewish false prophet, named Bar-Jesus. (7) He was with the proconsul, Sergius Paulus, a man of intelligence, who summoned Barnabas and Saul and sought to hear the word of God. (8) But Elymas the magician (for that is the meaning of his name) withstood them, seeking to turn away the proconsul from the faith. (9) But Saul, who is also called Paul, filled with the Holy Spirit, looked intently at him (10) and said, "You son of the devil, you enemy of all righteousness, full of all deceit and villainy, will you not stop making crooked the straight paths of the Lord? (11) And now, behold, the hand of the Lord is upon you, and you shall be blind and unable to see the sun for a time." Immediately mist and darkness fell upon him and he went about seeking people to lead him by the hand. (12) Then the proconsul believed, when he saw what had occurred, for he was astonished at the teaching of the Lord.

Acts 15:39-40: (39) there arose a sharp contention, so that they separated from each other; Barnabas took Mark with him and sailed away to Cyprus, (40) but

Paul chose Silas and departed, being commended by the brethren to the grace of the Lord.

Acts 21:3: When we had come in sight of Cyprus, leaving it on the left we sailed to Syria, and landed at Tyre; for there the ship was to unload its cargo.

Acts 21:15-16: (15) After these days we made ready and went up to Jerusalem. (16) And some of the disciples from Caesarea went with us, bringing us to the house of Mnason of Cyprus, an early disciple, with whom we should lodge.

Acts 27:4: (4) And putting to sea from there we sailed under the lee of Cyprus, because the winds were against us.

Apart from the short story about Paul, Barnabas, and the magician in Acts 13, there is really only modest mention of Cyprus in the New Testament.[1] Barnabas, an important character in Acts, and a certain Mnason, mentioned only in passing, were natives of the place, although they subsequently lived in or near Jerusalem (Acts 4:36-37; 21:15-16). After the persecution of Stephen, some followers of Jesus—no names are given, but they clearly belong to the group Luke dubs the "Hellenists" (6:1, 9:29)—reportedly left Palestine to evangelize Jews on Cyprus[2] and some Cypriot Christians went to Antioch and preached to Greeks (Acts 11:19-20).[3] Acts further reports that Barnabas and Mark, after a quarrel with Paul, went to Cyprus, although it says nothing about what they did there (15:39-40). Finally, two of the so-called we-sections of Acts have Paul and his companions sailing within sight of Cyprus but evidently not landing there (21:3; 27:4). And that is it.

Nevertheless, as one reflects on these passages in Acts and what they might mean, a line of thought suggests itself. It does not have to do directly with Cyprus but rather with the nature of the post-Easter Jesus movement and with some implications for modern critical scholarship. My point of departure is the simple observation that although Cyprus was not an important early Christian center in the way that Jerusalem, Antioch, or Ephesus was, an impressive number of important individuals nonetheless spent time there—Barnabas, John Mark, Paul, and unnamed missionaries who belonged to the so-called Hellenists of Jerusalem. All of these people found themselves at some point on Cyprus. Beyond that, Acts has it that certain "men of Cyprus" went to Antioch, where they missionized.

As one begins to think about this simple and obvious fact that so many prominent individuals are associated with the same island, Cyprus, another simple and obvious fact may dawn: all of these people—that is, Barnabas, John Mark, Paul, and the so-called Hellenists—are also, in Acts, associated with two other places, Jerusalem and Antioch.[4] This literary circumstance may in turn lead one to ruminate on the size and nature of the earliest Jesus movement and to ask the following question: During the first two or three decades—when the total number of Christians was, by our best estimate, probably no more than 1500[5]—is it not likely that everybody important knew pretty much everybody else who was important?[6]

The question may seem not worth asking, because is not the answer obvious? The picture that Acts paints is of local communities full of leaders and itinerants who travel around the Mediterranean world, individuals who, furthermore, keep in touch with one another. One cannot, to be sure, equate Acts with history, but on this matter the book clearly enshrines the historical truth, because Paul's epistles offer confirmation. His letters prove that he was in direct touch with James ("the Lord's brother"; cf. Gal 1:19), Peter (Cephas), and John (presumably John son of Zebedee). They place him in Syria, Asia Minor, and Greece and show his desire to go to Italy and even Spain. They additionally prove that he had numerous friends and acquaintances in all of these different parts of the world, even in places that he had not visited (cf. esp. Rom 16:1-16); and further that, among his coworkers, were some, such as Aquila and Prisca, who were like him in that they worked in multiple locations around the Mediterranean. It is, in addition, evident from Paul's letters that Christians in one place knew much about what was going on with Christians in other places.[7]

I confess that while I have always known all of this, I have until recently not seriously pondered at length the apparent implications. I did once write the following:

> If in the past we have tended to find too much unity in the early church, perhaps now, as citizens of a pluralistic and fragmented society, we are going too far the other way.[8] One may even wonder whether for its first decade or two early Christianity was not the complex thing modern scholars imagine but instead a very small movement with a few recognizable leaders who, as Paul tells us, agreed on quite a bit.[9]

But these sentences were, in effect, interrogatory, and until recently I pursued the issue no further.

Before unfolding my argument, I need to set it within its larger academic context. The books and articles that I read as a young scholar tended to put the accent on the independence and diversity of early Christian groups. I entered the guild at a time when it was quite common to speak about the Markan community, the Lukan community, the Matthean community, and the Johannine community. Each was often envisaged as though it were a group in its own place that had its own traditions, its own leaders, and its own distinctive version of the new faith.[10] This way of thinking was carried forward by work on Q in the 1970s, 1980s, and 1990s, in publications that sought to reconstruct the beliefs and history of what had come to be called the "Q community."[11] Many placed this community in Galilee and highlighted its theological distance from Mark, John, Acts, and Paul.[12]

All of this was part of a larger movement in New Testament studies, one that grew in part out of Walter Bauer's influential study of orthodoxy and heresy in the early church.[13] In reaction to an ecclesiastical tradition that saw all heresy as secondary and that did its best to iron out differences between canonical books—to show, for instance, that Matthew and Paul do not contradict each other on the subject of Torah, or that James and Paul are truly at one when it comes to faith and works, or that Luke's Christology is really the same as John's Christology—scholarship came fully to appreciate the different emphases and indeed contradictory ideas in early Christian texts, including the texts of the New Testament. Indeed, redaction criticism, scholarship on the Nag Hammadi library, literary readings of the New Testament, and renewed interest in so-called Jewish Christianity—a term with different meanings and functions for different scholars—seemed to many to antiquate altogether any notion of the theological unity of early Christianity.[14]

To my mind, the developments I have just catalogued have been, for the most part and in general, an effective antidote to the unhistorical harmonization that has ruled most of exegetical history. If we are playing the role of historian, we should interpret a text in the first place according to what it says, not according to what other early Christian sources say; and in the following pages I do not wish to be misunderstood as mounting an argument to the contrary. My concern is rather this: we need to take great care to separate the issue of theological diversity from the issue of historical connection. One can have diversity of thought because two individuals or groups have developed their ideas independently of one another. But, to state the obvious, individuals and groups who know each other or each other's writings can also hold diverse and conflicting opinions. The author of Matthew, for instance, belonged to a group that knew and used the Gospel of Mark, and yet Matthew's understanding of the Torah appears to be at odds with what we find in Mark.[15] Again, the Epistle of James does not speak about faith and works the way that Paul does; yet this is not because James and Paul represent two different early Christian currents that never crossed. On the contrary, it is due precisely to the fact that they did cross, and the result was antagonism.[16]

A Thought Experiment

In order to explore the consequences of the possibility that, as I have put it, in the first two or three decades of the early Jesus movement, everybody important knew pretty much everybody else who was important, I would like to conduct a thought experiment. Over the following pages I would like to entertain, for the sake of argument, the possibility that ecclesiastical tradition is correct about the authorship of both Mark and Luke-Acts. That is, I would like to presuppose, temporarily, that the John Mark known from Acts (12:12, 25; 13:5, 13; 15:37-40), who is named as a coworker of Paul in Col 4:10; 2 Tim 4:11; and Phlm 24, wrote the Second Gospel, and that the Luke mentioned in Col 4:14; 2 Tim 4:11; and Phlm 24 composed Luke and Acts, including the latter's "we sections." On this hypothetical scenario, three New Testament authors knew one another.

What would follow if this were true, if the author of Mark, the author of Luke, and Paul all knew one another face to face? In my judgment, the consequences both for our work on the historical Jesus and for our reconstruction of the history of early Christian theology would be far-reaching. Most of us would have to rethink much. Let me briefly elucidate by introducing five issues. Once I have done this, I will then explain why the thought experiment is worth our attention.

(1) **The Criterion of Multiple Attestation**. Modern Jesus research has often appealed to the criterion of multiple attestation. This tool assumes that Paul, Q, Mark, M, L, John (or at least parts of it), and (for some) the Gospel of Thomas are independent sources. The presumption is that, in general, the greater the number of independent sources witnessing to a particular saying, complex, or event, the higher the odds of it being rooted in the life and ministry of Jesus.[17]

Consider, as an illustration, the tradition of the last supper. The words of institution appear in Matt 26:26-29; Mark 14:22-25; Luke 22:17-20; and 1 Cor 11:24-25. Common scholarly wisdom has it that we have here two or three independent sources. Matthew's version is usually taken to depend upon Mark, from which it differs only slightly. Mark and Paul are regularly thought to represent two different streams of the tradition. As for Luke 22:17-20, with its notorious text-critical problem, it is commonly reckoned to depend upon Mark and/or a source closely related to 1 Cor 11:24-25. The task then becomes determining which of the three passages, if any, has the better chance of preserving what Jesus is likely to have said. Many opt for Mark. Some favor Paul. A few opt for Luke.[18]

Robert Webb offers an illustration of the usual procedure. Holding that Luke 22:17-20 depends upon Mark, he argues the following: the words of institution appear not only in the synoptics but also "in 1 Cor 11:23-25, a letter Paul wrote almost 20 years before Mark was written. And there is no evidence that Mark is dependent upon Paul's letter. Thus for at least a core of elements within this tradition there is multiple attestation—Paul and Mark—and so" we may judge those elements to have "a greater probability of historicity."[19]

Yet what if, to take up my thought experiment, the authors of Mark and Luke were onetime coworkers of Paul? If they were, then they must have participated in religious services with him. And if that is true, then they almost certainly were with him when some version of the words of institution were recited, because this was an important Pauline practice (cf. 1 Cor 11:17-34). In what sense, then, could we regard Mark 14:22-25 and Luke 22:17-20 as truly independent of 1 Cor 11:24-25? If Paul and the authors of the accounts in Mark and Luke were in the same place and the same time for celebrations of the Lord's Supper, then it is far from clear what, in such a case, multiple attestation could mean. This scenario does not, to be sure, rule out the possibility that Mark and Luke knew more than the Pauline tradition. That alternative would, however, need to be argued at greater length than it typically has been. Furthermore, how could one ever escape the suspicion that, with regard to the points of agreement, everything goes back to the single ritual conducted in the Pauline churches?[20] Indeed, some might even be moved to take seriously the hypothesis that Paul himself received the words of institution in a vision or revelation from the risen Lord,[21] for the standard counter to this, the appeal to multiple independent attestation, would fall to the ground.

One might counter all this by urging that at least John 6:53 ("unless you eat the flesh of the Son of man and drink his blood, you have no life in you") reflects independent knowledge of the words of institution.[22] Yet, apart from the real possibility that John has been influenced, directly or indirectly, by one or more of the synoptics,[23] the final edition of John is usually thought to have appeared two or three decades after Paul's death, so on chronological grounds alone one wonders whether John can be altogether unaffected by Paul. This is all the more true if one accepts the patristic tradition that John's Gospel was published in Ephesus,[24] for as Acts reports and as Paul's letters confirm, the apostle spent a good deal of time there.[25] And how could one ever be confident that celebration of the Lord's Supper in a city where Paul conducted a prolonged ministry was free of Pauline influence, especially as there are a number of contacts between John 6:51-58 and the eucharistic traditions in Paul?[26]

(2) **Mark and Q**. Because Paul's letters interact with the Jesus tradition so infrequently, the criterion of multiple attestation has been associated more commonly with the canonical gospels and their sources. Perhaps most important have been the overlaps between Q and Mark. To illustrate: on the assumption that these are two independent sources, Benedict Viviano has insisted that the traditions shared by Q and Mark are the sure footing upon which the quest for Jesus should erect its work.[27] "If Q and Mark are indeed independent of each other, the cases where they echo the same saying or phenomenon take on high significance as the most solidly grounded early sources available."[28]

Yet, once again, what if the authors of Mark and Luke were the figures who are named together in Phlm 23–24, where we find this: "Epaphras ... sends greetings to you, as do also Mark, Aristarchus, Demas, and Luke, my fellow workers" (cf. Col 4:10; 2 Tim 4:11)? What if the man behind Mark's Gospel was an occasional colleague of the author of Luke and so an associate of one who, on the common four source theory, knew and made extensive use of Q? If the two friends were sufficiently interested in the Jesus tradition so as to write gospels, how likely is it that they never spoke to one other at any length about the materials that ended up in their writings? Not very likely, or so it seems to me; and it would appear to follow that the all-inclusive independence of Mark over against Q would be imperiled. Indeed, if, sticking with my proposed scenario, the evangelists Luke and Mark were together in the 60s, as would be the case if Philemon was, as so often argued, written from Rome, and if, beyond that, Luke already knew Q,[29] it would be peculiar indeed if the latter were altogether ignorant of it.

In this connection one should recall that, even apart from my hypothetical scenario, a few have made a case that Mark's Gospel betrays an acquaintance with the Sayings Source.[30] Their thesis has the advantage of explaining why Mark, at least in comparison with the other canonical gospels and Thomas, preserves far fewer sayings of Jesus: perhaps the evangelist took his task to be something other than the duplication of Q. As B. H. Streeter once wrote: "Mark wrote expressly not to supersede Q, but, since Q contained practically nothing but discourse, to supplement Q with the biographical narrative for which a demand had arisen. Accordingly Mark quotes Q as little as he conveniently can without omitting features which no biography of our Lord could well do without."[31]

The view that Mark knew and used Q remains, to be sure, that of a minority.[32] Nonetheless, on the standard theory of synoptic relationships, there are somewhere around thirty significant overlaps between Mark and Q,[33] and Mark's acquaintance with someone with access to a copy of Q would be one way of explaining this circumstance.

(3) **Paul and the Jesus Tradition**. One of the great debates concerning Paul has been why he appears to cite and allude to the sayings of Jesus so infrequently. Some have thought the silence more apparent than real,[34] others that the apostle did not in fact know a whole lot about what Jesus taught.[35] If, however, the authors of two gospels were among his coworkers, the second of these alternatives would be hard to uphold. We would certainly have to dismiss the theory, associated with Wilhelm Heitmüller and, later on, Ulrich Wilckens, that the Jesus tradition was handed down in a wing of the church to which Paul did not belong.[36] In addition, the arguments for thinking that Paul alludes to the Jesus tradition on multiple occasions[37] would be greatly enhanced,

as would the contention of those who have urged that, at points, Paul's letters imply that the apostle was familiar with the notion of Jesus as "the Son of man,"[38] even though the extant correspondence nowhere employs that title. Anyone whose associates included the authors of Mark and Luke could not possibly have been unaware that tradition remembered Jesus speaking of himself as "the Son of man."

Yet a scenario in which Paul and the author of Luke knew each other would create its own problems for adjudicating Paul's indebtedness to the Jesus tradition. 1 Cor 10:27 reads: "If one of the unbelievers invites you to dinner and you are disposed to go, eat whatever is set before you (πᾶν τὸ παρατιθέμενον ὑμῖν ἐσθίετε) without raising any question on the ground of conscience." Luke 10:8 has this: "Whenever you enter a town and they receive you, eat what is set before you (ἐσθίετε τὰ παρατιθέμενα ὑμῖν)." Luke's line has no parallel in Matthew, and there is debate as to whether we should assign it to Q, Q[lk], L, or Lukan redaction. Whatever the answer to that, the nearness to 1 Cor 10:27 is remarkable. How do we explain it? One could suggest that Paul's sentence depends upon the Jesus tradition.[39] If, however, Luke knew Paul, one could very easily and just as plausibly claim that the former inspired the latter.[40] The direction of influence would be all but impossible to determine.

One can easily think of any number of additional ways in which one's reading of Paul might be altered, informed, or complicated were one to assume that, among his close friends, were the writers of two canonical gospels.[41] Here I observe only this: that those of us who have contended that Paul's minimal use of synoptic-like materials is due to something other than ignorance of such materials would have to be right.[42]

(4) **The Genealogy of Christian Theological Ideas**. In Rom 5:12-21; 1 Cor 15:21-22, 44-49; and perhaps Phil 2:5-11, Paul sets forth an Adam Christology.[43] Jesus, the last Adam, through his death and resurrection, has become a life-giving spirit from heaven; he has undone the reign of sin and death that entered the world through a man of dust, the first man Adam.[44] Critical discussion of Paul's doctrine of two Adams in Adam Christology has often explained its origins by reference to Philo's ruminations about a "first man" and a "second man," or to apocalyptic ideas within Judaism, or to Gnosticism's ideas about two Adams, or to rabbinic exegetical speculations about Adam.[45] But the singular focus on Paul misses the fact that traces of an Adam Christology appear elsewhere in early Christian literature.

Many exegetes have found the key to Mark's compressed and cryptic version of Jesus' temptation in traditions about the first Adam (1:13-14).[46] In paradise, Adam lived in peace with the animals[47] and was guarded by and/or honored by angels.[48] There too he was fed by angels[49] or (according to another tradition) ate the food of angels, manna.[50] But, after succumbing to the serpent's temptation, he was cast out (Gen 3:24 LXX: ἐξέβαλεν). This sequence of events is turned upside down in Mark. Jesus is first cast out (ἐκβάλλει). Then he is tempted. Then he gains companionship with the animals and the service of angels (which probably includes being fed by them, as in 1 Kgs 19:5-8).[51]

Adam succumbs to temptation

the beasts are "with" Adam no longer

the angels no longer serve Adam
Adam no longer enjoys the food of angels

Jesus overcomes temptation
↓
the beasts are with Jesus
the angels serve Jesus
Jesus has the food of angels

This typology appropriately follows the descent of the Spirit as a dove over the water in Mark 1:10, because that is a creation motif.[52] So, Mark's implicit point is analogous to T. Levi 18:10, which prophesies that the Messiah will open the gates of Eden and remove the sword that has guarded it since Adam and Eve fell—except in Mark, as in Paul, this hope has been realized in Jesus Christ.

It is likely that the author of Luke thought along similar lines, because he placed Jesus' genealogy immediately before his (very different) temptation narrative. The result is this juxtaposition: Jesus was "the son of Enos, the son of Seth, the son of Adam, the son of God. And Jesus, full of the Holy Spirit, returned from the Jordan, and was led by the Spirit for forty days in the wilderness, tempted by the devil" (3:38–4:2). Luke names Adam right before he relates how Jesus overcame the temptations of Satan.[53]

Heb 2:5-11 may also reflect an Adam Christology. These verses quote Psalm 8: "What is man (ἄνθρωπος) that you are mindful of him, or the son of man (υἱὸς ἀνθρώπου), that you care for him? You have made him for a little while lower than the angels; you have crowned him with glory and honor, subjecting all things under his feet" (vv. 6-8, quoting Ps 8:5-7 LXX). The lines quote a creation psalm, one that recalls Adam's creation in the image of God and his dominion over the animals (Gen 1:26), and transfer the words to Jesus Christ. It does not surprise that the older commentators on Hebrews often name Adam here[54] nor that Harold Attridge has written as follows: Hebrews may preserve

> the original anthropological meaning of the text, suggesting that the "world to come" is ultimately subject not to angels, but to human beings. The first and foremost of these is Jesus, who has already achieved the exalted status that is the destiny of all. Thus the association could be evoking an "Adamic" Christology. Hints of such a perspective may also be found in the following pericope, although in general Hebrews does not utilize the elements of such an Adamic Christology.[55]

It appears, then, that Paul was not the only early Christian to promote an Adam Christology; rather, there seems "to have been abroad in first generation Christianity an already quite sophisticated Adam christology."[56] But where did it come from? One might urge, given its likely presence in Mark, Luke, and Hebrews, that it was common property.[57] Hebrews, however, is not wholly outside the Pauline sphere of influence;[58] and if one stays with my thought experiment, the authors of Mark and Luke knew Paul. One could, then, trace everything back to Paul.[59] This would harmonize with Seyoon Kim's theory that Paul interpreted his experience on the Damascus road as a manifestation of the divine glory, which in turn led him to think of Christ as the new, eschatological Adam.[60] One might, in response, object that Phil 2:5-11 both preserves a traditional "hymn" and features an Adam Christology. The Adamic interpretation, however, is hardly secure.[61] Beyond that, even if Phil 2:5-11 is (as I think) largely a piece of tradition,[62] that tradition might well have originated in a community "founded by Paul."[63]

The difficulty of determining whether Paul invented his Adam Christology or developed a typology he inherited from his Christian tradition stands for a host of problems. How do we ascertain whether a theological theme that Paul advances was his invention or not? The usual strategy has been to suppose that the appearance of a theme outside of Paul implies his debt to tradition. If, however, two of Paul's onetime coworkers wrote the Gospels of Mark and Luke, using them in this way becomes dubious. If one further reckons, as I do, with the direct or indirect influence of Paul upon Hebrews, 1 Peter,[64] 2 Peter,[65] 1 Clement,[66] and (to a lesser extent) the Johannine literature, the procedure becomes even more difficult. One could in fact argue that the only first-century sources truly independent of Paul may be Matthew, James, Jude, Revelation, and the Didache (or its basic building blocks); yet two of those—Matthew and James—arguably contain anti-Pauline elements,[67] which of course entails acquaintance or familiarity with Paul.

The problem is obvious. The smaller the number of early Christian sources that we judge to lay beyond Pauline influence, the harder it is to know where the apostle was being innovative and where he was reworking tradition, and so the harder it is for us to construct a history of early Christian theological ideas.

Wilhelm Bousset once proposed that the title "Son of God" was "an independent creation of Paul."[68] I have never taken this idea seriously. The reason has always been my belief that a number of the relevant sources that employ the title, including Mark and Luke, supply evidence independent of Paul. If, however, I were to ponder the issue within the boundaries of my thought experiment, it would be more difficult to establish that Bousset must have been wrong.

(5) **Paul and Acts**. I leave to the last the most obvious implication of my thought experiment. It is this. If the person who wrote Acts was the Luke of Phlm 24 (cf. Col 4:14; 2 Tim 4:11), then he clearly knew Paul fairly well. What would be the consequences? It would not follow that the Pauline sections of Acts must be unsullied history. The idea that eye-witnesses always give us the past is left over from yesterday's apologetics. A sometime companion of Paul could have misremembered and/or misconstrued some things or even many things. He could, despite his admiration for the apostle, have disagreed with him on various matters and had his own theological agenda, which he wished to promote in his writings. He could have used Paul as a mouthpiece, just as Plato fictionalized Socrates and used him as a mouthpiece, to get across ideas he believed to be important. Luke could also have incorporated rumors and legends that he heard at second-hand, and he could have left out incidents or facts he thought unedifying.[69]

Yet if Luke had been Paul's coworker for a period of time, Acts is not likely to come from the second century, as a number of scholars today argue.[70] Additionally, we would have to be more open-minded about the possibility that, despite the idealized portrait of the apostle and of the early church in Acts, Luke has more things right than many of us have been wont to suppose.[71]

From Thought Experiment to History

So much for my thought experiment. Of what value is it? Despite the pose I have adopted until now, I here confess that, for me, it is not purely hypothetical. I say this for two reasons. The first is that the ecclesiastical traditions about Mark and Luke still have learned defenders, and for all I know those defenders may be correct. I do not claim to know that they are correct, only that they are not obviously wrong. Joseph Fitzmyer made a reasonable case for the Lukan authorship of Luke-Acts, and Claus-Jürgen Thornton and Maurice Casey have forwarded their own arguments for coming to the same verdict.[72] As for Mark, Joel Marcus has recently surveyed all the issues and arrived at the eminently reasonable conclusion: "not proven."[73] More expansively: "our Gospel probably was written by someone named Mark … The possibility cannot be excluded that this Mark was the John Mark of Acts and the Pauline correspondence."[74] Since I agree, I cannot dismiss as necessarily false the premise of my thought experiment, namely, that Paul, John Mark, and Luke all knew each other. The second reason why my thought experiment is more than theoretical for me is that even if the old traditions about authorship are mistaken, clear links between Mark, Luke, and Paul remain.[75] Luke, to state the obvious, was not outside the Pauline orbit. Even if the Third Evangelist was never Paul's coworker, he was acquainted with a very large number of "traditions and memories of Paul and his mission."[76]

The situation with Mark is more controversial. Nonetheless, several scholars have drawn our attention to strong connections between Mark and Paul, and the sole explanation is not likely to be general Christian tradition.[77] There are significant overlaps between Paul's letters and Mark's Gospel in both ideas and terminology, and it is hard to shake the sense of a direct connection between Rom 14:14 ("I know and am persuaded in the Lord Jesus that nothing is unclean [κοινόν] in itself; but it is unclean [κοινόν] for anyone who thinks it unclean [κοινόν]") and 20 ("Do not, for the sake of food [βρώματος], destroy the work of God. All things are pure [πάντα μὲν καθαρά]") on the one hand and Mark 7:14-23 ("there is nothing outside a person that by going in can defile [κοινῶσαι] him"; "whatever goes into a person from outside cannot defile [κοινῶσαι]"; "thereby purifying all foods [καθαρίζων πάντα τὰ βρώματα]") on the other.[78] This is Marcus' general judgment on the relationship between Mark and Paul:

> Mark writes in the Pauline sphere of activity and shows some sort of Pauline influence on his thought, although he is not a member of a Pauline "school" in the same sense that the authors of Colossians-Ephesians and the Pastorals are; unlike them, he has not studied, internalized, and imitated Paul's letters. But neither is he hermetically sealed off from the influence of Paul.[79]

As I concur with these words, I cannot dismiss my thought experiment as of no practical value. On the contrary, and even aside from the issue of who wrote Mark and who wrote Luke-Acts, I must entertain the possibility that my hypothetical state of affairs might approximate to some degree the real historical situation. This in turn, and as we have seen, would raise question marks over all sorts of assumptions—such as the independence of Mark and Q and the utility of the criterion of multiple attestation—that have been foundational for much historical work.

Final Reflections

I am left with two unanswered questions. The first is this. How influential were Paul and his theological ideas? We should not, in my view, seriously entertain the sensationalistic proposal that the apostle was the real founder of Christianity.[80] We may even, furthermore, wonder about the much lesser claim that he should be esteemed, in the words of N. T. Wright, as the individual who "effectively invented 'Christian theology.'"[81] Maybe such an evaluation overestimates Paul's originality by overlooking his large debts to a Christian tradition that was, already in the first two decades, substantial and rich.[82] Wright's judgment may also betray captivity to the apostle's self-estimation: the apostle and his mission were, in Paul's own mind, crucially significant on a worldwide scale. Self-perception is, however, often skewed, and all the more when filtered through large religious claims and aspirations. Acts, with its idealized image of the all-important Paul, may mislead here. Nonetheless, self-perception is not always misperception, and the idolization of Paul in Acts could be as much a response to the man's actual historical significance as a generator of it. Given, then, that the apostle's theological thought appears, to greater or lesser degree, to have influenced a majority of books that come to us from the first Christian century, his influence may have been as far-reaching as the New Testament implies.[83]

Yet I remain unsure. This is because there is a second, closely related question. How representative are the extant documents? That is, how characteristic or typical of early Christianity—or, if one prefers, early Christianities—are the sources that have survived? Maybe Paul appears to us to have been so prominent and influential because the existing evidence is—due to happenstance and/or to a biased process of selection—partial and lop-sided. Perhaps our sources do not allow us to get an accurate fix either on the degree of Paul's originality or on the extent of his theological influence. Maybe there was even more theological diversity than meets us in the New Testament—that seems plausible enough—and maybe Paul was, in his time and place, less significant than our witnesses make him out to have been. What might we learn if an epistle written by Stephen of Jerusalem were to come to light or one from Peter or James (as opposed to the pseudepigrapha attributed to them in the New Testament)?

Mark's Gospel, Luke-Acts, and the epistles attributed to Paul make up almost 60 percent of the New Testament. This means that they constitute a sizeable portion of the texts that remain from the first century. If, moreover, one concurs that Hebrews, 1 and 2 Peter, and (perhaps) the Johannine literature are not wholly unaffected by Pauline theology, it might appear that Paul's theological tentacles reached far and wide. Yet this may be an illusion, the result of a prejudice that favored the preservation mostly of documents promoting a faith compatible with Pauline theology and the law-free gospel of the Gentile churches. Only a few fragments remain of the Gospel of the

Hebrews and the Gospel of the Nazoraeans, and we have no idea how much else has disappeared from the historical record[84] or how much of great importance never made it into a written text at all. Without, however, a knowledge of what has ceased to be, the task of evaluating the theological novelty, importance, and influence of Paul may well be beyond us.

Notes

1. According to Martin Hengel, *Acts and the History of Earliest Christianity* (Philadelphia: Fortress, 1980), pp. 108–9, apart from Acts 13, Luke may have minimized reporting about Cyprus because he "was only interested in the development of the Pauline mission"; thus Acts 11:19-20 and 15:39-40 remain undeveloped notices.
2. There was a sizeable Jewish population in Cyprus; cf. Philo, *Legatio ad Gaiam* 282; Josephus, *Ant.* 13.284-87.
3. I am aware that, with reference to the pre-70 CE Jesus movement, some now reject "Christian" and "Christianity" as anachronistic; and I concede that the words may encourage us to confuse later circumstances with earlier realities. Nonetheless, the usual alternatives are long and clunky—e.g., "Jews and Gentiles who believed in Jesus," a circumlocution which has the additional disadvantage of perhaps implying that they all believed exactly the same things—or of limited scope—e.g., "Nazarenes" (cf. Acts 24:5), which cannot be used of Gentile followers of Jesus—or misleading and parochial—e.g., the use of the unmodified "believers," as though others, such as non-Christian Jews, were not also religious believers. Moreover, the use of "Christian" probably arose before 70 CE, as soon as outsiders found it expedient to distinguish followers of Jesus from other groups or associations; cf. Acts 11:26; 26:28; 1 Pet 4:16; Josephus, *Ant.* 18.64; Suetonius, *Nero* 16.2; Tacitus, *Ann.* 15.44; CIL 4.679; and see Christopher P. Jones, "The Historicity of the Neronian Persecution: A Response to Brent Shaw," *NTS* 63 (2017): 148–51. For convenience, then, and despite the problems, I continue to use the traditional term.
4. See Acts 4:36-37; 11:22, 30; 12:12, 25; 13:1-3, 5, 13; 15:12, 37.
5. Bart D. Ehrman, *The Triumph of Christianity* (New York: Simon & Schuster, 2018), pp. 170–3, 286–94.
6. On this issue, see the instructive essay of Michael B. Thompson, "The Holy Internet: Communication between Churches in the First Christian Generation," in *The Gospels for All Christians*, edited by Richard Bauckham (Grand Rapids, MI/Cambridge, UK: Eerdmans, 1998), pp. 49–70. Although my approach in this chapter is different, my conclusions are more than compatible with his. Note also pp. 30–44 of Bauckham's essay, "For Whom Were the Gospels Written?" in the same volume. He argues that "the early Christian movement" was "a network of communities with constant, close communication among themselves." On the relevance of social network theory in this connection, see n. 83.
7. Note Rom 1:8; 15:26; 16:19; 1 Cor 16:1, 8-9, 19-20; 2 Cor 8:1-5; 9:2-4; Gal 2:11-14; Phil 1:12-14; 2:25-26; 4:15-16, 22; Col 4:7-9, 16; 1 Thess 1:6-10; 2:14-16. Here again I can refer to Thompson, "Holy Internet."
8. Here I drew attention in a footnote to Arland J. Hultgren, *The Rise of Normative Christianity* (Philadelphia: Fortress, 1994).

9   Dale C. Allison., Jr., *The Jesus Tradition in Q* (Harrisburg, PA: Trinity Press Intl., 1997), p. 45. Melanie Johnson-DeBaufre, *Jesus among Her Children: Q, Eschatology, and the Construction of Christian Origins*, HTS 55 (Cambridge, MA: Harvard University Press, 2005), p. 32, quoted these words and commented: "For Allison, modern and ancient Christianity is primarily a single, unified movement." I confess to being perplexed by such careless reading. My honest historical musings, which in this case have nothing to do with my theology, are qualified by "may" and "perhaps," and they imply absolutely nothing about modern Christianity, which no informed individual could regard as "a single, unified movement."
10 Note the overview of early redaction criticism in Joachim Rohde, *Rediscovering the Teaching of the Evangelists* (Philadelphia: Westminster, 1968).
11 Influential, representative works include H. E. Tödt, *The Son of Man in the Synoptic Tradition*, NTL (London: SCM, 1965); Paul D. Meier, "The Community of Q" (unpublished Ph.D. dissertation, University of Iowa, 1967); John S. Kloppenborg, *The Formation of Q: Trajectories in Ancient Christian Wisdom Collections*, SAC (Philadelphia: Fortress, 1987).
12 Note, e.g., Burton Mack, *The Lost Gospel: The Book of Q and Christian Origins* (San Francisco: Harper, 1993). According to Mack's reconstruction, the Q group "did not think of Jesus as a messiah or the Christ. They did not take his teachings as an indictment of Judaism. They did not regard his death as a divine, tragic, or saving event. And they did not imagine that he had been raised from the dead to rule over a transformed world" (p. 4). For a more even-handed evaluation of the importance of Q for discussions of early Christian diversity, see John S. Kloppenborg Verbin, *Excavating Q: The History and Setting of the Sayings Gospel* (Edinburgh: T&T Clark, 2000), pp. 345–79.
13 Walter Bauer, *Orthodoxy and Heresy in Earliest Christianity* (Philadelphia: Fortress, 1971).
14 See James D. G. Dunn, *Unity and Diversity in the New Testament: An Inquiry into the Character of Earliest Christianity* (Philadelphia: Westminster, 1977); Hultgren, *Rise of Normative Christianity*; and Karen L. King, "Factions, Variety, Diversity, Multiplicity: Representing Early Christian Differences for the 21st Century," *MTSR* 23 (2011): 216–37.
15 David C. Sim, *The Gospel of Matthew and Christian Judaism: The History and Social Setting of the Matthean Community*, SNTW (Edinburgh: T&T Clark, 1998), pp. 123–39.
16 Dale C. Allison, Jr., "Jas 2:14-26: Polemic against Paul, Apology for James," in *Ancient and New Perspectives on Paul*, edited by Tobias Nicklas, Andreas Merkt, and Joseph Verheyden, NTOA 102 (Göttingen: Vandenhoeck & Ruprecht, 2013), pp. 123–49.
17 See, e.g., John Dominic Crossan, *The Historical Jesus: The Life of a Mediterranean Jewish Peasant* (San Francisco: HarperSanFrancisco, 1991).
18 For the issues, see Rudolf Pesch, *Das Abendmahl und Jesu Todesverständnis*, QD 80 (Freiburg/Basel/Vienna: Herder, 1978), and I. Howard Marshall, "The Last Supper," in *Key Events in the Life of the Historical Jesus: A Collaborative Exploration of Context and Coherence*, edited by Darrell L. Bock and Robert L. Webb (Grand Rapids, MI: Eerdmans, 2009), pp. 560–75.
19 Robert L. Webb, "The Historical Enterprise and Historical Jesus Research," in Bock and Webb, *Key Events*, p. 62. Cf. E. P. Sanders, *The Historical Figure of Jesus* (London: Penguin, 1993), p. 263: "The passage in general has the strongest possible support, putting it on a par with the saying on divorce in terms of certainty: there are two

slightly different forms, which have reached us through two independent channels, the synoptic tradition and the letters of Paul."

20 Cf. the judgment of some that the Pauline version has priority over the versions in both Mark and Luke; So Eduard Schweizer, *The Good News according to Mark* (Atlanta: John Knox, 1976), pp. 300–2, and B. D. Smith, "The More Original Form of the Words of Institution," *ZNW* 83 (1992): 166–86.

21 Cf. 1 Cor 11:23 ("for I received from the Lord") and see Hyam Maccoby, "Paul and the Eucharist," *NTS* 37 (1991): 247–67, and Francis Watson, "'I Received from the Lord …': Paul, Jesus, and the Last Supper," in *Jesus and Paul Reconsidered: Fresh Pathways into an Old Debate*, edited by Todd D. Still (Grand Rapids, MI: Eerdmans, 2007), pp. 102–24.

22 According to Rudolf Bultmann, *Theology of the New Testament*, vol. 2 (New York: Charles Scribner's Sons, 1955), p. 9, "John is not of the Pauline school and is not influenced by Paul; he is, instead, a figure with his own originality and stands in an atmosphere of theological thinking different from that of Paul." C. H. Dodd, *The Interpretation of the Fourth Gospel* (Cambridge: Cambridge University Press, 1953), p. 5, was more measured: "That the evangelist has not escaped the powerful influence of the first great Christian theologian whose works are extant, is probable enough. But the actual range of Pauline influence upon Johannine thought has been exaggerated." Although work since Bultmann and Dodd has not much dissented from them on this issue, in my view this subject is ripe for reconsideration, and the sort of investigation undertaken in Albert E. Barnett, *Paul Becomes a Literary Influence* (Chicago: University of Chicago Press, 1941), needs to be carried forward with today's tools and methods.

23 See my article "Reflections on Matthew, John, and Jesus," in *Jesus Research: The Gospel of John in Historical Inquiry*, edited by James H. Charlesworth with Jolyon G. R. Pruszinski, Jewish and Christian Texts 26 (London: T&T Clark, 2019), pp. 47–69.

24 The most important passages are Irenaeus, *Haer.* 3.1.1, 4; Clement of Alexandria, *Quis div.* 42; Polycrates *apud* Eusebius, *H.E.* 5.24.3-4; and Dionysius *apud* Eusebius, *H.E.* 7.25.16. Cf. the second-century *Acts of John*, which relates multiple tales about John of Zebedee in Ephesus.

25 Acts 18-20; 1 Cor 15:32; 16:8; also 1 Tim 1:3; 2 Tim 1:18; 4:12. Paul wrote 1 Corinthians while in Ephesus and also, according to some scholars, Philippians and Philemon.

26 See Peder Borgen, "John and the Synoptics: Can Paul Offer Help?" in *Tradition and Interpretation in the New Testament: Essays in Honor of E. Earle Ellis*, edited by Gerald F. Hawthorne and Otto Betz (Grand Rapids, MI/Tübingen: Eerdmans/Mohr Siebeck, 1987), pp. 80–94. It is ironic that, in response to recent criticisms of the standard criteria of authenticity—see esp. Anthony Le Donne and Chris Keith, eds., *Jesus, History, and the Demise of Authenticity: The Rise and Fall of the Search for an Authentic Jesus. Authenticity after the Third Quest* (London/New York: T&T Clark, 2012)—some evangelical historians have taken to defending those criteria; so, e.g., Michael Licona, "Is the Sky Falling in the World of Historical Jesus Research?" *BBR* 26 (2016): 353–68. But the criteria were initially developed by scholars who had discarded the old ecclesiastical traditions about who wrote the canonical gospels. If one accepts those traditions, it is unclear how the criterion of multiple attestation is supposed to work, at least when it comes to Mark, Luke, and Paul.

27 Benedict Thomas Viviano, "The Historical Jesus in the Doubly Attested Sayings: An Experiment," *RB* 103 (1996): 367–410; reprinted in *Trinity—Kingdom—Church:*

Essays in Biblical Theology, NTOA 48 (Freiburg/Göttingen: Universitätsverlag/ Vandenhoeck & Ruprecht, 2001), pp. 21-63.

28 Viviano, "Historical Jesus," p. 367. On pp. 408-9, Viviano speaks of "the increased historical certitude which accompanies the method of listening carefully to two independent and early witnesses."

29 According to Kloppenborg, *Excavating Q*, pp. 80-7, "a date [for Q] in the late 50s or very early 60s is certainly possible," although he tentatively posits a later date for the final form. For an argument for a much earlier date—possibly in the forties—see my *Jesus Tradition in Q*, pp. 54-60.

30 See, e.g., Harry T. Fleddermann, *Mark and Q: A Study of the Overlap Texts*, BETL 122 (Leuven: University Press, 1995); Harry T. Fleddermann, *Q: A Reconstruction and Commentary*, BTS 1 (Leuven/Dudley, MA: Peeters, 2005), pp. 180-3. For criticism, see Franz Neirynck, "Mark and Q," in Fleddermann, *Mark and Q*, pp. 263-97.

31 B. H. Streeter, "St. Mark's Knowledge and Use of Q," in *Studies in the Synoptic Problem*, edited by W. Sanday (Oxford: Clarendon, 1911), p. 165. He later changed his mind on the matter. Alternatively, if one believed in proto-Luke—a theory which, in my judgment, has undeservedly fallen on hard times—one could perhaps imagine that Mark knew proto-Luke and desired to highlight largely different materials. In any case, it is hard to disagree with Ulrich Luz, "Looking at Q through the Eyes of Matthew," in *New Studies in the Synoptic Problem. Oxford Conference, April, 2008: Essays in Honour of Christopher M. Tuckett*, edited by P. Foster, A. Gregory, J. S. Kloppenborg, and J. Verheyden, BETL 239 (Leuven/Paris/Walpole, MA: Peeters, 2011), p. 587: "We would certainly like to know why the Gospel of Mark did not convey more of Jesus' teaching. Given the value accorded it by Mark, it is probable that he knew more than he actually records."

32 For arguments for the literary independence of Mark and Q, see Rudolf Laufen, *Die Doppelüberlieferungen der Logienquelle und des Markusevangeliums*, BBB 54 (Königstein: Peter Hanstein, 1980), and Christopher M. Tuckett, "Mark and Q," in *The Synoptic Gospels: Source Criticism and the New Literary Criticism*, edited by Camille Focant, BETL 110 (Leuven: Leuven University Press/Peeters, 1993), pp. 149-75.

33 For an overview of the data, see Viviano, "Historical Jesus."

34 My own teacher, W. D. Davies, *Paul and Rabbinic Judaism*, rev. ed. (New York: Harper & Row, 1967), p. 140, argued that "Paul is steeped in the mind and words of his Lord." My more modest, onetime conclusion was that "in his role as missionary and pastor, Paul regularly had occasion to turn to the Jesus tradition"; see "The Missionary Discourse, Q 10:2-16: Its Use by Paul," in *Jesus Tradition in Q*, p. 119.

35 Cf. Günther Bornkamm, *Paul* (New York: Harper & Row, 1971), p. 110 (in Paul "the Jesus of history is apparently dismissed"), and more recently Michael Wolter, "Jesus bei Paulus," in *The Rise and Expansion of Christianity in the First Three Centuries of the Common Era*, edited by Clare K. Rothschild and Jens Schröter (Tübingen: Mohr Siebeck, 2013), pp. 205-32.

36 Wilhelm Heitmüller, "Zum Problem Paulus und Jesus," in *Das Paulusbild in der neueren deutschen Forschung*, edited by Karl Heinrich Rengstorf and Ulrich Luck, Wege der Forschung 24 (Darmstadt: Wissenschaftliche Buchgesellschaft, 1969), pp. 124-243, and Ulrich Wilckens, "Jesusüberlieferung und Christuskerygma–zwei Wege urchristlicher Überlieferungsgeschichte," *ThViat* 10 (1966): 310-39.

37 See esp. Michael Thompson, *Clothed with Christ: The Example and Teaching of Jesus in Romans 12.1-15.13*, JSNTSS 59 (Sheffield: JSOT Press, 1991), and my early article,

"The Pauline Epistles and the Synoptic Gospels: The Pattern of the Parallels," *NTS* 28 (1982): 1–32.

38 So, e.g., Oscar Cullmann, *The Christology of the New Testament*, rev. ed., NTL (Philadelphia: Westminster, 1963), pp. 166–81, and George W. E. Nickelsburg, "Son of Man," in *ABD* (1992) 6: 147–8.
39 See Allison, "Missionary Discourse," in *Jesus Tradition in Q*, pp. 109–10.
40 For this possibility (without the hypothesis that the author of Luke-Acts knew Paul), see C. M. Tuckett, "Paul and the Synoptic Mission Discourse," *ETL* 60 (1984): 378.
41 E.g., the debate as to whether Paul, in 1 Corinthians 15, assumes that Jesus' tomb was empty would be affected if the individuals who composed Mark 16 and Luke 24 were, at some point, members of the Pauline network.
42 See further Allison, "Missionary Discourse," pp. 111–19.
43 For the Adamic interpretation of Phil 2:5-11, see James D. G. Dunn, *The Theology of Paul the Apostle* (Grand Rapids, MI/Cambridge, UK: Eerdmans, 1998), pp. 281–8, and N. T. Wright, *Paul and the Faithfulness of God, Book II Parts III and IV* (Minneapolis, MN: Fortress, 2013), p. 686.
44 Cf. also Paul's use of the idea of "new creation" in 2 Cor 5:17 and Gal 6:15 and his understanding of Christ as the divine εἰκών ("image") Rom 8:29; 1 Cor 15:49; 2 Cor 3:18; 4:4; and Col 1:15.
45 See Andreas Lindemann, "Die Auferstehung der Toten: Adam und Christus nach 1.Kor 15," in *Eschatologie und Schöpfund: Festschrift für Erich Grässer zum siebzigsten Geburtstag*, edited by Martin Evang, Helmut Merklein, and Michael Wolter, BZNW 89 (Berlin: de Gruyter, 1997), pp. 155–67, and Stephen Hultgren, "The Origin of Paul's Doctrine of the Two Adams in 1 Corinthians 15.45-49," *JSNT* 25 (2003): 343–70.
46 Cf. Rudolf Pesch, *Das Markusevangelium 1 Teil. Kommentar zu Kap. 1,1-8,26*, 2nd ed., HTKNT 2/1 (Freiburg/Basel/Vienna: Herder, 1977), pp. 94–6, and H. Mahnke, *Die Versuchungsgeschichte im Rahmen der synoptischen Evangelien: Ein Beitrag zur frühen Christologie*, BBET 9 (Frankfurt am Main/Bern/Las Vegas: Peter Lang, 1978), pp. 28–38. This interpretation is in line with patristic tradition; cf. Justin, *Dial.* 103; Irenaeus, *Haer.* 5.21.2; Athanasius, *Frag. Matt* in PG 27:1368A; etc.
47 Cf. Gen 2:18-20 (Adam names the animals); Jub. 3:1-3, 28; LAE 8:1-3; 37:1-3; Apoc. Mos. 15:3; 16:2; 24:4; 29:14, 16; 2 En. 58:2-6.
48 LAE 13:3-15:3 (the angels worship Adam); 21:1-3 (the angels assist Eve even after the fall); 22:1-2 (Michael teaches Adam how to farm); 33:1-3 (two angels guard Adam and Eve); Apoc. Mos. 29:1-6, 14 (angels intercede for Adam after the fall); *Apocalypse of Sedrach* 5:2 (the angels worship Adam).
49 ARN A 1: "Adam was reclining in the Garden of Eden and the ministering angels stood before him, roasting meat for him and cooling wine for him."
50 LAE 4:2: "And Adam said to Eve, 'The Lord apportioned this for animals and beasts to eat, but for us there used to be the food of angels.'"
51 Mark has: "and the angels served (διηκόνουν) him." BDAG, s.v., gives the first meaning of διακονέω as "wait on someone at table," and this is the sense it has just a few verses later, in Mark 1:31, where Peter's mother-in-law "serves" Jesus and the disciples.
52 Cf. Joel Marcus, *Mark 1-8*, AB 27A (New York: Doubleday, 2000), p. 169, and see further my article "The Baptism of Jesus and a New Dead Sea Scroll," *Biblical Archaeology Review* 18 (1992): 58–60. Marcus also (on p. 246) suggests that Jesus is Adam's counterpart in Mark 2:27-28: "The sabbath was made for man, not man for the sabbath; so, the Son of man is lord even of the sabbath."

53 Cf. Charles Fox Burney, *The Aramaic Origin of the Fourth Gospel* (Oxford: Clarendon Press, 1922), pp. 47–8; Joachim Jeremias, "Ἀδάμ," *TDNT* 1 (1964): 141; John Nolland, *Luke 1–9:20*, WBC (Nashville: Thomas Nelson, 1989), p. 173; Gavin Ortlund, "Image of Adam, Son of God: Genesis 5:3 and Luke 3:38 in Intercanonical Dialogue," *JETS* 57 (2014): 673–88; and Yongbom Lee, "Jesus, Son of Adam and Son of God (Luke 3.38): Adam-Christ Typologies in Luke-Acts," in *The Earliest Perceptions of Jesus in Context: Essays in Honour of John Nolland on His 70th Birthday*, edited by Aaron W. White, Craig A. Evans, and David Wenham, LNTS 566 (London: Bloomsbury T&T Clark, 2018), pp. 120–8. The temptation narratives in the gospels certainly moved many church fathers to think about Adam; cf. Ambrose, *Comm. Luke* 4.7, 14, and see Klaus-Peter Köppen, *Die Auslegung der Versuchungsgeschichte, unter besonderer Berücksichtigung der Alten Kirche*, BGBE 4 (Tübingen: Mohr Siebeck, 1961), pp. 79–85.

54 E.g., Matthew Poole, *Annotations on the Holy Bible*, 3 vols. (London: Henry G. Bohn, 1846) 3.815, and John Wesley, *Explanatory Notes upon the New Testament* (London: Epworth, 1950), p. 814 ("The words here cited concerning dominion were doubtless in some sense applicable to Adam, although in their complete and highest sense they belong to none but the second Adam").

55 Harold Attridge, *The Epistle to the Hebrews: A Commentary on the Epistle to the Hebrews*, Hermeneia (Philadelphia: Fortress, 1989), p. 75; cf. Yongbom Lee, *The Son of Man as the Last Adam: The Early Church Tradition as a Source of Paul's Adam Christology* (Eugene, OR: Pickwick, 2012), pp. 63–8.

56 Dunn, *Theology of Paul*, 203.

57 One could in fact trace it back to the Jesus tradition if one interpreted words about the Son of man to be about the son of Adam; see Joel Marcus, "Son of Man as Son of Adam," *RB* 110 (2003): 1–24, 370–86, and Lee, *Son of Man*.

58 Cf. 13:23 ("our brother Timothy") and note Attridge, *Hebrews*, 30: Paul and the author of Hebrews "certainly derive from the same wing of the early church that took a critical attitude toward the Law and its applicability to followers of Christ."

59 Cf. Davies, *Paul*, 44. Davies suggests that if Jesus is implicitly compared to Adam in Luke 3:38–4:2, then "Luke may have owed this conception to Paul's doctrine of Christ as the Second Adam."

60 Seyoon Kim, *Paul and the New Perspective*, WUNT 2/140 (Tübingen: Mohr Siebeck, 2002).

61 For an overview of the problems, see Markus Bockmuehl, *The Epistle to the Philippians*, BNTC (London: A. & C. Black Ltd., 1998), pp. 131–3, and Larry W. Hurtado, *Lord Jesus Christ: Devotion to Jesus in Earliest Christianity* (Grand Rapids, MI/Cambridge, UK: Eerdmans, 2003), pp. 120–3.

62 But see the doubts of Bockmuehl, *Philippians*, pp. 117–20.

63 So Jerome Murphy-O'Connor, *Paul: A Critical Life* (Oxford: Clarendon, 1996), p. 226. Cf. Jerry L. Sumney, *Steward of God's Mysteries: Paul and Early Church Tradition* (Grand Rapids, MI: Eerdmans, 2017), p. 57: "While the liturgy was not composed by Paul, some do think that it was composed by someone within his sphere of influence. Thus we must be careful about how we use this piece to identify what the church before and outside Paul's influence believed."

64 See Paul J. Achtemeier, *1 Peter: A Commentary on First Peter*, Hermeneia (Minneapolis, MN: Fortress, 1996), pp. 15–19. His cautious conclusion is that "while there are some developments of Pauline ideas in 1 Peter, along with certain Pauline turns of phrase, 1 Peter is not a deliberate attempt to theologize in the Pauline mode, or to defend Paulinism as a way of carrying on theological reflections" (p. 19).

65 3:15-16 explicitly refers to Paul's letters.
66 Cf. the summary of Paul's work, suffering, and martyrdom in 1 Clem. 5:5-7. Clement knew 1 Corinthians and probably Romans; see Horacio E. Lona, *Der erste Clemensbrief*, KAV 2 (Göttingen: Vandenhoeck & Ruprecht, 1998), pp. 49–51, and Andrew F. Gregory, "1 Clement and the Writings That Later Formed the New Testament," in *The Reception of the New Testament in the Apostolic Fathers*, edited by Andrew Gregory and Christopher M. Tuckett (Oxford/New York: Oxford University Press, 2005), pp. 129–57.
67 For Matthew, see Sim, *Matthew and Christian Judaism*, pp. 188–211; Sim, "Matthew's Anti-Paulinism: A Neglected Feature of Matthean Studies," *HTS* 58 (2002): 767–83; Sim, "Matthew 7.21-23: Further Evidence of Its Anti-Pauline Perspective," *NTS* 53 (2007): 325–43. For James, see my article "Polemic against Paul." But for different verdicts regarding Matthew, see Joel Willitts, "Paul and Matthew: A Descriptive Approach from a Post-New Perspective Interpretative Framework," in Bird and Willitts, *Paul and the Gospels*, pp. 62–85, and Paul Foster, "Paul and Matthew: Two Strands of the Early Jesus Movement with Little Sign of Connection," in Bird and Willitts, *Paul and the Gospels*, pp. 86–114. My own inclination is to side with Sim, in part because I deem it unlikely that if we date Matthew 80–95, its author and his audience were unfamiliar with stories and controversies surrounding Paul.
68 Wilhelm Bousset, *Kryios Christos: A History of the Belief in Christ from the Beginnings of Christianity to Irenaeus* (Nashville/New York: Abingdon, 1970), pp. 206–7.
69 To argue that Luke's differences from Paul show that he could not have known him well is a fallacy. For this error, see Philipp Vielhauer, "On the 'Paulinism' of Acts," in *Studies in Luke-Acts: Essays Presented in Honor of Paul Schubert*, edited by Leander E. Keck and J. Louis Martin (Nashville/New York: Abingdon, 1996), p. 48. Contrast B. H. Streeter, *The Four Gospels: A Study of Origins, Treating of the Manuscript Tradition, Sources, Authorship, and Dates*, rev. ed. (London: Macmillan and Co., 1930), pp. 553–6: Luke could have known Paul well without adopting his characteristic theology; indeed, if Luke had become a Christian some time before "he became really intimate with Paul, we should not expect him in any fundamental way to change his own religious outlook." A friend or even coworker need not have been a disciple. Here the old argument of Adolf Harnack, *Luke the Physician: The Author of the Third Gospel and the Acts of the Apostles* (London/New York: Williams & Norgate/G. P. Putnam's Sons, 1907), pp. 121–45, retains its value.
70 E.g., Richard Pervo, *Acts: A Commentary*, Hermeneia (Minneapolis, MI: Fortress, 2009), pp. 5–7.
71 On the issues surrounding history in Acts, see esp. Charles Talbert, "What Is Meant by the Historicity of Acts?" in *Reading Luke-Acts in Its Mediterranean Milieu*, NovTSup 107 (Leiden/Boston: Brill, 2003), pp. 197–217.
72 Joseph A. Fitzmyer, *The Gospel according to Luke*, AB 28A (Garden City, NY: Doubleday, 1981), pp. 35–59; Joseph A. Fitzmyer, "The Authorship of Luke-Acts Reconsidered," in *Luke the Theologian: Aspects of His Teaching* (New York: Paulist Press, 1989), pp. 1–26; Claus-Jürgen Thornton, *Der Zeuge des Zeugen: Lukas als Historiker der Paulusreisen*, WUNT 56 (Tübingen: Mohr Siebeck, 1991), and Maurice Casey, *Jesus: Evidence and Argument or Mythicist Myths?* (London: Bloomsbury, 2014). Note also Craig Keener, *Acts: An Exegetical Commentary*, 4 vols. (Grand Rapids, MI: Baker Academic, 2012–15), 1:402-22; 3:2350-74.
73 Marcus, *Mark 1-8*, 24.
74 Ibid.

75   There is also, of course, the possibility that the tradition about Luke is correct and that about Mark incorrect, or vice versa, and likewise possible that both traditions are fiction and that Paul nonetheless knew the author of Mark and/or the author of Luke.
76   C. K. Barrett, *A Critical and Exegetical Commentary on the Acts of the Apostles*, vol. II: *Introduction and Commentary on Acts XV–XXVIII*, ICC (London/New York: T&T Clark Continuum, 1998), p. xxx. In this connection one should perhaps mention the opinion of some that the author of Luke-Acts was involved in the production of the pastoral epistles; see, e.g., Stephen G. Wilson, *Luke and the Pastoral Epistles* (London: SPCK, 1979), and Jerome D. Quinn, "The Last Volume of Luke: The Relation of Luke-Acts to the Pastoral Epistles," in *Perspectives on Luke-Acts*, edited by Charles H. Talbert (Edinburgh: T&T Clark, 1978), pp. 62–75. Those who date Acts to the second century can hold that our author studied the Pauline letters; so, e.g., Pervo, *Acts*, pp. 12–14.
77   E.g., K. Romaniuk, "Le Problème des Paulinismes l'Évangile de Marc," *NTS* 23 (1977): 266–77; Michael F. Bird, "Mark: Interpreter of Peter and Disciple of Paul," in *Paul and the Gospels: Christologies, Conflicts and Convergences*, edited by Michael F. Bird and Joel Willitts, LNTS 411 (London: T&T Clark, 2011), pp. 30–61; Joel Marcus, "Mark—Interpreter of Paul," in *Mark and Paul: Comparative Essays Part II: For and Against Pauline Influence on Mark*, edited by Eve-Marie Becker, Troels Engberg-Pedersen, and Mogens Müller, BZNW 199 (Berlin: de Gruyter, 2014), pp. 29–49; and Gerd Theissen, "'Evangelium' im Markusevangelium: Zum traditionsgeschichtlichen Ort des ältesten Evangelium," in Becker et al., *Mark and Paul*, pp. 63–86. For dissent, see Michael Kok, "Does Mark Narrate the Pauline Kerygma of 'Christ Crucified'? Challenging an Emerging Consensus on Mark as a Pauline Gospel," *JSNT* 37 (2014): 139–60. James G. Crossley, "Mark, Paul and the Question of Influences," in Bird and Willitts, *Paul and the Gospels*, pp. 10–29, is also critical, yet he ends his essay with this: "It seems reasonable enough to suggest that one [Paul or Mark] was at least aware of the other, perhaps one (or both) even taking a precise idea here and there from the other." For the novel hypothesis that Mark used 1 Corinthians, see Thomas P. Nelligan, *The Quest for Mark's Gospel: An Exploration of the Case for Mark's Use of First Corinthians* (Eugene, OR: Pickwick, 2015).
78   Cf. Thompson, *Clothed with Christ*, pp. 185–99; Robert Jewett, *Romans: A Commentary*, Hermeneia (Minneapolis, MI: Fortress, 2007), p. 859; and Bird, "Mark," pp. 49–51.
79   Marcus, *Mark 1-8*, 75.
80   One recalls William Wrede's *Paul* (London: Philip Green, 1907), in which Paul is "the second founder of Christianity," who turned Jesus' Jewish faith into a "religion of redemption." For a similar, more recent argument along these lines, see Hyam Maccoby, *The Mythmaker: Paul and the Invention of Christianity* (London: Weidenfeld and Nicholson, 1986). The idea has a long history; cf. the argument, from the eighteenth century, of Henry St. John and Viscount Bolingbroke, "Concerning Authority in Matters of Religion," in *The Works of Lord Bolingbroke*, 4 vols. (Philadelphia: Carey and Hart, 1841) 3: 422–9.
81   So N. T. Wright, *Paul and the Faithfulness of God, Book I, Parts I and II*, Christian Origins and the Question of God Volume 4 (Minneapolis, MI: Fortress, 2013), p. 26.
82   For an old statement of this view, see Archibald M. Hunter, *Paul and His Predecessors*, rev. ed. (Philadelphia: Westminster Press, 1961). For a more recent presentation, see Sumney, *Steward of God's Mysteries*, passim.

83   This is not historically incredible, for in the jargon of social network theory, Paul had, first, high "degree centrality," that is, he was linked face-to-face and through his letters to many others; second, he had high "betweenness centrality," that is, he was a bridge between otherwise unconnected network clusters (e.g., the communities he founded and those in Jerusalem, Antioch, and elsewhere); and third, he had "closeness centrality," that is, there were relatively few steps between him and most others in the early Christian network. For an introduction to social network theory, see Wenlin Liu, Anupreet Sidhu, Amanda M. Beacom, and Thomas W. Valente, "Social Network Theory," in *The International Encyclopedia of Media Effects*, edited by Patrick Rössler, Cynthia A. Hoffner, and Liesbet van Zoonen (New York: John Wiley & Sons, 2017), pp. 1–12.

84   According to Christoph Markschies, "The Canon of the New Testament in Antiquity: Some New Horizons for Future Research," in *Homer, the Bible, and Beyond: Literary and Religious Canons in the Ancient World*, edited by Margaret Finkelberg and Guy G. Stroumsa, Jerusalem Studies in Religion and Culture 2 (Leiden/Boston: Brill, 2003), p. 176, "we only possess 14% of the Christian literature of the 2nd century that, according to our sources, must have existed." Is there any reason to think that the situation for the first century is radically different? The Pauline corpus refers to at least three defunct letters (see 1 Cor 5:9; 2 Cor 2:3-4; Col 4:16), and one wonders whether the "many" (πολλοί) of Luke 1:1 should be dismissed as hyperbole.

10

Visions of Cyprus: A Phenomenological Background to Jewish and Christian Scripture

Jolyon G. R. Pruszinski

Under rare astronomical and meteorological conditions, a visual phenomenon known as the "Canigou Effect" allows a viewer from Marseille, France to see the Mt. Canigou Massif, a mountain in the Pyrenees which otherwise is totally obscured by the ocean due to the curvature of the earth (Figure 10.1). These rare conditions allow for the sudden "appearance" of an otherwise *invisible island* silhouetted against the setting sun. A nearly identically congruent geographic relationship exists between the biblical Mt. Zaphon, or "Jebel Aqra" as it is now known, on the Turkish-Syrian border and Cypriot Mt. Olympus. This parallel relationship could produce the same visual phenomenon—the appearance to a viewer on the slopes of Mt. Zaphon of an otherwise *invisible island* (actually the summit of Cypriot Mt. Olympus) in the sunset—under similar, rare conditions. Some of the Mt. Zaphon traditions that appear in the Hebrew Bible may themselves preserve traces of evidence of just such a phenomenon, but perhaps the best evidence comes from the late antique pseudepigraphon known as the *History of the Rechabites*, which purports to recount a vision of the *Isle of the Blessed Ones*. The attempt to locate the Isle of the Blessed Ones has, from antiquity, been inconclusive. However, it may have been unusual visions of Cyprus from the biblical Mt. Zaphon that provided the spark for literary appropriations of the Greek Blessed Isle legend in this popular, late antique text.

"Canigou Effect"

The visual phenomenon known as the "Canigou Effect," which has been observed in the western Mediterranean, may illuminate the possibility of an important visual relationship between Cyprus and the "Holy Land."[1] This atmospheric-astronomical effect allows a viewer from Marseille, France, to see, under particular, rare conditions, Mt. Canigou, a mountain in the Pyrenees, which is otherwise totally obscured by the ocean due to curvature of the earth.[4] This visual phenomenon

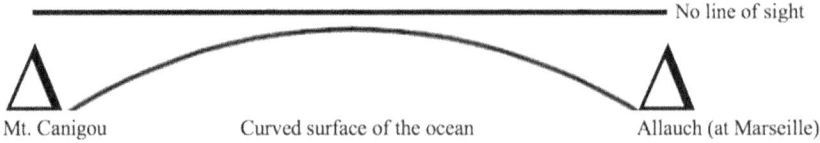

Figure 10.1 Line of sight between Marseille and Canigou.[2]

Figure 10.2 Canigou Effect.[3]

has been documented most extensively by Alain Origne, a research engineer at Laboratoire d'Astrophysique de Marseille.[5]

These conditions allow for the "appearance" of an otherwise invisible "island" silhouetted against the setting sun. This phenomenon is likely a subspecies of the Novaya Zemlya Effect,[6] which, through rare conditions[7] of atmospheric refraction, allows the viewing of objects at a distance which are actually below the horizon. When these atmospheric conditions occur in concert with the necessary astronomical conditions (during the alignment of the sunset with the Canigou Massif as seen from Marseille) the local effect is produced.[8]

As can be seen from Figure 10.2, even when the sun is very low on the horizon (though not yet behind the massif) there is still no land visible across the ocean. As the sun dips behind the Canigou Massif the mountain range "appears." Interestingly, the sun continues to shine through "below" the mountain at times.[9] This creates something of a floating effect, where the base of the "island" appears to glow brilliantly as it hovers slightly over the water.[10] Astronomically speaking, the setting sun must align with the mountain (Canigou) and the viewing location (Marseille).[11] Atmospherically, the sky must be entirely clear and the air must be stable over the ocean. These conditions typically occur when the low-altitude air is cold and dry.[12] Under these conditions, in Marseille, the phenomenon may be observed with the highest probability in November and in February (Figure 10.3).

Visions of Cyprus

Parallel Geography in the Eastern Mediterranean

Parallel favorable conditions appear to exist in the eastern Mediterranean as well.[13] Under normal circumstances, due to the curvature of the earth, Cyprus is not directly visible across the Mediterranean from the region of Antioch (Figure 10.4), now near the border of southern Turkey and western Syria.[14]

However, under similar astronomical[16] and meteorological[17] conditions to those required at Marseille, it should be possible to see across the ocean between the Antioch area and Cyprus due to their similar geographic relationship. These similarities include the time of year of sunset alignment (November 2 and February 8 at Marseille, and November 13 and January 28 in the Antioch region), the distance between the locations in question (263 kilometers from Marseille to Canigou and 306 kilometers from Jebel Aqra to Cypriot Mt. Olympus), and the aforementioned not quite tangential line of sight between respective observation points and mountaintops (Figure 10.5).

This congruency suggests the likelihood of rare Novaya Zemlya–type apparitions of the summit of the Cypriot Mt. Olympus from the coastal highland of the Antioch region during the calendrical periods of adequate alignment. The summit would appear as a small island visible only in the setting sun. It is, of course, prevented by significant cloud cover, and the summit of Cypriot Olympus, like many mountains, produces a micro-climate involving frequent localized cloud formation.

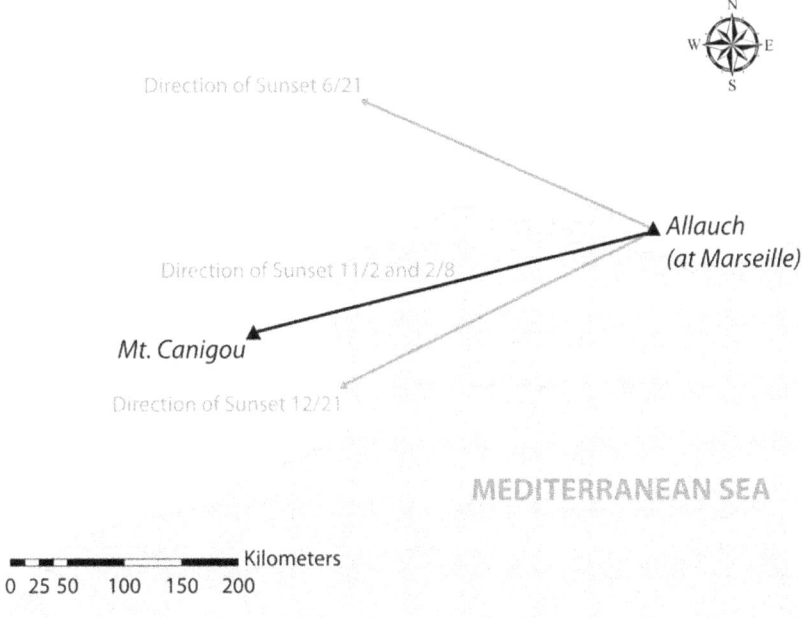

Figure 10.3 Calendrical conditions for sunset alignment between Marseille and Mt. Canigou.

No one would argue that Cyprus is continually wrapped in cloud, and yet in many of the texts we will discuss which are possibly linked to this phenomenon, obscuring cloud cover is a common theme. A common climatic effect that might account for such texts occurs normally when prevailing winds rise over higher elevations. The phenomenon is known as *orographic lift*. Air rises as it passes over a mountain. The water vapor present in the air condenses as it chills at elevation to produce clouds, typically up to heights well above the elevation of the summit. Such clouds then often continue in the direction of the prevailing wind. If such a mountain was not visible a significant distance downwind due to the curvature of the earth, the clouds produced by it would nevertheless be visible as they rose high above the mountain or continued downwind. Orographic lift produces this exact effect on Mount Olympus (Figure 10.6).[19]

Early Zaphon/Kasios Traditions

The location in the vicinity of Antioch that best matches the geographic parameters necessary for a Canigou Effect apparition of Cyprus is Jebel Aqra, the biblical Mt. Zaphon (on the modern-day Turkish-Syrian border). It is situated on the Mediterranean coast just south of the mouth of the River Orontes near Antioch (Figure 10.7).[20]

One might wonder if such a mountain would, in antiquity, have had anyone on it regularly enough to catch the proposed vision of the "Blessed Isle." The answer is "yes." Mt. Zaphon, known later as Mt. Kasios, was home in antiquity to a succession of cults, including Baal traditions preserved in both Ugaritic texts and the Hebrew Bible. While these traditions do not necessarily relate to a Canigou Effect–type vision explicitly, some of the themes and language preserved in the Zaphon traditions could be explained by the proposed phenomenon.[21]

The Baal Saphon (Zaphon) cult was active in several locations around the Mediterranean in antiquity, and in every instance, there was a relation to a geographic phenomenon that in some way replicated one of those present at Mt. Zaphon. The instances of worship in the near-environs of the mountain, like at Ugarit and Tyre, require no further explanation than proximity to the mountain itself. The locus of reverence in Egypt was related to a particular "mountain" and the nearby lake which produced a misty cloud cover reminiscent of that related to Baal's vanquished serpent foe.[23] But most significantly, we have record of recognition of Baal Sapon in *Marseille*,[24] which, as we have already mentioned, is the location in which the Canigou Effect has been observed and which exhibits such a congruency in its geographic relationships

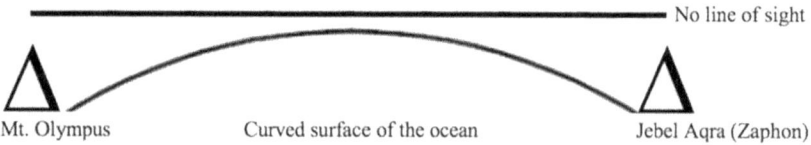

Figure 10.4 Line of sight between Mt. Zaphon and Cypriot Mt. Olympus.[15]

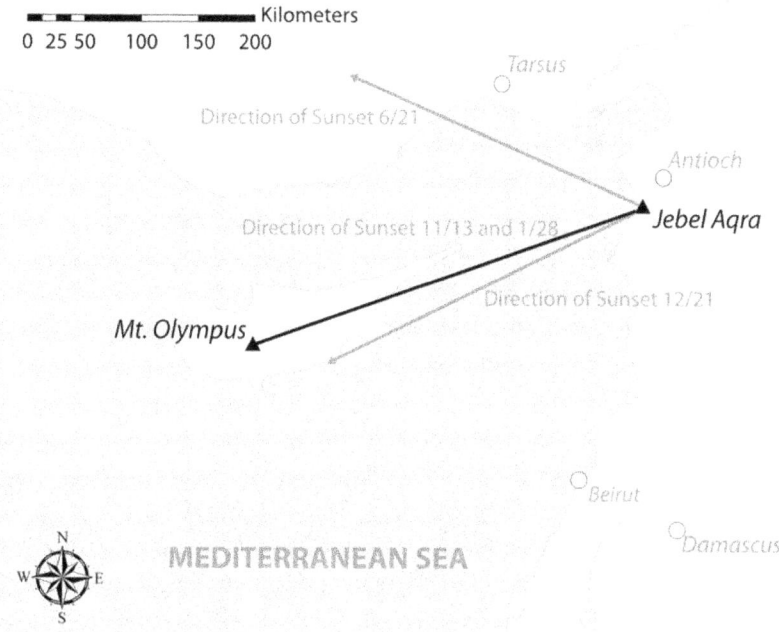

Figure 10.5 Calendrical conditions for sunset alignment between Jebel Aqra and Cypriot Mt. Olympus.

to Mt. Zaphon that we may conclude that the two likely produce similar visual phenomena. That Marseille was found to be a suitable location for the cult in the western Mediterranean would seem to confirm the strong connection between the two sites (postulated above).

The Hebrew Bible has of course appropriated and transformed many Zaphon traditions, some of which appear to preserve elements of a Canigou Effect–type phenomenon from Zaphon. Not only have many scholars suggested that Baal traditions were appropriated and attached, with some alteration, to YHWH in the Hebrew Bible, but holy mountain traditions from Zaphon came to be attached to holy mountains revered in the Hebrew Bible.[25]

The possibly Zaphon-connected Hebrew Bible texts are too numerous to catalog here exhaustively, so a few must suffice. One of the most obvious examples appears in the book of Exodus:

> [9] Then Moses and Aaron, Nadab, and Abihu, and seventy of the elders of Israel went up, [10] and they saw the God of Israel. Under his feet there was something like a pavement of sapphire stone, like the very heaven for clearness. [11] God did not lay his hand on the chief men of the people of Israel; also they beheld God, and they ate and drank. [12] The lord said to Moses, "Come up to me on the mountain, and wait there; and I will give you the tablets of stone, with the law and the commandment,

Figure 10.6 Satellite photo of a dust storm.[18] Clouds over Cypriot Mt. Olympus formed by orographic lift.

Figure 10.7 View south to Jebel Aqra/Zaphon/Kasios from the Turkish coast to the north.[22]

which I have written for their instruction." ¹³ So Moses set out with his assistant Joshua, and Moses went up into the mountain of God. ¹⁴ To the elders he had said, "Wait here for us, until we come to you again; for Aaron and Hur are with you; whoever has a dispute may go to them." ¹⁵ Then Moses went up on the mountain, and the cloud covered the mountain. ¹⁶ The glory of the lord settled on Mount Sinai, and the cloud covered it for six days; on the seventh day he called to Moses out of the cloud. ¹⁷ Now the appearance of the glory of the lord was like a devouring fire on the top of the mountain in the sight of the people of Israel. ¹⁸ Moses entered the cloud and went up on the mountain. Moses was on the mountain for forty days and forty nights.

(Exod 24:9-18, NRSV)

In this passage several relevant themes appear: (1) God, (2) the holy mountain, (3) shrouded in cloud, but at the same time the divinity has (4) the appearance of a bright fire, while being described as (5) standing on a clear-blue precious stone like lapis. Though not oceanic in location,[26] many later interpretative traditions still attribute the blue pavement under the feet of God as a reference to the waters of the ocean.[27]

Further Zaphon traditions likely appear in the book of Job:

⁵ The shades below tremble, the waters and their inhabitants.⁶ Sheol is naked before God, and Abaddon has no covering.⁷ He stretches out Zaphon over the void, and hangs the earth upon nothing.⁸ He binds up the waters in his thick clouds, and the cloud is not torn open by them.⁹ He covers the face of the full moon, and spreads over it his cloud. ¹⁰ He has described a circle on the face of the waters, at the boundary between light and darkness. ¹¹ The pillars of heaven tremble, and are astounded at his rebuke. ¹² By his power he stilled the Sea; by his understanding he struck down Rahab. ¹³ By his wind the heavens were made fair; his hand pierced the fleeing serpent. ¹⁴ These are indeed but the outskirts of his ways; and how small a whisper do we hear of him! But the thunder of his power who can understand?

(Job 26:5-14)

Baal traditions are being recycled in Job 26. This is shown not only by the use of "Zaphon" but also by reference to the "thunder of his power" and to the Baal legend of the defeat of the Sea/Death/Mot. Even beyond this recycling, there are clear resemblances to Canigou-Effect phenomena as previously described, the obscuring cloud and reference to the "face of the waters" as "the boundary between light and darkness." Most notable of all is the language of Zaphon stretched "over the void" (i.e., the sea) and the earth hung "upon nothing," as appears to be the case in a Canigou Effect.[28]

The book of Job not only preserves Zaphon traditions but also discusses the inaccessible dwelling-place of wisdom:

⁵ As for the earth, out of it comes bread; but underneath it is turned up as by fire.⁶ Its stones are the place of sapphires, and its dust contains gold .... ¹² But where shall wisdom be found? And where is the place of understanding? ¹³ Mortals do not

know the way to it, and it is not found in the land of the living .... ²⁰ Where then does wisdom come from? And where is the place of understanding? ²¹ It is hidden from the eyes of all living, and concealed from the birds of the air. ²² Abaddon and Death say, "We have heard a rumor of it with our ears." ²³ God understands the way to it, and he knows its place. ²⁴ For he looks to the ends of the earth and sees everything under the heavens.

(Job 28:5-6, 12-13, 20-24)

On the one hand, we see again the language of fire, shining blue gems, and gold underneath the earth, not unlike what we have seen earlier. Added to these elements, we also see a further connection to the idea of wisdom being located in a particular, hard-to-find place and to God knowing this location because he "looks to the ends of the earth." Given the combination of these themes as preserved in the book of Job, a perceptive Jew or Christian might think (had they seen a Canigou Effect–type vision from Zaphon) that they had managed to glimpse the dwelling of the wise.²⁹

Though it is unlikely that the New Testament book of Revelation is the direct result of a vision on biblical Mt. Zaphon,³⁰ there are many themes which appear in Revelation that are likely received and reinterpreted Zaphon traditions.³¹ Chapter 21 is particularly rich in the themes discussed above including the victory over the sea, victory over death, a heavenly vision, God as the source of life-giving water, a burning water-surface associated with the abyss or sea, vision from a mountain top, shiningly bright divine residence, and a jeweled foundation of the divine residence.³² Revelation 21 also emphasizes the idea of constant light in the heavenly city (21:23-25) which might preserve data derived from the viewing of a Canigou-Effect phenomenon.³³

Thus, themes preserved in these Jewish and Christian texts appear to have some Zaphon-linked background. They also include descriptions of visually perceived phenomena with marked similarities to those present in a Canigou Effect. The evidence is circumstantial but may suggest support for Zaphon-based viewing of a Canigou-Effect type of phenomenon.

Traditions Related to the Isle(s) of the Blessed Ones

No investigation of a mysterious "island" in the Mediterranean would be complete without consideration of the legend of the *Isle of the Blessed Ones*. Though the legend appears in many of the classic Greek works which have been preserved from antiquity, the attempt to locate the Isle of the Blessed Ones has, of course, met only with ambiguous results. Hesiod writes that to some very fortunate ancients:

Zeus the father, Cronus' son, bestowed life and habitations far from human beings and settled them at the limits of the earth; and these dwell with a spirit free of care on the Islands of the Blessed beside deep-eddying Ocean—happy heroes, for whom the grain-giving field bears honey-sweet fruit flourishing three times a year.³⁴

In other texts, such as Pindar's *Olympian Odes*[35] and Plato's *Gorgias*,[36] the righteous dead are assigned a life of ease and reward in the Blessed Isles.

Various locations have been proposed for this blessed island, based mostly on reports of mild climate, including Sicily, the Aeolian Islands, the Aegadian Islands, other small Sicilian islands, Bermuda, the Lesser Antilles, the Azores, Madeira, Cape Verde, and the Canary Islands. Indeed, the collective name for these latter four archipelagos, "Macaronesia," is derived specifically from the association with the Blessed Isles made by Greek geographers of antiquity.[37]

The legend is ultimately appropriated in a late antique Christian text, the *History of the Rechabites*. But why would Jews or Christians, who had already known of this renowned legend for centuries,[38] incorporate it into their own devotional literature in the *History of the Rechabites*? They had never done so previously in a literary sense.[39] My hypothesis is that unusual visions of Cyprus viewed from the coastal mountains of the Antioch region may have provided the spark for literary appropriations of the Greco-Roman Blessed Isle legend in this popular, late antique pseudepigraphic text.

History of the Rechabites

Not much is known about the Rechabites before the revelation of the abode of the Blessed which appears in our text. They are mentioned fleetingly in Jeremiah 35 as those who were faithful to the command of their ancestor Jonadab not to drink wine, nor to build houses, nor to engage in agriculture even when tempted. They are held up by Jeremiah—and indeed God—as an example against the rest of Judah.[40] The text of the core of the *History of the Rechabites* is thus something of a midrashic expansion on Jeremiah 35 which explains, among other things, how the Rechabites came to be preserved by God for all time in their blessed abode. Other traditions have been grouped with it, or around it, including the travelogue of the righteous man Zosimus.[41] As we have the extant text today in Greek and Syriac, an angel guides the holy Zosimus to the abode of the Rechabites where he learns of their blessed state and way of life. All commentators recognize the composite nature of the text and, as such, there are many speculations regarding the earliest literary stratum and whether this earliest form was Jewish or Christian.[42] The question, however, of what would have precipitated the appropriation of the Blessed Isle legend into the amalgamated *History of the Rechabites* remains entirely unanswered. Some data about the Isle from our text may be illuminating.

Data from *History of the Rechabites*

The Isle of the Blessed Ones is described in the text as a physical place, away from the world of corruption, that is, away from the contaminated world of men. And while it is away from the inhabited world and its corruption (HistRech 1:2), it is not heaven. Though Zosimus is guided on a journey by an angel (1:3, 2:1), it is not a heavenly journey as in many apocalypses. Although he is lifted up briefly into the heavens by means of two giant trees,[43] this brief elevation is only the means of conveyance from one physical, earthly location to another (3:1-4). This physical-earthly location of the abode of the Blessed Ones allows, presumably, for the faint, but real, possibility of glimpsing it on earth, which Zosimus does.[44]

The Greek Blessed Isle legends place it in the west.[45] In this detail our extant texts of *History of the Rechabites* agree—namely that the *Isle of the Blessed Ones* is across the great sea (2:6,[46] 2:6-7[47]), which is considered to be in the west.[48] Significantly, this reckoning corresponds to an alignment with the setting sun.

The abode of the blessed is described as being "in the midst" (2:8a) of a cloud and that "(something) like a dense bulwark of cloud" or "wall" (2:8) of cloud extends from the water up to heaven, separating the Isle from those who would see it (10:7, 11:5, 17:3a, 17:4b, 17:5b, [Syriac]; 4:2, 4:8-9, 10:8 [Greek]).

Another interesting aspect of the separation of the Isle is that the waters surrounding the island rise up around it (10:7), obscuring it.[49] In the Syriac manuscripts, the Rechabites claim that when they were settled in their abode: "God commanded and the waters rose up from the deep abyss and encircled this place" (10:7a).[50] In the Greek recensions, the description of this event suggests instead that God miraculously parted the water to expose an island, not unlike the parting of the Red Sea, and that "water came up out of the abyss" (ἀνῆλθεν ὕδωρ ἀπὸ τῆς ἀβύσσου, 10:7). In either case, the suggestion is that the Isle is obscured by the water which surrounds it in some supernatural fashion.

Finally, the *Isle of the Blessed Ones* is described as perpetually bathed in light. The Rechabites explain: "The land in which we are is filled with a glorious light so darkness and night do not enter it. And we possess a shining appearance and dwell in light" (11:5a-5b).[51]

As it pertains to the aforementioned proposed visual phenomenon, the Isle in question would be located across the "great sea" (2:6) just as Cyprus is from Syria.[52] The waters surrounding the island rise up around it (10:7), obscuring it, just as the ocean obscures Cyprus from Western Syria under normal conditions. Further, the island is always bathed in light (11:5 [Syriac]), and the proposed visual effect allows the sun, as it leaves the rest of the world in darkness, to appear to set into the location of the island and join it. The island becomes visible only in silhouette against the sun.

Perhaps the most convincing evidence from our text is the fact that a cloud normally conceals the island (2:8, 10:8). As we have seen, even if the astronomical and other atmospheric factors were otherwise perfectly aligned for a Canigou-Effect type of phenomenon, orographic lift might still cause the peak to be obscured, hiding it within a "bulwark of cloud," very like what is described in the *History of the Rechabites*.

Lacking Similar Detail in Greek and Roman Blessed Isle Legends

Many of the characteristics described above indicate a divergence from the most popular versions of the earliest legends of the Blessed Isle. Analysis of these "classical" texts is somewhat difficult, as the Blessed Isles legends are often conflated in Greco-Roman sources with legends of Elysium, Hades, Atlantis, and remote geographies like the dwelling of "the Aithiopians."⁵³ It is certainly true that the Greek and Roman legends regularly envision the Blessed Isles as a real earthly place. They are certainly to be found in the west across the great sea (or the encircling river), and antique geographic tropes certainly make use of the language of inaccessibility for remote or exotic locations.⁵⁴ However, it is typical in Greco-Roman traditions that a single *Island of the Blessed Ones* is not envisioned but rather *islands*.⁵⁵ There are similarly no well-established preexisting themes in early sources of constant light in the abode of the blessed ones,⁵⁶ nor shrouding or concealing of the place with a cloud,⁵⁷ nor of the surrounding water rising up around the place to protect or conceal it.⁵⁸

Environmental Phenomena as Literary Catalysts

Though it may seem strange, it is not at all unprecedented for environmental catalysts to act as literary inspiration for the location of mythic spaces. In *1 Enoch*, for example, it is likely that the presence of Mount Hermon suggested to the author the location of the descent of the angels. In *1 Enoch* 6 it is written:

> The angels ... said to one another, "Come, let us choose wives for ourselves from among the daughters of man and beget us children. ..." And they descended into 'Ardos, which is the summit of Hermon. And they called the mount Armon, for they swore and bound one another by a curse.⁵⁹
>
> (1 En. 6:2-6 [*OTP*])

And elsewhere in *1 Enoch* it appears that Hermon suggests the location of the Garden of Eden, paradise, or the throne of God:⁶⁰

> He [Michael] answered, saying, "This tall mountain which you saw whose summit resembles the throne of God is (indeed) his throne, on which the Holy and Great Lord of Glory, the Eternal King, will sit when he descends to visit the earth with goodness. And as for this fragrant tree, not a single human being has the authority to touch it until the great judgment, when he shall take vengeance on all and conclude (everything) forever. This is for the righteous and the pious. And the elect will be presented with its fruit for life. He will plant it in the direction of the northeast, upon the holy place—in the direction of the house of the Lord, the Eternal King."
>
> (1 En. 25:3-5)

In a similar vein, the tradition of Aphrodite being birthed from the sea off the coast of Cyprus is likely derived from observation of a natural phenomenon near Paphos. The action of crashing waves in a south-west wind forms a feature that "looks exactly like a human figure literally 'rising from the sea' and spreading long hair and dripping arms."⁶¹ Robin Lane Fox's magisterial, if at times speculative, *Travelling Heroes in the Epic Age of Homer* is brimming with further examples of correlative relationships between ancient literary traditions and physical geography.

Thus, it seems clear that a Canigou Effect–type vision could have provided an environmental catalyst which sparked the Jewish and Christian literary appropriation of the legend of the Blessed Isle. But are there any other indications that the Antioch region would have been a likely locus of provenience?

Provenience: Palestine/Syria

While there has been hearty disagreement over whether the earliest parts of the text of the *History of the Rechabites* had a Jewish or Christian provenience, most experts have agreed over a Palestinian or near-Palestinian origin in the northern Levant. Similarly, most experts have noted that the ascetic characteristics of the lives of the Rechabites, exaggerated in the descriptions of Zosimus' life at the beginning and end of the text, suggest if not actual composition in monastic or ascetic circles, then at least favorable reception in those communities.[62] While it is not in Palestine, Antioch could reasonably count as "near-Palestinian," and none of the arguments for Palestinian origin prevent a near-Palestinian origin.[63] Interestingly, the presence of two miraculously tall, heaven-scraping trees which serve as Zosimus' mode of transport across the ocean, may point to a provenience somewhere north of Palestine in the Lebanon range. Palestine was not known for its large trees, but the enormous "cedars of Lebanon" were renowned and could have inspired an author who had them to hand.[64] And additionally, the nearby city of Antioch was home to the kind of robust Jewish and Christian literary communities in late antiquity that might have generated a popular text like the *History of the Rechabites*.[65]

It has been established that there was probably significant enough cultic activity on Mt. Zaphon in antiquity to allow for viewing of the visual phenomenon in question. However, it is also necessary to consider whether in later years, when known as Mt. Kasios in the Hellenistic and Late Antique eras, the mountain would have had enough activity on it to allow the reasonable possibility for viewing the phenomenon in question.

During the Hellenistic era, Mt. Kasios was a prominent locus of the Olympian cult and was considered (one of) the home(s) of Zeus. The Emperor Julian is even reported, according to Libanius,[66] to have had an epiphanic vision of Zeus on Mt. Kasios in 363 CE. Robin Lane Fox suggests that coinage[67] from Seleucia at the time shows the pillared temple on the summit surrounding a conical rock, said to represent perhaps not the mountain per se but Zeus Kasios himself.[68] However, it is certainly possible that the conical rock represents the vision of the distant peak of Cypriot Olympus to the west as only rarely viewable from the summit of Mt. Kasios.

Christian hermits were also very active on the mountain in late antiquity and founded a monastery[69] near the tree line. They intended to supplant the "pagan" cult. The caves all over the high slopes were occupied by ascetics. Several Christian literary giants, like Diodorus, Chrysostom, and Theodore of Mopsuestia (the latter two of whom also studied under Libanius in Antioch), likely spent time here, as well as Simeon Stylites (the younger).[70]

Mt. Kasios was a very highly populated mountain at a time when Christian contestation with traditional Greco-Roman religion was very active. Against this historical background we should recognize that its highly trafficked summit region afforded ample opportunity for the religious in its vicinity to catch a fleeting glimpse of Cyprus (or the *Isle of the Blessed Ones*), possibly catalyzing its Christian appropriation of the earlier Blessed Isle legend in the *History of the Rechabites*.

Conclusion

According to the argument set forth in this chapter, it is likely that a visual phenomenon similar to the Canigou Effect is visible from the summit of Jebel Aqra under rare but predictable astronomical and atmospheric conditions. This phenomenon may have led to the development of traditions linked to the site which preserve evidence of the phenomenon, such as in the Baal cycle and the Hebrew Bible. The most compelling language which seems to preserve evidence of this visual phenomenon appears in the late antique pseudepigraphon known as the *History of the Rechabites*. It seems likely, based on the account of the location of the Isle of the Blessed preserved in the *History of the Rechabites*, that a Canigou Effect–type vision from the summit of Jebel Aqra provides the phenomenological catalyst which sparked the appropriation of the Blessed Isle legend by a Jewish or, more likely, Christian author, a legend which had otherwise been largely neglected in those traditions.

The primary objection to the proposal set forth in this chapter is the consideration that the description of the location of the Isle in the *History of the Rechabites* may be based solely on literary precedents[71] or tropes and not on an actual environmental-phenomenological spark. Unfortunately, no data, not even modern confirmation of the phenomenon from Jebel Aqra, could definitively prove that the proposed vision led to the appropriation of the legend of the Blessed Isle in the *History of the Rechabites*. Even that confirmation should not be expected any time soon since the summit of Jebel Aqra has been off-limits to civilians for decades due to its designation as a military zone. The recent Syrian conflict has not ameliorated the situation.[72]

We must make one final consideration, however, and it pertains to the importance of lines of sight in the evaluation of holy space and of the location of temples in particular. In her article "Beyond the Temple: Blurring the Boundaries of 'Sacred Space,'" Eleanor Grey has set forth excellent reasons to consider sacred space in the Greek and Roman cosmology as not simply involving the demarcated precincts of a temple, or holy site, but the spaces that are seen from that site.[73] Fascinatingly, Fox confirms this priority in his discussion of the siting of the Barlaam Monastery on Jebel Aqra with respect to lines of sight. He writes:

> As [Symeon Stylites the younger's] blessing and prophecies proved their worth, they attracted important patrons, including the Byzantine emperor Maurice who built the large stone church which still stands around the pillar. The siting is extremely significant: the view through its side chapels aligns exactly with the peak of Jebel Aqra, the demonic backdrop to Symeon's life on high …. [He] stood on high as an alternative Christian focus, contradicting an ancient pagan "high place" in the mountain landscape behind him.[74]

Certainly the vista-related implications of siting were not lost on those who built the cultic sites on the summit either.[75] This crucial dimension to the holiness of cultic sites, that their holiness is not based simply on the site itself but on what can be seen from the site, further militates in favor of the suggested hypothesis of this chapter: that the rare visions of Cyprus possible from the summit of Jebel Aqra led not only to preservation of evidence of this phenomenon in the Baal Cycle, Hebrew Bible, and other traditions but likely sparked the particular appropriation of the Blessed Isle legend by the author or redactor of the *History of the Rechabites*. This conclusion provides additional data for discussions of provenience and supports locating a significant stage in the text's production as linked to the Antioch region or western Syria.

Further, due to the likelihood of the visibility of "Canigou Effect" type phenomena in locations beyond the environs of the Canigou Massif, I propose the generic appellation "Atlantis Effect" for the visual phenomenon, due to its similarity to the description of Atlantis as it appears in Plato's *Critias*.[76] This phenomenon would involve several elements:

1. The Atlantis Effect involves the appearance of an "island" which is not normally visible from the viewing location. The natural curvature of the earth would prevent normal viewing without atmospheric refraction. Typically, the two locations involved would sit just below an ocean-surface-grazing tangential line. This change in visibility would require a Novaya Zemlya refraction effect, a subspecies of a superior mirage, which allows distant objects below the horizon to become visible due to atmospheric inversion.
2. The Atlantis Effect is visible in the setting sun. For most locations this requires twice-yearly predictable but narrow calendrical viewing windows in which there is an alignment of viewing location, target location, and sunset.
3. The Atlantis Effect at its most vivid appears to reveal an island with a brilliantly shining base. This requires refraction of some sunlight to occur differently from the light coming from the rest of the target "island." This effect is likely the result of "stacking" of superior mirages due to differential refraction. Atmospheric inversion would be necessary, but the "shining base" aspect is likely the result of more heavily refracted light moving through the coldest section of air along the ocean reflecting off of the ocean itself.

It is hypothesized that the effect is visible in many locations, not only those described herein.

From these geographic and scriptural observations, it is clear that the connection of Cyprus, not only with eastern Mediterranean coastal lands but with the Holy Land in particular, was an important shaping influence on the religious experiences and sacred scriptures of Jews and Christians for over a millennium. The scenic imagination, spurred by unusual visions from Zaphon/Kasios, enabled generations of believers to think beyond the borders of their immediate life experiences, to envision a divine "other" place, and at times, to envision themselves in that place.[77] Distant observations of Cyprus, and not exclusively spiritual revelations or speculations, may lie behind some of the vivid descriptions of biblical and apocalyptic authors.[78]

Notes

1. "Holy Land" here is understood according to the most extensive definitions from the Hebrew Bible, which puts the "northern" border of the land at "Zaphon."
2. Without atmospheric refraction.
3. Photo series of sunset over Roc Negre of the Canigou Massif from Allauch, France. Notice that no "island" is visible in the photo on the left, taken before Canigou appears in silhouette. Three photos: "Roc Negre depuis semaphore fevrier 2012 (16)," "Roc Negre depuis semaphore fevrier 2012 (25)," "Roc Negre depuis semaphore fevrier 2012 (33)" by flickr.com user "akunamatata" taken February 17, 2012. Images cropped and converted to grayscale. Used with permission.
4. Assuming that the radius of the earth is 6371 km, the distance "D" to the visible horizon from a location "h" high above sea level is given by the formula $D = (112.88 \text{ km}) \sqrt{h}$. Thus, from the summit of the Canigou Massif (2.75 km) the horizon across the sea would be 187.19 km distant. From the observation location "Allauch" in Marseille (0.31 km above sea level) without atmospheric refraction the horizon would appear 62.85 km distant. If the sum of these two distances were greater than the distance from Marseille to Canigou (263.1 km), then the mountain would be normally visible. However, the combined horizon viewing distance (250.04 km) is just a little less than the distance between the two locations, thus they are not mutually visible without significant atmospheric refraction.
5. See his website: http://canigou.allauch.free.fr/Photos-anims.htm.
6. This effect has been noted, among other instances, during polar expeditions. During the Barentsz expedition in 1597 expedition members observed the sun above the horizon a full two weeks before it would have been visible without atmospheric refraction. Gerrit de Veer, *The Three Voyages of William Barents to the Arctic Regions: 1594, 1959, and 1596*, translated by Charles T. Beke (London: The Hakylut Society, 1876).
7. Namely, atmospheric inversion, which will be described later in the chapter.
8. This particular local manifestation of the effect is categorized by William R. Corliss, *Rare Halos, Mirages, Anomalous Rainbows and Related Electromagnetic Phenomena: A Catalog of Geophysical Anomalies* (Glen Arm, MD: The Sourcebook Project, 1984), p. 144, as a "telescopic mirage," though no telescopic effect is required, and in spite of the fact that it is more akin to a "Novaya Zemlya Effect," which involves viewing an object below the horizon as a result of highly refracted light. Corliss catalogs a similar observation of Tahiti and surrounding islands from a distance of "210 miles away" (Corliss, *Rare Halos*, p. 144). In this latter instance, both a telescopic effect and a refraction around the surface of the earth allowed the observation. The whole chapter in Corliss (*Rare Halos*, pp. 137–57) on mirages is instructive, as many of these observed phenomena either defy easy categorization or display characteristics of multiple phenomena simultaneously. A better-known Mediterranean mirage is the "Fata Morgana" occasionally observable in the straits of Messina (Corliss, *Rare Halos*, pp. 139–41), though this mirage shares only some characteristics with that viewable from Marseille.
9. See canigou.allauch.free.fr/Anim-16nov08-1.htm for a similar, but animated, sequence which shows this brilliant "base" of the "island" very vividly, as documented by Alain Origne.
10. This aspect of the effect may result from a "Fata Morgana" mirage coincident with Novaya Zemlya refraction or may be due to some other category of mirage,

enabling reflection of differently refracted sunlight on the surface of the water (see the discussion of "multiple mirages" in Corliss, *Rare Halos*, pp. 147–9). The various naming conventions and categories of mirage are not well established and exhibit a good deal of variability of use. At the least it is necessary for two different refraction trajectories to be at work, one for the "island" and a separate one for the "shining base." The latter may be the result of differently, and more strongly, refracted light traveling through the coldest layer of air at the very surface of the water, allowing a sliver of sun to be visible at the base through what is known as a "superior" mirage. The observed effect would require two different superior mirages to be visible, one stacked on top of the other, but reversed in order from the actual objects' orientation, likely as a result of multiple atmospheric thermocline ducting effects. This is an otherwise documented phenomenon and not unprecedented: "The Novaya Zemlya Effect … may also be applicable to other optical phenomena occurring near the horizon, which are generally considered to be the consequence of simple refraction by atmospheric strata" (Corliss, *Rare Halos*, p. 151). The mechanism of the effect, however, is not the primary concern. Rather the fact of its occurrence, the description of it visually, and notation of the conditions under which it occurs are the concerns for this chapter.

11   However, due to the breadth and orientation of the Canigou Massif, the range of dates when the astronomical alignment is in some way possible is rather broad. For instance, perfect alignment of the peak occurs on November 2 and February 8; however, the above photos in Figure 10.2 were taken of the effect over the southeastern spur of the massif on February 17, 2012.
12   The Novaya Zemlya Effect is most frequently observed in polar regions due to this necessity of atmospheric inversion, that is, a temperature gradient from cold in lower elevations to warm in higher elevations. This enables greater concavity of refraction along the curvature of the earth. This effect is visible outside of polar regions when atmospheric inversion is present. See, e.g., W. H. Lehn, "The Novaya Zemlya Effect: An Arctic Mirage," *Journal of the Optical Society of America* 69 (1979): 776–81.
13   The phenomenon remains formally undocumented to my knowledge.
14   The summit of Cypriot Mt. Olympus, at 1.952 km, is not visible from sea level beyond 157.71 km without atmospheric refraction. The distance from Mt. Olympus to a comparable viewing location on the Turkish coast near Antioch is approximately 306 km.
15   Without atmospheric refraction.
16   The range of dates when the astronomical alignment is possible for viewing points in the region of Turkey/Western Syria is narrower than the date range for viewing the effect from Marseille. This is because of the different orientation of the Cypriot Olympus range. It presents a narrower viewing cross-section to points to the east-northeast than does the Canigou Massif.
17   Similar meteorological conditions occur in similar seasons due to the relative homogeneity of the Mediterranean climate. The parallel viewing windows for each location are favorable for the occurrence of the necessary conditions of atmospheric inversion.
18   Original photo by NASA. From https://commons.wikimedia.org/wiki/File:Cyprus.A2002292.1045.500m.jpg. Used with permission. Edited for publication.
19   I am not aware of a parallel data point in the earlier legends we will discuss. There are, of course, Hebrew Bible precedents for the shrouding of a holy place or thing in cloud, but it is likely that this has phenomenological background in natural summit shrouding.

20 The horizon from the summit of Jebel Aqra (1.717 km), without atmospheric refraction, is 147.91 km. That distance added to the distance from Cypriot Mt. Olympus to the horizon is 305.62 km. This is almost precisely the distance from Jebel Aqra to Cypriot Mt. Olympus and as such would not allow a viewer to see one from the other under normal, limited refraction conditions.

21 A good deal of attention in the Baal cycle is given to deliberation over whether to build a window into Baal's palace. Baal is against it from the beginning, concerned with others looking in upon the palace. Ultimately, he is prevailed upon to allow a single window. Baal's window is referred to not just in typical building terms but also as a "break in the clouds." Interestingly, the window is only built after the rest of the construction is completed. The palace is built through a multiday process of burning during which the ruder elements of construction are transformed into gold, silver, and lapis, all shining brilliantly. Lady Asherah of the sea is instrumental in inciting the building process and initial concerns regarding the window related to "Pidray, girl of light." However, once the palace is completed and glorious to behold Baal agrees to allow the window, which will allow glimpses of the palace. The narrative does not make sense if the temple to Baal on the summit of Zaphon is in mind. That temple would have been regularly visible from all around. However, a rare vision of an apparently "heavenly" location shining brilliantly where the sea and sun meet through a "window" in the clouds would do better justice to the details of the Baal cycle text.

22 Photo by Wikimedia.org user Anthiok. Used with permission. Edited for publication.

23 Robin Lane Fox, *Travelling Heroes in the Epic Age of Homer* (New York: Vintage, 2008), p. 254.

24 Mark Smith, *Where the Gods Are*, p. 88, derives his evidence for this conclusion from Herbert Donner and Wolfgang Röllig, *Kanaanäische und aramäische Inschriften*, 2nd ed. (Wiesbaden: Harrassowitz, 1966–9), 69.1.

25 Later discussion will touch on the possibility of literary borrowing from these and other Hebrew Bible texts as a possible literary background for the *History of the Rechabites*. The relevant data points in question from the Hebrew Bible are the ones most dependent on Zaphon traditions. They are therefore not a "clean" source, but rather are likely themselves to have been influenced by Zaphon or northern Lebanon range visual phenomena and traditions. With respect to the issue of adjudicating literary or phenomenological precedents behind HistRech, there has certainly been significant literary borrowing, but that does not preclude a likely phenomenological explanation or impetus for its unique synthesis. As for the "northern Lebanon range" locations, it is possible that the proposed phenomenon is viewable from certain northern Lebanon range locations, but the probability is much lower than at Jebel Aqra/Zaphon due to the sunset alignment occurring in warmer months, making the likelihood of favorable atmospheric conditions (i.e., stable cool surface air producing atmospheric inversion) much lower.

26 Frank Moore Cross (*Canaanite Myth and Hebrew Epic* [Cambridge, MA: Harvard University Press, 1973], pp. 166–7) asserts that previous scholars' contentions of a volcanic eruption as a phenomenological background to texts such as the Exodus 24 theophany are misguided, suggesting instead the mountainous storm imagery of Baal traditions as adequately explanatory. This chapter suggests that Canigou Effect–type phenomena observed from Zaphon may also (or instead) lie behind these appropriated traditions.

27 See, e.g., b. Ṣoṭ. 17a:24.

28 Many further connections can be made between Zaphon traditions and the Hebrew Bible, likely including Ps 48:2, Ps 68, Ps 89, Jer 10:10-13, Ezek 1:4 ff.
29 This is not unlike the scenario envisioned in HistRech. Ps 107 could have provided some suggestive background for the establishment of the Rechabites in their abode.
30 Though the vision of Rev 21:10 does occur on a mountaintop.
31 These would most likely have been received through their use in the Hebrew Bible. See also Smith, *Where the Gods Are*, p. 37.
32 Rev 21:1-4, 6-8, 10-11, 18-20, 23-25: "Then I saw a new heaven and a new earth; for the first heaven and the first earth had passed away, and the sea was no more.[2] And I saw the holy city, the new Jerusalem, coming down out of heaven from God, prepared as a bride adorned for her husband.[3] And I heard a loud voice from the throne saying, 'See, the home of God is among mortals. He will dwell with them; they will be his peoples, and God himself will be with them;[4] he will wipe every tear from their eyes. Death will be no more; mourning and crying and pain will be no more, for the first things have passed away. ... To the thirsty I will give water as a gift from the spring of the water of life.[7] Those who conquer will inherit these things, and I will be their God and they will be my children.[8] But as for the cowardly, the faithless, the polluted, the murderers, the fornicators, the sorcerers, the idolaters, and all liars, their place will be in the lake that burns with fire and sulfur, which is the second death. ... '[10] And in the spirit he carried me away to a great, high mountain and showed me the holy city Jerusalem coming down out of heaven from God.[11] It has the glory of God and a radiance like a very rare jewel, like jasper, clear as crystal.... [18] The wall is built of jasper, while the city is pure gold, clear as glass.[19] The foundations of the wall of the city are adorned with every jewel; the first was jasper, the second sapphire, the third agate, the fourth emerald,[20] the fifth onyx, the sixth carnelian, the seventh chrysolite, the eighth beryl, the ninth topaz, the tenth chrysoprase, the eleventh jacinth, the twelfth amethyst ....[23] And the city has no need of sun or moon to shine on it, for the glory of God is its light, and its lamp is the Lamb.[24] The nations will walk by its light, and the kings of the earth will bring their glory into it.[25] Its gates will never be shut by day—and there will be no night there."
33 This is very similar to the scenario described in the *History of the Rechabites*.
34 Hesiod, *Op.* 168-73 (Most, LCL).
35 Pindar, *Ol.* 2.61-78 (Race, LCL): "But forever having sunshine in equal nights and in equal days, good men receive a life of less toil, for they do not vex the earth or the water of the sea with the strength of their hands to earn a paltry living. No, in company with the honored gods, those who joyfully kept their oaths spend a tearless existence, whereas the others endure pain too terrible to behold. But those with the courage to have lived three times in either realm, while keeping their souls free from all unjust deeds, travel the road of Zeus to the tower of Cronos, where ocean breezes blow round the Isle of the Blessed, and flowers of gold are ablaze, some from radiant trees on land, while the water nurtures others; with these they weave garlands for their hands and crowns for their heads, in obedience to the just counsels of Rhadamanthys, whom the great father keeps ever seated at his side, the husband of Rhea, she who has the highest throne of all."
36 Plato, *Gorg.* 523a (Lamb, LCL): "Socrates: Give ear then, as they say, to a right fine story, which you will regard as a fable, I fancy, but I as an actual account; for what I am about to tell you I mean to offer as the truth. By Homer's account, Zeus, Poseidon, and Pluto divided the sovereignty amongst them when they took it over from their father. Now in the time of Cronos there was a law concerning mankind,

and it holds to this very day amongst the gods, that every man who has passed a just and holy life departs after his decease to the Isles of the Blest, and dwells in all happiness apart from ill; but whoever has lived unjustly and impiously goes to the dungeon of requital and penance which, you know, they call Tartarus. Of these men there were judges in Cronos' time, and still of late in the reign of Zeus—living men to judge the living upon the day when each was to breathe his last; and thus the cases were being decided amiss. So Pluto and the overseers from the Isles of the Blest came before Zeus with the report that they found men passing over to either abode undeserving."

37 Certainly, there is also some literary conflation with the Elysian Plain, Hades, the White Isle, and Atlantis.
38 Perhaps as much as a millennium.
39 At least, there is no prior appropriation to our knowledge. Atlantis themes are at times conflated with Blessed Isle themes in Greco-Roman sources, but the Jewish and Christian writers who transmit or appropriate Atlantis traditions do not seem to transmit those aspects which relate to the Blessed Isle. Philo refers to the Platonic Atlantis story in *Aet*. 26, but only to relate it to destruction by flood. Jerome refers negatively, and only in passing, to the legend as part of a polemic against those who suggest that the righteous are geographically confined after death (*Vigil*. 6). But there is no suggestion there that Christians have appropriated the legend. Tertullian may refer to the legend in a polemic against those Christian heretics who speculate about the living quarters of the heavens (*Adversus Valentinianos* 7). But again, here there is only reference to the legend and not a suggestion that Christians have appropriated it. Hippolytus refers to the Isle of the Blessed legend to suggest that the Greeks derived it from Jewish Essene traditions (*Haer*. 9.22). This is the text that most suggests a Jewish connection to the legend. The only early Christian writer who makes a reference of any kind to a similar legend, favorably received, is Clement of Rome in 1 Clement 20:8. There he writes vaguely that ωκεανος ανθρωποις απερατος και οι μετ αυτον κοσμοι ταις αυταις ταγαις του δεσποτου διευθυνονται. Whether these "worlds" beyond the ocean refer to Atlantis or the Blessed Isle or something else entirely is unclear. What is clear is that this is nothing close to the scale of appropriation of the legend of the Blessed Isle that we find in HistRech.
40 "Then the word of the lord came to Jeremiah: Thus says the lord of hosts, the God of Israel: Go and say to the people of Judah and the inhabitants of Jerusalem, Can you not learn a lesson and obey my words? says the lord. The command has been carried out that Jonadab son of Rechab gave to his descendants to drink no wine; and they drink none to this day, for they have obeyed their ancestor's command. But I myself have spoken to you persistently, and you have not obeyed me. I have sent to you all my servants the prophets, sending them persistently, saying, 'Turn now every one of you from your evil way, and amend your doings, and do not go after other gods to serve them, and then you shall live in the land that I gave to you and your ancestors.' But you did not incline your ear or obey me. The descendants of Jonadab son of Rechab have carried out the command that their ancestor gave them, but this people has not obeyed me. Therefore, thus says the lord, the God of hosts, the God of Israel: I am going to bring on Judah and on all the inhabitants of Jerusalem every disaster that I have pronounced against them; because I have spoken to them and they have not listened, I have called to them and they have not answered. 'But to the house of the Rechabites Jeremiah said: Thus says the lord of hosts, the God of Israel: Because you have obeyed the command of your ancestor Jonadab, and kept all his precepts, and done all that he

commanded you, therefore thus says the lord of hosts, the God of Israel: Jonadab son of Rechab shall not lack a descendant to stand before me for all time'" (Jer 35:12-19).

41 For whom the work is sometimes named the *Story of Zosimus* or the *Apocalypse of Zosimus* or the *Testament of Zosimus*.

42 One does wonder about whether there is a connection between prefix *mem* (place of) the *rekabim* (rechabites) and *merkabah* (chariot) mysticism (which was typically oriented around descriptions of inaccessible holy places and which seems to have been increasingly heavily criticized and prohibited in the Talmudim). It is possible that our text comes out of a Jewish background in which *merkabah* legends are increasingly suspect and may have been sanitized through the euphemism of the "Rechabites." However, such an investigation is well beyond the limited scope of this chapter.

43 These trees may refer to the two Edenic trees: that of the knowledge of good and evil and that of life, which were also represented by the pillars at the entrance to the second Jerusalem Temple.

44 The *Isles of the Blessed Ones* are also literal places in the Greek and Roman accounts. This element in the text does much to mitigate criticisms, à la D. F. Strauss' criticisms of Eichorn and Paulus in *The Life of Jesus, Critically Examined*, of interpretive approaches that seek to understand possible naturalistic explanations. HistRech identifies itself as a text that describes seeing a literal, albeit hidden, place. Some philosophers of religion may object that the argument put forward in this chapter does too much to resurrect the de-mythologizing tendencies popularized by the work of Friedrich Max Müller, from which the field of religious studies has sought to distance itself over the past century. The concern here may be that the present argument too easily conflates scientific discourse with religious discourse. The issue merits consideration; however, the underpinnings of this argument are derived more from Marxist epistemological frameworks based in the field of geography, which maintain the essential nature of analysis from material phenomena.

45 Ptolemy (*Geogr.* 7.5.14), Plutarch (*Sert.* 8), Strabo (*Geogr.* 3.2.13), and Philostratus (*Vit. Apoll.* 5.3), among others, all agree upon this.

46 English translations of the Syriac text are from James H. Charlesworth, "The History of the Rechabites: A New Translation and Introduction," in *OTP* 2.443-61. Syriac text comes from manuscript BnF syr. 236.

47 In Greek traditions the great sea is synonymous with the "encircling river." English translations of the Greek text are from James H. Charlesworth, *The History of the Rechabites, Volume 1: The Greek Recension* (Chico, CA: Scholars Press, 1982). Greek text comes from Cod. Par. Gr. 1217 of BnF.

48 These two words "west" and "sea" are of course the same in Hebrew: *yam*.

49 I am not aware of a parallel data point in the Greek and Roman legends. Although some kind of separation would be tropologically expected with a holy place.

50 *OTP* 2:455.

51 Syriac translation from *OTP* 2:456.

52 This is basically similar to Greco-Roman accounts.

53 Ethiopian legends appear in Homer, as noted by Brent Landau, "'One Drop of Salvation from the House of Majesty': Universal Revelation, Human Mission and Mythical Geography in the Syriac Revelation of the Magi," in *The Levant: Crossroads of Late Antiquity. History, Religion and Archaeology*, edited by Ellen Bradshaw Aitken and John M. Fossey (Leiden: Brill, 2013), p. 98: "The Aithiopians are situated at the boundaries of Okeanos (*Iliad* 23.205), in a land accessible only to the gods. As a sign

of their favor in the eyes of the gods, their land is blessed with extreme fecundity and a most pleasant climate."

54 E.g., Atlantis in Plato's *Critias* 113d-e (Bury, LCL): "Poseidon, being smitten with desire for her, wedded her; and to make the hill whereon she dwelt impregnable he broke it off all round about; and he made circular belts of sea and land enclosing one another alternately, some greater, some smaller, two being of land and three of sea, which he carved as it were out of the midst of the island; and these belts were at even distances on all sides, so as to be impassable for man; for at that time neither ships nor sailing were as yet in existence." But even this legend is attributed to the ancient past, subsequent development of Atlantis as described in *Critias* involving bridging these barriers and cutting shipping channels through them. The base of the outer edges were still walled though and these were plated with metals, including brass, "which sparkled like fire" in the sun (Plato, Critias 116c [Bury, LCL]). The towers of the temple at the center (and highest point) of Atlantis were coated in gold. These features seem reminiscent of elements of a Canigou Effect, especially the shining through of the sun underneath or at the base of the "island."

55 Plato has it in the plural (*Menex*. 235c; *Gorgias* 523a, 526c; *Symp*. 179e). Others similarly (Strabo, *Geogr*. 3.2.13; Antoninus Liberalis, *Metam*. 33; Athenaeus, *Deipn*. 15.695; Apollodorus *Library* 3.10.1; Hesiod, *Op*. 155–73; Philostratus, *Vit. Apoll*. 5.3). Only Pindar (*Ol*. 2.55-75), Euripides (*Hel*. 1676), and Herodotus (*Hist*. 3.26.1) envision one island, and Herodotus' account is very garbled.

56 Though Pindar, *Ol*. 2.55-75, could arguably preserve such a tradition, and if we consider Atlantis traditions, then Plato's descriptions in *Critias* include a "shining" base and high points.

57 Although, one could interpret the Greek myths regarding Atlas (Atlantis) as the father of Calypso (literally "I will conceal" or "I will cover") to be a possible indirect suggestion of this idea in a tradition that may sometimes be conflated with the Blessed Isle tradition, the relation is clearly very speculative.

58 There are, of course, many examples of various kinds of obstacles preventing access to remote, and often sacred, locations. For a discussion of some of these tropes, particularly "extreme inaccessibility," as they pertain to various locales as appearing in late antique texts, see Landau, "'One Drop of Salvation from the House of Majesty': Universal Revelation, Human Mission and Mythical Geography in the Syriac Revelation of the Magi," p. 98.

59 *OTP* 1.15 (E. Isaac trans.).

60 1 En 25:5, 32:1, 77:4 (*OTP*)/77:3 (in George W. E. Nickelsburg and James C. VanderKam, *1 Enoch 2: A Commentary on the Book of 1 Enoch, Chapters 37–82* [Hermeneia: Fortress Press, 2011]).

61 J. L. Myres, "Aphrodite Anadyomene," *ABSA* 41 (1945): 99.

62 James R. Davila, in his paper for the SBL Pseudepigrapha Group at the November 24, 2003, meeting in Atlanta ("Is the Story of Zosimus Really a Jewish Composition"), asserts a monastic/ascetic provenience and notes that both Brian McNeil and Christopher Knights agree concerning the favorable reception such a work would have received in monastic/ascetic communities. See https://www.st-andrews.ac.uk/divinity/rt/otp/abstracts/zosimus/.

63 The reasons scholars argue for Palestinian provenience do not rule out Antiochene provenience: There is a setting in a monastic or ascetic community, there is interest in Jerusalem (particularly in manuscript "BnF syr. 234" in which Zosimus is described as a monk living in a monastery in Jerusalem, but, as Davila points out, interest in

Jerusalem does not necessitate Palestinian provenience), further mention at the end of "BnF syr. 234" that Zosimus was ultimately settled in a different non-Jerusalemite *Palestinian* monastery, and the translation history in *OTP*'s manuscript D (British Museum Add. 12174) which suggests that "it was translated from [an original Hebrew] … by the Hands of the Reverend Mar Jacob of Edessa" (*OTP* 1:444, 461). These seem to indicate more the provenience of particular manuscript traditions rather than provenience of the first unified Ur-text. While a Palestinian provenience is of course possible, the composite nature of the text, including likely elements that originated in two different languages (chapters 8–12 and 14–16:7 Greek; 1–7, 13, 16:8-18 Syriac; see Davila, "Is the Story of Zosimus Really a Jewish Composition" for helpful demarcation) increases the probability that the text came together as a whole in a more northerly locale like Antioch.

64 James H. Charlesworth shared this idea with me, *viva voce*, at the 2018 Larnaca conference.
65 See, e.g., J. H. Charlesworth, *Jesus as Mirrored in John: The Genius in the New Testament* (London: T&T Clark, 2018), pp. 364, 388, 427, n. 13, and for discussion of the library at Antioch dating to 221 BCE, see pp. 525–6.
66 Libanius, *Or.* 18.172.
67 K. Butcher, *Coinage in Roman Syria: Northern Syria 64BC-AD253*, Royal Numismatic Society 34 (Ann Arbor: University of Michigan Press, 2004), pp. 413–25.
68 Fox, *Travelling Heroes*, p. 282.
69 St. Barlaam's Monastery.
70 See the illuminating discussion in Peter Brown, "The Rise and Function of the Holy Man in Late Antiquity," *The Journal of Roman Studies* 61 (1971): 83.
71 Though no source available to us appears to contain all the relevant elements before their usage in the HistRech. It appears to present, for its time, a unique synthesis.
72 See Figure 15.
73 E. Grey, "Beyond the Temple: Blurring the Boundaries of 'Sacred Space,'" in *Proceedings of the Fourteenth Annual Theoretical Roman Archaeology Conference, Durham 2004*, edited by J. Bruhn, B. Croxford, and D. Grigoropoulos (Oxford: Oxbow Books, 2005), pp. 109–18.
74 Fox, *Travelling Heroes*, p. 250.
75 In fact, there are many indications in the Baal cycle that the views from Zaphon were of particular relevance and importance, as, for example, previously mentioned with respect to the window controversy. This is in spite of protestations against the importance of geographic referents from some scholars such as Simon Parker, *The Pre-Biblical Narrative Tradition*, SBL Resources for Biblical Study 24 (Atlanta: Scholars Press, 1989), p. 55. For a perspective supportive of the importance of geography and to this issue, see B. Margalit, "The Geographical Setting of the AQHT Story and Its Ramifications," in *Ugarit in Retrospect: Fifty Years of Ugarit and Ugaritic*, edited by D. G. Young (Winona Lake, IN: Eisenbrauns, 1981), pp. 131–58.
76 These elements include location in the west, across a large body of water, a brilliantly shining base and being now, or typically, invisible (in *Critias* this is due to the destructive flood that obliterated the island). There are enough distinctive additional elements in HistRech that it likely prevents exclusive literary borrowing from *Critias*.
77 As suggested by the logic of spatial imagination described in M. Merleau Ponty, *The Phenomenology of Perception*.
78 I would like to thank the "Islands, Islanders, and Scripture" SBL Group for their helpful feedback on a preliminary version of the paper in Boston, MA, in November

2017. I would also like to thank George L. Parsenios, James H. Charlesworth, Dale C. Allison, Anders K. Petersen, Nate C. Johnson, M. J. P. O'Connor, Jim Neumann, Devlin McGuire, and Steve Bohannon for their kind feedback and suggestions. For a more extended treatment, see Jolyon G. R. Pruszinski, *An Ecology of Scriptures: Experiences of Dwelling behind Early Jewish and Christian Texts* (London: T&T Clark, 2021).

Conclusions Regarding Cyprus and the Holy Land in the Biblical Period

James H. Charlesworth and
Jolyon G. R. Pruszinski

The robust connectivity of the Mediterranean world has long been a well-known feature of life in antiquity. The intimacy of these relations is captured in the classic quip attributed to Socrates referring to that great sea as a "pond" ringed with cities (*Phaedo* 109). This is such a salient feature of the historic understanding of the region that Peter Brown begins his classic *The World of Late Antiquity* with a vignette of these interrelations.[1] The question we have considered in this congress is whether (and if so, how) the Holy Land, specifically the land of ancient Israel, the land of early Judaism, and of early Christianity, is related to Cyprus. The former has often been categorized as separate from, and marginally affected by, the deeply interconnected world of the Mediterranean, of which Cyprus is clearly a part. This assumption of alienation has especially been prevalent in consideration of periods prior to the Hellenistic and Roman eras. However, the effect of this congress has been to establish the connection throughout the biblical period of the land of Israel, a "forbidding highland" to use Brown's terminology,[2] with the land of Cyprus, a land clearly fully enmeshed within, and critical to, ancient Mediterranean culture and commerce.

In considering the relations between Cyprus and the Holy Land, it is instructive to be reminded of Brown's famous dictum that "it cost less to bring a cargo of grain from one end of the Mediterranean to another than to carry it another seventy-five miles inland."[3] Jerusalem, the center of gravity of the Holy Land, is, of course, only half that distance from the coast, but the principle holds. We readily recognize the interrelations of Alexandria or Antioch and Israel, but Cyprus has been neglected though equidistant by sea. Conversely, travel to a city like Damascus from Jerusalem is far costlier from the standpoint of trade because of the necessity of overland travel. Connections through overland trade routes could and did exist, but the comparative ease of maritime transport dwarfs them by sheer volume. Archaeological excavations in ancient Palestine have shown that the Israel of the biblical period was by no means isolated from the cities of the Mediterranean, though certainly it was more isolated from them than they were from each other. As such, the time has come to acknowledge the important mutual shaping influence of Cyprus and the Holy Land in the biblical period not only through commerce but also through culture.

The Cyprus Congress concluded with discussions that were cohesive. We agreed that experts have too often assumed that borders are barriers. The Mediterranean was a border of ancient Palestine but not a barrier, especially from earliest times to the period of Herod the Great. In the late first century BCE, the western border of ancient Palestine became increasingly porous as Herod built Caesarea Maritima in the orderly aftermath of the Roman campaigns to end piracy.[4] Ships now could moor near the beach and passengers and desirable commodities be brought from Egypt, Rome, Greece, and Cyprus. Resinated wine, for example, was and is appreciated on Cyprus and, according to one Qumran Scroll, was known by the Essenes living at Qumran. Excavations in Jerusalem, and throughout Israel-Palestine, demonstrate that Cyprus and Cypriote ware helped shape Canaanite, Israelite, Jewish, and Christian cultures in "the Land." All attendees, including those who were unable to provide final papers for publication, agreed that for the study of ancient Israelite and subsequent cultures to be more complete, it must attend not only to textual evidence but to the material remains from Cyprus, including elegant pottery, ships, jewelry, weapons, and wines.

Notes

1 Peter Brown, *The World of Late Antiquity: AD 15–750* (London: Thames and Hudson Ltd., 1971), pp. 11–13.
2 Ibid., 12.
3 Ibid., 13.
4 These were begun in earnest under Pompey.

Cyprus and the Holy Land in History, Archaeology, and Scripture: A Selected Bibliography

Jolyon G. R. Pruszinski

The following bibliography records those works of modern authors in the realms of history, archaeology, and biblical studies which offer the most relevant scholarship on the relations of Cyprus and ancient Israel/Palestine in the biblical period and particularly those works germane to the papers presented at the 2018 Larnaca Congress. Select additional publications that have appeared since the Congress, or which might be of especial benefit of the reader, have been included as well. Of special note is the recently published *From Roman to Early Christian Cyprus* from Mohr Siebeck (2020), edited by Laura Nasrallah, Charalambos Bakirtzis, and AnneMarie Luijendijk (WUNT 437). The focus of that excellent volume, and its bibliography, is largely the period of Late Antiquity, providing an exceptional complement to the present volume, the focus of which is largely the biblical period.

Achtemeier, Paul J. *1 Peter: A Commentary on First Peter*. Hermeneia. Minneapolis, MN: Fortress, 1996.
Aharoni, Yohanan. *The Archaeology of the Land of Israel*. Philadelphia: Westminster, 1982.
Ahituv, Shmuel. *Handbook of Ancient Hebrew Inscriptions from the Period of the First Commonwealth and the Beginning of the Second Commonwealth*. Jerusalem: Bialik Institute, 1992 (Hebrew).
Albright, William F. *The Archaeology of Palestine*. Harmondsworth: Penguin, 1961.
Alexander, Loveday. "Luke's Political Vision." *Interpretation* 66.3(2012): 283–4, 290.
Alexander, P. S. *Toponymy of the Targumim with Special Reference to the Table of Nations and the Boundaries of the Land of Israel*. Oxford: University of Oxford, 1974.
Allison, Dale C., Jr. "The Pauline Epistles and the Synoptic Gospels: The Pattern of the Parallels." *NTS* 28 (1982): 1–32.
Allison, Dale C., Jr. "The Baptism of Jesus and a New Dead Sea Scroll." *Biblical Archaeology Review* 18 (1992): 58–60.
Allison, Dale C., Jr. *The Jesus Tradition in Q*. Harrisburg, PA: Trinity Press Intl., 1997.
Allison, Dale C., Jr. "Jas 2: 14-26: Polemic against Paul, Apology for James." Pages 123–44 in *Ancient and New Perspectives on Paul*. Edited by Tobias Nicklas, Andreas Merkt, and Joseph Verheyden. NTOA 102. Göttingen: Vandenhoeck & Ruprecht, 2013.
Allison, Dale C., Jr. "Reflections on Matthew, John, and Jesus." Pages 47–69 in *Jesus Research: The Gospel of John in Historical Inquiry*. Edited by James H. Charlesworth with Jolyon G. R. Pruszinski. Jewish and Christian Texts 26. London: T&T Clark, 2019.
Alpert Nakhai, Beth. "Where to Worship? Religion in Iron II Israel and Judah." Pages 90–101 in *Defining the Sacred: Approaches to the Archaeology of Religion in the Near East*. Edited by Nicola Lanery. Oxford: Oxbow Books, 2015.

Amorai-Stark, Shua, and Malka Hershkovitz. *Ancient Gems, Finger Rings and Seal Boxes from Caesarea Maritima: The Hendler Collection*. Tel Aviv: Shay Hendler (privately published), 2016.

Attridge, Harold. *The Epistle to the Hebrews: A Commentary on the Epistle to the Hebrews*. Hermeneia. Philadelphia: Fortress, 1989.

Aubet, Maria E. *The Phoenicians and the West: Politics, Colonies, and Trade*. Cambridge: Cambridge University Press, 2001.

Aubet, Maria. E. "Phoenicia during the Iron Age II Period." Pages 706–16 in *Oxford Handbook of the Archaeology of the Levant, c. 8000–332 BCE*. Edited by Margreet L. Steiner and Ann E. Killebrew. Oxford: Oxford University Press, 2014.

Aus, Roger D. "Paul's Travel Plans for Spain and the 'Full Number of the Gentiles' of Romans 11.25." *Novum Testamentum* 21 (1979): 232–62.

Avissar Lewis, R. S. "Childhood and Children in the Material Culture of the Land of Israel, from the Middle Bronze Age to the Iron Age." PhD diss., Bar-Ilan University, 2010 (Hebrew with English abstract).

Avissar Lewis, R. S. "How Are Children Identified in the Archaeological Record?" Pages 170–3 in *The Five-Minute Archaeology*. Edited by C. Shafer Eliiott. London: Equinox Publishing, 2016.

Avissar Lewis, R. S. "A Matter of Perception: Children in Pre-Israelite and Philistine Houses in the Iron Age I." Pages 242–53 in *Tell It in Gath. Studies in the History and Archaeology of Israel, Essays in Honor of Aren M. Maeir on the Occasion of His Sixtieth Birthday*. Edited by I. Shai, J. R. Chadwick, L. Hitchock, A. Dagan, C. McKinny, and J. Uziel. Ägypten und Altes Testament 90. Münster: Zaphon, 2018.

Avissar Lewis, R. S. *Children in Antiquity, Archaeological Perspectives on Children and Childhood in the Land of Israel*. Haifa: Haifa University Press, 2019 (Hebrew with English abstract).

Backhouse, J. "Figures Ostraca from Deir El-Medina." Pages 25–39 in *Current Research in Egyptology 2011 Proceedings of the Twelfth Annual Symposium Which Took Place at Durham University, United Kingdom, March 2011*. Edited by H. Abd El Gawad, N. Andrews, M. Correas-Amador, V. Tamorri, and J. Taylor. Oxford/Oakville: Oxbow Books, 2015.

Baltrusch, Ernst. *Die Juden und das Römische Reich: Geschichte einer konfliktreichen Beziehung*. Darmstadt: Wissenschaftliche Buchhandlung, 2002.

Barclay, J. M. G. *Jews in the Mediterranean Diaspora: From Alexander to Trajan (323 BCE – 117 CE)*. Edinburgh: T&T Clark, 1996.

Barclay, William. *And He Had Compassion on Them*. Edinburgh: Church of Scotland, 1955.

Barkay, Gabriel. "The Iron Age II–III." Pages 302–73 in *The Archaeology of Israel*. Edited by Amnon Ben-Tor. New Haven: Yale University Press, 1992.

Barkay, Gabriel. "Burial Caves and Burial Practices in Judah in the Iron Age." Pages 96–164 in *Graves and Burial Practices in Israel in the Ancient Periods*. Edited by Itamar Singer. Jerusalem: Yad Ben-Zvi, 1994 (Hebrew).

Barker, Craig. *Aphrodite's Island: Australian Archaeologists in Cyprus. The Cypriot Collection of the Nicholson Museum*. Sydney: Nicholson Museum, University of Sydney, 2012.

Barnett, Albert E. *Paul Becomes a Literary Influence*. Chicago: University of Chicago Press, 1941.

Barrett, C. K. *A Critical and Exegetical Commentary on the Acts of the Apostles. Vol. II: Introduction and Commentary on Acts XV–XXVIII*. ICC. London/New York: T&T Clark Continuum, 1998.

Bauer, Walter. *Orthodoxy and Heresy in Earliest Christianity*. Edited by R. A. Kraft and G. Krodel. Philadelphia: Fortress, 1971.

Bauckham, Richard. "For Whom Were the Gospels Written?" Pages 9–48 in *The Gospels for All Christians*. Edited by Richard Bauckham. Grand Rapids, MI/Cambridge, UK: Eerdmans, 1998.

Beckman, G. M. *Hittite Birth Rituals: An Introduction*. Malibu: Undena Publications, 1982.

Beckman, G. M. *Hittite Birth Rituals*. 2nd Revised ed. Studien zu den Bogazkoy-Texten heft 29. Wiesbaden: Otto Harrassowitz, 1983.

Belfer-Cohen, A., L. A. Schepartz, and B. Arensberg. "New Biological Data for the Natufian Populations in Israel." Pages 411–24 in *The Natufian Culture in the Levant*. Edited by O. Bar Yosef and F. R. Valla. Ann Arbor: International Monographs in Prehistory, 1991.

Ben-Shlomo, David. "Material Culture." Pages 63–246 in *Ashdod VI: The Excavations at Areas H and K (1968-1969)*. Edited by Moshe Dothan and David Ben-Shlomo. Jerusalem: Israel Antiquities Authority, 2005.

Ben-Shlomo, David. *Decorated Philistine Pottery: An Archaeological and Archaeometric Study*. Oxford: British Archaeological Reports, 2006.

Ben-Shlomo, David. *Philistine Iconography: A Wealth of Style and Symbolism*. Friborg: Academic Press, 2010.

Ben-Shlomo, David, Itzahk Shai, and Aren M. Maeir. "Late Philistine Decorated Ware 9 ('Ashdod Ware'): Typology, Chronology, and Production Centers." *BASOR* 335 (2004): 1–35.

Berman, Joshua A. *Created Equals: How the Bible Broke with Ancient Political Thought*. Oxford: Oxford University Press, 2008.

Bikai, P. M., and M. A. Perry. "Petra North Ridge Tombs 1 and 2: Preliminary Report." *BASOR* 324 (2001): 59–78.

Biran, Avraham, and Joseph Naveh. "An Aramaic Stele Fragment from Tel Dan." *IEJ* 43 (1993): 81–98.

Biran, Avarham, and Joseph Naveh. "The Tel Dan Inscription: A New Fragment." *IEJ* 45 (1995): 1–18.

Bird, Michael F. "Mark: Interpreter of Peter and Disciple of Paul." Pages 30–61 in *Paul and the Gospels: Christologies, Conflicts and Convergences*. Edited by Michael F. Bird and Joel Willitts. LNTS 411. London: T&T Clark, 2011.

Blanton, Richard E. "Beyond Centralization: Steps toward a Theory of Egalitarian Behavior in Archaic States." Pages 135–72 in *Archaic States*. Edited by Gary M. Feinman and Joyce Marcus. Santa Fe: Institute of Advanced Studies, 1998.

Bloch-Smith, Elisabeth. *Judahite Burial Practices and Beliefs about the Dead*. Sheffield: Sheffield Academic Press, 1992.

Bloch-Smith, Elisabeth. "Resurrecting the Iron I Dead." *IEJ* 54 (2004): 77–91.

Bloch-Smith, Elisabeth, and Beth Alpert Nakhai. "A Landscape Comes to Life: The Iron I Period." *Near Eastern Archaeology* 62.2 (1999): 62–127.

Bockmuehl, Markus. *The Epistle to the Philippians*. BNTC. London: A. & C. Black Ltd., 1998.

Bonazzo, J. "Scientists Just Discovered a Major Part of King Solomon's 3,000-Year-Old Mines." *Observer* (January 27, 2017).

Borg, M. J., and J. D. Crossan. *The First Paul: Reclaiming the Radical Visionary behind the Church's Conservative Icon*. San Francisco: HarperOne, 2010.

Borgen, Peder. "John and the Synoptics: Can Paul Offer Help?" Pages 80–94 in *Tradition and Interpretation in the New Testament: Essays in Honor of E. Earle Ellis*. Edited by

Gerald F. Hawthorne and Otto Betz. Grand Rapids, MI/Tübingen: Eerdmans/Mohr Siebeck, 1987.
Bornkamm, Günther. *Paul*. New York: Harper & Row, 1971.
Bousset, Wilhelm. *Kryios Christos: A History of the Belief in Christ from the Beginnings of Christianity to Irenaeus*. Nashville/New York: Abingdon, 1970.
Branch, R. G. "Barnabas: Early Church Leader and Model of Encouragement." *In die Skriflig* 41.2 (2007): 295–322.
Braun, David. P. "Why Decorate a Pot? Midwestern Household Pottery 200 B.C.–A.D. 600." *Journal of Anthropological Archaeology* 10 (1991): 360–97.
Braunsberger, O. *Der Apostel Barnabas: Sein Leben und der ihm beigelegte-Brief*. Mainz: Florian Kupferberg, 1876.
Breen, A.E. "Bethany beyond the Jordan." Page 532 in *The Catholic Encyclopedia*. Vol. 2. New York: Robert Appleton Company, 1907.
Brehme, Sylvia et al. *Ancient Cypriote Art in Berlin*. Nicosia: A. G. Leventis Foundation and the Staatliche Museen zu Berlin, 2001.
Broshi, Magen, and Israel Finkelstein. "The Population of Palestine in the Iron Age II." *BASOR* 287 (1992): 47–60.
Brown, Peter. "The Rise and Function of the Holy Man in Late Antiquity." *The Journal of Roman Studies* 61 (1971): 80–101.
Brown, Peter. *The World of Late Antiquity: AD 15–750*. London: Thames and Hudson Ltd., 1971.
Brown, Raymond E. *The Gospel according to John*. AB 29A. Garden City: Doubleday, 1970.
Budin, Stephanie L. "Creating a Goddess of Sex." Pages 315–24 in *Engendering Aphrodite: Women and Society in Ancient Cyprus*. Edited by D. Bolger and N. Serwint. ASOR Archaeological Reports 07. Boston: ASOR, 2002.
Budin, Stephanie L. *Images of Woman and Child from the Bronze Age. Reconsidering Fertility, Maternity, and Gender in the Ancient World*. Cambridge: Cambridge University Press, 2011.
Bultmann, Rudolph. *Theology of the New Testament*. London: SCM, 1955.
Bunimovitz, Shlomo. "The Late Bronze Age." in *Archaeology of the Land of Israel: From the Neolithic to Alexander the Great*. Edited by Avraham Faust and H. Katz. Ra'anan: The Open University of Israel, in press (Hebrew).
Bunimovitz, Shlomo. "On the Edge of Empires—the Late Bronze Age (1500–1200 BCE)." Pages 320–31 in *The Archaeology of Society in the Holy Land*. Edited by Thomas E. Levy. London: Leicester University Press, 1995.
Bunimovitz, Shlomo. "Lifestyle and Material Culture: Behavioral Aspects of 12th Century B.C.E. Aegean Immigrants in Israel and Cyprus." Pages 146–60 in *Material Culture, Society and Ideology: New Directions in the Archaeology of the Land of Israel*. Edited by Avraham Faust and Aren M. Maeir. Ramat-Gan: Bar-Ilan University, 1999 (Hebrew).
Bunimovitz, Shlomo, and Assaf Yasur-Landau. "Philistine and Israelite Pottery: A Comparative Approach to the Question of Pots and People." *TA* 23 (1996): 88–101.
Bunimovitz, Shlomo, and Avraham Faust. "Ideology in Stone: Understanding the Four Room House." *BAR* 28.4 (2002): 32–41, 59–60.
Bunimovitz, Shlomo, and Avraham Faust. "Building Identity: The Four Room House and the Israelite Mind." Pages 411–23 in *Symbiosis, Symbolism and the Power of the Past: Canaan, Ancient Israel and Their Neighbors from the Late Bronze Age through Roman Palestine*. Edited by William G. Dever and Seymour Gitin. Winona Lake: Eisenbrauns, 2003.

Burney, Charles Fox. *The Aramaic Origin of the Fourth Gospel*. Oxford: Clarendon Press, 1922.

Burrows, M. *What Mean These Stones? The Significance of Archeology for Biblical Studies*. New Haven: American Schools of Oriental Research, 1941.

Butcher, Kevin. *Coinage in Roman Syria: Northern Syria 64BC–AD253*. Royal Numismatic Society 34; Ann Arbor: University of Michigan Press, 2004.

Cameron, A., and A. Kuhrt, eds. *Images of Women in Antiquity*. London: Routledge, 1993.

Campbell, Edward F. "Archaeological Reflections on Amos's Targets." Pages 32–52 in *Scripture and Other Artifacts*. Edited by Michael David Coogan, J. Cheryl Exum, and Lawrence E. Stager. Louisville: Westminster/John Knox Press, 1994.

Campbell, W. *Paul and the Creation of Christian Identity*. London: T&T Clark, 2008.

Campbell, W. "The Addressees of Paul's Letter to the Romans: Assemblies of God in House Churches and Synagogues?" Pages 146–68 in *Between Gospel and Election: Explorations in the Interpretation of Romans 9-11*. Edited by Florian Wilk and J. Ross Wagner. WUNT 257. Tübingen: Mohr Siebeck, 2010.

Campbell, W. *Unity and Diversity in Christ: Interpreting Paul in Context*. Eugene, OR: Cascade Books, 2013.

Campbell, W. *The Nations in the Divine Economy: Paul's Covenantal Hermeneutics and Participation in Christ*. Lanham, MD: Lexington/Fortress Academic, 2018.

Caraher, William R., Scott Moore, and David K. Pettegrew. *Pyla-Koutsopetria I: Archaeological Survey of an Ancient Coastal Town*. Archaeological Reports 21. Boston, MA: ASOR, 2014.

Carter, Warren. *The Roman Empire and the New Testament*. Nashville, TN: Abingdon, 2005.

Casey, Maurice. *Jesus: Evidence and Argument or Mythicist Myths?* London: Bloomsbury, 2014.

Cayla, Jean-Baptiste. *Les inscriptions de Paphos: La cité chypriote sous la domination lagide et à l'époque impérial*. Travaux de la Maison de l'Orient 74. Lyon: Maison de l'Orient et de la Méditerranée Jean Pouilloux, 2018.

Chamberlain, A. *Demography in Archaeology*. Cambridge: Cambridge University Press, 2006.

Chapman, Stephen B. "Saul/Paul: Onomastic Typology and Christian Scripture." Pages 214–43 in *The Word Leaps the Gap: Essays on Scripture and Theology in Honor of Richard B. Hays*. Edited by J. R. Wagner, C. K. Rowe, and Katherine Grieb. Grand Rapids, MI: Eerdmans 2009.

Charlesworth, James H. *The History of the Rechabites, Volume 1: The Greek Recension*. Chico, CA: Scholars Press, 1982.

Charlesworth, James H. "Cesarea Maritima." Pages 62–5 in *The Millennium Guide for Pilgrims to the Holy Land*. North Richland Hills, TX: BIBAL Press, 2000.

Charlesworth, James H. "Introduction: Devotion to and Worship in Jerusalem's Temple." Pages 1–17 in *Jesus and Temple: Textual and Archaeological Explorations*. Edited by James H. Charlesworth. Minneapolis: Fortress Press, 2014.

Charlesworth, James H. *Jesus as Mirrored in John*. London/New York: T&T Clark, 2019.

Charlesworth, James H., and Jolyon G. R. Pruszinski, eds. *Jesus Research: The Gospel of John in Historical Inquiry*. Jewish and Christian Texts 26. London: T&T Clark, 2019.

Charlesworth, James H., and Michael Medina. *Walking through the Land of the Bible: Historical 3D Adventure*. Jerusalem: The Hebrew University Magnes Press, 2014.

Chotzakoglou, Charalampos G. *Church of Saint Lazarus in Larnaka*. Lefkosia: Thekona Printing Works, LTD, 2004.

Cline, Eric. *1177 B.C.: The Year Civilization Collapsed*. Princeton: Princeton University Press, 2014.
Collins, Raymond F. "Lazarus." *ABD* 4 (1992): 265–6.
Corbell, Anthony. *Nature Embodied: Gesture in Ancient Rome*. Princeton: Princeton University Press, 2004.
Corliss, William R. *Rare Halos, Mirages, Anomalous Rainbows and Related Electromagnetic Phenomena: A Catalog of Geophysical Anomalies*. Glen Arm, MD: The Sourcebook Project, 1984.
Cross, Frank M. *Canaanite Myth and Hebrew Epic*. Cambridge: Harvard University Press, 1973.
Cross, Frank M. "Reuben, First-Born of Jacob." *ZAW* 100 Supplement (1988): 46–65.
Crossan, John Dominic. *The Historical Jesus: The Life of a Mediterranean Jewish Peasant*. San Francisco: HarperSanFrancisco, 1991.
Crossley, James G. "Mark, Paul and the Question of Influences." Pages 1–29 in *Paul and the Gospels: Christologies, Conflicts and Convergences*. Edited by Michael F. Bird and Joel Willitts. LNTS 411. London: T&T Clark, 2011.
Cullmann, Oscar. *The Christology of the New Testament*. Revised ed. NTL. Philadelphia: Westminster, 1963.
Cunningham, H. *Children and Childhood in Western Society since 1500*. London/New York: Longman, 1995.
Daniels, J. B. "Barnabas." *ABD* 1 (1992): 610–11.
David, Nicholas, Judy Sterner, and Kodzo Gavua. "Why Pots Are Decorated." *Current Anthropology* 29 (1988): 365–89.
Davies, W. D. *Paul and Rabbinic Judaism*. Revised ed. New York: Harper & Row, 1967.
Davila, James R. "Is the Story of Zosimus Really a Jewish Composition?" Paper presented in the Pseudepigrapha Group at the Annual Meeting of the SBL, Atlanta, GA, November 24, 2003. https://www.st-andrews.ac.uk/divinity/rt/otp/abstracts/zosimus/
Dayagi-Mendels, Michal, and Silvia Rozenberg, eds. *Chronicles of the Land: Archaeology in the Israel Museum Jerusalem*. Jerusalem: The Israel Museum, 2010.
Deetz, James. *In Small Things Forgotten, An Archaeology of Early American Life*. New York: Anchor, 1996.
Depla, A. "Women in Ancient Egyptian Wisdom Literature." Pages 24–52 in *Women in Ancient Societies, An Illusion of the Night*. Edited by L. J. Archer, S. Fischler, and M. Wyke. London: The Macmillan Press, 1994.
Dever, William G. *Gezer VI*. Annual of the Nelson Glueck School of Biblical Archaeology IV. Jerusalem: Hebrew Union College, 1986.
Dever, William G. "How to Tell a Canaanite from an Israelite?" Pages 26–56 in *The Rise of Ancient Israel*. Edited by Hershel Shanks. Washington: Biblical Archaeology Society, 1992.
Dever, William G. "Cultural Continuity, Ethnicity in the Archaeological Record, and the Question of Israelite Origins." *ErIsr* 24 (1993): 22–33.
Dever, William G. "Ceramics, Ethnicity, and the Questions of Israel's Origins." *BA* 58.4 (1995): 200–13.
Dever, William G. "Ceramics, Syro-Palestinian Ceramics of the Neolithic, Bronze and Iron Ages." Pages 459–65 in *OEANE* 1. Edited by Eric Meyers. New York: Oxford University Press, 1997.
Dever, William G. *Who Were the Israelites and Where Did They Come From?* Grand Rapids: Eerdmans, 2003.

Dever, William G. *Beyond the Texts: An Archaeological Portrait of Ancient Israel and Judah*. Atlanta: Society of Biblical Literature, 2017.
Dodd, C. H. *The Interpretation of the Fourth Gospel*. Cambridge: Cambridge University Press, 1953.
Donner, Herbert, and Wolfgang Röllig. *Kanaanäische und aramäische Inschriften*. 2nd ed. Wiesbaden: Harrassowitz, 1966-9.
Dothan, M. and D. N. Freedman. *Ashdod I. The First Season of Excavations 1962*. Jerusalem: The Department of Antiquities and Museums in the Ministry of Education and Culture, 1967.
Dothan, Moshe. *Ashdod II-III: The Second and Third Seasons of Excavations 1963, 1965, Soundings in 1967*. Atiqot 9-10. Jerusalem: Department of Antiquities and Museums, Ministry of Education and Culture; Department of Archaeology. Hebrew University of Jerusalem; Israel Exploration Society, 1971.
Dothan, Moshe, and Yosef Porath. *Ashdod IV: Excavation of Area M*. Atiqot XV. Jerusalem: The Department of Antiquities and Museums, 1982.
Dothan, Trude, *The Philistines and Their Material Culture*. New Haven: Yale University and the Israel Exploration Society, 1982.
Dothan, Trude, and Amnon Ben-Tor. *Excavations at Athienou, Cyprus 1971-1972*. Qedem 16. Jerusalem: Institute of Archaeology, Hebrew University of Jerusalem, 1983.
Duff, Paul B. *Jesus Followers in the Roman Empire*. Grand Rapids, MI: Eerdmans, 2017.
Dunn, James D. G. *Unity and Diversity in the New Testament: An Inquiry into the Character of Earliest Christianity*. Philadelphia: Westminster, 1977.
Dunn, James D. G. "The New Perspective on Paul." Pages 183-206 in *Jesus, Paul and the Law: Studies in Mark and Galatians*. London: SPCK, 1990.
Dunn, James D. G. *The Theology of Paul the Apostle*. Grand Rapids, MI/Cambridge, UK: Eerdmans, 1998.
Dunn, James D. G. *Beginning from Jerusalem: Christianity in the Making*. Vol. 2. Grand Rapids, MI: Eerdmans, 2009.
Eck, Werner. *Rom und Judaea. Fünf Vorträge zur römischen Herrschaft in Palaestina*. Tübingen: Mohr, 2007.
Efron, J., St. Weitzman, and M. Lehmann. *The Jews: A History*. London/New York: Routledge, 2016.
Ehrensperger, Kathy. *Paul and the Dynamics of Power: Communication and Interaction in the Early Christ-Movement*. London: T&T Clark, 2007.
Ehrensperger, Kathy. *Paul at the Crossroads of Cultures: Theologizing in the Space Between*. London/New York: Bloomsbury T&T Clark, 2013.
Ehrman, Bart D. *The Triumph of Christianity*. New York: Simon & Schuster, 2018.
Eisenstadt, Irina, Khaled Arabas, and Zur Ablas. "A Late Bronze Age Burial Cave at Zawata." Pages 77-106 in *Burial Caves and Sites in Judea and Samaria From the Bronze and Iron Ages*. Edited by Hananya Hizmi and Alon De Groot. Judea and Samaria Publications 4. Jerusalem: Staff Officer of Archaeology—Civil Administration of Judea and Samaria and Israel Antiquities Authority, 2004.
Elayi, Josette. *Histoire de la Phénicie*. Paris: Perrin, 2013.
Elliott, Neil. *The Arrogance of Nations: Reading Romans in the Shadow of Empire*. Minneapolis: Fortress, 2008.
Ellis, Earle. *Paul's Use of the Old Testament*. Grand Rapids, MI: Eerdmans, 1957.
Eph'al, Israel, and Joseph Naveh. *Aramaic Ostraca of the Fourth Century BC from Idumaea*. Jerusalem: The Magnes Press, the Hebrew University, and the Israel Exploration Society, 1996.

Eriksen, T. H. *Ethnicity and Nationalism*. 3rd ed. London: Pluto, 2010.
Eriksen, T. H. "Ethnicity: from boundaries to frontiers." Pages 280–98 in *The Handbook of Sociocultural Anthropology*. Edited by J. G.Carrier and D. B. Gewertz. London: Bloomsbury, 2018.
Erikson, E. H. *Childhood and Society*. New York: W. W. Norton, 1950.
Erman, A. *Life in Ancient Egypt*. Translated by H. M. Tirard. New York: Dover Publications, 1971.
Esler, Philip F. *Lazarus*. Philadelphia: Fortress, 2006.
Esse, Douglas L. "The Collared Store Jar: Scholarly Ideology and Ceramic Typology." *SJOT* 2 (1991): 99–116.
Esse, Douglas L. "The Collared Pithos at Megiddo: Ceramic Distribution and Ethnicity." *JNES* 51 (1992): 81–103.
Farber, Zev I. "Religion in Eighth-Century Judah: An Overview." Pages 431–53 in *Archaeology and History of Eighth-Century Judah*. Edited by Zev I. Farber and Jacob L. Wright. Atlanta: Society of Biblical Literature, 2018.
Faust, Avraham. "Socioeconomic Stratification in an Israelite City: Hazor VI as a Test-Case." *Levant* 31 (1999): 179–91.
Faust, Avraham. "Ethnic Complexity in Northern Israel during the Iron Age II." *PEQ* 132 (2000): 1–27.
Faust, Avraham. "Burnished Pottery and Gender Hierarchy in Iron Age Israelite Society." *Journal of Mediterranean Archaeology* 15.1 (2002): 53–73.
Faust, Avraham. "Mortuary Practices, Society and Ideology: The Lack of Highlands Iron Age I Burials in Context." *IEJ* 54 (2004): 174–90.
Faust, Avraham. *The Israelite Society in the Period of the Monarchy: An Archaeological Perspective*. Jerusalem: Yad Ben-Zvi, 2005 (in Hebrew).
Faust, Avraham. *Israel's Ethnogenesis: Settlement, Interaction, Expansion and Resistance*. London: Equinox, 2006.
Faust, Avraham. "Trade, Ideology and Boundary Maintenance in Iron Age Israelite Society." Pages 17–35 in *A Holy Community*. Edited by Marcel Purthuis and Joshua Schwartz. Leiden: Brill, 2006.
Faust, Avraham. "The Sharon and the Yarkon Basin in the Tenth Century BCE: Ecology, Settlement Patterns and Political Involvement." *IEJ* 57 (2007): 65–82.
Faust, Avraham. "The Archaeology of the Israelite Cult: Questioning the Consensus." *BASOR* 360 (2010): 23–35.
Faust, Avraham. "How Were the Israelites Buried: The Lack of Iron Age I Burial Sites in the Highlands in Context." Pages 12–32 in *In the Highlands Depth: Ephraim Range and Binyamin Research Studies*. Edited by Aharon Tavger, Zohar Amar, and Miriam Billig. Bethel: Midreshet Harei Gofna, 2011.
Faust, Avraham. "The Israelites and the Sea: Ecology, World Views and Coastal Settlements." *UF* 43 (2011): 117–30.
Faust, Avraham. *The Archaeology of Israelite Society in Iron Age II*. Winona Lake: Eisenbrauns, 2012.
Faust, Avraham. "Decoration versus Simplicity: Pottery and Ethnic Negotiations in Early Israel." *Ars Judaica* 9 (2013): 7–18.
Faust, Avraham. "From Regional Power to Peaceful Neighbor: Philistia in the Iron I–II Transition." *IEJ* 63 (2013): 174–204.
Faust, Avraham. "Pottery and Society in Iron Age Philistia: Feasting, Identity, Economy and Gender." *BASOR* 373 (2015): 167–98.

Faust, Avraham. "Settlement in the Sharon and in the Northern and Southern Coastal Plain during the 8th Century BCE: Settlement, Culture, Ecology, and World-Views." *Jerusalem and Eretz Israel* 10 (2018): 19–38 (Hebrew).

Faust, Avraham, and Hayah Katz. "The Archaeology of Purity and Impurity: A Case-Study from Tel 'Eton, Israel." *Cambridge Archaeological Journal* 27 (2017): 1–27.

Faust, Avraham, and Shlomo Bunimovitz. "The Four Room House: Embodying Iron Age Israelite Society." *NEA* 66 (2003): 22–33.

Faust, Avraham, and Shlomo Bunimovitz. "The Judahite Rock-Cut Tomb: Family Response at a Time of Change." *IEJ* 58 (2008): 150–70.

Faust, Avraham, and Shlomo Bunimovitz. "The House and the World: The Israelite House as a Microcosm." Pages 143–64 in *Family and Household Religion: Toward a Synthesis of Old Testament Studies, Archaeology, Epigraphy, and Cultural Studies*. Edited by Rainer Albertz, Beth Alpert Nakhai, Saul M. Olyan, and Rüdiger Schmitt. Winona Lake: Eisenbrauns, 2014.

Faust, Avraham, and Justin Lev-Tov. "The Construction of Philistine Identity: Ethnic Dynamics in 12th-10th Centuries Philistia." *Oxford Journal of Archaeology* 30 (2011): 13–31.

Faust, Avraham, and Yair Sapir. "The "Governor's Residency" at Tel 'Eton, The United Monarchy, and the Impact of the 'Old House Effect' on Large-Scale Archaeological Reconstructions." *Radiocarbon* 60 (2018): 801–20.

Faust, Avraham, and Justin Lev-Tov. "Philistia and the Philistines in the Iron Age I: Interaction, Ethnic Dynamics and Boundary Maintenance." *HIPHIL Novum* 1 (2014): 1–24.

Faust, Avraham, and Zeev Safrai. "Salvage Excavations as a Source for Reconstructing Settlement History in Ancient Israel." *PEQ* 137 (2005): 139–58.

Faust, Avraham, and Zeev Safrai. *The Settlement History of Ancient Israel: A Quantitative Analysis*. Ramat Gan: Rennert Center for Jerusalem Studies, Bar-Ilan University, 2015 (in Hebrew).

Faust, Avraham, Hayah Katz, Yair Sapir, Assaf Avraham, Ofer Marder, Guy Bar-Oz, Ehud Weiss, Chen Auman-Chazan, Anat Hartmann-Shenkman, Tehila Sadiel, Oren Vilnay, Michael Tsesarsky, Sarah Pariente, Oren Ackermann, Natasha Timmer, Ofir Katz, Dafna Langgut, and Mordechai Benzaquen. "The Birth, Life and Death of an Iron Age House at Tel 'Eton, Israel." *Levant* 49.2 (2017): 136–73.

Fitzmyer, Joseph A. *The Gospel according to Luke*. AB 28A. Garden City, NY: Doubleday, 1981.

Fitzmyer, Joseph A. "The Authorship of Luke-Acts Reconsidered." Pages 1–26 in *Luke the Theologian: Aspects of His Teaching*. New York: Paulist Press, 1989.

Fleddermann, Harry T. *Mark and Q: A Study of the Overlap Texts*. BETL 122. Leuven: University Press, 1995.

Fleddermann, Harry T. *Q: A Reconstruction and Commentary*. BTS 1. Leuven/Dudley, MA: Peeters, 2005.

Foster, Paul. "Paul and Matthew: Two Strands of the Early Jesus Movement with Little Sign of Connection." Pages 86–114 in *Paul and the Gospels: Christologies, Conflicts and Convergences*. Edited by Michael F. Bird and Joel Willitts. LNTS 411. London: T&T Clark, 2011.

Fotiou, Stavros S. *St. Lazarus and His Church in Larnaca*. Translated by A. P. Vittis. Larnaca: The Ecclesiastical Committee of the Holy Church of St Lazarus, 2016.

Fowler, M. D. "Excavated Figurines: A Case for Identifying a Site as Sacred." *ZAW* 97.3 (1985): 333–44.

Fox, Robin Lane. *Travelling Heroes: In the Epic Age of Homer*. New York: Vintage Books, 2008.

Frankel, David. "Cyprus during the Middle Bronze Age." Pages 482–94 in *Oxford Handbook of the Archaeology of the Levant, c. 8000–332 BCE*. Edited by Margreet L. Steiner and Ann E. Killebrew. Oxford: Oxford University Press, 2014.

Franken, Hank M., and Gloria London. "Why Painted Pottery Disappeared at the End of the Second Millennium BCE." *BA* 58 (1995): 214–22.

Franken, Hank M., and Margreet L. Steiner. *Excavations in Jerusalem 1961–1967, Volume II*, London: Oxford University Press, 1990.

Fredriksen, Paula. "If It Looks Like a Duck, and It Quacks Like a Duck … On Not Giving Up the Godfearers." Pages 25–34 in *A Most Reliable Witness: Essays in Honor of Ross Shepard Kraemer*. Edited by Susan Ashbrock Harvey et al. Providence, RI: Brown Judaic Studies, 2015.

Fredriksen, Paula. *Paul, the Pagans' Apostle*. New Haven: Yale University Press, 2017.

Freeman, David. "Strange 'Magical' Amulet Has Scientists Buzzing." *Huffington Post* (January 7, 2015).

Fujii, Takashi. *Imperial Cult and Imperial Representation in Roman Cyprus*. Stuttgart: Steiner, 2013.

Galil, G. *The Lower Stratum Families in the Neo-Assyrian Period*. Leiden: Brill, 2007.

Garroway, K. H. *Children in the Ancient Near Eastern Household*. Winona Lake: Eisenbrauns, 2014.

Gehlken, E. "Childhood and Youth, Work and Old Age in Babylonia—A Statistical Analysis." Pages 89–120 in *Approaching the Babylonian Economy, Proceedings of the START Project Symposium Held in Vienna, 1–3 July 2004*. Edited by H. D. Baker and M. Jursa. Alter Orient und Altes Testament, Band 330. Munster: Ugarit-Verlag, 2005.

Georgiades, Cleanthis P. *History of Cyprus*. Nicosia: Demetrakis Christophorou, 1993.

Georgiou, Giorgos, Jennifer M. Webb, and David Frankel. *Psematismenos-Trelloukkas: An Early Bronze Age Cemetery in Cyprus*. Nicosia: Department of Antiquities, 2011.

Gigante, M. *Il fungo sul Vesuvio secondo Plinio il Giovane*. Rome: Lucarini, 1989.

Gilboa, Ayelet. "The Southern Levant (Cisjordan) during the Iron I Period." Pages 624–48 in *Oxford Handbook of the Archaeology of the Levant, c. 8000–332 BCE*. Edited by Margreet L. Steiner and Ann E. Killebrew. Oxford: Oxford University Press, 2014.

Gilboa, Ayelet. "Iron Age I–II Cypriot Imports and Local Imitations." Pages 483–507 in *The Ancient Pottery of Israel and Its Neighbors from the Iron Age to the Hellenistic Period*. Edited by inSeymour Gitin. Jerusalem: IES, 2015.

Gilboa, Ayelet, Ilan Sharon, and Elisabeth Bloch-Smith. "Capital of Solomon's Fourth District? Israelite Dor." *Levant* 47.1 (2015): 51–74.

Gilboa, Ayelet, Paula Waiman-Barak, and Ilan Sharon. "Dor, the Carmel Coast and Early Iron Age Mediterranean Exchanges." Pages 85–110 in *The Mediterranean Mirror: Cultural Contacts in the Mediterranean Sea between 1200 and 750 B.C.* Edited by Andrea Babbi, Friederike Bubenheimer-Erhart, Beatriz Marín-Aguilera, and Simone Mühl. Mainz: Verlag des Römisch-Germanischen Zentralmuseums, 2015.

Gitin, Seymour, Trude Dothan, and Joseph Naveh. "A Royal Dedicatory Inscription from Ekron." *IEJ* 47 (1997): 1–16.

Gonen, Rivka. *Burial Patterns and Cultural Diversity in Late Bronze Age Canaan*. Winona Lake: Eisenbrauns, 1992.

Gonen, Rivka. "The Late Bronze Age." Pages 211–57 in *The Archaeology of Israel*. Edited by Amnon Ben-Tor. New Haven: Yale University Press, 1992.

Goodman, A. H., and G. J. Armelagos. "Infant and Childhood Morbidity and Mortality Risks in Archaeological Populations." *World Archaeology* 21.2 (1990): 225–43.

Gordis, Robert. "Primitive Democracy in Ancient Israel." Pages 45–60 in *Poets, Prophets and Sages, Essays in Biblical Interpretation*. Edited by Robert Gordis. Bloomington/London: Indiana University Press, 1971.

Gottwald, Norman K. *The Tribes of Yahweh*. New York: Orbis Books, 1979.

Granqvist, H. *Birth and Childhood among the Arabs: Studies in a Muhammadean Village in Palestine*. Helsingfors: Soerstrom and Forlagsaktiebolag, 1947.

Greener, Aaron. *Late Bronze Age Imported Pottery in the Land of Israel: Between Economy, Society and Symbolism*. PhD diss., Bar-Ilan University, Ramat Gan, 2015.

Gregory, Andrew F. "1 Clement and the Writings That Later Formed the New Testament." Pages 129–57 in *The Reception of the New Testament in the Apostolic Fathers*. Edited by Andrew Gregory and Christopher M. Tuckett. Oxford/New York: Oxford University Press, 2005.

Grey, Eleanor. "Beyond the Temple: Blurring the Boundaries of 'Sacred Space.'" Pages 109–18 in *Proceedings of the Fourteenth Annual Theoretical Roman Archaeology Conference, Durham 2004*. Edited by J. Bruhn, B. Croxford, and D. Grigoropoulos. Oxford: Oxbow Books, 2005.

Griffiths, Sarah. "Mysterious 1,500-year-old Charm Unearthed: Palindrome Amulet that Reads the Same Backwards and Forwards Sheds Light on Ancient Religious Beliefs." *Mailonline* (January 5, 2015).

Gruen, Er. S. *Diaspora: Jews amidst Greeks and Romans*. Cambridge: Harvard University Press, 2004.

Gunneweg, A. H. J. *Leviten und Priester*. FRLANT 89. Göttingen: Vandenhoeck & Ruprecht, 1965.

Haacker, Kl. "Paul's Life." Pages 19–33 in *The Cambridge Companion to St Paul*. Edited by J. D. G. Dunn. Cambridge: Cambridge University Press, 2004.

Hadjidemetriou, K. *A History of Cyprus*. 2nd ed. Nicosia: I. G. Kassoulides & Sons, Ltd., 2007.

Hadjisavvas, S. "The Destruction of the Archaeological Heritage of Cyprus." Pages 133–9 in *Trade in Illicit Antiquities: The Destruction of the World's Archaeological Heritage*. Edited by N. Brodie, J. Doole, and C. Renfrew. McDonald Institute Monographs. Cambridge: McDonald Institute for Archaeological Research, 2001.

Haenchen, E. "Barnabas." *RGG* 1 (1957): 879.

Hallo, William W. "Introduction: The Bible and the Monuments." Pages xxi–xxvi in *The Context of the Scripture, Volume Two: Monumental Inscriptions from the Biblical World*. Edited by William W. Hallo and K. Lawson Younger. Leiden: Brill, 2003.

Halpern, Baruch. "Levitic Participation in the Reform Cult of Jeroboam I." *JBL* 95 (1976): 31–42.

Hamann, Richard. "Lazarus in Heaven." *The Burlington Magazine for Connoisseurs* 63.364 (July 1933): 3–5, 8–11.

Haran, Menahem. *Temples and Temple Service in Ancient Israel*. Winona Lake, IN: Eisenbrauns, 1985.

Harden, Donald B. *The Phoenicians*. London: Thames & Hudson, 1963.

Harden, Donald B. *Catalogue of Greek and Roman Glass in the British Museum 1*. London: British Museum, 1981.

Harnack, Adolf. *Luke the Physician: The Author of the Third Gospel and the Acts of the Apostles*. London/New York: Williams & Norgate/G. P. Putnam's Sons, 1907.

Harrington, N. "Children and the Dead in New Kingdom Egypt." Pages 52–65 in *Current Research in Egyptology 2005, Proceedings of the Sixth Annual Symposium University of Cambridge 2005*. Edited by R. Mairs and A. Stevenson. Oxford: Oxbow Books, 2007.

Harris, R. *Gender and Aging in Mesopotamia: The Gilgamesh Epic and Other Ancient Literature*. Norman: University of Oklahoma Press, 2000.

Hassan, F. A. "Determination of the Size, Density, and Growth Rate of Hunting-Gathering Populations." Pages 27–53 in *Population, Ecology, and Social Evolution*. Edited by S. Polgar. Mouton: The Hague, 1975.

Heitmüller, Wilhelm. "Zum Problem Paulus und Jesus." Pages 124–243 in *Das Paulusbild in der neueren deutschen Forschung*. Edited by Karl Heinrich Rengstorf and Ulrich Luck. Wege der Forschung 24. Darmstadt: Wissenschaftliche Buchgesellschaft, 1969.

Hengel, M., and A. M. Schemer. *Paul between Damascus and Antioch*. London: SCM, 1997.

Hengel, Martin. *Acts and the History of Earliest Christianity*. Philadelphia: Fortress, 1980.

Heszer, Catherine. *Rabbinic Body Language: Non-verbal Communication in Palestinian Rabbinic Literature of Late Antiquity*. Leiden: Brill, 2017.

Hodder, Ian, and Scott Hutson. *Reading the Past*. 3rd ed. Cambridge: Cambridge University Press, 2003.

Holloway, April. "Ancient Greek Amulet with Strange Palindrome Inscription Discovered in Cyprus." *Ancient Origins* (January 2, 2015).

Horgan, Maurya P. "Pesharim." Pages 1–193 in *The Dead Sea Scrolls: Hebrew, Aramaic, and Greek Texts with English Translations. Vol 6B, Pesharim, Other Commentaries, and Related Documents*. Edited by James H. Charlesworth et al. Princeton Theological Seminary Dead Sea Scrolls Project 6B. Tübingen: Mohr Siebeck/Westminster John Knox, 2002.

Horrell, David. "No Longer Jew or Greek: Paul's Corporate Christology and the Construction of Christianity." Pages 320–44 in *Christology, Controversy and Community: New Testament Essays in Honour of David R. Catchpole*. Edited by David G. Horrell and Christopher M. Tuckett. Leiden: Brill, 2000.

Horster, Marietta, Doria Nicolaou, and Sabine Rogge, eds. *Church Building in Cyprus (Fourth to Seventh Centuries): A Mirror of Intercultural Contacts in the Eastern Mediterranean*. Münster: Waxman Verlag, 2018.

Hultgren, Arland J. *The Rise of Normative Christianity*. Philadelphia: Fortress, 1994.

Hultgren, Stephen. "The Origin of Paul's Doctrine of the Two Adams in 1 Corinthians 15.45-49." *JSNT* 25 (2003): 343–70.

Hummel, B. S. "Copper." Page 278 in *Eerdmans Dictionary of the Bible*. Vol. 1. Edited by D. N. Freedman, A. C. Myers, and A. B. Beck. Grand Rapids, MI: Eerdmans, 2000.

Humphrey, S. C. *Anthropology and the Greeks*, London: Routledge and Kegan Paul, 1978.

Hunter, Archibald M. *Paul and His Predecessors*. Revised ed. Philadelphia: Westminster Press, 1961.

Hurtado, Larry W. *Lord Jesus Christ: Devotion to Jesus in Earliest Christianity*. Grand Rapids, MI/Cambridge, UK: Eerdmans, 2003.

Hutton, J. M. "Southern, Northern, and Transjordanian Perspectives." Pages 149–74 in *Religious Diversity in Ancient Israel and Judah*. Edited by F. Stavrakopoulou and J. Barton. London/New York: T&T Clark, 2010.

Hutton, J. M. "The Levitical Diaspora (II): Modern Perspectives on the Levitical Cities Lists (A Review of Opinions)." Pages 45–81 in *Levites and Priests in Biblical History and Tradition*. Edited by M. Leuchter and J. M. Hutton. SBL Ancient Israel and Its Literature 9. Atlanta: SBL, 2011.

Iacovou, Maria. "Cyprus during the Iron Age through the Persian Period: From the 11th Century BC to the Abolition of the City-kingdoms (ca. 300 BC)." Pages 795–824 in *Oxford Handbook of the Archaeology of the Levant, c. 8000-332 BCE*. Edited by Margreet L. Steiner and Ann E. Killebrew. Oxford: Oxford University Press, 2014.

Ilan, David. "Burial Sites." Pages 384–6 in *OEANE* 1. Edited by Eric Meyers. New York: Oxford University Press, 1997.

Ilan, David. "Tombs." Pages 218–21 in *OEANE* 5. Edited by Eric Meyers. New York: Oxford University Press, 1997.

Israeli, Yael. *Ancient Glass in the Israel Museum: The Eliahu Dobkin Collection and Other Gifts*. Jerusalem: The Israel Museum, 2003.

Janssen, R. M., and J. J. Janssen. *Growing Up in Ancient Egypt*. London: The Rubicon Press, 1990.

Jarus, Owen. "Ancient Amulet Discovered with Curious Palindrome Inscription." *Live Science* (January 1, 2015).

Jeremias, Joachim. "Ἀδάμ." *TDNT* 1 (1964): 141.

Jewett, Robert. *Romans: A Commentary*. Hermeneia. Minneapolis, MI: Fortress, 2007.

Jobling, David. "'The Jordan a Boundary': Transjordan in Israel's Ideological Geography." Pages 88–133, 142–7, in *The Sense of Biblical Narrative*. Vol. 2. JSOTSup 39. Sheffield: JSOT Press, 1986.

Johnson-DeBaufre, Melanie. *Jesus among Her Children: Q, Eschatology, and the Construction of Christian Origins*. HTS 55. Cambridge, MA: Harvard University Press, 2005.

Jones, Christopher P. "The Historicity of the Neronian Persecution: A Response to Brent Shaw." *NTS* 63 (2017): 148–51.

Jones, Sian. *The Archaeology of Ethnicity: Constructing Identities in the Past and Present*. London: Routledge, 1997.

Kalman, A. "Timna Copper Mines Dated to King Solomon Era." *The Times of Israel* (September 8, 2013).

Kamen, H. A. F. *European Society 1500–1700*. London: Unwin Hyman, 1984.

Kang, Hoo-Goo, and Yosef Garfinkel. "Ashdod Ware I: Middle Philistine Decorated Ware." Pages 151–60 in *Khirbet Qeiyafa. Vo. 1: Excavation Report 2007–2008*. Edited by Yosef Garfinkel and Saar Ganor. Jerusalem: Israel Exploration Journal and the Hebrew University of Jerusalem, 2009.

Karageorghis, Jacqueline. *Kypris: The Aphrodite of Cyprus: Ancient Sources and Archaeological Evidence*. Nicosia: The A. G. Leventis Foundation, 2005.

Karageorghis, Vassos. *Salamis in Cyprus, Homeric, Hellenistic and Roman*. New York: Thames and Hudson, 1969.

Karageorghis, Vassos. *Two Cypriote Sanctuaries of the End of the Cypro-Archaic Period*. Rome: Consiglio Nazionale Delle Ricerche, 1977.

Karageorghis, Vassos. *Cyprus Museum and Archaeological Sites on Cyprus*. Athens: Ekdotike Athenon S.A., 1985.

Karageorghis, Vassos. *The Cyprus Ancient Monuments*. Nicosia: C. Epiphaniou Publications, 1989.

Karageorghis, Vassos. *The Cyprus Museum*. Nicosia: Epiphaniou Publications, 1989.

Karageorghis, Vassos. *Aspects of Everyday Life in Ancient Cyprus, Iconographic Representations*. Nicosia: A. G. Leventis Foundation, 2006.

Karageorghis, Vassos, and M. Demas. *Excavations at Kition V*. Nicosia: Department of Antiquities Cyprus, 1985.

Keel, Othmar. *Symbols of the Biblical World: Ancient Near-Eastern Iconography and the Book of Psalms*. New York: Seabury Press, 1978.
Keel, Othmar, and C. Uehlinger. *Gods, Goddesses and Images of God in Ancient Israel*. Minneapolis: Fortress Press, 1998.
Keener, Craig. *Acts: An Exegetical Commentary*. 4 vols. Grand Rapids, MI: Baker Academic, 2012–15.
Keener, Craig S. *The Gospel of John*. Vol. 2. Peabody, MA: Hendrickson, 2003.
Kelly, R. L. *The Foraging Spectrum: Diversity in Hunter-Gatherer Lifeways*. Washington: Smithsonian Institution Press, 1995.
Kelso, James L. *The Excavations of Bethel (1934–1960)*. AASOR 39. Cambridge, MA: ASOR, 1968.
Kempinski, Aharon. "Area A." Pages 73–81 in *Engebnisse der Ausgrabungen auf der Hirbet el-Msas (Tel Masos) 1972–1975 (vol 1: textband)*. Edited by Volkmar Fritz and Aharon Kempinski. Wiesbaden: Otto Harrassowitz, 1983.
Killebrew, Anne E. *Biblical Peoples and Ethnicity: An Archaeological Study of Egyptians, Canaanites, Philistines, and Early Israel 1300–1100 B.C.E*. Archaeology and Biblical Studies 9. Atlanta: Society of Biblical Literature, 2005.
Kim, Seyoon. *Paul and the New Perspective*. WUNT 2/140. Tübingen: Mohr Siebeck, 2002.
Kimbel, W. H., R. Lavi, Y. Rak, and E. Hovers. "Hominid Remains from Amud Cave in the Context of the Levantine Middle Paleolithic." *Paléorient* 21.2 (1995): 47–61.
King, Karen L. "Factions, Variety, Diversity, Multiplicity: Representing Early Christian Differences for the 21st Century." *MTSR* 23 (2011): 216–37.
King, Philip J., and Lawrence E. Stager. *Life in Biblical Israel*. Louisville: Westminster John Knox Press, 2001.
Kletter, Raz. *The Judean Pillar-Figurines and the Archaeology of Asherah*. BAR International Series 636. Oxford: Tempus Reparatum, 1996.
Kletter, Raz. "People without Burials? The Lack of Iron Age Burials in the Central Highlands of Palestine." *IEJ* 52 (2002): 28–48.
Kloppenborg, John S. *The Formation of Q: Trajectories in Ancient Christian Wisdom Collections*. SAC. Philadelphia: Fortress, 1987.
Kloppenborg, John S. *Excavating Q: The History and Setting of the Sayings Gospel*. Edinburgh: T&T Clark, 2000.
Kok, Michael. "Does Mark Narrate the Pauline Kerygma of 'Christ Crucified'? Challenging an Emerging Consensus on Mark as a Pauline Gospel." *JSNT* 37 (2014): 139–60.
Kollmann, Bernd. *Joseph Barnabas: His Life and Legacy*. Translated by M. Henry. Collegeville, MN: Liturgical Press, 2004.
Köppen, Klaus-Peter. *Die Auslegung der Versuchungsgeschichte, unter besonderer Berücksichtigung der Alten Kirche*. BGBE 4. Tübingen: Mohr Siebeck, 1961.
Kostsova, A. *The Subjects of Early Russian Icons*. Saint Petersburg: Iskusstvo Publishers, 1994.
Kremer, J. "The Awakening of Lazarus." *TD* 33 (1986): 135–8.
Lancy, D. F. *The Anthropology of Childhood: Cherubs, Chattel, Changelings*. Cambridge: Cambridge University Press, 2008.
Landau, Brent. "'One Drop of Salvation from the House of Majesty': Universal Revelation, Human Mission and Mythical Geography in the Syriac Revelation of the Magi." Pages 83–104 in *The Levant: Crossroads of Late Antiquity. History, Religion and Archaeology*. Edited by Ellen Bradshaw Aitken and John M. Fossey. Leiden/Boston: Brill, 2013.
Lapp, Nancy L. "Pottery, Pottery Chronology of Palestine." *ABD* (1992) 5:433–44.

Laufen, Rudolf. *Die Doppelüberlieferungen der Logienquelle und des Markusevangeliums.* BBB 54. Königstein: Peter Hanstein, 1980.
Le Donne, Anthony, and Chris Keith, eds. *Jesus, History, and the Demise of Authenticity: The Rise and Fall of the Search for an Authentic Jesus. Authenticity after the Third Quest.* London/New York: T&T Clark, 2012.
Lee, Yongbom. *The Son of Man as the Last Adam: The Early Church Tradition as a Source of Paul's Adam Christology.* Eugene, OR: Pickwick, 2012.
Lee, Yongbom. "Jesus, Son of Adam and Son of God (Luke 3.38): Adam-Christ Typologies in Luke-Acts." Pages 120–8 in *The Earliest Perceptions of Jesus in Context: Essays in Honour of John Nolland on His 70th Birthday.* Edited by Aaron W. White, Craig A. Evans, and David Wenham. LNTS 566. London: Bloomsbury T&T Clark, 2018.
Lehn, Waldemar H. "The Novaya Zemlya Effect: An Arctic Mirage." *Journal of the Optical Society of America* 69 (1979): 776–81.
Lenski, Gerhard. "Review of N. K. Gottwald, The Tribes of Yahweh." *Religious Studies Review* 6 (1980): 275–8.
Leuchter, M. "From Levite to Maskil in the Persian and Hellenistic Eras." Pages 215–32 in *Levites and Priests in Biblical History and Tradition.* Edited by M. Leuchter and J. M. Hutton. Atlanta: Society of Biblical Literature, 2011.
Leuchter, M., and J. M. Hutton, eds. *Levites and Priests in Biblical History and Tradition.* SBL Ancient Israel and Its Literature 9. Atlanta: SBL, 2011.
Levy, S., and Gershon Edelstein. "Cinq années de fouilles a Tel 'Amal." *Revue Biblique* 79 (1972): 325–45.
Lewis, Theodor J. "Israel, Religion of." Pages 332–6 in *The Oxford Companion to the Bible.* Edited by Bruce M. Metzger and Michael David Coogan. Oxford: Oxford University Press, 1993.
Lichty, E. "Demons and Population Control." *Expedition* 13.2 (1971): 22–6.
Licona, Michael. "Is the Sky Falling in the World of Historical Jesus Research?" *BBR* 26 (2016): 353–68.
Lillehammer, G. "A Child Is Born: The Child's World in an Archaeological Perspective." *Norwegian Archaeological Review* 22.2 (1989): 89–105.
Lindemann, Andreas. "Die Auferstehung der Toten: Adam und Christus nach 1.Kor 15." Pages 155–67 in *Eschatologie und Schöpfund: Festschrift für Erich Grässer zum siebzigsten Geburtstag.* Edited by Martin Evang, Helmut Merklein, and Michael Wolter. BZNW 89. Berlin: de Gruyter, 1997.
Liu, Wenlin, Anupreet Sidhu, Amanda M. Beacom, and Thomas W. Valente. "Social Network Theory." Pages 1–12 in *The International Encyclopedia of Media Effects.* Edited by Patrick Rossler, Cynthia A. Hoffner, and Liesbet van Zoonen. New York: John Wiley & Sons, 2017.
Livingstone, A. "The Pitter-Patter of Tiny Feet in Clay: Aspects of the Liminality of Childhood in the Ancient Near East." Pages 15–27 in *Children, Childhood and Society.* Edited by S. Crawford and G. Shepherd. BAR International Series 1696. Oxford: Archaeopress, 2007.
Livingstone, David. "A Middle Bronze Age II and Iron Age I Tomb (No. 65) at Khirbet Nisya." *Atiqot* 43 (2002): 17–35.
Lods, Alfred. *Israel, from Its Beginning to the Middle of the Eighth Century.* New York: A. A. Knauf, 1932.
Loffreda, S. "Due tombe a Betania presso le Suore della Nigrizia." *LA* 19 (1969): 349–66
Loffreda, S. "La tomba n. 3 presso le Suore della Nigrizia a Betania." *LA* 24 (1974): 142–69.

Lona, Horacio E. *Der erste Clemensbrief.* KAV 2. Göttingen: Vandenhoeck & Ruprecht, 1998.
Lorentz, K. "Cultures of Physical Modification: Child Bodies in Ancient Cyprus." Pages 203–10 in *SOMA 2001, Symposium on Mediterranean Archaeology.* Edited by G. Muskett, A. Koltsida, and M. Georgiadis. International Series 1040. British Archaeological Reports. Oxford: Archeopress, 2002.
Loulloupis, M. C. "An Archaic Classical Tomb at Kornos." Pages 126–67 in *Report of the Department of Antiquities of Cyprus 1967.* Nicosia: Department of Antiquities, 1967.
Lund, John. "On the Circulation of Goods in Hellenistic and Early Roman Cyprus: The Ceramic Evidence." Pages 31–49 in *Panayia Ematousa II: Political, Cultural, Ethnic and Social Relations in Cyprus: Approaches to Regional Studies.* Edited by L. Wreidt Sørensen and K. Winther Jacobson. Athens: Danish Institute of Athens, 2006.
Luz, Ulrich. "Looking at Q through the Eyes of Matthew." Pages 571–89 in *New Studies in the Synoptic Problem. Oxford Conference, April, 2008: Essays in Honour of Christopher M. Tuckett.* Edited by P. Foster, A. Gregory, J. S. Kloppenborg, and J. Verheyden. BETL 239. Leuven/Paris/Walpole, MA: Peeters, 2011.
Lyzhenkova, Maria, and Valery Fateyev, eds. *The Hermitage.* St. Petersburg: P-s Art Publishers, 2008.
Maccoby, Hyam. *The Mythmaker: Paul and the Invention of Christianity.* London: Weidenfeld and Nicholson, 1986.
Maccoby, Hyam. "Paul and the Eucharist." *NTS* 37 (1991): 247–67.
Mack, Burton. *The Lost Gospel: The Book of Q and Christian Origins.* San Francisco: Harper, 1993.
MacKnight, James. *A New Literal Translation from the Original Greek of All the Apostolical Epistles.* 4th ed. London: Longman & Company, 1809.
Magda, Ksewnija. *Paul's Territoriality and Mission Strategy.* Tübingen: Mohr Siebeck, 2009.
Mahnke, H. *Die Versuchungsgeschichte im Rahmen der synoptischen Evangelien: Ein Beitrag zur frühen Christologie.* BBET 9. Frankfurt am Main/Bern/Las Vegas: Peter Lang, 1978.
Marcus, Joel. *Mark 1-8.* AB 27A. New York: Doubleday, 2000.
Marcus, Joel. "Son of Man as Son of Adam." *RB* 110 (2003): 1–24, 370–86.
Marcus, Joel. "Mark—Interpreter of Paul." Pages 29–49 in *Mark and Paul: Comparative Essays Part II: For and Against Pauline Influence on Mark.* Edited by Eve-Marie Becker, Troels Engberg-Pedersen, and Mogens Müller. BZNW 199. Berlin: de Gruyter, 2014.
Margalit, Baruch. "The Geographical Setting of the AQHT Story and Its Ramifications." Pages 131–58 in *Ugarit in Retrospect: Fifty Years of Ugarit and Ugaritic.* Edited by D. G. Young. Winona Lake, IN: Eisenbrauns, 1981.
Mark, Jos J. "Zeno of Citium." *Ancient History Encyclopedia* (February 15, 2011).
Markschies, Christoph. "Barnabas." Page 452 in *Der Neue Pauly: Enzyklopädie der Antike.* Vol. 2. Edited by August Fr. Pauly et al. Stuttgart: J. B. Metzler, 1997.
Markschies, Christoph. "The Canon of the New Testament in Antiquity: Some New Horizons for Future Research." Pages 175–94 in *Homer, the Bible, and Beyond: Literary and Religious Canons in the Ancient World.* Edited by Margaret Finkelberg and Guy G. Stroumsa. Jerusalem Studies in Religion and Culture 2. Leiden/Boston: Brill, 2003.
Marshall, I. Howard. "The Last Supper." Pages 560–75 in *Key Events in the Life of the Historical Jesus: A Collaborative Exploration of Context and Coherence.* Edited by Darrell L. Bock and Robert L. Webb. Grand Rapids, MI: Eerdmans, 2009.
Marsman, H. J. *Women in Ugarit and Israel. Their Social and Religious Position in the Context of the Ancient Near East.* Leiden/Boston: Brill, 2003.

Master, Daniel M., Penelope A. Mountjoy, and Hans Mommsen. "Imported Cypriot Pottery in Twelfth-Century B.C. Ashkelon." *BASOR* 373 (2015): 235–43.

Mazar, Amihai. "The Israelite Settlement in Canaan in the Light of Archaeological Excavations." Pages 61–71 in *Biblical Archaeology Today—1984: Proceedings of the International Congress on Biblical Archaeology, Jerusalem*. Edited by J. Amitai. Jerusalem: Israel Exploration Society, 1985a.

Mazar, Amihai. "Temples of the Middle and Late Bronze Age and the Iron Age." Pages 161–87 in *The Architecture of Ancient Israel from the Prehistoric to the Persian Period*. Edited by Aharon Kempinski and Ronny Reich. Jerusalem: Israel Exploration Society, 1992a.

Mazar, Amihai. "The Iron Age I." Pages 258–301 in *The Archaeology of Israel*. Edited by Amnon Ben-Tor. New Haven: Yale University Press, 1992b.

Mazar, Eilat. "Edomite Pottery at the End of the Iron Age." *IEJ* 35 (1985b): 253–69.

McCarter, P. Kyle. *Ancient Inscriptions*. Washington, DC: Biblical Archaeology Society, 1996.

McDonough, Sean. "Small Change: Saul to Paul, Again." *JBL* 125 (2006): 390–1.

McGovern, Patrick E. *Ancient Wine: The Search for the Origins of Viniculture*. Princeton: Princeton University Press, 2003.

McGovern, Patrick E., Donald L. Glusker, Lawrence J. Exner, and Mary M. Voigt. "Neolithic Resinated Wine." *Nature* 381.6582 (June 6, 1996): 480–1.

McGovern, P. E., S. J. Fleming, and S. H. Katz, eds. *The Origins and Ancient History of Wine*. New York: Gordon and Breach, 1995.

Meier, John P. *A Marginal Jew: Rethinking the Historical Jesus*. Vol. 2. New York/London: Doubleday, 1994.

Meier, Paul D. "The Community of Q." Ph.D. diss., University of Iowa, 1967.

Mendenhall, George. The Hebrew Conquest of Palestine. *BA* 25 (1962): 66–87.

Merleau-Ponty, Maurice. *Phenomenology of Perception*. Translated by Colin Smith. London: Routledge, 1962.

Merrillees, R. S. "Mother and Child: A Late Cypriote Variation on an Eternal Theme." *Mediterranean Archaeology* 1 (1988): 42–56.

Metcalf, Peter, and Richard Huntington. *Celebrations of Death, the Anthropology of Mortuary Ritual*. Cambridge: Cambridge University Press, 1991.

Meyers, Carol. *Discovering Eve: Ancient Israelite Women in Context*. New York/Oxford: The University Press, 1988.

Meyers, Carol. *Rediscovering Eve: Ancient Israelite Women in Context*. New York/Oxford: The University Press, 2013.

Meyers, Carol. "Contributing to Continuity: Women and Sacrifice in Ancient Israel." Pages 1–19 in *Women, Religion, and the Gift: An Abundance of Riches*. Edited by Morny Joy. Sophia Studies in Cross-cultural Philosophy of Traditions and Cultures 17. Springer: Cham, 2017.

Michaelides, Demetrios, ed. *Historic Nicosia*. Nicosia: Rimal Publications, 2012.

Mitchell, Stephen, and Philipp Pilhofer, eds. *Early Christianity in Asia Minor and Cyprus: From the Margins to the Mainstream*. Leiden: Brill, 2019.

Munck, Johannes. "Romans 15: 14-33 and Paul's Conception of His Mission." *JBL* 83 (1964): 1–11.

Murphy-O'Connor, Jerome. *Paul: A Critical Life*. Oxford: Clarendon, 1996.

Murphy-O'Connor, Jerome. "Bethany." Pages 133–5 in *The Holy Land: An Oxford Archaeological Guide from Earliest Times to 1700*. 4th ed. Oxford: Oxford University Press, 1998.

Myres, John L. "Aphrodite Anadyomene." *Annual of the British School at Athens* 41 (1940–5): 99.
Na'aman, Nadav. *Borders and Districts in Biblical Historiography*. Jerusalem Biblical Studies. Jerusalem: Simor, 1986.
Na'aman, Nadav. *The Past That Shapes the Present: The Creation of Biblical Historiography in the Late First Temple Period and after the Downfall*. Jerusalem: Yeriot, 2002.
Nasrallah, Laura, Charalambos Bakirtzis, and AnneMarie Luijendijk, eds. *From Roman to Early Christian Cyprus*. WUNT 437. Tübingen: Mohr Siebeck, 2020.
Neirynck, Franz. "Mark and Q." Pages 263–97 in *Mark and Q: A Study of the Overlap Texts*. Edited by Harry T. Fleddermann, BETL 122. Leuven: University Press, 1995.
Nelligan, Thomas P. *The Quest for Mark's Gospel: An Exploration of the Case for Mark's Use of First Corinthians*. Eugene, OR: Pickwick, 2015.
Nickelsburg, George W. E. "Son of Man." *ABD* 6 (1992): 147–8.
Nickelsburg, George W. E. and James C. VanderKam. *1 Enoch 2: A Commentary on the Book of 1 Enoch, Chapters 37–82*. Edited by Klaus Baltzer. Hermeneia. Minneapolis, MN: Fortress Press, 2011.
Noël Hume, Ivor. *A Guide to Artifacts of Colonial America*. New York: Knopf, 1974.
Nolland, John. *Luke 1-9:20*. WBC. Nashville: Thomas Nelson, 1989.
Notley, R. Steven, and Jeffrey P. Garcia. "Queen Helena's Jerusalem Palace—In a Parking Lot?" *BAR* 40 (May/June 2014): 28–39, 62–5.
Nurmela, Risto. *The Levites: Their Emergence as a Second-Class Priesthood*. South Florida Studies in the History of Judaism 193. Atlanta: Scholars Press, 1998.
Olsen, B.A. "Women, Children and the Family in the Late Aegean Bronze Age; Differences in Minoan and Mycenaean Constructions of Gender." *World Archaeology* 29.3 (1998): 380–92.
Ortlund, Gavin. "Image of Adam, Son of God: Genesis 5:3 and Luke 3:38 in Intercanonical Dialogue." *JETS* 57 (2014): 673–88.
Papadopoullos, Theodoros, ed. Ιστορία τῆς Κύπρου. 6 vols. Leukosia: Hidryma Archiepiskopou Makariou, 1995.
Papageorgiou, Athanasios, and Ioannis A. Eliades. *Guide to the Byzantine Museum and Art Gallery of the Archbishop Makarios III Foundation*. Nicosia: Byzantine Museum of the Archbishop Makarios III Foundation, 2008.
Papantoniou, Giorgos. *Religion and Social Transformations in Cyprus: From the Cypriot Basileis to the Hellenistic Strategos*. Mnemosyne Supplements: History and Archaeology of Classical Antiquity 347. Leiden: Brill, 2012.
Parker, Simon. *The Pre-Biblical Narrative Tradition*. SBL Resources for Biblical Study 24; Atlanta: Scholars Press, 1989.
Parker Pearson, Michael. "Mortuary Practices, Society and Ideology: An Ethnoarchaeological Case Study." Pages 99–113 in *Symbolic and Structural Archaeology*. Edited by Ian Hodder. Cambridge: Cambridge University Press, 1982.
Pearce, K. "The Lucan Origins of the Raising of Lazarus." *ExpTim* 96 (1985): 359–61.
Peleg, Yuval. "Early Roman Farmhouse and Late Bronze Age Burial Cave East of Otniel." Pages 260–84 in *Burial Caves and Sites in Judea and Samaria From the Bronze and Iron Ages* Edited by Hananya Hizmi and Alon De Groot. Judea and Samaria Publications 4. Jerusalem: Staff Officer of Archaeology—Civil Administration of Judea and Samaria and Israel Antiquities Authority, 2004.
Peleg, Yuval, and Irina Eisenstadt. "A Late Bronze Age Tomb at Hebron (Tell Rumeideh)." Pages 21–259 in *Burial Caves and Sites in Judea and Samaria From the Bronze and Iron Ages*. Edited by Hananya Hizmi and Alon De Groot. Judea and Samaria Publications 4.

Jerusalem: Staff Officer of Archaeology—Civil Administration of Judea and Samaria and Israel Antiquities Authority, 2004.
Pesch, Rudolf. *Das Markusevangelium 1 Teil. Kommentar zu Kap. 1,1-8,26*. 2nd ed. HTKNT 2/1. Freiburg/Basel/Vienna: Herder, 1977.
Pesch, Rudolf. *Das Abendmahl und Jesu Todesverständnis*. QD 80. Freiburg/Basel/Vienna: Herder, 1978.
Pickup, Sadie, Marianne Bergeron, and Jennifer M. Webb, eds. *Cypriote Antiquities in Reading: The Ure Museum at the University of Reading and the Reading Museum (Reading Borough Council)*. Studies in Mediterranean Archaeology XX:30. Corpus of Cypriote Antiquities 30. Uppsala: Åströms Förlag, 2015.
Pilides, Despina, and Maria Mina, eds. *Four Decades of Hiatus in Archaeological Research in Cyprus: Towards Restoring the Balance. Proceedings of the International One-Day Workshop, Held in Lefkosia (Nicosia) on 24th September 2016, Hosted by the Department of Antiquities, Cyprus*. Κυπριακά—Forschungen zun antiken Zypern 2. Vienna: Holtzhausen Verlag, 2017.
Pilides, Despina, and Nikolas Papadimitriou, eds. *Ancient Cyprus: Cultures in Dialogue*. Nicosia: Department of Antiquities, Cyprus, 2012.
Polyviou, Ev. "The Jewish Diaspora in Cyprus in Roman Times: The Limitations of Evidence," *Kypriakai Spoudai* 75 (2011): 69–84.
Polyviou, Ev. "Jews in Ancient Cyprus: Apostles, Rabbis, Magicians, Rebels." *Citizen: Chronicle* 6 (April 2018). ["Οι Ιουδαίοι στην Αρχαία Κύπρο: Απόστολοι, ραββίνοι, μάγοι, επαναστάτες." Πολίτης: Χρονικό, τεύχος 6 (Απρίλιος 2018)].
Poole, Matthew. *Annotations on the Holy Bible*. 3 vols. London: Henry G. Bohn, 1846.
Press, M. D. *The Leon Levy Expedition to Ashkelon. Ashkelon 4, The Iron Age Figurines of Ashkelon and Philistia*. Winona Lake: Eisenbrauns, 2012.
Price, T. H. *Kourotrophos: Cults and Representations of the Greek Nursing Deities*. Leiden: Brill, 1978.
Pruszinski, Jolyon G. R. *An Ecology of Scriptures: Experiences of Dwelling behind Early Jewish and Christian Texts*. London: T&T Clark, 2021.
Quinn, Jerome D. "The Last Volume of Luke: The Relation of Luke-Acts to the Pastoral Epistles." Pages 62–75 in *Perspectives on Luke-Acts*. Edited by Charles H. Talbert. Edinburgh: T&T Clark, 1978.
Rabens, Volker. "Von Jerusalem aus und rings umher … (Röm.15,19). Die paulinische Missionsstrategie im Dickicht der Städte." Pages 219–37 in *Das frühe Christentum und die Stadt*. Edited by Reinhard von Bendemann and Markus Tiwald. BWANT 198. Stuttgart: Kohlhammer, 2012.
Ran, Nahman, ed. נתיבים לארץ ישראל. Tel Aviv: 1987 ישראל ארץ אמנות ,.
Reed, Annette Yoshiko, and Nathalie B. Dohrmann. "Rethinking Romanness, Provinicializing Christendom." Pages 1–21 in *Jews, Christians and the Roman Empire in Late Antiquity*. Edited by Annette Yoshiko Reed and Nathalie B. Dohrmann. Philadelphia: University of Pennsylvania Press, 2013.
Reiner, E. "Babylonian Birth Prognoses." *ZAW* 72 (1982): 124–38.
Rendsburg, Garry. "No Stelae, No Queens: Two Issues concerning the Kings of Israel and Judah." Pages 95–107 in *The Archaeology of Difference: Gender, Ethnicity, Class and the 'Other' in Antiquity*. Edited by Douglas R. Edwards and C. Thomas McCollough. Boston: American Schools of Oriental Research, 2007.
Reviv, Hanoch. *The Society in the Kingdoms of Israel and Judah*. Jerusalem: Bialik, 1993 (Hebrew).
Robins, G. *Women in Ancient Egypt*. Cambridge, MA: Harvard University Press, 1993.

Rohde, Joachim. *Rediscovering the Teaching of the Evangelists*. Philadelphia: Westminster, 1968.

Romaniuk, K. "Le Problème des Paulinismes l'Évangile de Marc." *NTS* 23 (1977): 266–77.

Rüsemann, Frank C. *Das Alte Testament als Wahrheitsraum des Neuen: Die neue Sicht der christlichen Bibel*. Gütersloh: Gütersloher Verlaghaus, 2011.

Rutgers, L.V. "The Jews of Italy, c. 235–638." Pages 492–508 in *The Cambridge History of Judaism. Vol. IV. The Late Roman-Rabbinic Period*. Edited by S. T. Katz. Cambridge: Cambridge University Press, 2006.

Saller, S. J. *Excavations at Bethany (1949–53)*. PSBF 12. Jerusalem: Franciscan, 1957.

Salopek, Paul. "Ghosts of the Vine: In Georgia, Science Probes the Roots of Winemaking." *National Geographic* (April 14, 2015).

Samet, Inbal. "Pottery Consumption and International Trade in Middle Bronze Age Kabri and Other Canaanite Palatial Polities." PhD diss., University of Haifa, 2017.

Sanders, E. P. *Paul, the Law and the Jewish People*. Philadelphia: Fortress, 1983.

Sanders, E. P. *The Historical Figure of Jesus*. London: Penguin, 1993.

Sapir, Yair, Assaf Avraham, and Avraham Faust. "Mud-brick Composition, Archaeological Phasing and Pre-Planning in Iron Age Structures: Tel 'Eton (Israel) as a Test-Case." *Archaeological and Anthropological Sciences* 10 (2018): 337–50.

Schenke, L. *Die Urgemeinde: Geschichtliche und theologische Entwicklung*. Stuttgart: Kohlhammer, 1990.

Schreiber, Nicola. *The Cypro-Phoenician Pottery of the Iron Age*. Leiden: Brill, 2003.

Schweizer, Eduard. *The Good News according to Mark*. Atlanta: John Knox, 1976.

Scott, James. *Paul and the Nations*. Tübingen: Mohr Siebeck, 1995.

Seibert, I. *Women in the Ancient Near East*. New York: Abner Schram, 1974.

Shai, Itzhak, and Aren M. Maeir. "The Late Iron Age IIA Pottery Assemblage from Stratum A3." Pages 313–63 in *Tell es-Safi/Gath I (The 1996–2006 Seasons)*. Edited by Aren M. Maeir. Wiesbaden: Harrassowitz, 2012.

Shapira, Amnon. *Democratic Values in the Hebrew Bible*. Tel-Aviv: Hakibbutz Hameuchad, 2009 (Hebrew).

Shaw, I., and P. Nicholson. *Dictionary of Ancient Egypt*. London: The British Museum Press, 2002.

Sherratt, Susan E. "Globlization at the End of the Second Millennium B.C.E." Pages 37–62 in *Symbiosis, Symbolism and the Power of the Past: Canaan, Ancient Israel and Their Neighbors from the Late Bronze Age through Roman Palestine*. Edited by William G. Dever and Seymour Gitin. Winona Lake: Eisenbrauns, 2003.

Sim, David C. *The Gospel of Matthew and Christian Judaism: The History and Social Setting of the Matthean Community*. SNTW. Edinburgh: T&T Clark, 1998.

Sim, David C. "Matthew's Anti-Paulinism: A Neglected Feature of Matthean Studies." *HTS* 58 (2002): 767–83.

Sim, David C. "Matthew 7.21-23: Further Evidence of Its Anti-Pauline Perspective." *NTS* 53 (2007): 325–43.

Śliwa, Joachim. "Magical Amulet from Paphos with the ιαεω-Palindrome." *Studies in Ancient Art and Civilization* 17 (2013): 293–301.

Smith, B. D. "The More Original Form of the Words of Institution." *ZNW* 83 (1992): 166–86.

Smith, Mark. *Where the Gods Are: Spatial Dimensions of Anthropomorphism in the Biblical World*. Anchor Yale Bible Reference Library. New Haven: Yale University Press, 2016.

Smith, P., E. Bornemann, and J. Zias. "The Skeletal Remains." Pages 110–20 in *Excavations at Ancient Meiron, Upper Galilee, Israel 1971–72, 1974–75, 1977*. Edited by

E. M. Meyers, J. F. Strange, and C. L. Meyers. Cambridge, MA: The American Schools of Oriental Research, 1981.

Spaer, Maud. *Ancient Glass in the Israel Museum*. Jerusalem: The Israel Museum, 2001.

Speiser, Ephraim A. "The Manner of the Kings." Pages 280–7 in *The World History of the Jewish People, Vol. 3 (Judges)*. Edited by Benjamin Mazar. Jerusalem: Masada, 1971.

Stager, L. E., and P. J. King. *Life in Biblical Israel*. Louisville, KY: Westminster John Knox Press, 2001.

Stager, L. E., A. Walker, and G. E. Wright, eds. *American Expedition to Idalion, Cyprus*. Supplement to the Bulletin of the American Schools of Oriental Research 18. Cambridge, MA: ASOR, 1974.

Stark, Rodney. *Cities of God: The Real Story of How Christianity Became an Urban Movement and Conquered Rome*. New York: HarperOne, 2007.

Steel, Louise. "Cyprus during the Late Bronze Age." Pages 577–91 in *Oxford Handbook of the Archaeology of the Levant, c. 8000–332 BCE*. Edited by Margreet L. Steiner and Ann E. Killebrew. Oxford: Oxford University Press, 2014.

Stefani, Grete, ed. *Man and the Environment in the Territory of Vesuvius: The Antiquarium of Boscoreale*. Archeologia Vesuviana. Pompeii: Flavius Edizioni Pompeii, 2010.

Stein, Gil. "Economy, Ritual and Power in 'Ubaid Mesopotamia." Pages 35–46 in *Chiefdoms and Early States in the Near East: The Organizational Dynamics of Complexity*. Edited by Gil Stein and Mitchell S. Rothman. Madison, WI: Prehistory Press, 1994.

St. John, Henry, and Viscount Bolingbroke. "Concerning Authority in Matters of Religion." Pages 422–9 in *The Works of Lord Bolingbroke*. Vol. 3. Philadelphia: Carey and Hart, 1841.

Stol, M. *Birth in Babylonia and the Bible, Its Mediterranean Setting*. Cuneiform Monographs 14. Groningen: STYX Publication, 2000.

Stoltz, F. "Sea." Pages 1390–402 in *Dictionary of Deities and Demons in the Bible*. Edited by K. Van der-Toorn, B. Becking, and P. W. Van der Horst. Leiden: Brill, 1995.

Stone, L. *Family, Sex and Marriage in England 1500–1800*. London: Harper and Row, 1977.

Strange, John. *Caphtor/Keftiu: A New Investigation*. Acta Theologica Danica 14. Leiden: Brill, 1980.

Strauss, David Friedrich. *The Life of Jesus Critically Examined*. Edited by Peter C. Hodgson. Translated by George Eliot. Philadelphia: Fortress, 1972.

Streeter, B. H. "St. Mark's Knowledge and Use of Q." Pages 165–83 in *Studies in the Synoptic Problem*. Edited by W. Sanday. Oxford: Clarendon, 1911.

Streeter, B. H. *The Four Gospels: A Study of Origins, Treating of the Manuscript Tradition, Sources, Authorship, and Dates*. Revised ed. London: Macmillan and Co., 1930.

Sumney, Jerry L. *Steward of God's Mysteries: Paul and Early Church Tradition*. Grand Rapids, MI: Eerdmans, 2017.

Swiny, Stuart et al., eds. *Res Maritimae: Cyprus and the Eastern Mediterranean from Prehistory to Late Antiquity*. ASOR Archaeological Reports 4. Atlanta: Scholars Press, 1997.

Talbert, Charles. "What Is Meant by the Historicity of Acts?" Pages 197–217 in *Reading Luke-Acts in Its Mediterranean Milieu*. NovTSup 107. Leiden/Boston: Brill, 2003.

Tappy, Ron. "Did the Dead Ever Die in Biblical Judah." *BASOR* 298 (1995): 59–68.

Theissen, Gerd. "'Evangelium' im Markusevangelium: Zum traditionsgeschichtlichen Ort des ältesten Evangelium." Pages 63–86 in *Mark and Paul: Comparative Essays Part II: For and Against Pauline Influence on Mark*. Edited by Eve-Marie Becker, Troels Engberg-Pedersen, and Mogens Müller. BZNW 199. Berlin: de Gruyter, 2014.

Thompson, Michael. *Clothed with Christ: The Example and Teaching of Jesus in Romans 12.1-15.13*. JSNTSS 59. Sheffield: JSOT Press, 1991.

Thompson, Michael B. "The Holy Internet: Communication between Churches in the First Christian Generation." Pages 49–70 in *The Gospels for All Christians*. Edited by Richard Bauckham. Grand Rapids, MI/Cambridge, UK: Eerdmans, 1998.

Thornton, Claus-Jürgen. *Der Zeuge des Zeugen: Lukas als Historiker der Paulusreisen*. WUNT 56. Tübingen: Mohr Siebeck, 1991.

Tödt, H. E. *The Son of Man in the Synoptic Tradition*. NTL. London: SCM, 1965.

Tucker, J. Brian. *You Belong to Christ: Paul and the Formation of Social Identity in 1 Corinthians 1-4*. Eugene, OR: Pickwick, 2010.

Tuckett, C. M. "Paul and the Synoptic Mission Discourse." *ETL* 60 (1984): 378.

Tuckett, C. M. "Mark and Q." Pages 149–75 in *The Synoptic Gospels: Source Criticism and the New Literary Criticism*. Edited by Camille Focant. BETL 110. Leuven: Leuven University Press/Peeters, 1993.

Ulbrich, A. "The Great Goddess at Marani-Vournes." *Cahiers du centre d' Études Chypriotes* 45 (2015): 201–9.

Uziel, Josef. "The Development Process of Philistine Material Culture: Assimilation, Acculturation and Everything in Between." *Levant* 39 (2007): 165–73.

Vandervondelen, M. "Childbirth in Iron Age Cyprus: A Case Study." Pages 143–55 in *Engendering Aphrodite, Women and Society in Ancient Cyprus*. Edited by D. Bolger, and N. Serwint. ASOR Arch Reports Book 7. Boston, MA: American Schools of Oriental Research, 2002.

Van Deun, P., ed. *Sancti Barnabae Apostoli Laudatio*. Corpus Christianorum Series Graeca 26. Leuven: University Press, 1993.

Van Gennep, A. *The Rites of Passage*. Translated by M. B. Vizedom and G. L. Caffee. Chicago: The University of Chicago Press, 1972.

de Veer, Gerrit. *The Three Voyages of William Barents to the Arctic Regions: 1594, 1595, and 1596*. Translated by Charles T. Beke. London: The Hakylut Society, 1876.

Vermes, G., F. Millar, and M. Goodman. *The History of the Jewish People in the Age of Jesus Christ (175 B.C.–AD 135)*. Vol. 2. Edinburgh: T&T Clark, 1986.

Vickers, Michael, and David Gill. *Artful Crafts, Ancient Greek Silverware and Pottery*. Oxford: Oxford University Press, 1994.

Vielhauer, Philipp. "On the 'Paulinism' of Acts." Pages 33–50 in *Studies in Luke-Acts: Essays Presented in Honor of Paul Schubert*. Edited by Leander E. Keck and J. Louis Martin. Nashville/New York: Abingdon, 1996.

Viezel, E. "Why Does the Torah Describe Babies Born Hands First?" *TheTorah.com* (November 28, 2018).

Viviano, Benedict Thomas. "The Historical Jesus in the Doubly Attested Sayings: An Experiment." *RB* 103 (1996): 367–410; reprinted as Pages 21–63 in *Trinity—Kingdom—Church: Essays in Biblical Theology*. NTOA 48. Freiburg/Göttingen: Universitätsverlag/Vandenhoeck & Ruprecht, 2001.

Wagner, Joseph. *Auferstehung und Leben: Joh 11, 1-12, 19 als Spiegel johanneischer Redaktions-und Theologiegeschichte*. Regensburg: F. Pustet, 1988.

Ward, William A., and Martha S. Joukowsky. *The Crisis Years: The 12th Century B.C., From beyond the Danube to the Tigris*. Dubuque: Kendall-Hunt, 1992.

Watson, Francis. "'I Received from the Lord …': Paul, Jesus, and the Last Supper." Pages 102–24 in *Jesus and Paul Reconsidered: Fresh Pathways into an Old Debate*. Edited by Todd D. Still. Grand Rapids, MI: Eerdmans, 2007.

Webb, Jennifer M., and David Frankel. *Ambelikou Aletri: Metallurgy and Pottery Production in Middle Bronze Age Cyprus*. Studies in Mediterranean Archaeology 138. Jonsered: Åströms Förlag, 2013.

Webb, Robert L. "The Historical Enterprise and Historical Jesus Research." Pages 9–93 in *Key Events in the Life of the Historical Jesus: A Collaborative Exploration of Context and Coherence*. Edited by Darrell L. Bock and Robert L. Webb. WUNT 247. Grand Rapids, MI: Eerdmans, 2009.

Weinfeld, Moshe. "The Extent of the Promised Land: The Status of Transjordan." Pages 59–75 in *Das Land Israel in biblischer Zeit*. Edited by G. Strecker. Göttingen: Vandenhoeck & Ruprecht, 1983.

Welch, John J. "Miracles, *Maleficium*, and *Maiestas* in the Trial of Jesus." Pages 349–83 in *Jesus and Archaeology*. Edited by James H. Charlesworth. Grand Rapids: Eerdmans, 2006.

Wenkel, David H. "From Saul to Paul: The Apostle's Name Change and Narrative Identity in Acts 13.9." *Asbury Journal* 66 (2011): 67–76.

Wesley, John. *Explanatory Notes upon the New Testament*. London: Epworth, 1950.

Westcott, Brooke F. *The Gospel according to St. John*. Edited by Arthur Westcott. London: J. Murray, 1908.

Weyl Carr, Annemarie, and Andréas Nicolaïdès, eds. *Asinou Across Time: Studies in the Architecture and Murals of the Panagia* Phorbiotissa, *Cyprus*. Washington, DC; Dumbarton Oaks Research Library and Collection; Cambridge, MA: Harvard University Press, 2012.

Weymouth, R. F. *The New Testament in Modern Speech*. London: James Clarke & Co., 1903.

Whipps, H. "Mythic Birthplace of Zeus Said Found." *Live Science* (February 9, 2000).

Wilckens, Ulrich. "Jesusüberlieferung und Christuskerygma–zwei Wege urchristlicher Überlieferungsgeschichte." *ThViat* 10 (1966): 310–39.

Wilkinson, R. H. *The Complete Gods and Goddesses of Ancient Egypt*. London: Thames & Hudson, 2003.

Willett, E. A. R. "Infant Mortality and Women's Religion in the Biblical Periods." Pages 79–98 in *The World of Women in the Ancient and Classical Near East*. Edited by B. Alpert Nakhai. Newcastle: Cambridge Scholars Publishing, 2009.

Willitts, Joel. "Paul and Matthew: A Descriptive Approach from a Post-New Perspective Interpretative Framework." Pages 62–85 in *Paul and the Gospels: Christologies, Conflicts and Convergences*. Edited by Michael F. Bird and Joel Willitts. LNTS 411. London: T&T Clark, 2011.

Wilson, Brittany. "Hearing the Word and Seeing the Light: Voice and Vision in Acts." *JSNT* 38.4 (2016): 456–81.

Wilson, Stephen G. *Luke and the Pastoral Epistles*. London: SPCK, 1979.

Wolf, C. Umhau. "Traces of Primitive Democracy in Ancient Israel." *JNES* 6 (1947): 98–108.

Wolter, Michael. "Jesus bei Paulus." Pages 205–32 in *The Rise and Expansion of Christianity in the First Three Centuries of the Common Era*. Edited by Clare K. Rothschild and Jens Schröter. Tübingen: Mohr Siebeck, 2013.

Wrede, William. *Paul*. London: Philip Green, 1907.

Wright, N. T. *Paul and the Faithfulness of God*. Minneapolis, MN: Fortress, 2013.

Yon, Marguerite, and William A. P. Childs. "Kition in the Tenth to Fourth Centuries B.C." *Bulletin of the American Schools of Oriental Research* 308 (November 1997): 9–17.

Zevit, Z. *The Religions of Ancient Israel, A Synthesis of Parallactic Approaches*. London/New York: Continuum, 2001.

Ancient Sources Index

Old Testament / Hebrew Bible

Genesis
1:26	134
1:27–28	42
2:18–20	142n.47
3:16	44
3:24 LXX	133
5:3	143n.53
9:1	42
9:7	42
10	13, 117, 124n.11
10:4	13–14
22:17	42
17	42, 93
24	42
26	42
27	42
28	93
29:1–37	93
29:32–34	42
29:34	96
30:20	42
35:16–20	44

Exodus
1:16	44
6:16–20	94
6:25	94
12:1–20	93
12:43–49	93
24	163n.26
24:9–18	151, 153
27:3	19
28–29	93

Leviticus
1	95
1–16	93
25:32	94

Numbers
1:50	94
3–4	94, 95
3:2–13	93
3:6	94
3:8	94
4:1–3	94
8:5–13	94
8:14–19	93
8:16–18	95
16:9	94
18:2	94
24:24	11, 14
26:58–59	94
35:2	94

Deuteronomy
	94
10:8	95
13	81n.38
21:5	95
31:9	95
31:25	95

Joshua
21:3–7	94

1 Samuel
	44
4:19	44

2 Samuel
8:18	100n.6

1 Kings
7:14	19
7:45–46	19
19:5–8	133

1 Chronicles
	12
1:7	12, 13
9:22	94

9:26–27	94	12:14–16	117
9:33	94	35	155
15:19	19	35:12–19	165–166n.40
23:2–4	94		
23:28	94	Ezekiel	13, 93
27:17	94	1:4 ff.	164n.28
		7:7	12
2 Chronicles		27:6	11–12, 14
17:7–9	94	27:7	14
35:3	94	40–48	94
		44:10–14	93
Ezra		44:13	93
3:8–9	94		
		Daniel	
Nehemiah	16	11:30	12, 14
8:7	94		
9:2	94	Amos	
		9:7	5
Job			
26	153	**New Testament**	
26:5–14	153		
28:5–6	153–154	Matthew	79n.15, 130, 135,
28:12–13	153–154		139n.15, 141n.31,
28:20–24	154		144n.67
		2:1	112n.13
Psalms		7:21–23	144n.67
8	134	9:18–25	66
8:5–7 LXX	134	10:9	19
48:2	164n.28	26:26–29	131
68	164n.28		
75:9	23n.67	Mark	76, 130, 131, 132,
89	164n.28		133, 134, 135, 136,
107	164n.29		137, 140n.20, 140n.26,
			141nn.30–32, 145n.75,
Proverbs			145nn.77–78
23:19–21	15	1–8	142n.52, 144n.73,
			145n.79
Isaiah	16	1:1–8	142n.46
10	23n.52	1:10	134
23:1	14	1:13	142n.51
23:12	14	1:13–14	133
66	117	1:26	142n.46
66:18–19	124n.11	1:31	142n.51
66:19	117	2:27–28	142n.52
		5:21–43	66
Jeremiah	16	7:14–23	136
1:10	88n.2	12:42	19
2:10	11	14:22–25	131
10:10–13	164n.28	16	142n.41

Luke	113n.23, 117, 123, 130, 131, 133, 134, 135, 136, 137, 140n.20, 140n.26, 141n.31, 142n.40, 143n.53, 144n.69, 144n.72, 145nn.75–76	11:25	65
		11:27 f.	75
		11:28	74
		11:30	74
		11:31	74
		11:32	74
		11:33	74
1:1	146n.84	11:35	74
1:1–9:20	143n.53	11:36	66
2:34	108	11:37	75
3:38	143n.53	11:38	74
3:38–4:2	134, 143n.59	11:38–44	67
7:11–17	66	11:44	74, 75
8:40–56	66	11:45–48	76
10:1	86	11:45–57	67
10:8	133	11:47	67
10:23	108	11:48	68
10:25–37	94	11:55	75
10:38–42	67	11:57	66, 68
13:43–45	108	12:1–8	68
16:19–31	65	12:9	76
17:4	108	12:9–11	68
21:2	19	12:10	68
22:17–20	131	12:18	68
24	142n.41	15–17	65
24:31	108	20	78
		21	65
John	13, 65, 76, 130, 131, 135, 137, 140n.23, 140n.26, 143n.53	Acts	9, 76, 86, 87, 93, 103, 104, 106, 107, 109, 111, 112n.6, 113n.22–23, 115, 117, 121, 128, 129, 130, 131, 135, 136, 137, 142n.40, 143n.53, 144n.69, 144nn.71–72, 145n.75
6:35	131		
6:51–58	131		
11	65, 66, 78n.11		
11:1–12	78n.3		
11:1–44	67		
11:3	66		
11:4	75	1–12	103
11:5	66, 74	4:26	117
11:6	74	4:36	12, 85, 89n.9
11:7	75	4:36–37	85, 93, 127, 128, 138n.4
11:8	67	6:1	128
11:11	66	7:58	86
11:11 f.	75	8:1–3	86
11:14	67	9:8–9	107, 108
11:16	67	9:17–19	108
11:17	67	9:26	86
11:18	74	9:27–28	86
11:19	74, 78n.3	9:29	128
11:24	75	10	122

10–11	104	15	104, 116, 121
10:36	106	15:1–3	91n.60
11:19	12, 13, 84, 89n.11	15:1–35	86
11:19–20	13, 127, 128, 138n.1	15:2	87
11:19–26	87, 90n.48, 117	15:12	86, 112n.4, 115, 138n.4
11:20	12, 89n.9	15:18–21	116
11:22	138n.4	15:20	116
11:22–23	86	15:22–32	91n.60
11:24	85	15:23	115
11:25–26	86, 88	15:24	115
11:25–30	88	15:25	112n.4, 115
11:26	138n.3	15:36–40	87
11:27–30	86, 90n.41	15:36–41	115
11:30	138n.4	15:37	138n.4
12:12	85, 130, 138n.4	15:37–39	87
12:25	86, 130, 138n.4	15:37–40	130
12:25–13:3	85, 90n.48	15:37–41	9
13	9, 103, 128, 138n.1	15:38	115
13:1	88	15:39	12, 13
13:1–3	105, 115, 138n.4	15:39–40	127–128, 138n.1
13:1–12	108	15:39–41	115
13:2	87	16:3	118
13:4	12, 13	16:7	120
13:4–5	9	16:10	120
13:4–7	73	17:7	110
13:4–12	90n.48, 103, 127	17:8	110
13:5	84, 96, 105, 130, 138n.4	18–20	140n.25
13:6	9, 84, 105	18:21	120
13:6–11	87	21:3	12, 13, 128
13:7	105, 109	21:4	120
13:8–12	90n.47	21:15–16	13, 128
13:8	99	21:16	12
13:9	90n.47, 107, 113n.17, 115	21:37–39	103
		23:16	85
13:10	107, 108	24:5	84, 138n.3
13:11	108	24:10–27	103
13:11b	108	25–26	111
13:12	9	25:6–12	103
13:13	90n.47, 91n.56, 130, 138n.4	27:4	12, 13, 128
		28:24	108
13:27	110	28:31	103, 112
13:43	87, 90n.47		
13:46	90n.47, 115	Romans	144n.66, 145n.79
13:47	105, 106, 109	1:8	138n.7
13:48	87	5:12–21	133
13:50	90n.47	8:29	142n.44
14:1	87	9–11	126n.31
14:8–18	87	11:25	115, 124n.2
14:14	86	11:28	107

11:28b-29	107	2:3-4	146n.84
12:1–15:13	141n.37	3	125n.27
12:3	119	3:18	142n.44
14	122	4:4	142n.44
14–15	123	5:17	142n.44
14:4	125n.31	8:1–5	138n.7
14:9–15:3	126n.32	8:16–24	120
14:14	136	9:2–4	138n.7
14:20	136	10	119
15:8	118	10:12	119
15:14–33	124n.1	10:13	119
15:19	124n.2, 124n.7	11:24	9
15:24	115		
15:26	138n.7	Galatians	
16:1–16	129	1:7	107
16:19	138n.7	1:13–17	86
		1:15–17	106
1 Corinthians	140n.25, 144n.66	1:19	129
1–4	112n.10	2:9	90n.45
4:19	120	2:9–10	90n.41
5:9	146n.84	2:11–13	91n.57, 91n.59
7:17	117, 118	2:11–14	138n.7
7:17–24	119	2:13	91n.59, 123
7:17-32a	125n.20	3:1	107
7:19	118, 119	6:15	119, 142n.44
7:22	120		
7:24	118	Ephesians	136
7:29–31	118		
8	122	Philippians	140n.25
9:6	87	1:12–14	138n.7
10:27	133	2:5–11	133, 135, 142n.43
11:17–34	131	2:25–26	138n.7
11:23	140n.21	3:7–8	119
11:23–25	131	4:15–16	138n.7
11:24–25	131	4:22	138n.7
15	142n.41, 142n.45		
15:21–22	133	Colossians	136
15:32	140n.25	1:15	142n.44
15:44–49	133	4:7–9	138n.7
15:45–49	142n.45	4:10	89n.25, 130, 132
15:49	142n.44	4:14	135
16:1	138n.7	4:16	138n.7, 146n.84
16:8	140n.25		
16:8–9	138n.7	1 Thessalonians	
16:19–20	138n.7	1:6–10	138n.7
		2:14–16	138n.7
2 Corinthians			
1:15–2:4	120	1 Timothy	136
2:1	120	1:3	140n.25

2 Timothy	136	25:5	167n.60
1:18	140n.25	32:1	167n.60
4:11	91n.56, 130, 132, 135	77:3	167n.60
4:12	140n.25	77:4 (*OTP*)	167n.60
Titus	136	1 Maccabees	85
		1:1	12
Philemon	132, 140n.25	8:5	12
23–24	132	15:23	88n.4, 89n.9
24	130, 135		
		2 Baruch	7
Hebrews	86, 134, 135, 137, 143n.55	*2 Enoch*	
2:5–11	134	58:2–6	142n.47
2:6–8	134		
13:23	143n.58	2 Maccabees	
		12:2	88n.4
James	130, 135, 137		
2:14–26	139n.16	*4 Ezra*	7
1 Peter	135, 137, 143n.64	*Apocalypse of Moses*	
4:16	138n.3	15:3	142n.47
		16:2	142n.47
2 Peter	135, 137	24:4	142n.47
3:15–16	144n.65	29:1–6	142n.48
		29:14	142nn.47–48
1 John	135, 137	29:16	142n.47
2 John	135, 137	*Apocalypse of Sedrach*	
		5:2	142n.48
3 John	135, 137		
		Epistle of Aristeas	
Jude	135	12–14	88n.5
Revelation	135, 154	*History of the*	
21	154	*Rechabites*	147, 155, 156, 158, 159, 160, 163n.25, 164n.29, 164n.33, 166nn.46–47, 167n.62, 168n.71, 168n.76
21:1–4	164n.32		
21:6–8	164n.32		
21:10	164n.30		
21:10–11	164n.32		
21:18–20	164n.32	1–7	168n.63
21:23–25	154, 164n.32	1:2	155
		1:3	155
Old Testament Apocrypha and Pseudepigrapha		2:1	155
		2:6	156
		2:6 syr.	156
1 Enoch	157	2:6–7 gk.	156
6:2–6	157	2:8a	156
25:3–5	157	2:8	156

3:1–4	156	**New Testament Apocrypha and Pseudepigrapha**	
4:2 gk.	156		
4:8–9 gk.	156		
8–12	168n.63	*Acts of Barnabas*	86
10:7a syr.	156	23	86
10:7	156		
10:7 gk.	156	*Acts of John*	140n.24
10:7 syr.	156		
10:8	156	*Acts of Paul*	9
10:8 gk.	156		
11:5a-5b syr.	156	*Gospel of the Hebrews*	137–138
11:5 syr.	156		
13	168n.63	*Gospel of the Nazoreans*	138
14–16:7	168n.63		
16:8–18	168n.63	*Gospel of Thomas*	130, 132
17:3a syr.	156		
17:4b syr.	156	Pseudo-Clement	13
17:5b syr.	156	*Homilia*	
		1 9.1	13
Jubliees		*Recognitiones*	
3:1–3	142n.47	1.7.7	13
3:28	142n.47		
8–9	125n.13	**Dead Sea Scrolls**	
Life of Adam and Eve		*Apocryphon of Levi* (4Q541)	96
4:2	142n.50		
8:1–3	142n.47	*Beatitudes* (4QBéat / 4Q525)	14, 16
13:3–15:3	142n.48	Frag. 24	14
21:1–3	142n.48	Frag. 24.7–8	15
22:1–2	142n.48	Frag. 25.4	14
37:1–3	142nn.47–48		
		Damascus Document (CD)	
Prayer of Jacob		4.2–4 (MS A)	96
10–11	99	13:2–11	89n.23
Testament of Levi	97	*Isaiah Pesher* (4QpIsa^a / 1Q161)	
18:10	134	4	12
Testaments of the Twelve Patriarchs	96	*Pseudepigraphon of Benjamin ar* (4Q538)	96
Sirach (Ben Sira)		*Pseudepigraphon of Levi* (4Q540)	96
31:29	15, 85		
		Rule of the Community (1QS)	
Tobit		6:8–11	89n.23
4:15	15	8:1–3	89n.23

Temple Scroll	65	**Apostolic Fathers**	
Testament of Joseph ar (4Q539)	96	1 Clement	135
		5:5–7	144n.66
Testament of Judah (3Q7, 4Q484)	96	20:8	165n.39
		37–38	85
Testament of Levi (1Q21, 4Q213, 4Q213ᵃ⁻ᵇ, 4Q214, 4Q214ᵃ⁻ᵇ)	96	40–41	85
		40.5	85
		Didache	135
Testament of Naphtali (4Q215)	96	*Epistle of Barnabas*	86

Papyri, Ostraca, and Inscriptions

Testament of Qahat ar (4Q542) 96

Corpus Inscriptionum Latinarum
    4.679   138n.3

Vision and Testament of Jacob ar (4Q537) 96

pKahun and Gurob
    prescriptions 21–23   52n.6

*Visions of Amram*ᵃ⁻ᵍ (4Q543-49) 96

pRam IV (Gardiner, C 2–3)   52n.6

Greek and Latin Works

Rabbinic Texts

Ambrose
   Comm. Luke
    4.7   143n.53
    4.14   143n.53

Babylonian Talmud
  Kerithot 6a   89n.24
  Sotah 17a:24   163n.27

Ammianus Marcellinus
   Res Gestae
    14 8.14   5

The Fathers According to Rabbi Nathan (ARN), Version A
  1   142n.49

Antoninus Liberalis
   Metamorphōseōn synagōge
    33   167n.55

Jerusalem Talmud
  Yoma 4:5   85

Apollodorus
   Library
    3.10.1   167n.55

Mishnah
  Middoth 2:5–6   85

Rashi
  Exod 1:16   44, 52n.18

Apostolic Church Order (*Constitutio Ecclesiastica Apostolorum*)
    15–29   89n.23

Targum Pseudo-Jonathan
  Gen 37:25   14
  Gen 43:11   14

Aristotle
   Physics   22n.37

Athanasius
  Frag. Matt
    PG 27:1368A   142n.46

Athenaeus
  Denipnosophistae
    15.695   167n.55

Benedictus Arias Montanus
  Sacrae Geographiae   14

Bordeau Pilgrim
  Itinerarium Burdigalense 71

Cicero
  Tusculan Disputations
    1.1.2   104–105

Clement of Alexandria 13
  Quis dives salvetur
    42   140n.24
  Stromateis
    2 116.3   23n.63
    2.6   90n.36
    2.7   90n.36
    2:20 116.3.5   90n.35

Cyprian
  Epistulae
    1.1   89n.23
    52.5   85

Dio Cassius
  Historiae Romanae
    68.32   89n.17
    68.32.3   84, 89n.18

Dio Chrysostom
  Historia
    49 32.5   22n.41

Diodorus of Sicily
  Bibliotheca historica
    1.68, 6   6

Epiphanius   13
  De incarnatione
    4.4   23n.63

  Panarion
    20   23n.63
    37.6   74

Euripedes
  Helena
    1676   167n.55

Eusebius   13
  Historia ecclesiastica
    1 12.1   23n.63
    2 1.4   23n.63
    5.24.3–4   140n.24
    7.25.16   140n.24
  Onomastikon
    58 lines 15–17   71, 79n.22

Gervase of Tilbury
  Otia Imperialia   71

Herodotus   62
  Historiae
    1.105   3
    2.182   6
    3.26.1   167n.55
    3.89   62
    3.91   55
    5.104   6
    7.90   3

Hesiod
  Opera et dies
    155–173   167n.55
    168–173   154, 164n.34
  Theogony
    195   3, 21n.16

Hippolytus of Rome
  Refutatio omnium haeresium
    9.22   165n.39
  Against Noetus
    18   70

Homer
  Hymns
    5   21n.16

Ancient Sources Index

Iliad
    23.205   166n.53
Odyssey   21n.16
    17.485–87   91n.51

Iamblichus
    On the Mysteries
        1.1   91n.53

Irenaeus
    Adversus haereses
        3.1.1   140n.24
        3.1.4   140n.24
        5.21.2   142n.46

Jacobus de Varagine
    Golden Legend   66, 70

Jerome   65, 71
    Adversus Vigilantium
        6   165n.39
    Epistulae
        52.5   85
    Psalm VIII   99

John Chrysostom
    On the Four-day [Dead] Lazarus
        PG 132, 513B   73

Josephus
    Antiquitates Judaicae
        1, 128   14
        12.3–7   88n.5
        13.10.4   83
        13.284–287   89n.9, 138n.2
        16.4.5   84
        17.285–295   112n.15
        18.64   138n.3
        20.216   85
        20.218   89n.21
    Jewish War
        4.8.1   80n.30
        5.25   32

Justin
    Dialogus cum Tryphone
        103   142n.46

Libanius
    Oratio
        18.172   168n.66

Lucius Columella
    De Re Rustica
        12.20.3   16
        12.22.2   16

Martial
    Epigrammaton libri
        4.441   7, 22n.40

Ovid
    Metamorphoses
        8.618–724   91n.52

Philo
    De Aeternitate Mundi
        26   165n.39
    Legatio ad Gaium
        282   89n.9, 138n.2
        282.3   84, 89n.13
    De Specialibus Legibus
        156   89n.22

Philostratus
    Vita Apollonii
        5.3   166n.45, 167n.55

Pindar
    Olympionikai
        2.55–75   167nn.55–56
        2.61–78   155, 164n.35

Plato
    Critias   160, 167n.56, 168n.76
        113d-e   167n.54
        116c   167n.54
    Gorgias
        523a   155, 164–165n.36, 167n.55

526c	167n.55	Strabo	
Menexenus		*Geographica*	
235c	167n.55	3.2.13	166n.45,
Phaedo			167n.55
109	171	14 6.5	9–10
Symposium			
179e	167n.55	Tertullian	
180e	21n.16	*Adversus Valentinianos*	
		7	165n.39
Pliny the Elder	9	*De Pudicitia*	
Naturalis Historia		20	86
14.124	16		
16.60	16	Tacitus	
		Annales	
Plutarch		15.44	138n.3
Sertorius			
8	166n.45	Virgil	
Vita Antonii		*Aeneid*	
36.3	22n.41	4.331–332	107
		Xenophon	
Ptolemy		*Cyropaedia*	
Geographica		7 4.1–2	6
7.5.14	166n.45		
		Other Ancient Texts	
Simplicius			
Physics	22n.37	Atra-hasis	
		1:281–295	44
Suetonius			
Nero		Sarcophagus Text	
16.2	138n.3	Utterance 366 § 632	42, 52n.5

Modern Authors Index

Ablas, Z. 40n.57
Achtemeier, P. 143n.64
Ackermann, O. 39n.25, 39n.29
Aharoni, Y. 39n.28
Ahituv, S. 40n.45
Albright, W. 39n.34, 39n.37
Alexander, L. 106, 112n.16
Alexander, P. S. 125n.13
Allison, D. C. xv, 20n.3, 127–146, 139n.9, 139n.16, 142n.39, 142n.42, 169n.77
Alpert Nakhai, B. 39n.22, 39n.26, 40n.40, 40n.42
Amorai-Stark, S. 24n.77
Arabas, K. 40n.57
Arensberg, B. 52n.10
Armelagos, G. J. 52n.10
Attridge, H. 134, 143n.55, 143n.58
Aubet, M. E. 38n.6, 39n.19
Auman-Chazan, C. 39n.25, 39n.29
Aus, R. D. 124n.2, 125n.12
Avissar Lewis, R. S. xv, 41–53, 52n.3
Avraham, A. 39n.25, 39n.29

Backhouse J. 45, 52n.24, 53n.27
Bakirtzis, C. 20n.2, 173
Baltrusch, E. 112n.12
Bar-Oz, G. 39n.25, 39n.29
Barclay, J. M. G. 88n.1, 88n.6, 89n.15
Barclay, W. 78n.8
Barkay, G. 39n.28, 39n.30, 40n.50
Barnett, A. E. 140n.22
Barrett, C. K. 145n.76
Bauer, W. xxvi, 73, 80n.27, 99, 101n.17, 129, 139n.13
Bauckham, R. 138n.6
Baumgarten, J. M. 96
Beacom, A. M. 146n.83
Beckman, G. M. 52n.9, 52n.23
Belfer-Cohen, A. 52n.10
Ben Artzi, A. xi-xii

Ben-Shlomo, D. 29–30, 38nn.14–15, 39n.17, 39n.30
Ben-Tor, A. 21n.22
Benzaquen, M. 39n.25, 39n.29
Berman, J. A. 39n.34
Bikai, P. M. 52n.10
Biran, A. 40n.46
Bird, M. F. 144n.67, 145nn.77–78
Blanton, R. E. 40n.49
Bloch-Smith, E. 37, 39n.22, 39n.26, 40n.40, 40n.52, 40n.56
Bockmuehl, M. 143nn.61–62
Bolingbroke, V. 145n.80
Bonazzo, J. 22n.44
Borg, M. J. 90n.40, 90n.42, 90n.46, 91n.54, 91n.59
Borgen, P. 140n.26
Bornemann, E. 52n.10
Bornkamm, G. 141n.35
Bousset, W. 135, 144n.68
Bowers, W. P. 116
Branch, R. G. 88, 88n.3, 88n.7, 90nn.28–30, 90n.33, 90n.36–37, 90n.39, 90n.44, 91n.55, 91n.58, 91nn.61–62
Brashear, W. M. 98
Braun, D. P. 39n.32
Braunsberger, O. 23n.61
Breen, A. E. 79n.24
Brehme, S. 21n.29
Broshi, M. 38n.12
Brown, P. 168n.70, 171, 172n.1
Brown, R. E. 67, 78n.7
Budin, S. L. 21n.15, 47, 53nn.32–33, 53n.41, 53n.43, 53n.45
Bultmann, R. 118, 140n.22
Bunimovitz, S. 35, 38n.4, 38n.7, 40n.44, 40n.53, 40n.55, 40n.58
Burney, C. F. 143n.53
Burrows, M. 52n.9, 53n.38
Butcher, K. 168n.67

Cameron, A. 52n.8
Campbell, E. F. 39n.29
Campbell, W. S. xv, 23n.65, 115–126, 124n.5, 125n.17, 125n.20, 125n.25, 125n. 27, 125–126n.31
Carter, W. 112n.15
Casey, M. 136, 144n.72
Chamberlain, A. 52n.10
Chapman, S. B. 113n.17
Charlesworth, J. H. xi-xii, xv, xxvii, 1–24, 20n.11, 21n.17, 23n.57, 23n.62, 24n.76, 65–81, 78n.2, 78n.4, 79n.26, 80nn.35–36, 93–101, 140n.23, 166nn.46–47, 168nn.64–65, 169n.77, 171–172
Childs, W. A. P. 79n.16
Chotzakoglou, C. G. 79n.19, 79n.21, 79n.25
Cline, E. 38n.5
Collins, R. F. 66, 78n.1, 78n.5
Corbell, A. 113nn.19–20
Corliss, W. R. 161n.8, 162n.10
Cross, F. M. 39n.34, 100n.2, 163n.26
Crossan, J. D. 90n.40, 90n.42, 90n.46, 91n.54, 91n.59, 139n.17
Crossley, J. G. 145n.77
Cullmann, O. 142n.38
Cunningham, H. 52n.12

Daniels, J. B. 23n.55
David, N. 39n.32, 39n.35
Davies, W. D. 141n.34, 143n.59
Davila, J. R. 167–168nn.62–63
Dayagi-Mendels, M. 1–3, 20n.7
Deetz, J. 34, 39n.35
Depla, A. 52n.8
Demas, M. 21n.30
Dever, W. G. 29, 39n.22, 39n.26, 39n.28, 39n.34, 39nn.36–37, 40nn.42–43, 40n.50
Dodd, C. H. 140n.22
Dohrmann, N. B. 112nn.7–8
Donner, H. 163n.24
Dothan, M. 29, 30, 38n.10
Dothan, T. 21n.22, 39n.16, 40n.46
Duff, P. B. 125n.23
Dunn, J. D. G. 90nn.31–32, 90n.34, 90n.44, 90n.47, 90n.49, 91n.50, 91n.59, 91n.63, 122, 139n.14, 142n.43, 143n.56

Eck, W. 112n.12
Edelstein, G. 29
Efron, J. 89n.17
Ehrensperger, K. xv, 22n.48, 103–113, 125n.14, 126n.33
Ehrman, B. D. 138n.5
Eisenstadt, I. 40n.57
Elayi, J. 39n.19
Eliades, I. A. 80n.33
Elliott, N. 112n.15
Ellis, E. 124n.10, 140n.26
Eph'al, I. 22n.51
Erikson, E. H. 53n.51
Eriksen, T. H. 38
Esler, P. F. 78n.6
Esse, D. L. 39n.37

Farber, Z. I. 40n.42
Fateyev, V. 22n.42
Faust, A. xiv, 20n.9, 25–40, 38nn.10–11, 38n.13, 39n.18, 39nn.20–21, 39n.23, 39n.25, 39n.29, 39nn.32–33, 40nn.41–42, 40n.44, 40n.50, 40nn.58–61, 40nn.63–65
Finkelstein, I. 38n.12
Fitzmyer, J. A. 136, 144n.72
Fleddermann, H. T. 141n.30
Fleming, S. J. 24n.70
Foster, P. 141n.31, 144n.67
Fotiou, S. S. 69–70, 79nn.12–13, 79n.17, 79n.20, 80n.28
Fowler, M. D. 53n.38
Fox, R. L. 157–159, 163n.23, 168n.68, 168n.74
Frankel, D. 38n.2
Franken, H. M. 39n.28, 39n.31
Fredriksen, P. 112n.11, 122–123, 125n.28
Freeman, D. 100n.8
Freedman, D. N. xxv, 24n.78, 30, 38n.10

Galil, G. 52n.15
Ganschinietz, R. 98
Garcia, J. P. 20n.8
Garfinkel, Y. 30
Garroway, K. H. 52n.10
Gavua, K. 39n.32, 39n.35
Gehlken, E. 52n.16
Georgiades, C. P. 22n.35
Gibson, S. 47

Gigante, M. 22n.40
Gilboa, A. 37, 38n.6, 38nn.8–9
Gill, D. 39n.24
Gitin, S. 40n.46
Gonen, R. 38nn.3–4, 39n.39, 40n.51, 40n.54, 40n.57
Goodman, A. H. 52n.10
Goodman, M. 88n.5
Gordis, R. 39n.34
Gottwald, N. K. 39n.34
Granqvist, H. 53n.51
Greener, A. 26, 38nn.2–3
Gregory, A. F. 141n.31, 144n.66
Grey, E. 159, 168n.73
Griffiths, S. 100n.8
Gruen, Er. S. 88n.1, 89n.9
Gunneweg, A. H. J. 23n.54

Haacker, Kl. 91n.63
Hadjidemetriou, K. 8, 20n.12, 21n.23, 21n.26, 21nn.31–32
Hadjisavvas, S. 64n.10
Haenchen, E. 23n.55
Hallo, W. W. 35
Halpern, B. 100n.2
Haran, M. 23n.58, 94, 100n.5
Harden, D. B. 22n.46, 55
Harnack, A. 144n.69
Harrington, N. 52n.10
Harris, R. 52n.8, 52n.22
Hartmann-Shenkman, A. 39n.25, 39n.29
Hassan, F. A. 52n.10
Heitmüller, W. 132, 141n.36
Hengel, M. 23n.55, 138n.1
Hershkovitz, M. 24n.77
Heszer, C. 113n.19
Hodder, I. 39n.27, 39n.35
Holloway, A. 101n.9
Horgan, M. P. 23n.52
Horrell, D. 125n.16
Hovers, E. 52n.10
Hume, I. N. 34
Hultgren, A. J. 138n.8, 139n.14
Hultgren, S. 142n.45
Hummel, B. S. 24n.78
Humphrey, S. C. 39n.34
Hunter, A. M. 145n.82
Huntington, R. 40n.60
Hurtado, L. W. 143n.61

Hutson, S. 39n.27, 39n.35
Hutton, J. M. 23nn.53–54, 24n.75, 89nn.19–20, 94, 100nn.3–4

Iacovou, M. 38nn.8–9
Ilan, D. 40n.50
Israeli, Y. 22n.46

Janssen, J. J. 52n.4, 52n.7, 52n.9, 53nn.25–26
Janssen, R. M. 52n.4, 52n.7, 52n.9, 53nn.25–26
Jarus, O. 101n.9, 101n.13
Jeremias, J. 143n.53
Jewett, R. 119, 124n.6, 145n.78
Jobling, D. 24n.75, 100n.4
Johnson-DeBaufre, M. 139n.9
Jones, C. P. 138n.3
Jones, S. 39n.27
Joukowsky, M. S. 38n.5

Kalman, A. 22n.44
Kamen, H. A. F. 52n.12
Kang, H-G. 30
Karageorghis, V. 20n.5, 21n.25, 21nn.27–28, 21n.30, 21n.33, 22n.38, 53n.39, 53nn.45–49, 64n.4, 79n.16, 80n.29
Katz, H. 39n.25, 39n.29
Katz, O. 39n.25, 39n.29
Katz, S. H. 24n.70
Keel, O. 40n.64, 53nn.29–33, 53nn.35–37
Keener, C. S. 67, 78n.7, 144n.72
Kelly, R. L. 52n.12
Kelso, J. L. 39n.34
Keith, C. 140n.26
Kempinski, A. 30, 38n.10
Killebrew, A. E. 38nn.3–4, 38n.7
Kim, S. 134, 143n.60
Kimbel, W. H. 52n.10
King, K. L. 139n.14
King, P. J. 37, 39n.26, 39n.37, 52n.17
Kletter, R. 36, 39n.36, 40n.52, 53n.35, 53n.38
Kloppenborg, J. S. 139nn.11–12, 141n.29, 141n.31
Kok, M. 145n.77
Kollek, T. 1
Kollmann, B. 13, 22n.41, 22n.50, 23n.55, 23n.60, 23n.63
Köppen, K.-P. 143n.53

Kostsova, A. 79n.11
Kremer, J. 78n.3
Kuhrt, A. 52n.8

Lancy, D. F. 52n.12
Landau, B. 166n.53, 167n.58
Landau, Y. 35
Landenberg, S. 28–29
Langgut, D. 39n.25, 39n.29
Lapp, N. L. 39n.28
Laufen, R. 141n.32
Lavi, R. 52n.10
Le Donne, A. 140n.26
Lee, Y. 143n.53, 143n.55, 143n.57
Lehmann, M. 89n.17
Lehn, W. H. 162n.12
Lenski, G. 39n.34
Leuchter, M. 23nn.53–54, 89nn.19–20, 100n.3
Lev-Tov, J. 39n.18
Levy, S. 29
Lewis T. J. 40n.64
Lichty, E. 52n.9, 52n.22
Licona, M. 140n.26
Lillehammer, G. 52n.10
Lindemann, A. 142n.45
Liu, W. 146n.83
Livingstone, A. 52n.5, 52n.23
Livingstone, D. 40n.56
Lods, A. 39n.34
Loffreda, S. 79n.22
Lona, H. E. 144n.66
Lorentz, K. 52n.10, 53n.49
Loulloupis, M. C. 64n.6
Luijendijk, A. 20n.2, 173
Lund, J. 112n.5
Luz, U. 141n.31
Lyzhenkova, M. 22n.42

Maccoby, H. 140n.21, 145n.80
Mack, B. 139n.12
MacKnight, J. 125n.24
Maeir, A. M. 39n.15, 39n.30
Magda, K. 124n.3, 125n.11, 125n.13
Mahnke, H. 142n.46
Marcus, J. 136, 142n.52, 143n.57, 144n.73, 145n.77, 145n.79
Marder, O. 39n.25, 39n.29
Margalit, B. 168n.75

Mark, J. J. 22n.36
Markschies, C. 23n.55, 146n.84
Marmelshtein, M. 28–29
Marshall, I. H. 139n.18
Marsman, H. J. 52nn.8–9, 52nn.22–23
Master, D. M. 38n.7
Mazar, A. 39n.26, 39n.37, 39n.39, 40n.40
Mazar, E. 39n.30
McCarter, P. K. 40n.46
McDonough, S. 113n.17
McGovern, P. E. 15, 23–24nn.70–72
Medina, M. 20n.11, 24n.76
Meier, J. P. 69, 78n.10
Meier, P. D. 139n.11
Mendenhall, G. 39n.34
Merleau-Ponty, M. 168n.77
Merrillees, R. S. 53n.45
Metcalf, P. 40n.60
Meyers, C. 40n.42
Millar, F. 88n.5
Munck, J. 124n.1
Murphy-O'Connor, J. 79n.23, 143n.63
Myres, J. L. 169n.61

Na'aman, N. 24n.74, 35, 40n.48
Nasrallah, L. 20n.2, 173
Naveh, J. 22n.51, 40n.46
Neirynck, F. 141n.30
Nelligan, T. P. 145n.77
Nicholson, P. 53n.25
Nickelsburg, G. W. E. 142n.38, 167n.60
Noël Hume, I. 34
Nolland, J. 143n.53
Notley, R. S. 20n.8
Nurmela, R. 23n.54, 100n.1

Olsen, B. A. 53n.45
Origne, A. 148, 161n.9
Ortlund, G. 143n.53

Papadimitriou, N. xvi, 21n.20, 21n.33, 80n.29
Papageorgiou, A. 80n.33
Pariente, S. 39n.25, 39n.29
Parker, S. 168n.75
Parker Pearson, M. 40n.60
Pearce, K. 78n.3
Peleg, Y. 40n.57

Perry, M. A. 52n.10
Pesch, R. 139n.18, 142n.46
Pilides, D. xvi, 21n.20, 21n.33, 80n.29
Polyviou, Ev. 88nn.4–5, 88n.8, 89n.10, 89nn.16–17, 89n.26
Poole, M. 143n.54
Porath, Y. 29
Press, M. D. 53n.34
Price, T. H. 53n.45
Pruszinski, J. G. R. xiv, 20n.4, 78n.4, 140n.23, 147–169, 169n.77, 171–172, 173–195
Pruszinski, K. N. xv, 64nn.3–10

Quinn, J. D. 145n.76

Rabens, V. 124n.7
Ran, N. 23n.66
Rak, Y. 52n.10
Reed, A. Y. 112nn.7–8
Reiner, E. 52n.7
Rendsburg, G. 35
Reviv, H. 38n.13
Robins, G. 52n.7, 52n.9, 53nn.25–26
Rohde, J. 139n.10
Röllig, W. 163n.24
Romaniuk, K. 145n.77
Rozenberg, S. 20n.7
Rüsemann, F. C. 125n.19
Rutgers, L.V. 113n.18

Sadiel, T. 39n.25, 39n.29
Safrai, Z. 38n.11
Saller, S. J. 79n.22
Salopek, P. 23n.69
Sanders, E. P. 124n.2, 124n.5, 139n.19
Sapir, Y. 32, 39n.25, 39n.29
Sari, K. xiv, 21n.21, 55–64
Schemer, A. M. 23n.55
Schenke, L. 13, 23n.59
Schepartz, L. A. 52n.10
Schreiber, N. 28, 38nn.9–10, 39n.17
Schwartz, D. R. 96
Schweizer, E. 140n.20
Scott, J. 125n.11, 125n.13
Seibert, I. 52n.8, 52n.22
Shai, I. 39n.15, 39n.30
Sharon, I. 37, 38n.6
Shapira, A. 39n.34

Shaw, I. 53n.25
Sherratt, S. 38n.7
Sidhu, A. 146n.83
Sim, D. C. 139n.15, 144n.67
Śliwa, J. 97–99, 100n.8, 101nn.10–12, 101n.15
Smith, B. D. 140n.20
Smith, M. 163n.24, 164n.31
Smith, P. 52n.10
Sørensen, L. W. 1, 112n.5
Spaer, M. 22n.46
Speiser, E. A. 39n.34
Stager, L. E. 23n.53, 24n.79, 37, 39n.26, 39n.37, 52n.17, 94
Stark, R. 116, 124n.4
Steel, L. 38n.6
Stefani, G. 22n.40
Stein, G. 40n.49
Steiner, M. L. 39n.28
St. John, H. 145n.80
Stol, M. 52n.4, 52n.9, 52nn.22–23
Stoltz, F. 40n.64
Stone, L. 52nn.10–12
Strange, J. 5, 21n.24
Strauss, D. F. 166n.44
Streeter, B. H. 132, 141n.31
Sterner, J. 39n.32, 39n.35
Sumney, J. L. 143n.63
Swiny, S. 20n.1

Talbert, C. 144n.71, 145n.76
Tappy, R. 40n.50
Theissen, G. 145n.77
Thompson, M. B. 138n.6, 141n.37, 145n.78
Thornton, C-J. 136, 144n.72
Timmer, N. 39n.25, 39n.29
Tödt, H. E. 135n.11
Tsesarsky, M. 39n.25, 39n.29
Tucker, J. B. 112n.10
Tuckett, C. M. 125n.16, 141nn.31–32, 142n.40, 144n.66

Uehlinger, C. 53nn.29–33, 53nn.35–37
Ulbrich, A. 53n.45
Uziel, J. 39n.16

Valente, T. W. 146n.83
Van Deun, P. 23n.56

Van Gennep, A. 53n.51
VanderKam, J. C. 167n.60
De Veer, G. 161n.6
Vermes, G. 88n.5
Vickers, M. 39n.24
Vielhauer, P. 144n.69
Viezel, E. 53n.53
Vilnay, O. 39n.25, 39n.29
Viviano, B. T. 132, 140–141nn.27–28, 141n.33

Wagner, J. 78n.3
Waiman-Barak, P. 38n.6
Ward, W. A. 38n.5
Watson, F. 140n.21
Webb, R. L. 131, 139nn.18–19
Weinfeld, M. 24n.75, 100n.4
Weiss, E. 39n.25, 39n.29
Weitzman, S. 89n.17
Welch, J. W. 73, 77, 79n.26, 80n.38
Wenkel, D. H. 113n.17

Wesley, J. 143n.54
Westcott, B. F. 74–75, 80n.32
Weymouth, R. F. 118, 125n.15
Whipps, H. 20n.14
Wilckens, U. 132, 141n.36
Wilkinson, R. H. 52n.20
Willet, E. A. R. 52n.9, 52n.22, 53n.38
Willitts, J. 144n.67, 145n.77
Wilson, B. 113n.22
Wilson, S. G. 145n.76
Wolf, C. U. 39n.34
Wolter, M. 141n.35, 142n.45
Wrede, W. 145n.80
Wright, N. T. 137, 145n.81

Yasur-Landau, A. 35
Yon, M. 79n.16

Zarras, K. Th. xv, 22n.47, 83–91, 93, 96
Zevit, Z. 53n.35
Zias, J. 52n.10

Subject Index

Aaron (Aaronite) 13, 85, 93–96, 100n.2, 151, 153
Abraham and Sarah 42
Abydos 45
Adam Christology 133–135, 142nn.43–52, 143nn.53–64, 144nn.65–68
Adiabene 2
Aegadian Islands 155
Aegean colony 3
Aegean style pottery 30, 39n.15
Aeolian Islands 155
Africa 1, 43
Agia Kiraki 9
Agios Lazaros in Larnaca 70–71
Agrippa and Festus 111
Ai 19
Alain Origne 149, 161n.9
Alexander the Great 6, 12, 73, 88n.1
Alexandria 13, 23n.63, 69, 86, 90nn.34–36, 104, 140n.24, 171
Allauch, France 161nn.3–5, 161n.9
Amasis, Pharaoh 6
Amphilochius of Iconium 69
amphora(e) xiv, 16, 29
Amram 96
amulets 43, 45, 97, 98, 99, 100n.8, 101n.9
Andrew of Crete 70
Annas 95
Anthony (or Antony) and Cleopatra 7–8, 83–84
Antilles, Lesser 155
Antioch 1, 13, 23n.55, 73, 74, 83, 84, 86–88, 90n.34, 90n.41, 90n.49, 91n.57, 105, 112n.4, 115, 117, 121, 122, 123, 127, 128, 146n.83, 149, 150, 155, 158, 160, 162n.14, 167–168n.63, 168n.65, 171
Antioch "Incident" 91n.57, 121–122
Antioch, Patriarchate of 74
Antiochus IV 12
Antoninus Pius 84, 96

Aphek 27, 46
Aphrodite (*See also* Kypris) 1–3, 7, 11, 17, 21nn.15–17, 48–49, 80n.37, 83, 104, 157, 167n.61
apocalypse (apocalyptic) 7, 133, 155, 160, 166n.41
apostles xii, 13, 70, 73, 75, 78–79n.11, 83, 85–89, 93, 112n.6, 113n.17, 116, 119, 121–123, 124n.5, 124n.8, 125n.21, 125n.28, 127, 131–133, 135, 137, 142n.43, 144n.69, 145n.76
Aquila and Prisca 129
Arabia 40n.60, 117
Aramaic 13–14, 16, 22n.51, 143n.53
Arbanassi, Bulgaria 77
archaeology 1, 3, 20n.6, 21n.22, 24n.71, 25–53, 55–64, 71, 79n.26, 97, 142n.52, 166n.53, 168n.73, 173–183, 185–186, 188–191, 193, 195
Aristotle 6, 22n.37
Ashdod 18, 25, 27, 29–30, 56
Ashdod Ware (*See also* Late Philistine Decorated Ware) 25, 29–31, 39n.15
Ashkelon 3, 18, 27, 46, 56
Asia 1, 5, 14, 16, 83, 87, 129
Asia Minor 5, 14, 16, 83, 87, 129
Asshur 14
Assyrian Empire 4
Assyrians 5–6, 55, 57
Atlantis 156, 160, 165n.37, 165n.39, 167n.54, 167nn.56–57
Atlantis Effect 160
Atlas 167n.57
Atlit 62, 64n.3
atmospheric inversion 160, 161n.7, 162n.12, 162n.17, 163n.25
atmospheric refraction (*See also* Novaya Zemlya, Canigou Effect, Atlantis Effect) 148, 160, 161n.2, 161n.4, 161n.6, 161n.8, 162n.10, 162n.12, 162nn.14–15, 163n.20

Atra-hasis 44
Augustus (*See also* Octavian) 104
Autun Cathedral 69
Avallon, church at 69
Azores 155

Baal cycle 150–151, 153, 159–160, 163n.21, 163n.26, 168n.75
Barentsz expedition 161n.6
Babylonia xxiv, 16, 43, 95
Babylonians 42, 55
Babylonian Exile 95
Bacchus 7
Bar Jesus 9, 73, 103, 105–110, 127
Barlaam Monastery 159, 168n.69
Barnabas xv, 9, 13, 18–19, 22n.41, 22n.47, 22n.50, 23n.55, 23nn.60–61, 23n.63, 70, 73, 79n.15, 83–91, 93, 96, 97, 100, 104–106, 108–109, 112n.4, 115, 117, 120–123, 127–128
Bashan 11, 14
Basil of Seleucia 70
Beijing 5
Benedictus Arias Montanus 14
Berlin 5–6, 19
Bermuda 155
Bes 44
Bethany (el-'Azariyeh) 65–68, 71–74, 79nn.22–24, 80n.38
Beth Shean 18, 24n.76, 27, 46
Beth-Shemesh 19, 27
Bethzatha pool 76
Bilbel jar 9
Birth of Venus The (Botticelli) 3
Bithynia 120
Black on Red (BoR) Ware (*See also* Cypro-Phoenician pottery) xx, 28–30, 38
Black Sea 3
borders vs. barriers xiii–xiv, 17–20, 24n.74, 97, 99–100, 172
Britain (*See also* England) 5
bronze 2–3, 5, 8–9, 17, 19, 21n.17, 46, 56–57, 60
Bronze Age xi, xiv, xvi, xx, 5, 9, 17, 20n.9, 22n.46, 25–26, 35–36, 40n.66, 41, 46, 47–48
Building of Eustolios 4
Byblos 6
Byzantine period xvi, 9, 71, 159

Caesarea Maritima 3, 18, 24nn.76–77, 69, 71, 77–78, 128, 172
Caesarion (Julius Caesar's son) 8
Caiaphas 68, 80–81n.38
calling (Pauline, in Acts, etc.; *See also* mission) 107, 116–120, 121
Calypso 167n.57
Canaan/Canaanite xiii–xv, 5–6, 9, 22n.46, 25, 34, 36–37, 41, 46, 51, 53n.52, 100n.2, 163n.26, 172
  burial practice 36
childbirth and delivery 41, 46, 51
Canary Islands 155
Canigou Effect 147–151, 153–154, 156, 158–160, 161nn.3–10, 162nn.10–11, 163n.26, 167n.54
Cape Verde 155
Carthage 6, 107
cedar 5, 31, 158
Chethim (*See also* Kittim, Cyprus) 14
childbirth 41–53. *See also* delivery
China 5, 15
Christianity xii–xiv, 1, 4, 9, 11, 13, 19, 20nn.2–3, 65, 69–71, 73–74, 76, 80n.27, 80n.33, 83–85, 88, 89n.12, 90nn.31–32, 90n.34, 90n.44, 90n.47, 90n.49, 91n.50, 91n.59, 94, 99, 101n.17, 107, 112n.7, 113n.17, 123, 124n.4, 125n.16, 125n.25, 127–146, 147, 154–155, 158–160, 165n.39, 171–173
Christian theology, early
  genealogy of 133–135
  Mark and Q 132
  multiple attestation, criterion 130–131
  Paul and Acts 135
  Paul and the Jesus Tradition 132–133
Chrysostom, John 69, 73, 158
Church, the (ἐκκλησία) (*See also* Christianity, Christian theology, early) 13, 71, 73, 85–91, 115–117, 120–123, 126nn.31–32, 129, 131, 132, 135
Cicero 6, 104, 112n.9
Citium (*see also* Kitium, Kition, Larnaca) 3–4, 21n.18, 22n.36
Clement of Alexandria 13, 23n.63, 86, 90nn.35–36, 140n.24
Cleopatra (*see* Anthony and Cleopatra)

coin (coins, coinage; *See also* widow's
    mite, Jewish prutah) 7, 19, 104, 158,
    168n.67
conception 42–44. *See also* fertility
Constantia (*See also* Salamis) 74
Constantine II, Emperor 74
copper xiv, 2, 5, 8–10, 19, 22n.44, 24n.78,
    55, 62, 69, 84, 88n.2
Corinth 64n.4, 104
Council of Nicea 71, 99
Crete 3, 5, 70, 83–84
Cronos 164–165nn.35–36
cynocephalus 98
Cyprians (*see also* Cypriots) 3, 5, 9, 95
Cypriot Mt. Olympus 147, 149–152, 158,
    162n.14, 162n.16, 163n.20
Cypriots (*see also* Cyprians) xiv, 3, 5–6,
    9, 19, 83–91, 93, 95–100, 103–113,
    115, 117, 120–121, 123, 127–128
  imports and international trade xi,
    xiii–xiv, 2–12, 14–16, 19, 30, 55–64,
    112n.5, 171–172
  pottery 25–30, 37–38
  style of decoration 28–30
  Syllabic Script 6
Cypro-Phoenician pottery (*See also* Black
    on Red Ware) 28–31
Cyprus (*See also* Elishah, isles of Elisha,
    Kittim, Kypris) 1–24, 25–40, 41–53,
    55–64, 65–66, 69–70, 72–74, 76–80,
    83–91, 93, 95–101, 103–105, 108,
    111–112, 115, 117, 120–121, 123,
    127–128, 138nn.1–2, 147–152,
    155–157, 159–160, 162n.18,
    171–173
  childbirth and delivery 41, 44–51
  church to Lazarus 65
  fertility issues (*See also* fertility,
    conception) 42–43
  historical significance 1–11
  New Testament on 127–128
  number of children 43–44
Cyrenaica (Cyrene) 83, 117, 127
Cyril of Alexandria 69
Cythera 3, 21n.16

Damascenus of Studios 70
Damascus 17, 23n.55, 107, 134, 171
Darius III 6, 64n.9

David 8, 17, 19, 44, 94, 110
Deir El-Medina 45, 52n.24
delivery 41, 44–51
Delos 97
De Re Rustica 16
Deuteronomist 94
Dikteon Cave 3, 20n.13
Diodorus of Sicily 6
Diodorus of Tarsus 158
Dodanim (*See also* Rodanim) 14
Dor 17–18, 26–27, 37, 64n.8

Early Bronze Age xvi, 5, 47, 48
Eastern Mediterranean xviii, 20n.1
  geography 1–2, 83, 160
  Jewish communities 83–84
  maritime connections 25, 31
  parallel geography 149–150
  trade 5, 25, 31, 83–84
Eber 14
Eden 134, 142n.49, 166n.44
Edict of Milan 4
Edom 34
egalitarian ideology 34–37, 40n.60, 40n.62
Egypt xi, 2, 4–6, 8, 15–16, 18–19, 20n.10,
    22n.46, 37, 42, 44–46, 52n.5, 52–
    53n.24, 53n.52, 55, 60, 62, 73–74,
    89n.18, 96–99, 150, 172
Egyptians xi, 5–6, 8, 18–19, 22n.46, 42, 55
  delivery practice 44–45
Eleutheropolis 74
Elishah (*See also* Cyprus, isles of Elisha,
    Kittim, Kypris) 11–12, 14
Elymas of Paphos (*See also* Bar Jesus) 9,
    80n.27, 87, 90n.47, 99, 105–110, 127
Elysium 156, 165n.37
England (*See also* Britain) 19, 40n.60
English delftware 34
Enkomi 5, 21nn.27–28, 79n.16
Ephesus 120, 128, 131, 140nn.24–25
Ephraim 68
Epipaleolithic 43
Epiphanius 13, 23n.63, 74
Eratosthenes 10
Esau 42
eschatology (eschatological) 117, 135,
    139n.9, 142n.45
Essenes (*See also* Qumran) 93, 96, 97,
    165n.39, 172

Ethiopia (or Aithiopia) 1, 3, 16, 97, 157, 166n.53
Euboea 70, 84
Eudemus of Rhodes 6
Eusebius 13, 13n.63, 71, 79n.22, 140n.24
Euthymius Zigabenus 70
Evagoras (King) 6
Even-Shoshan's lexicon 15
Ewdoksia Papuci-Wladyka 99, 101n.16

Famagusta, Cyprus 5
Fata Morgana 161n.8, 161n.10
fertility 10, 21n.15, 42–44, 46–49, 51
Festus (*See* Agrippa and Festus)
figurine 42–43, 46–51
four-room house 35, 36
fretensis 6–7

Gaius Octavius 6
Galatia, Lycaonian 90n.42, 91n.51, 104
Galilee 13, 55, 75, 97, 129
Gamaliel 86
Gaza 18
Gee-Sin 44
Gentiles (*See also* non-Jews) 78, 83, 86–88, 91n.59, 109, 116–118, 121–123, 124n.2, 124n.5, 137, 138n.3
Georgia 15, 23n.69
Gerizim 69
Gershon (Gershonites) 94, 96
Gezer 27, 29, 46, 57, 64n.5, 64n.7
glass 5, 9, 22n.46, 60, 164n.32
Gnosticism 133
goddess 3, 21n.15, 43–49, 51
Golden Legend 66, 70
graves (*See also* tombs) 43, 47, 51, 52n.10
Greco-Roman 89n.17, 104, 155–158, 165, 165n.39, 166n.52
Greece xiii, 3–5, 15–16, 19, 43, 60, 62, 84, 97, 105, 129, 172
Greek palindrome 97–99, 100n.8, 101n.9
Greeks xi, 3–6, 12, 14, 18–19, 20n.14, 69, 73–74, 86, 88n.1, 89n.9, 99, 104, 127–128, 165n.39
Gregory of Nazianzus 88

Hades 156, 165n.37
Hadrian 9
Hagia Sophia 72

Hajji Firuz Tepe 15
Harasim, Tel 27, 46
hard liquor 15
Harpocrates 98
Hasmoneans xiv, 12, 17
Hathor 44
heaven 42, 78n.9, 79n.11, 133, 151, 153–156, 158, 163n.21, 164n.32, 165n.39
Hebrew 2, 7, 11–16, 37, 44, 65, 90n.43, 97–99, 100n.2, 147, 150–151, 159–160, 161n.1, 162n.19, 163nn.25–26, 164n.28, 164n.31, 166n.48, 168n.63
Hebrews (people) 5, 13, 14, 44, 86, 88
Hellenistic period xvi, 6, 48, 50, 56, 60–61, 71, 80n.29, 89nn.19–20, 99, 112n.5, 158, 171
henotheists 98
Heraclides 86
Herculaneum (Hercules' glory) 7
Hermes 87, 91nn.51–53
Hermitage, The (Museum) 3, 8, 11, 17, 22n.42, 24n.73
Hermon, Mt. 157
Herodotus 3, 5–6, 55, 62, 167n.55
Herod the Great 3, 8, 18, 19, 94–95, 172
Hesiod 3, 21n.16, 154, 165n.34, 167n.55
Hippolytus of Rome 69–70, 165
History of the Rechabites (HistRech; *See also* Ancient Texts Index) 147, 155–160, 163n.25, 164n.29, 165nn.39–40, 166n.44, 166nn.46–47, 168n.71
Hittites xi, 5, 42
Holy Land xiii, xv, 3, 79n.23, 80n.36, 99, 147, 160, 161n.1, 171–173
  Cyprus, visual relationship with 147–151, 161
Holy Spirit 9, 85, 87, 90n.30, 120, 123, 127, 133–134, 164n.32
households 31, 41, 43, 46–47, 49, 51, 52n.1, 109, 118, 122–123, 125n.31
Horus 46

Ideon Cave 3
Idumea (Idumeans) 117
Idylion (Idalion) 5, 19, 24n.79
Illyricum 116
imports 25–26, 29–31, 33–34, 37–38

India 5, 97
Indo-Scythian arrowhead 60
infant mortality rates 43
infertility 42
international /intercultural trade 25–26,
    29–31, 37–38, 60, 171
Iran 4–5, 15, 56, 60
Irano-Scythian arrowhead 56, 60
Iron Age xv, xvi, 9, 17, 19, 25, 29–31,
    34–38, 39n.15, 39n.27, 39n.38,
    40n.62, 41, 46–48, 56, 60–62
Iron Age II xv, xvi, 29–31, 34–38, 40n.62,
    46–47
Ishmael 117
Ishtar 42
Isis 42, 44, 46
island of Aphrodite 1, 3, 83, 157
Isle of the Blessed Ones xiv, 147, 150,
    154–160, 164n.35, 165n.39,
    166n.44, 167n.57
isles of Elisha (*See also* Cyprus, Elishah,
    Kittim, Kypris) 11–12, 14
Israel xiii-xiv, 1–6, 9–12, 17, 23n.53, 25–
    26, 30–31, 34–38, 39n.27, 39n.38,
    40n.48, 40n.58, 40n.62, 42–43,
    48, 52n.10, 55–64, 80n.34, 83, 85,
    93–94, 96, 100nn.4–5, 106, 108,
    110–111, 117, 119, 122, 125n.13,
    151, 153, 165–166n.40, 171–173
    types of bowls 33, 57–58, 60–61
Israeli littoral (coastal strip) 58, 60, 62–63,
    64n.1
Israelite xiii-xiv, 3, 9, 17, 25, 30, 31, 34–35,
    37–38, 39n.27, 39n.38, 40n.48,
    40n.62, 42, 80n.34, 85, 172
    ceramic assemblage 30–37
    four-room house 35–36
    international trade xiv, 9, 25, 30–37
    lack of burials 36–37
    lack of (royal) inscriptions 3, 31, 34–36
    negative attitudes 37
    pottery 31–37
    rarity of imports and temples 25, 31,
        33, 35–37
Italy 4, 7, 13–14, 16, 19, 97, 104, 113n.18,
    129

Jacob 42, 97, 99
    and Leah 96

James (*See also* Ancient Sources index)
    68, 91n.59, 122, 129–130, 135, 137,
    139n.16, 144n.67
Jastro 14
Javan 12, 14
Jebel Aqra 147, 149–152, 159–160,
    163n.20, 163n.25
Jericho 3, 27, 69
Jeroboam I 17, 100n.2
Jerome 65, 71, 85, 99, 165n.39
Jerusalem 2–3, 6–7, 13, 19, 20n.8, 23n.57,
    27, 47, 65–73, 75–76, 78, 80n.38,
    84–88, 90nn.31–32, 90n.34,
    90n.41, 90n.44, 90n.47, 90n.49,
    91n.50, 91n.56, 90n.59, 93, 95,
    96, 100, 103, 110–111, 112n.4,
    116–117, 120–124, 128, 137,
    146n.83, 164n.32, 165n.40, 166n.43,
    167–168n.63, 171–172
Jesus' crucifixion 13, 72, 75–76, 80n.31,
    110, 145n.77
Jewish Christianity 123, 129–130, 138n.3
Jewish Diaspora 84–85, 88n.1, 88n.6,
    89n.9, 89nn.15–16, 89n.26, 90n.38,
    94, 106, 122–123, 124n.5
Jews xi, xiii, xiv, 1, 3, 9, 11, 13–14, 16,
    18–19, 66–70, 72–76, 78, 78n.10,
    79n.11, 79n.15, 80n.30, 83–87,
    88n.1, 88nn.4–6, 88n.8, 89nn.9–10,
    89nn.15–18, 89n.26, 90n.38,
    94, 96–100, 103–111, 112n.7,
    113nn.18–19, 116–123, 124n.2,
    124n.5, 124n.8, 125n.16, 127–129,
    138nn.2–3, 139n.12, 145n.80, 147,
    154, 155, 158, 159–160, 165n.39,
    166n.42, 167n.62, 168n.63, 172
John of Euboea 70
John of Euroia, Saint 74
Jonadab 155, 165–166n.40
Jordan (River, Valley, region) 3, 5, 17–18,
    24n.75, 64n.7, 100n.4, 134
Josephus (*See also* Ancient Sources index)
    2, 14, 80n.30, 83–85, 88n.5, 89n.9,
    89n.21, 112n.15, 138nn.2–3
Joses (*See also* Barnabas) 13
Joshua 5, 8, 17, 153
Judaism xii, 1, 16, 19, 68, 75, 94–100, 108,
    133, 139n.12, 139n.15, 141n.34,
    144n.67, 171

Judea 55, 66–70, 72, 74–76, 93, 105
Julius Caesar 6–8, 111

Kakopetria 60, 64n.4, 64n.6
Kasios, Mt. 150, 152, 158, 160
kerygma 66, 141n.36, 145n.77
Khirokitia 3
Khnum 44
Kinnereth (Sea of Galilee, Chinnereth) 17, 26–27
Kition (*See also* Citium, Kitium, Larnaca) 3, 6, 21n.30, 69–70, 78, 79n.12, 79n.16, 83
Kittim (*See also* Cyprus, Elishah, isles of Elisha, Kypris) 11–14, 19, 88n.2
Kitium (*See also* Citium, Kition, Larnaca) 12, 13, 74
Kohath (*See also* Qohath) 96
Kohal 57
Kouklia 56, 64n.4, 64n.10
Kourion 4
Kourotrophoi 47, 49, 53n.42
Kypris (*See also* Aphrodite, Cyprus, Elishah, isles of Elisha, Kittim) 3, 48

Lachish 17, 27, 46
Lamashtu 44
Lapithos 49, 50
Larnaca (or Larnaka; *See also* Citium, Kition, Kitium) xii, xix, 4, 65, 67, 69–72, 78, 79n.12, 79n.19, 79n.21, 79n.25, 80n.28, 80n.34, 83, 168n.64, 173
Late Antiquity 1, 20nn.1–2, 112n.7, 113n.19, 147, 155, 158, 159, 166n.53, 167n.58, 168n.70, 171–173
late Bronze Age xvi, xx, 9, 17, 22n.46, 25–26, 35–36, 38, 40n.66, 46, 48
Late Philistine Decorated Ware (LPDW) (*See also* Ashdod Ware) xx, 30–31, 39n.15
Lazarus xv, 65–81
  burial in Bethany 65, 71–73
  connection with Mary and Martha 66–68
  death in Cyprus 66–67, 70–73
  fleeing from Jerusalem to Cyprus 13, 19, 66, 68–70, 72, 76–78
  killing of 68–70, 76

misleading identity 69
  name, significance 65
  New Testament on 65, 66, 68
  "resurrection" of (*See also* resuscitation) 65, 67–70, 73, 75
  skull and bones 66–67, 70–72
  story in the Gospel of John 65–70, 74–78
  tomb of 70–72
Lebanon 2, 12, 158, 163n.25
Leo VI, Emperor 72
Levant (*See also* Southern Levant, Palestine) xvi, 3, 19, 25–26, 30, 37–38, 55, 83, 166n.53
Levi 13, 94–97
Levites xv, 13, 19, 23nn.53–54, 83–91, 33–101, 117, 127
Levitical cities 23n.53, 94, 100n.3
Levitical Diaspora 23n.53, 94, 100n.3
Libya (*See also* Cyrenaica) 4, 97
Louvre 3
LXX (*See* Septuagint)
Lystra 87, 91nn.51–52

Macaronesia 155
Macedonia 120
Madeira 155
magos 105–108
maiestas 73, 79n.26
maleficium 73, 79n.26
mammisi 44
Maurice, Emporer (Byzantine) 159
Mark (John Mark) 9, 13, 76, 85, 87, 91n.56, 115, 121, 123, 127–137
Marseille 70, 79n.19, 147–151, 161n.4, 161n.8, 162n.16
Martial 7, 22n.40
martyr 9, 13, 68, 71, 74, 75, 86, 144n.66
Mary and Martha 66–68, 75
Mediterranean (*See also* Eastern Mediterranean) xii–xv, xviii, 1–3, 5, 14, 16–20, 25–26, 31, 37–38, 56, 62, 83–84, 97, 107, 128–129, 147–152, 154, 160, 161n.8, 162n.17, 171–172
Mediterranean coast (coastal strip, littoral) xiii–xv, 1–3, 5–6, 14, 17, 55, 58, 60, 62–63, 64n.1, 69, 75, 83, 97, 149–150, 152, 160, 162n.14, 171
Merari (Merarites) 94, 96

merkabah mysticism 166n.42
Mesopotamian traditions (deliveries) 44, 46, 52n.21
Messina, Straits of 161n.8
Metropolitan Chrysostomos of Kition 69
Metspe Yamim 57, 64n.7
Middle Bronze Age xvi, 25, 41, 46–47
Middle East 6, 16
Midian 34
mines (mining) 5, 8, 10, 19, 22n.44
Miriam 96
miscarriages 42
mission (Pauline, in Acts, etc.; *See also* calling) 9, 70, 72, 73, 76, 83, 85–88, 90n.42, 91n.50, 91n.56, 103, 115–126, 128, 136, 137, 138n.1, 141n.34, 142nn.39–40, 142n.42, 166n.53, 167n.58
Mnason of Cyprus 13, 128
Moab 17, 34
monotheists 98
Moses 3, 79n.11, 94, 96, 142nn.47–48, 151, 153
Mount of Olives 65, 71, 80n.38
Mt. Canigou 147–149, 160
Mt. Zaphon traditions 147, 150–151, 153–154, 158
Muslims 71, 76
Mycenaean Age 3, 5–6, 30, 46

Nabateans 117, 124n.11
Nablus 62, 64n.8
Nag Hammadi library 129
Nain 66
Naples 7
narratology 103–106
NASA 162n.18
Naturalis Historia 16
Nazarenes 84, 138n.3
Negev 17
Neo-Assyrian period 43
Neolithic culture xvi, 15, 20n.13
Nestorians 5
New Testament (*See also* "New Testament" in Ancient Texts Index) 9, 12, 65–66, 68, 75, 90n.29, 112n.15, 120, 125nn.15–16, 125n.18, 127–130, 137, 139n.14, 140n.22, 140n.26, 142n.38, 143n.54, 144n.66, 146n.84, 154

Nintu Mami 44
non-Jew (*See also* Gentile) 104, 106–109, 115–123
Novaya Zemlya Effect 148–149, 160, 161n.8, 161–162n.10, 162n.12
Nysa 7

Octavian (*See also* Augustus) 84
Omrides 37
orographic lift 150, 152, 156
Orontes 87, 150
Osiris 42, 98
ostraca (*See also* Ancient Sources Index) xxiv, 12, 22n.51, 35, 45, 52n.24

Palaipaphos, temple of Aphrodite at (*See also*, Aphrodite, Paphos, Temple) 104
Palestine (*See also* Levant, Southern Levant) xiii–xiv, 1, 3, 5–6, 8–9, 16, 18–19, 55, 65, 68, 71, 74, 80n.31, 83, 94, 96–97, 99–100, 128, 158, 171–173
palindrome 97–99, 100n.8, 101n.9
Pamphylia (Pamphilia) 91n.56, 109, 115
Panagia Chrysopolitissa Basilica 9
Paphos 9, 60, 63, 64n.4, 73, 84, 89n.14, 90n.47, 97–101, 103–105, 109, 111, 115, 127, 157
papyrus (papyri) (*See also* Ancient Sources index) xxiv, 16, 42
Parthia 2, 97
Passover (Pesach) 68, 75, 110
Paul xv, 3, 9–10, 13, 19, 23n.55, 68, 70, 72–73, 75–76, 78, 83–88, 90n.40, 90n.42, 90nn.46–47, 91n.54, 91n.56, 91n.59, 91n.63, 97, 103–113, 115–126, 127–146
  at Antioch 115, 117, 121–123
  on circumcision 86, 88, 117–119, 123
  on commandments of God 109, 118–120
  convictions, differing 107–108, 115, 122–123
  encounter with non-Jews 104–113, 117–120, 122–123
  relations with the Corinthians 120–121
  separation from Barnabas 9, 13, 87–88, 115, 120–123

stance or value system 117–118
travel proposal 115–117
Pazuzu 44
pendants 46
Pentateuch 94, 96
Pentecost 70
Perge 109
Persepolis 58, 64n.9
Persian period, Cyprus and Israel xiv,
 xvi, 9, 19, 21n.17, 21n.21, 21n.46,
 55–64, 71, 83, 89nn.19–20
 archaeological excavations 55–56
 arrowheads 56–57, 60, 63
 bowls 57–58, 60–61
 daily use objects 57–59, 60
 flat-leaf arrowhead 60
 furniture 57–59, 62
 helmet 56
 jewelry 61–62
 ladles 57, 59
 metal objects, dating 60, 63
 new weapons 60
 situla 57, 59
 vessels 57–59, 62
 weapons 56–57
Persians xi, 4, 6, 19, 73, 76
Pesharim 12
Peter (Cephas) 76, 87, 89n.27, 91n.59,
 103–104, 109, 116, 121–123,
 124n.5, 124n.8, 129, 137, 142n.51,
 145n.77
Petra tou Romiou 3–4
Phanagoria cemetery 3
Pharisees 13, 66–68, 80n.38, 86, 97
Philippi 104
Philistia 17, 26, 30–31, 34, 38, 39n.15
Philo of Alexandria (*See also* Ancient
 Source index) 69, 84, 89n.9, 89n.13,
 89n.22, 97, 133, 138n.2, 165n.39
Phoenicia 3, 6, 34, 84, 127
Phoenicians xi, 3, 5–6, 18, 30–31, 39n.19,
 55, 61–63
 Metal jewelry 5, 19, 21n.29, 55–56,
 60–62
Phrygia 91n.52
Plato 21n.16, 135, 155, 160, 164n.36,
 165n.39, 167nn.54–56
Pliny the Elder 5, 9, 16
Pluto 164–165n.36

Poland 19, 97
Pompeii 6
Poseidon 164n.36, 167n.54
post-Chaldean period 43
potters 25, 34
pottery (*See also* Aegean style pottery,
 Black on Red Ware, Cypriot
 pottery, Cypro-Phoenician pottery,
 Israelite pottery, Late Philistine
 Decorated Ware) xiv, xx, 2–3, 9,
 25–40, 55, 60, 71, 172
pregnancy 42–44, 46, 48, 51
Priestly Code 93–94
priests 13, 23nn.53–54, 35, 66, 67, 68, 69,
 76, 80n.38, 85, 89nn.19–20, 93–96,
 100nn.1–3, 100n.6, 110
Prisca (*See* Aquila and Prisca)
Proclus of Constantinople 70
prutah, Jewish (*See also* coin, widow's
 mite) 19
pseudepigraphon (pseudepigrapha)
 xxiii, xxvii, 96, 137, 147, 159,
 167n.62
Pseudo-Clement 13
P Source 13
Ptolemaeus I Lagos 83
Ptolemies 6, 73, 83–84, 166n.45
Ptolemy Lathyrus 83
Punic Wars 6
Pyrenees (*See also* Mt, Canigou, Canigou
 Effect) 147

Q (source) 129, 130, 132, 133, 137, 139n.9,
 139nn.11–12, 141nn.29–32,
 141n.34, 142n.39
Qohath (Qohathites; *See also* Kohath) 94
Queen Helena of Adiabene. 2, 20n.8
Qumran (*See also* Essenes) 12, 14, 16,
 89n.23, 93, 96, 97, 116, 172

Rashi 44, 52n.18
Rebekah and Isaac 42
Rechab 165–166n.40
Rechabites 147, 155, 156, 158, 159, 160,
 163n.25, 164n.29, 164n.33, 165n.40,
 166n.42, 166nn.46–47
refugees 5
Rehoboam 17
resinated wine 3, 14–16, 23n.70, 172

resurrection (*See also* Lazarus,
    resuscitation) 65, 67–70, 73, 75, 78,
    110, 133
resuscitation (*See also* Lazarus,
    resurrection) 65–67, 71, 73, 76
Retsina Malamatina (wine) 15
Revadim 46
Rodanim (*See also* Dodanim) 12, 14
Roman Empire 4, 6, 90n.34, 111, 112n.7,
    112n.15, 123, 125n.23
Romanos the Melodist 70
Romans xi, 3–6, 8, 12, 14, 16–18, 20n.2,
    68–69, 73–74, 80n.29, 80n.37,
    81n.38, 84–85, 88n.1, 89n.9, 89n.14,
    89n.17, 95, 103–111, 116, 122–123,
    172, 173
Rome xiv, 5–6, 12–13, 69–70, 76, 83,
    90n.34, 103–106, 110–111,
    113nn.18–19, 116, 123, 124n.4,
    124n.8, 126n.32, 132, 165n.39, 172

Sacrae Geographiae 14
sacrifices 43, 80n.38, 83, 87, 94, 95, 122
Sadducees 78
Saint John of Euroia 74
Saint of Larnaca 69, 79n.12, 79n.19,
    79n.21, 79n.25
Saint Petersburg 3
Salamis (*See also* Constantia) 5, 9, 22n.38,
    73–74, 79n.15, 80n.29, 80n.37,
    84–86, 88, 89n.10, 89n.14, 89n.17,
    95–96, 104, 127
Salt Sea (Dead Sea) 17
Samaria (Samaritans, Good Samaritan
    Parable) 46, 62, 64n.9, 69, 94, 96, 97
Sanhedrin 67, 80n.38, 85
Sarah and Abraham 42
Sargon II 4, 6
Saul (*See* Paul)
Scorpion I (King) 15
Scythian 3, 56, 60
Second World War 18
Sedasa 91n.51
Seleucia 9, 70, 73, 87, 115, 127, 158
Septuagint (LXX) 12, 94, 100n.6, 133–134
Sergius Paulus 9, 19, 73, 80n.27, 87,
    90n.47, 103, 105–106, 109–111, 127
Settlement phenomenon 31, 37
Sharon 37, 69

Shiqmona 56
shipbuilding 5, 12
Shulaveri-Shomu 15, 23n.68
Sicily 6, 14, 155
Sidon 6, 55
Signs Source 65–66, 68–69
Silas 87, 115, 120, 121, 128
Silicia 115
Siloam inscription 40n.47
Siloam pool 76
Simeon (Symeon) Stylites (the younger)
    158–159
Sinai, Mt. 153
Society of Biblical Literature xxvii, 76,
    167n.62
Socrates 135, 164n.36, 171
Solomon 8, 17, 19, 22n.44, 94–95
Southern Levant (*See also* Levant,
    Palestine) 25–26, 30, 37
Spain xiv, 5, 14, 116–117, 124n.2, 124n.9,
    125n.12, 129
Sparta 7
St. Trophîme at Arles 69
Stavros S. Fotiou 69–70, 79n.12, 80n.28
stelae 6, 45
Stephen (Stephanus) 13, 68, 72, 75, 78,
    84–84, 109, 127–128, 137
    stoning of 13, 68, 72, 75, 78, 84–85
stillbirths 42
Strabo 5, 9, 166n.45, 167n.55
StudiorumNovi Testamenti Societas 76
Sumerians 8, 42
superior mirage (*See also* Atlantis Effect,
    Canigou Effect, thermocline
    ducting) 160, 162n.10
synagogues 9, 73, 84, 95, 96, 120, 126n.31,
    127
Syria xiv, 1–3, 5–6, 16, 20n.4, 55, 83, 86,
    90n.34, 99, 115, 128–129, 147,
    149–150, 156, 158–160, 162n.16,
    168n.67

Tabernacle 94–95
Table of Nations 117, 124–125n.11,
    125n.13
Tahiti 161n.8
Taman Peninsula 3
Tamassos 10
Targum of Pseudo Jonathan 14

Tarshish 12, 14, 117
Tarsus 13, 56, 60, 83, 97, 117
Tawrat 44
Telamon 89n.10
Tel el-Agul 46
Tel 'Eton 31–33
Tel Michal 27, 62, 64n.3, 64n.5, 64n.8
Tell Beit Mirsim 27, 46
Tell Qasile 19
Tell Tenim 46
Temple (Jerusalem) 7, 13, 23nn.57–58, 65, 68, 75–76, 78, 80–81n.38, 84–85, 93–96, 99–100, 100n.5, 166n.43
temple (e.g. of Aphrodite, of Atlantis, of Baal, at Golgoi, of Zeus, etc.) 3, 6, 35, 44, 49–50, 104, 158–159, 163n.21, 167n.54, 168n.73
Temple Scroll 65
Tenth Legion (Legio X Fretensis) 6–7
terra incognita 16
Tertullian 86, 165n.39
tetragrammaton 97, 99
Teucer 89n.10
Theodore of Mopsuestia 158
Theodore of Studios (Theodoros of Stoudites) 70, 74
Theodosius I 4
Theophanes Kerameus 70
Theophylact of Bulgaria 70
Therapeutae 97
thermocline ducting (*See also* Atlantis Effect, Canigou Effect, superior mirage) 162n.10
Thessalonica 104
Thomas 67, 75, 130, 132
thought experiment. (*See* also Christian theology, early) 130–135
Timna 8, 19, 22n.44
tin 5
tombs (*See also* graves, Lazarus) 15, 36, 40n.58, 49, 61, 64n.9, 65, 67, 70–73, 78n.11, 79n.22, 80n.38, 142n.41

Torah 75, 94, 129–130
Trajan 84, 89n.18, 96
Trans-Jordan 3, 24n.75, 55, 100n.4
travelers 18–19
Trojan War 89n.10
Troodos range 8
Turkey 1, 4, 56, 60, 97, 149, 162n.16
Tyre 1, 6, 12–13, 26, 55, 128, 150

Ugarit (Ugaritic, Ugarits) 42, 150, 168n.75

Vesuvius 6–7, 22n.40
Vézelay 69

Wadi Arabah 19
widow's mite (See also coin, prutah) 19
wine (*See also* resinated wine) xiv, 2–3, 5, 9–10, 14–16, 23n.67, 23–24nn.69–70, 24n.72, 71, 85, 142n.49, 155, 165n.40, 172
wisdom 14, 15, 16, 131, 139n.11, 153, 154

Xenophon 6

Yahweh (YHWH; *See also* tetragrammaton) 97–99, 151
Yatnana 6

Zadok 13, 94, 96
Zagros Mountains 15
Zaphon 147, 150–154, 158, 160, 161n.1, 163n.21, 163nn.25–26, 164n.28, 168n.75
Zeno of Kition 6, 22n.36, 74
Zeus 3, 20nn.13–14, 87, 91nn.51–52, 104, 154, 158, 164–165nn.35–36
Zion, Mount 47, 69
Zosimus 155–156, 158, 166n.41, 167–168nn.62–63

www.ingramcontent.com/pod-product-compliance
Lightning Source LLC
Chambersburg PA
CBHW072144290426
44111CB00012B/1973